# opera

# opera

## THE DEFINITIVE ILLUSTRATED STORY

ALAN RIDING &
LESLIE DUNTON-DOWNER

**SECOND EDITION**

| | |
|---|---|
| Senior Editors | Victoria Heyworth-Dunne, Scarlett O'Hara |
| Senior Art Editor | Helen Spencer |
| US Senior Editor | Megan Douglass |
| US Executive Editor | Lori Cates Hand |
| Senior Picture Researcher | Myriam Megharbi |
| Managing Editor | Gareth Jones |
| Senior Managing Art Editor | Lee Griffiths |
| Jacket Designer | Surabhi Wadhwa |
| Jacket Design Development Manager | Sophia MTT |
| Art Director | Karen Self |
| Associate Publishing Director | Liz Wheeler |
| Publishing Director | Jonathan Metcalf |
| Design Director | Phil Ormerod |
| Media Archive | Romaine Werblow |
| Production Editor | Gillian Reid |
| Senior Production Controller | Rachel Ng |

**DK INDIA**

| | |
|---|---|
| Senior Editor | Tina Jindal |
| Project Art Editor | Meenal Goel |
| Editor | Shambhavi Thatte |
| Senior Managing Editor | Rohan Sinha |
| Managing Art Editor | Sudakshina Basu |
| Senior DTP Designers | Harish Aggarwal, Vishal Bhatia, Jagtar Singh |
| DTP Designer | Jaypal Chauhan |
| Senior Jackets Coordinator | Priyanka Sharma Saddi |
| Pre-Production Manager | Balwant Singh |
| Production Manager | Pankaj Sharma |
| DK India Editorial Head | Glenda Fernandes |
| DK India Design Head | Malavika Talukder |

**FIRST EDITION**

| | |
|---|---|
| Project Editor | Sam Atkinson |
| Project Art Editor | Victoria Clark |
| DTP Designer | Laragh Kedwell |
| Production Controller | Melanie Dowland |
| Managing Editor | Debra Wolter |
| Managing Art Editor | Karen Self |
| Publisher | Jonathan Metcalf |
| Art Director | Bryn Walls |
| Picture Researcher | Sarah Smithies |
| Editorial Assistant | Oussama Zahr |
| US Editor | Anne Plume |
| Indexer | Hilary Bird |

**STUDIO CACTUS LTD**

| | |
|---|---|
| Project Editor | Jennifer Close |
| Project Designer | Dawn Terrey |
| Designers | Sharon Cluett, Claire Moore, Sharon Rudd |
| Editorial Assistance | Jane Baldock, Aaron Brown, Rob Walker |

This American Edition, 2022
First American Edition, 2006
Published in the United States by DK Publishing
1450 Broadway, Suite 801, New York, NY 10018

Text copyright © 2006 Alan Riding and Leslie Dunton-Downer
Text copyright additional material © 2022 Alan Riding
Copyright © 2006, 2022 Dorling Kindersley Limited
DK, a Division of Penguin Random House LLC
22 23 24 25 26 10 9 8 7 6 5 4 3 2 1
001–325057–Aug/2022

A catalog record for this book is available from the Library of Congress.
ISBN: 978-0-7440-5631-0

DK books are available at special discounts when purchased in bulk for sales promotions, premiums, fund-raising, or educational use. For details, contact: DK Publishing Special Markets, 1450 Broadway, Suite 801, New York, NY 10018
SpecialSales@dk.com

Printed and bound in China

**For the curious**
www.dk.com

**MIX**
Paper | Supporting responsible forestry
**FSC™ C018179**

This book was made with Forest Stewardship Council ™ certified paper—one small step in DK's commitment to a sustainable future. For more information go to www.dk.com/our-green-pledge

# Contents

# Preface

Even passionate music fans may be forgiven for considering opera over-the-top. After all, how better to describe an art form that flaunts convoluted plots, incomprehensible lyrics, stormy orchestration, hyperbolic acting, exotic staging, and temperamental singers? Another word might be "operatic."

And yet, opera continually adds new converts to its legions of worshipful followers. It may first touch the unsuspecting soul through a diva's charisma on television, a haunting chorus on the radio, or the thrill of a live performance. Whatever the impetus may be, people have a way of remembering the moment when opera began to change their lives.

## An invitation

We both came to opera along different paths. But it has since led us to see the world—and ourselves—with fresh eyes. It has taken us on imaginary journeys and has accompanied us on our travels. And now, through this book, we hope to share the many pleasures that opera has afforded us.

Opera is, of course, an emotional, even intimate experience. Its dramatic essence cannot be overlooked: story, lyrics, and music come together to express powerful feelings. The words themselves may be sung in any number of languages—those we address here are in Italian, German, French, Russian, Czech, Hungarian, and English—but the music itself requires no translation.

It may be tempting to think of opera as an artificial, even contrived form of art. Barely four centuries old, it was born in the European land that provided its name and many of its greatest composers: Italy. Yet, in reality, singing—of love, betrayal, suffering, or joy—is older than recorded history, inseparable from human passion itself. Thus, what opera's earliest creators did was to give age-old emotional truths a new lyrical and dramatic form.

Successive generations of composers and librettists have captured the operatic sentiments of their own times. And as opera grew in popularity, spawning theaters designed around its needs, it also became an international art form. Singers, composers, poets, and designers criss-crossed Europe, and soon they carried opera to the New World and beyond.

◀ **Thousands of fans** brave the damp weather as the great Italian tenor Luciano Pavarotti celebrates 30 years in opera with a free concert in Hyde Park, London, in July 1991.

▲ **Crowds arrive** for *La traviata* at the "old" Metropolitan Opera in New York in 1961, five years before it was replaced by today's larger Metropolitan Opera at Lincoln Center.

## A thrilling adventure

No single book could cover every surviving opera: they number in the thousands. Instead, we have chosen those of enduring popularity, as well as those that played a crucial role in opera's evolution. Thus, while highlighting 182 operas and their composers, the book also aims to tell the story of opera itself.

This is a story of how the art form appeared and changed over the centuries. But it is also a story of composers who were worshipped like gods and others who died in misery; of operas banned as subversive and others that became patriotic banners; of arias, duets, and choruses that became popular hits; of electrifying singers and dazzling stagecraft; of opera houses burned to the ground and lovingly rebuilt; and, not least, of the devoted audiences who make opera what it is.

As authors, we, too, have been on a voyage. We both began with our own favorite operas, composers, and musical periods. But in selecting works for detailed examination, our research led us to discover new operatic treasures, and to admire the extraordinary variety and continuity of opera through the ages.

Opera is a richly rewarding world and it can be entered through myriad doors. We trust that this book will serve as a welcome companion to anyone exploring this unique realm.

# INTRODUCING OPERA

# WHAT IS
# OPERA?

Four centuries ago, music, theater, and dance came together in Italy to create a new art form called opera. It soon caught on and, by 1700, it was entertaining commoners and royalty alike across Europe. Over time, the sound of its music would change, yet the essence of opera has not: accompanied by an orchestra, with scenery, costumes, and light adding drama, singers tell a story.

Music's unique power to move people is no secret, but opera's special appeal lies in the voice, arguably the most affecting of all instruments. It conveys emotion even when the lyrics are not understood, while talented voices can enliven the most familiar of scores and plots. Indeed, the pleasure of revisiting beloved operas explains how an entire art form can rest on the genius of Mozart, Verdi, and Wagner and a core repertoire of some 150 works.

Still, it remains a mystery why relatively few operas have survived and many thousands are forgotten. Some operas, sell-outs in their day, are now never performed. Others, heckled at their premieres, have become firm favorites. There are also fashions: once considered the summit of the art, French *grand opéra* has vanished; in contrast, Renaissance and Baroque opera have been rediscovered with enthusiasm. Today, contemporary opera is a minority taste, yet works are continually being composed and a few have entered the repertoire.

Opera's stories also matter. Its scores can be recorded in studios or presented in concert version, yet opera was born as music theater—that is, music set to a libretto for the stage. True, most people only remember the name of the opera's composer, yet even the greatest composers have always valued a good libretto. It may borrow its plot from Greek mythology or Roman history, from Shakespeare or Schiller, from historical epics, romantic dramas, or the occasional farce of life. More importantly, it should use the poetry of language to express a spectrum of emotions. The composer taps into all these ingredients of human drama. Thus, the greatest operas can be about violence, greed, ambition, intrigue, betrayal, reconciliation, and death, but they may also be shaped by humor, joy, passion, and love. »

◄ **The magnificent horseshoe-shape auditorium** of Milan's Teatro alla Scala, which opened in 1778, was the model until recent decades for opera houses around the world.

## A possessive public

Score and libretto become an opera through the voices of soloists and chorus, supported by orchestra and staging. And when all work together, the opera's creators can feel satisfied. Except, of course, they are rarely alive. Instead, the role of judge and jury is played by the public—some newcomers to opera, others veterans of myriad productions, all with opinions flowing from strong passions. Indeed, if opera audiences often proclaim their verdicts with loud cheers or boos, it is because they feel deeply possessive about opera.

Yet rare is the opera devotee who likes all operas. In fact, some verge on the sectarian, worshipping one composer, disdaining another. Wagner lovers, for instance, resemble a cult. Then there are those who prefer Verdi's dramatic operas, while others yearn for the

bel canto—"beautiful singing"—of, say, Bellini. Russian and Czech audiences are strongly loyal to their own national operas, while the French have led the revival of Baroque opera.

At the same time, an art form once mocked by Samuel Johnson as "an exotick and irrational entertainment" continues to win converts. In this, glamorous stars make a difference. And even in the absence of mega-divas like Maria Callas, stars keep appearing: with Elīna Garanča or Juan Diego Flórez on a bill, a full house can be assured. Spectacles like *The Three Tenors* were also successful in attracting new audiences. To satisfy this demand, opera houses are renovated and new ones are built. Opera festivals keep multiplying, while crowds watch live performances on screens in squares and parks. Four centuries after its inception, opera is still alive and well.

## How it all began

Opera was yet another fruit of the Italian Renaissance. And, as such, it is no accident that its roots lie in the creative exuberance of Florence. In the final decade of the 16th century, a group of artists, musicians, and poets, calling themselves the "Camerata," met there to promote a revival of Greek drama. What they came

◀ **Michele Marieschi's view** of the courtyard of the Palazzo Ducale in Venice, where for the first time opera was staged in public theaters for paying audiences.

▲ **At the 100th anniversary** of the Metropolitan Opera in New York on October 22, 1983, performers at a gala evening filled the stage to receive a standing ovation from an ecstatic audience.

up with instead was the idea that these stories could be told as an *opera in musica*—"a work in music."

Claudio Monteverdi is considered the father of opera because he took the Florentine experiment a step further: with *L'Orfeo*, presented in Mantua in 1607, he absorbed his audience in a lyrical drama. The new art quickly spread to other courts and soon arrived in Venice. There, with the opening of the city's first opera house in 1637, opera reached a new public. By the end of the century, Venice boasted 17 opera houses and the Italian love for opera was sealed.

The city was never short of composers, with Antonio Vivaldi its early 18th-century star. Europe's royal courts also wanted the new *divertimento*, or entertainment, and Italians often provided it, with Jean-Baptiste Lully introducing opera to France as Louis XIV's official composer. George Frideric Handel, a German, made opera popular in 18th-century London, although the first opera in English, Henry Purcell's *Dido and Aeneas*, was performed as early as 1689.

## Opera's reform

The prevailing model for much of the 17th and 18th centuries was *opera seria*, with the narrative recounted in sung dialogue, called recitatives, and moments of high emotion provided by arias, which allowed soloists—frequently castratos, men castrated before puberty to preserve their high voices—to show off their virtuosity. Neapolitan opera broke with this solemnity by introducing humorous *opera buffa*, but this, too, demanded great technical prowess of singers.

In the late 18th century, two figures broke the mold. The Viennese-based composer Christoph Willibald Gluck emerged as the key figure in a so-called *reforma* by moving opera away from vocal exhibitionism toward expression of the drama. His *Orfeo ed Euridice*, in particular, paved the way for opera's first undisputed genius, Wolfgang Amadeus Mozart.

Mozart inherited a legacy of *opera seria* and *opera buffa* as well as German Singspiel, a form of opera with spoken dialogue instead of sung recitative. But while he exploited these genres, he also transformed them, responding to the audacity of his librettists with music of rare inspiration. Today, his reputation rests on four late masterpieces: *Le nozze di Figaro*, *Don Giovanni*, *Così fan tutte*, and *Die Zauberflöte*. In practice, opera history can be divided into pre-Mozart and post-Mozart.

## Rise of national operas

The clearest way of tracking what followed is through space rather than time. The 19th century, for instance, was an era when Italy, Germany, and the Czech region were forging themselves as nation states, while Czarist Russia was opening itself up to Europe. At the same time, travel also encouraged cross-fertilization. With so much change in the air, opera was inevitably affected.

Influenced by Gluck and Mozart, and with its instinct for melody, Italian music spawned five monumental 19th-century composers. Gioachino Rossini wrote 39 operas between the ages of 17 and 37, then abandoned composition. In comic operas like *Il barbiere di Siviglia* and *La Cenerentola*, he refined *bel canto*, a florid and virtuoso form of singing that was adopted by his successors, Vincenzo Bellini and Gaetano Donizetti. A still greater opera composer followed. Giuseppe Verdi not only created a stream of memorable works but also came to personify the *Risorgimento*, Italy's revolt against Austrian occupation. Several of his operas, notably *Nabucco*, were metaphors for this struggle, although his most popular works, *Rigoletto*, *Il trovatore*, and *La traviata*, are deeply romantic. His successor, Giacomo Puccini, was no less drawn to tragic love stories. Rich in memorable tunes, his greatest operas, *Manon Lescaut*, *La bohème*, *Tosca*, and *Madama Butterfly*, all portray ill-fated heroines.

◄ **In the 18th century**, the operas of Christoph Willibald Gluck (1714–1787) increased the dramatic aspect of the art form.

## The Paris crossroads

Although Italian opera held its own, from the 1820s Paris became Europe's opera capital, drawing composers from across Europe. Their influence was considerable. Rossini, Donizetti, and Verdi all worked there. A German expatriate, Giacomo Meyerbeer, created the spectacle known as *grand opéra*, comprising five-act operas with historical »

► **The artist Thomas Rowlandson** captures the social dimension of opera-going in the 18th century in this lively and crowded scene.

## Genres of opera

In the 18th century, *opera seria* and its comic cousin, *opera buffa*, were the dominant models, with sung recitatives and strict aria structures. Many other types were also popular. Gluck's *Orfeo ed Euridice* was a *tragédie opéra*. The German Singspiel and the French *opéra comique* both used spoken dialogue, while French *grand opéra* required five acts and ballet. But many composers named their operas as they wished. Mozart's *Don Giovanni* was called a *dramma giocoso* ("jocose" opera). Verdi often chose *melodramma*, Wagner varied the description of his operas, and Mussorgsky came up with "national music drama" for *The Khovansky Affair*.

## Types of voices

Voices are defined by their tessitura, a palette of notes that for professional singers, usually covers two octaves. However, while composers write roles to fit these tessituras, the singer's range may be expected to surpass them, above all when sopranos and tenors are assigned exceptionally high notes. The tonal ranges of the six different voice types are shown to the right, from soprano (the highest) to bass (the lowest). There are also subdivisions of each type that define whether they are light or heavy, lyric or dramatic. For instance, there are at least six categories of sopranos and tenors. A Wagnerian tenor is thus unlikely to sing a Mozartian tenor aria.

Soprano

Tenor

Mezzo-soprano

Baritone

Contralto

Bass

librettos, rich decor, and lengthy ballet interludes. Another German, Jacques Offenbach, invented the operetta, or *opéra-bouffe*, which earned him great popularity in Paris and a following across Europe.

French opera as such had to carve its own path. Hector Berlioz turned away from *grand opéra* for his few lyrical works. Charles Gounod and Jules Massenet, who both studied in Rome, made their names with melodious Italianate operas. Georges Bizet was less prolific, yet his *Carmen*, with its exotic setting, fiery love story, and catchy tunes, carried his name around the world. However, it was another maverick, Claude

▼ **An 1826 stage design for** the port of Damietta (now Dumyat) in Egypt, the setting of Act I of Giacomo Meyerbeer's crusader opera, *Il crociato in Egitto*, shows the elaborate sets that are so often a feature of opera.

Debussy, whose work *Pelléas et Mélisande* would be considered the most revolutionary French opera of its time.

### German Romanticism

Puzzlingly, of the great 19th-century Germanic composers of instrumental music, only Beethoven was drawn to opera and he wrote just one, *Fidelio*. Richard Wagner, in contrast, was interested only in opera and, by the mid-century, he was transforming the art form with through-composed music, expressionist orchestration, unorthodox harmonies, and grand "arches" of melody. Seeking inspiration for his librettos in German Romanticism, he embraced Teutonic story material with almost religious fervor. With his early operas *Tannhäuser* and *Lohengrin* he forged a Romantic style that reached its apex with *Tristan und Isolde*. But he is most revered for his monumental four-opera cycle known as *Der Ring des Nibelungen*.

Wagner's influence was such that two generations of composers wrestled to escape his shadow. One of the first to do so successfully was Richard Strauss. He took Wagner's radicalism to a new plane in his early operas. He then built on Wagner's Romanticism and even tapped Mozart in his ever-popular *Der Rosenkavalier*, *Ariadne auf Naxos*, *Arabella*, and *Capriccio*.

The 19th century also saw the rise of other national "sounds". In Russia, Mikhail Ivanovich Glinka borrowed Slavic folk music, while Modest Mussorgsky brought Russian history to the stage with *Boris Godunov*. But it was the Romantic composer Piotr Ilyich Tchaikovsky who entered the Western repertoire with *Eugene Onegin* and *The Queen of Spades*. Similarly, in the Czech lands, while Bedřich Smetana is hailed as the father of nationalist opera, Leoš Janáček wrote works of greater

▲ **Wagner's Valkyries have** long been caricatured as symbols of opera's otherworldliness. Today, with Wagner's *Ring* cycle ever more popular, these female warriors often appear in modern dress.

sophistication, such as *Jenůfa* and *Katya Kabanova*, which are now performed alongside the works of Mozart.

### Modern opera's many faces

The notion that different opera movements can exist simultaneously was never clearer than in the 20th century. Richard Strauss's *Salome* and *Elektra* sent shock waves through the opera world. Soon afterward, Arnold Schoenberg broke with traditional ideas about music by rejecting harmony in favor of atonality (music organized without reference to a musical key). He and Alban Berg then brought dissonance (unresolved notes or chords) to opera in the 1920s, Schoenberg with *Erwartung* and *Moses und Aron*, and Berg with *Wozzeck* and *Lulu*. Yet, while they were redefining modern music, more conventional operas were still being composed.

Since the end of World War II, however, opera has resembled a laboratory, with composers like Karlheinz Stockhausen, Luciano Berio, and Philip Glass testing different idioms, from serialism (in which tones, tempos, and other variables are set in sequences) and minimalism (characterized by the repetition of musical elements) to electronic music and even explorations of silence and noise. Yet so far, among post-war composers, only Benjamin Britten is regularly performed around the globe. With *Peter Grimes* and *Billy Budd*, he successfully achieved the ideal of setting powerful librettos to deeply stirring music.

Today, as in the past, it remains the composer's challenge to keep opera moving forward with verve and originality. Encouragingly, some opera houses are

▲ **Kaija Saariaho's** *Adriana Mater*, which premiered in Paris in 2006, sets a story of maternal love in a conflict reminiscent of the Bosnian war of the 1990s.

assuring opera's future by commissioning new works, even at the risk of losing audiences who prefer old favorites over experimentation. After all, opera history proves that amid today's strangest sights and sounds may lie tomorrow's masterpieces.

### Musicals

Musical comedy is an American invention, but its roots are in Europe. Just as *opera buffa* inspired Offenbach, Lehár, and Gilbert and Sullivan to write operettas, when the operetta met American jazz, music hall, and folk music, the musical was born. George Gershwin, Cole Porter, Irving Berlin, and Richard Rodgers were drawn to it, and landmark musicals followed, from *Show Boat* to *West Side Story*. Then, after London adopted the genre, Andrew Lloyd Webber created global hits like *Cats* and *Phantom of the Opera*. Today, musicals dominate both Broadway and the West End, yet they can also serve as a gateway to opera.

▶ **The link between** popular musicals and opera was underlined by the hit show *Rent*, which borrowed its story from Puccini's opera *La bohème*.

# LIBRETTOS & LIBRETTISTS

In 1786, Antonio Salieri wrote a short entertainment called *Primo la musica e poi le parole*, making a claim in its title—"first the music, then the words"—that has kept composers and librettists arguing ever since. But the dispute is largely specious: for an opera to succeed, the music must suit the lyrics—and vice versa.

In truth, opera composers have always valued talented librettists. Wagner and Janáček wrote their own librettos, but masterworks by Mozart, Bellini, Verdi, Puccini, Richard Strauss, and Britten all resulted from close collaborations with gifted librettists. Yet librettists are often the unsung heroes of opera. Once their stories are set to music, the opera is remembered for its composer. Worse, a failed opera is often blamed on a weak libretto. At the birth of opera, there was no such dispute. In Monteverdi's *L'Orfeo*, scored to a poetic libretto by Alessandro Striggio, words formed the center of gravity: music served the text by expressing the musical qualities of the language and the action.

Nonetheless, each opera had to match the conventions and possibilities of its time. Thus, the raw material used by the librettist had to be similarly adapted, whether borrowed from such timeless storytellers as Aeschylus, Ovid, Shakespeare, or Goethe, beloved playwrights such as France's Beaumarchais, national poets like Russia's Pushkin, or history or folklore. When the courtly, quasi-academic operas of Mantua and Florence led to the rise of commercial opera, top librettists needed to hold the attention of a new, mixed public. Giovanni Faustini ruled the day in mid-17th-century Venice, where his librettos, such as *La Calisto* for composer Francesco Cavalli, featured pastoral love and comical or satirical action, often spiced with erotic tension. Giovanni Francesco Busenello took a new tack in the 1640s, when he was the first librettist to use history, rather than fiction, as his source. The result was Monteverdi's absorbing *L'incoronazione di Poppea* (1643), which invited Venetians to see the past through the new prism of music theater.

When opera traveled beyond Italian courts and cities, librettists adapted their texts to suit indigenous languages, stories, and theater traditions. Like the early librettists of Venice, some wrote for public opera houses, where a key to success was to unleash the greatest passions of paying opera-goers. Others wrote for court productions, where the task was to please the sovereign who commissioned the opera. In either case, the opera's subject had to be worthy of emotional and theatrical grandeur. Costly to mount, operas also required an unusual mix of talents and energies to stage. Already in 1627, the Spanish court tested Florentine ideas in the nascent art of *recitar cantando*, or "sung recitative," in *La selva sin amor*, with text by Spain's great dramatist Lope de Vega. »

▶ **In opera's earliest days**, both score and libretto were written with ink and quill before the composer prepared the completed work, which would then be copied by hand for singers and instrumentalists.

◀ "Orpheus, Leading Eurydice Out of Hell, Looks Back Upon Her and Loses Her Forever", a 1731 engraving by Bernard Picart, captures a mythological moment of interest to librettists since opera's earliest days.

Lully's long-time librettist, Philippe Quinault, drew on the heroic French epic for *Roland*, given at Versailles in 1685. Composing for a more hybrid London theater audience, Henry Purcell set John Dryden's libretto for *King Arthur* in 1691, and the next year adapted Shakespeare's *A Midsummer Night's Dream* for *The Fairy Queen*. As opera proliferated, its librettos gained new languages, forms, and stories.

### The 18th century

Many librettists collaborated closely with composers to shape words and music into opera. But the most famous librettist of the 18th century was a stranger to most of the composers who set his words. Metastasio, an Italian who served the court theater of Vienna, wrote dozens of librettos used by many composers, including Vivaldi, Handel, Gluck, Mozart, and even the 19th-century Meyerbeer. *Artaserse*, a libretto about the great Persian Emperor Xerxes I, was so popular that it was put to music some 50 times by various composers. Through his influential librettos, Metastasio defined the contours of *opera seria*, a form that dominated the 18th century until the momentous arrival of Mozart.

The Italian Lorenzo da Ponte collaborated with fellow countryman Antonio Salieri, as well as with Spain's Vicente Martín y Soler and the German Peter Winter. But da Ponte's legendary collaboration—indeed, one of the greatest in opera history—was with the Austrian Mozart. Da Ponte's fresh-sounding language and vibrant dramatic action inspired Mozart's best opera music, beginning with *Le nozze di Figaro*. It was called an *opera buffa*, but its characters and story were far from mere farce. For *Don Giovanni*, da Ponte went even further in mixing serious and comical strains. Along with *Così fan tutte*, such works possessed a new lyricism and energy, dynamic characterizations, and

lively dramatic structure and pacing—all perfectly suited to Mozart's musical palette. In the wake of these operas, the old Metastasian categories of *opera seria* and *opera buffa* no longer held up. As Europe's old social order crumbled following the French Revolution, a new kind of audience called for more relevant stories. Plots derived from mythical antiquity suddenly seemed distant and stale, and gave way to stories about more recognizable people struggling to achieve glory, or to find love.

### The 19th century

In France, the leading librettist was Eugène Scribe, who wrote almost 60 librettos for operas appealing to the expanding middle classes of Paris. For 30 years, a libretto by Scribe, whose stories often explored heroism of historical magnitude, served as a passport for composers seeking sure entry into the venerable Paris Opéra. Daniel Auber and Giacomo Meyerbeer

◀ **The first opera to draw its story** from historical chronicles was Monteverdi's *L'incoronazione di Poppea*, with a plot set in Emperor Nero's ancient Rome.

### Carlo Goldoni

Carlo Goldoni (1707–1793) was the greatest Italian comic stage writer of his era. As a theater reformer, he rejected stereotypes to create lifelike characters. Goldoni ran away from school as a boy to join a touring acting company. He became a lawyer, but at age 40 left the bar for the stage. He wrote for theaters in Venice until 1762, when he became director of the Comédie-Italienne in Paris. Later, he tutored Louis XV's daughters in Italian, only to die in poverty after the French Revolution. He wrote more than 150 plays and 80 opera librettos, some set by Mozart and Haydn.

▼ **As well as being a sought-after librettist**, Carlo Goldoni (shown center, with a company of traveling actors) was also an accomplished playwright.

◀ **Giacomo Puccini** (left) collaborated with Giuseppe Giacosa (center) and Luigi Illica (right) on several major operas at the turn of the 20th century.

turned to him repeatedly, but Scribe also wrote librettos for Rossini, Donizetti, Bellini, and even Verdi. The most important librettists for Verdi, though, were Francesco Maria Piave and Arrigo Boito. Piave wrote *Macbeth*, *Rigoletto*, and *La traviata*, among many other works, for Verdi, while Boito was the librettist for *Otello* and *Falstaff*. As the 19th century waned, Wagner changed the course of opera history, in part by serving as his own librettist. With his grand vision of opera as *Gesamtkunstwerk*, or "total art work," Wagner could only have realized his masterpiece, the cycle *Der Ring des Nibelungen*, by fusing his music to his own words and action. By the end of the century, Giuseppe Giacosa and Luigi Illica coauthored librettos in the Romantic Italian mold for Puccini's *La bohème*, *Tosca*, and *Madama Butterfly*. And though Puccini constantly hounded his librettists, together they created some of the world's best-loved operas.

### The modern libretto

Some remarkable librettist–composer collaborations played a large role in keeping opera alive in the 20th century. The Austrian Hugo von Hofmannsthal supplied Richard Strauss with exquisite

▶ **US president Richard Nixon's** state visit in 1972 inspired Adams' *Nixon in China*, which in the late 20th century set new trends for operas based on news events.

librettos for a string of masterpieces, beginning with *Elektra* and including *Der Rosenkavalier*. Germany's Bertolt Brecht teamed up with Kurt Weill to make opera history with original librettos for *Rise and Fall of the City of Mahagonny* and *The Threepenny Opera*. And the American Gertrude Stein penned original librettos for Virgil Thomson, whose musical voice came alive through Stein's rhythmic and flowing verses for *Four Saints in Three Acts* and *The Mother of Us All*. But the librettist of widest influence from the time of World War II was the English-born American poet W. H. Auden. His lyrical ear and keen sense of dramatic action placed him in high demand for three decades. Initially writing *Paul Bunyan* for Britten, Auden— with Chester Kallman—was later librettist to Hans Werner Henze for *Elegy for Young Lovers* and *The Bassarids*, and to Igor Stravinsky for *The Rake's Progress*. He even contributed to *Un re in ascolto*, Luciano Berio's avant-garde opera inspired by Shakespeare's *The Tempest*. By the end of the 20th century, new kinds of storytelling had found their way into opera. Robert Wilson's visual approach led him to use artwork instead of words to inspire Philip Glass's *Einstein On the Beach*. And Alice Goodman's libretto for John Adams' *Nixon in China* took its cues from television news. Yet, whatever its source material, what really counts is whether the libretto inspires a composer to weave musical magic that will take audiences on an operatic journey.

### Faust

Some stories are so operatic that they have spawned more than a handful of operas. One of these is the legend of Doctor Faust, who sold his soul to the devil to gain forbidden knowledge of the earthly world. Faust inspired literary works by Christopher Marlowe, Johann Wolfgang Goethe, and Thomas Mann, and held enduring appeal for librettists. Operas based on the legend include Hector Berlioz's *La damnation de Faust*, Charles Gounod's *Faust*, Arrigo Boito's *Mephistopheles*, and Ferruccio Busoni's *Doktor Faust*. Faustian operas of the 21st century include *Faust, The Last Night* by the French composer Pascal Dusapin.

▼ **The devil who lures Faust** is shown on the cover of a score for *La damnation de Faust*, the 1846 opera by Hector Berlioz.

# STAGING
## OPERA

Opera can be enjoyed in recordings, but it only truly comes alive when music and words meet interpretation, decor, lighting, and costumes. It is then that the audience decides if the alchemy has succeeded. For conductor and singers no less than director and designers, staging an opera is the moment of truth. And when the curtain falls on opening night, they face the public's verdict.

From opera's earliest days, audiences wanted spectacle along with music and drama. In Venice, with its rich experience of *commedia dell'arte* (a form of popular theater), public theaters soon found ingenious ways of conveying the magic of the stories being told. Louis XIV's court at Versailles then borrowed from Venice to embellish its own productions. In the strange, unreal world of opera, it seems, imaginative new machinery made everything possible. Scenes were rapidly changed between acts; gods would "fly" on and off stage on invisible wires; mountains, storms, and monsters appeared unexpectedly; flames would engulf assorted scoundrels.

Then, once Mozart had brought a fresh naturalism to operatic characters in, for example, *Le nozze di Figaro*, the Paris Opéra was free to step further toward realism with historical epics. Crowds—peasants, soldiers, courtiers—were represented by large choruses and armies of extras. Scenery became more complicated, while period costumes used velvets and silks for authenticity. Acrobats and fire-eaters peopled the stage, while real animals joined hunt scenes and royal processions. *Grand opéra*'s trademark was opulence, and Paris being Paris, opera houses in Vienna, Milan, London, and St. Petersburg followed its example.

Lighting also played a central role in shaping the aesthetics of opera. In the 17th and 18th centuries, candlelight prevailed despite the accompanying risk of fire, with metal screens sometimes masking candles placed directly in front of the stage. In the 19th century, gaslight was introduced to theaters, and, here again, techniques were developed to create mysterious color effects. Finally, from the 1880s, electricity began to reach major opera houses, allowing the auditorium to be darkened, while events on stage were transformed by spotlights, colors, and shadows. **»**

◀ **Mozart's last great opera**, *Die Zauberflöte*, or *The Magic Flute*, has always invited visually imaginative productions, as was apparent at Glyndebourne, England, in 2004.

## Enter the age of artists and directors

In the early 20th century, as Modernism swept both music and art, what opera audiences saw and heard also changed. The new art was as revolutionary as the new music of Schoenberg and Stravinsky. Diaghilev's Ballets Russes took the lead in showing it. Among the artists recruited to design decor and costumes were Pablo Picasso, Natalya Goncharova, Henri Matisse, Jean Cocteau, and Salvador Dalì. The staging of opera also mirrored new art movements, like Constructivism, Cubism, and Surrealism.

But the rise of Fascism in the 1930s drove avant-garde art from German and Italian stages. Across Europe and the United States, opera came under the sway of musicians, personified by the composer Richard Strauss and Arturo Toscanini, opera's reigning *maestro* until the 1950s. In fact, conductors ruled the roost, among them Wilhelm Furtwängler, Herbert von Karajan, Carlos Kleiber, Leonard Bernstein, Karl Böhm, and Georg Solti.

In the late 1960s, however, yet another era began in opera, prompted less by the creation of new operas than by a perceived need to make the standard opera repertory seem relevant to modern audiences. Following the example of post-war playwrights and theater directors, the idea now was to focus not on physical staging, but on interpretation. This might be supported by decor and costumes, but the approach was principally intellectual.

### Putting on an opera

An opera house must book top singers years ahead of an engagement, but its most important decision involves picking the director of a new production. Once named, this person chooses set, lighting, and costume designers, who together give form to the director's concept of the opera. Next, theater workshops start building scenery, computerizing lighting plans, and making costumes and wigs. Then, several weeks before opening night, rehearsals begin. Soloists and chorus should know their parts, but the director must define how they act. The conductor then shapes the sound of the opera, but its look is already fixed.

▲ **Making the scenery** for Offenbach's *Orphée aux enfers* at the workshop of the Paris Opéra.

Productions in modern dress became fashionable, while 19th-century operas were portrayed as 20th-century political struggles. It was to prove a watershed: the rise to operatic power of stage directors.

Unsurprisingly, the theater world supplied many influential opera directors. Patrice Chéreau was already a theater star when he directed a famous centenary production of Wagner's *Ring* cycle at the Bayreuth Festival between 1976 and 1980. Acclaimed theater directors like Peter Brook, Giorgio Strehler, and Harry Kupfer also engaged in opera with notable success, as did Ingmar Bergman, the Swedish movie and theater director. And, with directors like Richard Eyre,

Deborah Warner, Peter Stein, Stéphane Braunschweig, and Katie Mitchell, theater's influence on opera continues to this day.

### Singers as actors

The most important result has been to turn singers into actors. Since the birth of opera, they have provided most of the electricity that draws crowds to opera. From *castratos* like Farinelli, through tenors like Enrico Caruso, to soprano divas like Maria Callas, their voices and charisma have provoked hysteria. But with the new generation of directors, more was wanted of singers: now they were expected to bend to a coherent dramatic vision of an opera. The two leading tenors of the late 20th century illustrate the change. Luciano Pavarotti represented the old school of singers, who relied on the magic of their voices, while Plácido Domingo, a true actor–singer, set the theatrical standard now required of opera.

Today, singers must learn to live their roles, to convey emotion through physical and facial expression as well as through voice, to interact intensely with friends and foes alike, to sing in seemingly impossible positions, occasionally to bare themselves, and even to feign death convincingly. At times, they complain that a theater director has little understanding of their need to breathe properly as well as to act. And on such occasions, conductors and costume designers may come to their rescue.

Still, appearance is more important than ever: singers are expected to look their parts, and soloists who are handsome

◀ **Giorgio Strehler** (right), a theater director who also turned his hand to opera, marks out stage positions for *Fidelio* at the Théâtre du Châtelet, Paris, in 1989.

or beautiful and can act well are avidly courted by opera houses. And there is always a demand for opera "couples"—such as once-married Roberto Alagna and Angela Gheorghiu or Jonas Kaufmann and Anna Netrebko—for romantic roles.

## New looks on stage

As a crossroads of the arts, opera has also drawn other outsiders. Some film directors—notably Joseph Losey with *Don Giovanni* and Francesco Rosi with *Carmen*—have adapted operas for the screen. Many more—Baz Luhrmann, Julie Taymor, Anthony Minghella, and Michael Haneke among them—have brought the pace of cinema to the opera stage. Their show-business aura has helped attract a younger public to opera.

Leading choreographers have also turned to directing opera, with the lengthy musical interludes in 17th- and 18th-century works offering the best opportunity to combine song and dance. Trisha Brown's first venture

◄ **Arturo Toscanini**, pictured conducting at Milan's La Scala, was an inspirational figure in 20th-century opera.

into opera led her to Monteverdi's *L'Orfeo*, but she then applied her modern dance vocabulary to a new opera, Salvatore Sciarrino's *Luci mie traditrici*. For her magical production of Gluck's *Orfeo ed Euridice*, Pina Bausch doubled singers and dancers in the three main roles, while the chorus sang from the orchestra pit. Mark Morris, who also directed *Orfeo ed Euridice*, chose to place the singers in theater boxes, leaving the stage entirely to dancers.

There are some polymath directors who are known principally for their opera productions. Franco Zeffirelli's visual extravagance is identified with the Metropolitan Opera in New York. Other directors have been more daring, and three Americans stand out. Peter Sellars, who presented Mozart's *Così fan tutte* as a contemporary story, invariably approaches opera with a fresh eye: for Wagner's *Tristan und Isolde*, he incorporated large-screen videos by the American artist Bill Viola. Robert Wilson's minimalist productions in turn blend the stylized gestures of Japan's kabuki theater with remarkable lighting effects, while Francesca Zambello exploits the technical wizardry of modern stages.

Then there are opera directors, led by the Catalan Calixto Bieito, who set out to shock audiences with sex and gore. They often draw full houses and loud protests, but their antics can also distract from the music, leading many conductors to feel that their authority has been further eroded. More than ever, then, the opera stage is an arena in which different artistic elements vie for dominance. It is a high-risk business in which many directors become

▲ **The live performers look tiny** in this massive, quasi-Surrealist set for Puccini's *La bohème* at the Bregenz Festival in Austria in 2001.

unstuck. Yet when music, story, interpretation, decor, and costumes come together with a certain flair, opera blossoms in many colors.

### Stage fashions

Until the 20th century, costumes evoked the era in which an opera was set. Today, costumes are used to define the mood of a production: period costumes declare a traditional approach; modern dress anticipates a social or political message. And yet, stage characters may also be clothed in a peculiarly operatic melange: heroines in bejeweled gowns opposite heroes in martial Roman-style uniforms, women in brightly colored chiffon with men in black leather. But, since costumes are expensive to tailor, they are never an afterthought. In practice, while they may fit no exact period, they form an intrinsic part of every production.

▲ **Ornate costumes**, like these at the Palais Garnier in Paris, may be used in different operas, adjusted before each production to fit the singers' needs.

# OPERA HOUSES &
# FESTIVALS

Opera houses are more than just theaters. Their imposing facades suggest temples to a pagan cult, their ornate interiors reinforce the mystique for those who pass through their doors, and their stages present beauty in the form of ritual. Still more critically, they keep the art of opera alive by commissioning new works and bringing cherished classics to new audiences.

Opera houses can also be troublesome. Enormously costly to run, they live off government subsidies or private patronage. They are often arenas for fierce political struggles and are themselves variously attacked as elitist or populist. They are vulnerable to last-minute strikes by the technicians who make every performance happen. And they can present productions that send audiences into paroxysms of rage. Yet for all the headaches they cause, opera houses are loved with a passion.

A typical opera house is still one built in the late 18th or 19th centuries—its exterior is neoclassical; a marble foyer leads to a red and gold horseshoe auditorium, with boxes that originally offered a perfect view of the presiding monarch or nobles in the royal box. Indeed, for a long time, the social life of the opera house was as important as what occurred on stage. Dressed in their finery, the wealthy went to the opera to observe each other, while the less prosperous crowded the highest gallery; waited in a nearby bar; or stood below, eating and talking, until some stirring aria demanded their attention.

Certainly, the earliest opera houses, built in 17th-century Venice, reached out to all classes. It was this accessibility that quickly turned opera into popular entertainment across the Italian peninsula and beyond. First in Venice, soon in Bologna, Naples, and Milan, and later in London, Vienna, and Paris, opera houses multiplied and competed for audiences. Of these, few survive. But by the 19th century, notably in the Italian states and German principalities, every self-respecting European city boasted an opera house as a symbol of status. Then, to these were added opera festivals, starting with Wagner's Bayreuth Festival in Bavaria in 1876, followed by Austria's Salzburg Festival in 1920, and the Glyndebourne Festival in England in 1934. »

▶ **Built on the orders of Napoleon III** and inaugurated in 1875, after his overthrow, the Palais Garnier in Paris has long been considered the pinnacle of operatic opulence.

### Italy's opera shrines

In Italy, three opera houses stand as monuments to the golden age of Italian opera. The Teatro di San Carlo in Naples, arguably Italy's most beautiful theater, was inaugurated in 1737 and, while destroyed by fire in 1816, was rebuilt in just six months. Operas by Rossini, Bellini, Donizetti, and Verdi all had their premieres there. The Teatro La Fenice in Venice, a jewel squeezed among the city's canals, opened in 1792 and, though ravaged by fire in 1836 and again in 1996, was twice rebuilt, living up to its name of The Phoenix. Verdi premiered operas at La Fenice, as did Igor Stravinsky and Benjamin Britten in the 20th century. To this day, Venetians walk through its doors with a sense of pride. Milan's Teatro alla Scala, or simply La Scala,

has long been the true home of opera in Italy. Every 19th-century Italian composer wanted his opera to premiere there, with none more present than Verdi. For rising soloists, consecration at La Scala also became a vital rite of passage. Badly damaged by Allied bombing in 1943, the theater opened anew in 1946. Then, in 2001, it was closed for three years to undergo modernization of its backstage, although its glorious auditorium remains much as when Austria's Empress Maria Theresa inaugurated it in 1778.

Elsewhere in Europe, the history of opera houses is no less a record of fires and war damage. Before the Paris Opéra occupied the seemingly impregnable Palais Garnier in 1875, no fewer than six of its previous homes were razed by fire. In Vienna, several opera houses preceded the opening of the grand Hofopernhaus in 1869. In 1920, after the collapse of the Hapsburg monarchy, the Hofopernhaus became the Wiener Staatsoper. Then, while

▲ **Venice's glorious Teatro La Fenice** burned down in 1996, allegedly the result of arson, but it was rebuilt and reopened with a larger backstage in 2003.

it functioned under the Nazi occupation, it, too, was damaged by Allied bombers in 1945 and only reopened in 1955.

### The German operatic motor

Inevitably, German opera houses suffered most during World War II, with those of Berlin, Cologne, Dresden, Hamburg, Leipzig, and Stuttgart among dozens destroyed. The elegant 18th-century Staatsoper Unter den Linden in Berlin and the Bayerische Staatsoper in Munich were reconstructed, but in most cases new buildings were necessary. What was not affected was Germany's devotion to opera. To this day, no country has more opera houses than Germany, most working on a repertory system: singers from around the world head to sing in Germany, the only country where they can quickly build up a roster of roles.

▼ **Inaugurated in 1778**, Milan's world-famous Teatro alla Scala (La Scala) was at the heart of the city's social and political life throughout the 19th century.

### The opera boss

Opera houses only prosper when they have strong leaders. In 18th-century London, Handel managed his own theaters, while Domenico Barbaia shaped 19th-century Italian opera at both La Scala in Milan and the San Carlo in Naples. Sometimes, the drive comes from conductors, such as Richard Strauss at Vienna's Staatsoper; Arturo Toscanini at La Scala; and, more recently, James Levine at the Metropolitan Opera in New York. In the 1970s, it was the theater manager and composer Rolf Liebermann who brought innovation to the Paris Opéra. Whether a theater presents top singers, exciting productions, or new operas depends on who is in charge.

In England, too, war disrupted opera, with the Royal Opera House at Covent Garden used as a dance hall and the Sadler's Wells Theatre as a shelter for homeless Londoners. Inaugurated in 1858, the Royal Opera House survived the war and was finally modernized and expanded in the late 1990s. The Sadler's Wells Opera moved in 1968 to the London Coliseum, where in 1974 it was renamed the English National Opera. The Welsh National Opera, founded in 1943, was in turn given a new home at the Wales Millennium Centre in Cardiff Bay in 2004.

Until World War II, it was traditional for operas to be sung in the language of the audience. For instance, while Paris had a Théâtre-Italien, even Donizetti and Verdi had to use French librettos to gain access to the Paris Opéra. In fact, audiences everywhere wanted to hear words sung in their own language. It was also easier for the singers, who were usually employed by opera houses. Today, however, operas are performed in their original language almost everywhere: the English National Opera; the Komische Oper in Berlin; and the Opera Theatre in St. Louis, Missouri, are among the few exceptions. The reason for the change was practical. Opera has become so internationalized that major stages now present singers from all over the world. And peripatetic soloists have no time to learn the same role in several languages. The preferred solution, then, is to provide translation, either above the proscenium stage or on the backs of seats.

### Forever Salzburg

In a calendar crowded with summer festivals, one held in Mozart's birthplace clearly has special appeal. With Richard Strauss among its founders in 1920, the Salzburg Festival flourished until the Nazis occupied Austria in 1938. Then, in the post-war era, with the Vienna Philharmonic again its resident orchestra, it became the fiefdom of Herbert von Karajan who, in 1967, added the Salzburg Easter Festival. Today, with top conductors, orchestras, and singers on their programs, the festivals remain among Europe's most prestigious.

▶ **A busy night** in the Festival Quarter in Salzburg.

### Opera's long reach

Opera itself had no trouble traveling, spawning opera houses in Prague—its Estates Theatre premiered Mozart's *Don Giovanni* in 1787—and across Eastern Europe. Russia's czars also wanted opera, building the Mariinsky Theatre in St. Petersburg and the Bolshoi Theatre in Moscow. The opera fad spread still further afield: the Cairo Opera House opened in 1869, the Manaus Opera House in the heart of the Amazon in 1896, the Teatro Colón in Buenos Aires in 1908, and the Hanoi Opera in French Indochina in 1911.

With its large European immigrant population, the United States also quickly embraced opera: gold and silver boom towns in the West were among the first to build opera houses. But the turning-point was to come in New York in 1883 with the opening of the Metropolitan Opera, which was soon featuring top soloists in the best European operas. And it preserved its reputation for showcasing star singers after it moved to its far larger current home in Lincoln Center in 1966.

Meanwhile, most American cities presented opera. In 1857, Philadelphia's Academy of Music auditorium was modeled on La Scala. San Francisco, which lost many theaters in the 1906 earthquake, moved its new opera company into the War Memorial Opera House in 1932. Today, opera houses flourish across America, from Seattle to Washington, Los Angeles to Miami, Chicago to Houston.

For the Soviet Union, too, opera represented status and political power, and, by the mid-20th century, the capital of every Soviet republic, from Kiev to Tashkent, had its own opera house. And elsewhere, pride continues to generate opera houses. None is more iconic than the Sydney Opera House, which opened in 1973. But Paris now also has the Opéra Bastille, while Copenhagen and Valencia have new opera houses. Festivals have also multiplied, with Aldeburgh in England, Aix-en-Provence in France, Verona in Italy, and Santa Fe in the United States among the most popular. There is also a growing interest in European opera in Asia, with opera houses opening in Seoul in 1993, Tokyo in 1997, Shanghai in 1998, and Beijing in 2008.

◀ **The Staatsoper Unter den Linden**, Berlin's oldest opera house, has recovered its former glory since German reunification.

Idols of opera

# IDOLS OF
# OPERA

Opera is inseparable from diva worship. Over the centuries, a small number of singers with exceptional voices and powerful personalities have come to personify all the passion and drama of opera. And opera fans have always responded to them—with excitement, adulation, even hysteria. Onstage and off, opera's idols fuel the entire art form with their love of high drama.

arger-than-life opera stars are almost always sopranos—*divas*, or "goddesses" in Italian—but they can also be tenors. In an earlier age, they were often castratos. Together, they have played a central role in perpetuating the mysterious appeal of opera. What is their secret?

A talent for reaching extraordinarily high notes is almost a must: a high C, well sung and long held by a soprano or a tenor, electrifies audiences. The reigning opera vocalists are also gifted actors, bringing roles to life with the conviction of their singing. Yet just as important are their glamorous and volatile personalities. It is little wonder that many divas became muses to the best opera composers and conductors.

But it is among opera lovers that diva addiction thrives. They follow their favorite singers around the world; they toss bouquets of flowers at curtain calls; and they collect the minutiae of divas' lives, from stories of lovers to pets, hairstyles, and diets. The reigning diva, or *diva assoluta*, can even acquire a telling alias. The ultra-revered 20th-century Greek-American soprano Maria Callas was known as *La Divina* ("The Divine One"), while her rival Renata Tebaldi was dubbed *La Regina* ("The Queen").

Certainly, top singers can be moody and demanding, and many have been infamously capricious and narcissistic. But they can afford to be: their mere presence sells out an opera house. So, along with enduring weighty costumes, itchy wigs, ungainly props, and bizarre special effects, they carry heavy commercial responsibilities. And, since the early period of public opera houses in Venice, they have commanded exorbitant fees. Even today, they are often paid in cash in their dressing-rooms during the first interval of an opera performance. »

◄ **Maria Callas was acclaimed** for a final time by her English fans at London's Royal Festival Hall in November 1973 as part of her year-long farewell tour accompanied by the Italian tenor Giuseppe di Stefano. She died in Paris four years later.

### The long march

Audiences cheering a popular singer at a curtain call rarely wonder how success is forged. The answer invariably involves years of toil in music conservatories and small companies and then, crucially, a stroke of luck. With Luciano Pavarotti, it was when the soprano Joan Sutherland needed a tenor taller than herself for a tour to Australia. For the Russian soprano Aida Garifullina (right), winning the 2013 Operalia competition led to three years at the Vienna Staatsoper, then major roles on world stages. Stepping in as an understudy when the lead singer is sick can also transform a career. But even divas need thick skins: rare is the singer who has never been booed.

### Castratos

The entire diva saga can be traced back to opera's castratos, whose voices evolved out of sacred choir music, and whose techniques were passed down to future vocalists through the Italian tradition of *bel canto* singing. Castratos were the first opera stars, and established the rules for the divas who followed. For some castratos, special treatment began with vocal training. Even before opera emerged, promising boy singers schooled in Italian conservatories were fed richer foods, and lodged more comfortably than other classmates, all in the name of enhancing their voices. With females in the Papal Roman states forbidden to sing in church or in public over the first 200 years of opera, castratos were highly prized.

Potentially dangerous and occasionally fatal, castration involved the severing of a duct, and not the removal of an organ. Officially banned, it was nonetheless practiced since medieval times in order to supply church choirs with glorious, high male voices. When opera appeared in the 17th century, castratos readily sang male as well as female roles. The most popular dazzled fans far and wide, among them Carlo Broschi, who made his debut in Naples in 1720. Under the name Farinelli, he earned cult followings in opera houses and courts throughout Europe. Another 18th-century castrato, Luigi Marchesi, had such a following that opera houses accepted his outrageous demands: he was to enter the stage sporting a plumed helmet, riding a horse, and singing any aria his heart desired, even if it was not in the opera he was performing.

Castratos also bequeathed to divas their often stormy natures. Gaetano Majorano riveted audiences under the name Caffarelli in the 18th century, but he also skipped rehearsals, canceled appearances on a whim, loudly criticized other singers during performances, and even physically attacked fellow artists.

▼ **Farinelli, whose real name was** Carlo Broschi (1705–1782), traveled throughout Europe. For a time, he appeared with the Opera of the Nobility in London.

▶ **Renata Scotto's vocal** daring made her the Puccini interpreter *par excellence*, in roles such as Musetta (right), Mimì, Cio-Cio-San, and the three heroines of *Il trittico*.

### Prima donnas

Where women were allowed to appear on stage in the 17th and 18th centuries, prima donnas (first ladies) were cherished. Venice anointed Anna Renzi, the first female singer to fill opera houses; her roles included Ottavia in Monteverdi's 1643 *L'incoronazione di Poppea*. By Handel's era, the Italians Faustina Bordoni and Francesca Cuzzoni were known throughout Europe as much for combustible tempers as for vocal fireworks. By the end of the 18th century, Caterina Gabrielli had also spread diva joy—and wreaked diva havoc—from Russia to Sicily. Like her castrato compatriot Caffarelli, the headstrong Gabrielli served a brief prison sentence for outrageous conduct while performing.

The Romantic era ushered out the castrato, but welcomed new voice types and divas to go with them. Soprano Angelica Catalani drove Europe wild with her voice and stage presence, even as her high fees and defiance scandalized imperial leaders from Catherine the Great to Napoleon. Roles scored by Rossini produced mezzo-soprano divas, such as the legendary Maria Malibran.

◀ **The Three Tenors** sang their debut concert on the eve of the 1990 World Cup in Rome. Their signature song was "Nessun dorma" from Puccini's *Turandot*, with its climactic moment on the word *vincerò* ("I will win").

And in the 1830s, soprano Giuditta Pasta shook La Scala with her creations of Bellini roles, including Norma.

But the golden age for divas arrived with Verdi. Any pretender to the title of reigning diva had to leave her mark on Violetta of *La traviata*, or the title role of *Aïda*. And with opera houses and conservatories opening across the world in his era, Verdi was the first to score roles that instantly spoke to international audiences. Puccini's touching prima donnas—Tosca, Manon Lescaut, Cio-Cio-San, Mimì—would gain a place of their own in the pantheon of diva-making roles. Glamorous Czech soprano Emmy Destinn was among the first of many to bring Puccini's suffering females fame on a global scale.

Wagnerian opera demanded more stamina and distinct vocal technique. The controversial *vibrato*, with the voice seeming to wobble, allowed voices to be heard over a more sonorous and sizable orchestra. The noted Wagnerian soprano diva Lilli Lehmann blazed trails, inspiring generations of Sieglindes and Brünnhildes

in her wake. Operas by Richard Strauss called for yet another kind of prima donna to set singing on a new course over the 20th century. But with few exceptions, the modern-day diva prefers the dramatic characters of former eras over the more abstract roles of contemporary opera.

For the past 100 years, too, star singers have gained still greater notoriety as recording artists. German soprano Elisabeth Schwarzkopf, *diva assoluta* Maria Callas, Italian mezzo-soprano Cecilia Bartoli, and American soprano Renée Fleming are among them. But even fine recordings of top singers fail to capture the thrill of a live performance in an opera house.

### Tenors

Since the wane of the castrato, noted male voices have mainly been tenors. Early divos—although the term is rarely used—were passionate romantic lovers or historical saviors; later, the Wagnerian Heldentenor (literally "heroic tenor") produced a more forceful sound suited to mythical themes and larger orchestras.

In the 1820s, the Italian Giovanni Battista Rubini amazed opera houses with a high voice modeled on florid castrato effects. And the French tenor Adolphe Nourrit made audiences swoon and scream in the 1820s and 1830s, especially at the Paris Opéra, where he created countless roles. But the sensuous voice of Frenchman Gilbert-Louis Duprez, who in 1836 became the first tenor to float up from the chest to a high C, is credited with setting off a tenor craze that continues to this day. Venerated as opera performers and recording stars alike were Enrico Caruso, the Italian whose glorious voice brought new audiences to opera, and Danish Wagnerian Heldentenor Lauritz Melchior, whose performances and recordings of the early half of the 20th century remain legendary.

Unusually for the history of opera, the biggest stars of the late 20th century were tenors: Luciano Pavarotti and Plácido Domingo, who not only stirred frenzies among opera-goers but also, with José Carreras, took opera's most popular tunes to a mass audience as The Three Tenors. Such was their importance to opera houses, recording companies, and fans, that expectations rise every time an impressive young tenor—and potential successor— appears on stage. And the same applies to striking new sopranos who show promise.

Certainly, it is hard to imagine that opera would have survived 400 years without its beloved vocalists. Indeed, they inspire composers, excite audiences, and fill theaters far and wide. They also stir the deep passions that continue to assure opera's future.

### Diva vs. diva

In 1727, the Italian sopranos Faustina Bordoni and Francesca Cuzzoni broke into fisticuffs while singing on stage in London. Bookings for both performers soared, and John Gay immortalized the duo in *The Beggar's Opera* (1728). Paris in the 1840s saw mezzo-soprano rivalry, when Rosine Stoltz, mistress of the director of the Opéra, drove the threatening Julie Dorus-Gras from the company; Stoltz was later ejected herself when Paris tired of her diva tyranny. Methods differed at London's Covent Garden, where Australian soprano Nellie

Melba barred Luisa Tetrazzini. But their rivalry exploded in 1907, when Melba returned from a trip to learn that her nemesis had taken 20 curtain calls as Violetta in Verdi's *La traviata*. The Verdi role unleashed diva fury again in 1951, when Maria Callas told Renata Tebaldi that her Violetta was deficient. Tebaldi, who refused to appear at Milan's La Scala whenever Callas did, snapped that "a chicken coop doesn't hold two roosters." Callas, the Greek-American diva, had recently declared her own voice champagne to Tebaldi's Coca-Cola in a 1956 cover story for *Time* magazine.

▲ **Tetrazzini and Melba**, aptly caricatured as dueling gramophones in *Punch* magazine, 1908.

# MONTEVERDI TO MOZART

(c. 1600–1800)

# Monteverdi to Mozart c. 1600–1800

When Claudio Monteverdi fashioned a new kind of entertainment at the Gonzaga family's court in Mantua in 1607, few could have foreseen its rapid rise and far reach. From Sicily to St. Petersburg, more than 1,000 operas were created before Mozart's birth in 1756. With its mix of music, drama, and spectacle, opera awakened powerful appetites for a new art form.

## Opera before Mozart

In recent decades, operas composed between 1600 and 1750 have returned to vogue. One reason for this is the rediscovery that early opera's seeming restraint hides contrasting expressions of love and jealousy, bliss and torment, or yearnings to live or even die. Often portrayed are larger-than-life figures borrowed from mythology or chivalric romances, their emotional turmoil amplified through beautiful music, stunning costumes and scenery, and pyrotechnical stagecraft.

## Venice

Opera moved rapidly from Renaissance courts to popular forums, starting in Venice, where the first theater to welcome a paying public opened in 1637. Already in the 1640s, theaters teemed with innovation. Monteverdi's *L'incoronazione di Poppea*, set in the time of Emperor Nero, was the first opera to take history, rather than mythology, as its source. The sensual music of Francesco Cavalli, often to risqué librettos by Giovanni Faustini, captivated decades of opera-goers in works such as *La Calisto*. Venice in the 1730s was besotted with new sounds arriving from Naples, not least that of castrato singers such as Farinelli. The "Neapolitan style" was all about vocal virtuosity and, to the Venetian Antonio Vivaldi's distress, it became all the rage in his hometown.

## Naples

The city of Naples boasted four conservatories, music masters, and a steady supply of budding talents who readily adapted to the growing demand for opera singers. Most prized in Naples was the gifted and studious young castrato whose exquisite high voice

◀ **A mid-18th-century painting** of music-makers by Pietro Fabris depicts the vibrant cultural life of an aristocratic household in Naples.

would be preserved into adulthood. In principle sacrilegious, and also dangerous, castration was usually performed by family members who were willing to imperil a boy's welfare in the hope of assuring him a well-paid career. The castrato's moment of operatic glory came in the 18th century, with the da capo aria; its first section was repeated with elaborate improvisation and vocal ornaments, such as trills. Like the castratos, Neapolitan composers and librettists often served foreign courts and theaters.

## London

England's Civil War in the mid-17th century shut down theaters, which only reopened after the Restoration of 1660. Henry Purcell, influenced by Shakespeare's plays and pageant-like masques, wrote numerous "semi-operas." But the sole true opera in English, and indeed the only great opera in English before the 20th century, was Purcell's *Dido and Aeneas* of 1689, with "Dido's Lament" a popular solo to this day. Eighteenth-century London would welcome the prolific German George Frideric Handel, in whose hands the *opera seria*, or "serious opera," reached its zenith. His Baroque masterpieces *Giulio Cesare* and *Tamerlano*, sung in Italian, were both given in 1724, when he ran the Royal Academy of Music. But competition for audiences was stiff. *The Beggar's Opera* (1728), for instance, was a groundbreaking "ballad opera" by John Gay that sparkled with satirical irreverence. By 1741, the time of Handel's final opera, London opera-goers had had their fill of *opera seria* sung in Italian.

## Paris

Spectacular entertainments were integral to the Versailles of King Louis XIV, with the Italian Jean-Baptiste Lully the court's reigning composer. His love of dance, shared by his monarch, left a strong mark on French opera, with dance featuring prominently in the operas of Jean-Philippe Rameau a century later. More popular entertainment came with the arrival in Paris of Neapolitan *opera buffa*, or "comic opera." But it was Vienna that sparked a more radical reform of French musical formalism thanks to the influence of Christoph Willibald Gluck. His approach to language and orchestration heralded the arrival of Classical opera when his works premiered in Paris in the 1770s. Indeed, for many scholars, Gluck paved the way for Mozart.

# Claudio Monteverdi

Born: May 9, 1567, Cremona (Italy) • Died: November 29, 1643, Venice, Italy

Claudio Monteverdi is regarded as opera's founding father. His *L'Orfeo*, first performed in 1607, was the first work to unite opera's basic ingredients in an enduring manner. Monteverdi's early lyric dramas were the fruit of courtly Mantua, while his late operatic masterpieces were for public audiences in Venice. No other opera composer made such a leap.

### FIRST PERFORMANCES

- 1607 *L'Orfeo*

- 1608 *L'Arianna* (only a lament survives) • *Il ballo delle ingrate*

- 1624 *Il combattimento di Tancredi e Clorinda*

- 1640 *Il ritorno d'Ulisse in patria*

- 1641 *Le nozze d'Enea con Lavinia* (lost)

- 1643 *L'incoronazione di Poppea*

◀ **Danielle de Niese as Poppea** embraces Alice Coote as Nerone in a 2008 Glyndebourne production of *L'incoronazione di Poppea*, directed by Robert Carsen, with the Orchestra of the Age of Enlightenment conducted by Emmanuelle Haïm.

W hen Monteverdi arrived in Mantua in 1590 as a young string player for Duke Vincenzo Gonzaga, the court was bubbling with cultural innovation. The setting was ideal for a rising composer with an ear for polyphony and a keen sense of dramatic action. Monteverdi had already spent time in Cremona, studying with the director of music at the cathedral and composing many popular madrigals.

But Mantua offered new musical horizons. By the late 15th century, the court had assembled musicians, poets, dancers, and painters to stage heroic and pastoral stories. A century later, Monteverdi performed as a musician in the latest of these, and by 1602 became Mantua's music director. There, in 1607, his momentous *L'Orfeo* premiered.

In 1613, Monteverdi became the music director at the Basilica of St. Mark in Venice. In 1637, Venice saw the opening of the first commercial opera house. Until then, operas addressed the noble and mythological themes preferred by their commissioners. But success was now in the hands of paying audiences. They wanted marvelous sets, gripping dramas, and exhilarating arias delivered by virtuoso singers. At first, Monteverdi failed to appreciate this, offering a revision of his ill-suited *L'Arianna*, an opera originally composed for Mantua's court. But he struck Venetian gold with *Il ritorno d'Ulisse in patria* (1640) and *L'incoronazione di Poppea* (1643).

## "How can I move the passions?"

CLAUDIO MONTEVERDI

# Il ritorno d'Ulisse in patria

THE RETURN OF ULYSSES TO HIS HOMELAND Opera in a prologue and five acts, 3 hours • Composed: Year unknown • First performed: Carnival in February 1640, Teatro San Cassiano, Venice, Italy • Libretto: Giacomo Badoaro, based on Books 12–23 of Homer's *The Odyssey* (late 8th century BCE)

*Il ritorno d'Ulisse in patria*, Monteverdi's first opera for the public theater world of Venice, premiered when he was 73. Even so, he adapted to the tastes of his new audience, introducing comic figures, such as the glutton Iro, and stage effects, including those that would deliver the goddess Minerva from the heavens. The opera was successful enough to be given in Bologna the same year as its Venice premiere, and to return to Venice the following year. Monteverdi's first opera, *L'Orfeo*, composed more than 30 years earlier, was built of more rigid recitatives and arias. But *Il ritorno d'Ulisse in patria* uses another approach, freeing orchestra and voices to explore a more fluid palette of expression.

## Prologue
L'Humana Fragilità (Human Frailty) deplores Time, Fortune, and Love.

## Act I
Penelope bitterly awaits her husband's return following the Trojan War. Her servant, Melanto, hopes that Penelope will choose one of her many suitors. At sea, Nymphs quiet the winds so that Ulisse may sleep through his return to Ithaca, but the sea god Nettuno, angry at Ulisse, turns the ship to stone. Ulisse awakens confused on shore ("Dormo ancora"). But he soon recognizes his protector goddess, Minerva, who has taken the form of a shepherd. She gives Ulisse the appearance of an old man so he may face his rivals incognito. Learning that his servant Eumete awaits him, and that his son Telemaco will arrive, he rejoices in the strength that allows mortals to bear joy and torment.

## Act II
In the palace, Penelope rejects the idea of accepting a suitor. At a nearby fountain, Eumete chases the gluttonous Iro from his flock and offers refuge to Ulisse, whom he takes to be a beggar. From her chariot, Minerva presents Telemaco. He watches in awe as the earth appears to swallow up the "beggar" and regurgitate his father ("Che veggio, ohimè"). Reunited, Telemaco and Ulisse weep with joy.

## Act III
In the palace, Melanto and Eurimaco, another servant, celebrate love while suitors fail to amuse Penelope with songs and dances. Eumete announces Telemaco's return, and, when he suggests that Ulisse may follow, suitors brace for vengeance ("Amor è un'armonia"). In a wood, Minerva instructs Ulisse: she will assure his victory in a game to avenge him against his rivals.

## Act IV
Telemaco tells his mother that Helen of Troy was worth warring for ("Del mio lungo viaggio"). Eumete ushers in a "beggar," who defeats Iro in a wrestling match. Governed by Minerva's power, Penelope proposes that whoever best shoots an arrow from Ulisse's bow will win wife and kingdom. All suitors fail even to bend the bow. But the "beggar" sends an arrow flying. Minerva guides the arrow to slay the suitors.

## Act V
The slain Iro prepares for his well-fed body to feed worms ("Oh dolor"). The suitors' ghosts departed, Penelope refuses to believe that the bowman is Ulisse. In heaven, Nettuno finally agrees to forgive Ulisse. Within the palace, Penelope at first suspects sorcery when she sees the undisguised Ulisse. He reminds his wife of images of Diana that she wove into their bed sheets. Penelope begs his forgiveness and the couple rejoice.

### PRINCIPAL ROLES

**Ulisse** *tenor* King of Ithaca

**Penelope** *soprano*
Faithful wife to Ulisse

**Telemaco** *tenor*
Son to Ulisse and Penelope

**Ericlea** *mezzo-soprano*
Childhood nurse to Ulisse

**Melanto** *soprano*
Servant to Penelope

**Eumete** *tenor*
A poor old shepherd

**Iro** *tenor* A gluttonous nobleman

▼ **Michael Chance as Ulisse** at the English National Opera in 1992. Reunited with his powerful bow, he prepares to use it against his enemies.

Opera's first great tragic heroine, Penelope sings exclusively in grief-stricken recitative until the opera's final scene. Then, when she recognizes her husband, Ulisse, she joins him in a glorious duet.

# L'Orfeo

ORPHEUS *Favola in musica* in a prologue and five acts, 1¾ hours • Composed: c. 1607 • First performed: February 24, 1607, Palazzo Ducale, Mantua • Libretto: Alessandro Striggio, Jr., after *L'Euridice* (1600) by Ottavio Rinuccini

*L'Orfeo* is often called the first opera, but opera's evolution was in fact too gradual to support such a pat claim. Still, *L'Orfeo* presents the earliest successful synthesis of elements that define opera: sung words, dramatic impersonation, scenery, and music. The opera opens in joy, and passes through shock and grief before descending further, into regions of hell. Indeed, the work oscillates between hope and despair, praise and lament. Immortalized, Orfeo finally transcends his extreme passions. Following Monteverdi, strong emotions would remain the essence of great opera.

## PRINCIPAL ROLES

**La Musica** *soprano* Music personified

**Orfeo** *tenor* Shepherd and musician

**Euridice** *soprano* Wife to Orfeo

**Silvia** *soprano* Member of Euridice's entourage

**Speranza (Hope)** *soprano*
Orfeo's escort to Hades

**Caronte** *bass* Ferryman of the River Styx

**Plutone** *bass* God of the underworld

## Prologue

La Musica celebrates the power of music to "incline men's souls to heaven."

## Act I

On the open fields of Thrace, shepherds and nymphs celebrate the union of Orfeo and Euridice, and the end of Orfeo's lovesickness ("Lasciate i monti"). Orfeo invites the "Rose of Heaven," the Sun, to witness his joy, and sings to Euridice of his love for her. Euridice returns his love, and all prepare to pray that the gods preserve her life. Nymphs and shepherds note that joy is all the greater following its absence, and Orfeo's laments have given way to rousing praise.

## Act II

Orfeo addresses the groves of trees, reminding them how his laments had extracted pity even from stones. He sings of the former suffering that makes present joy all the more blissful. Suddenly, Silvia reports horrifying news: Euridice, bitten by a snake, died in her arms ("In un fiorito prato"). Orfeo is determined to use the power of song to soften the hard heart of Plutone, the ruler of Hades, and thus either return Euridice to life on earth, or else remain in hell himself ("Tu se morta").

The Mantuan courtier Carlo Magno wrote on the day before *L'Orfeo*'s premiere that the work was unusual because "all the actors sing their parts." He also worried that the hall would be too crowded for him to attend.

◀ **Gyula Orendt's** Orfeo is overwhelmed with despair by the death of Euridice, sung by Mary Bevan in a 2015 production by the Royal Opera House, London.

▲ **Simon Keenlyside interprets the role** of Orfeo in a production conducted by René Jacobs and choreographed by Trisha Brown for the Festival d'Aix-en-Provence, France, in 1998.

### Act III

Speranza (Hope) escorts Orfeo to the threshold of Hades, where he is warned by Caronte, ferryman of the River Styx, to proceed no further ("O tu ch'innanzi morte"). Orfeo attempts to gain access with his music ("Possente spirto"), but Caronte is unmoved. When a new tune lulls the ferryman to sleep, Orfeo passes unnoticed into hell. Underworld spirits sing of human success achieved through the courageous defiance of obstacles.

### Act IV

In Hades, Proserpina appeals to her husband Plutone to grant Orfeo's prayers. Moved, Plutone agrees that Euridice may regain life, on the condition that Orfeo does not behold her during their return journey from hell. Spirits note Plutone's orders, while Orfeo praises his lyre for bringing him success. Yet, unsure that Euridice follows him, Orfeo turns to behold his beloved. He briefly sees her before she disappears, then cries out in song for losing what he loved too much. Orfeo is drawn back into daylight as spirits note that he is defeated by his own affections.

### Act V

Back in the fields of Thrace, the stricken Orfeo vows to lament always amid Nature's hills and stones. Echo, the signal voice of bereavement, returns his words. Orfeo praises Euridice's soul and body, but sings angrily of all other women. His father, the god Apollo, descends from heaven to discourage ignoble excess of both joy and grief. Virtue is rewarded as father and son ascend into the heavens ("Saliam cantando al cielo").

### Orpheus and opera

With its immortal singer-hero, tragic love story, and emotional intensity, the Orpheus myth has inspired operas through the ages, beginning with Jacopo Peri's 1600 *Euridice*. Christoph Willibald Gluck used the story for his Classical *Orfeo ed Euridice* (1762) and revised *Orphée* (1774). With *Orphée aux enfers* (1858), Jacques Offenbach set the myth as operetta. In the 1990s, Jean Cocteau's films inspired American Philip Glass to compose an Orpheus opera trilogy.

▶ **A film poster** by Jean Cocteau for his *Le Testament d'Orphée*.

# L'incoronazione di Poppea

THE CORONATION OF POPPEA Opera in a prologue and three acts, 3½ hours • Composed: 1642 • First performed: Carnival in 1643, Teatro Santi Giovanni e Paolo, Venice, Italy • Libretto: Giovanni Francesco Busenello, after Tacitus, Suetonius, and perhaps Seneca

*L'incoronazione di Poppea*, an early masterpiece, is the first opera to be based on a historical rather than a mythological or fictional subject. The libretto draws on ancient Roman biographical portraits of Emperor Nero to explore adultery, lust, and ambition. The opera premiered during Carnival, when license to push moral boundaries was freer than usual. More than other Monteverdi operas, *L'incoronazione di Poppea* relies on the strengths of vocalists in its many commanding lead roles. The opera's authorship has been questioned, and the hands of other composers, including Cavalli, have been detected in the score.

## PRINCIPAL ROLES

**Nerone** *soprano* Roman Emperor

**Ottavia** *mezzo-soprano* Roman Empress

**Poppea** *soprano* Lover to Nerone

**Drusilla** *soprano* Servant to Ottavia

**Ottone** *male soprano* In love with Poppea

**Arnalta** *alto* Confidante to Poppea

**Seneca** *bass* Adviser to Nerone

**Lucano** *tenor* Poet serving Nerone

**Venere (Venus)** *soprano* Goddess of Beauty

### Prologue
On clouds, Fortuna, Virtù, and Amore ("Fortune," "Virtue," and "Love") debate which of them is sovereign. All agree: Love commands the world.

### Act I
Ottone stands before his beloved Poppea's home near Rome, crushed that she is sharing her bed with Emperor Nerone ("E pur io torno qui"). Inside, Poppea learns with joy that Nerone plans to divorce his wife, Empress Ottavia. Arnalta, Poppea's confidante, warns against her affair with Nerone, but Poppea dreams of becoming empress. In Rome, Ottavia laments the lot of women ("Disprezzata regina"). Her nurse urges her to forget Nerone's infidelity, but she cannot. Seneca notes the virtuous strength her fate has given her. Alone, he considers the sufferings of the crowned, and greets Athena, who descends from heaven to forewarn him of his death. Then, Nerone tells Seneca that Poppea will be empress, and is enraged when Seneca questions the wisdom of this. During their next tryst, Poppea provokes Nerone to order Seneca's death. Ottone talks himself out of his love for Poppea and welcomes the attentions of his former lover Drusilla, who serves Ottavia. But in his heart he knows that he still belongs to Poppea.

### Act II
Seneca receives Nerone's death sentence. Once it is carried out, Nerone requests a love song from Lucano. Ottone realizes he is still deeply in love with Poppea,

The notoriously decadent Emperor Nero inspired Busenello to write scenes that sizzle with erotic energy. A line of Nero's to Poppea: "As I behold you, my eyes take back the flaming spirit that I spent inside you."

◀ **Malena Ernman's Nerone** receives a steamy kiss from Carmen Giannattasio's Poppea at Berlin's Staatsoper in 2006.

but Ottavia commands him on pain of death to disguise himself as a woman and slay Poppea. He confides in Drusilla, who offers clothes for his disguise. In her garden, Poppea rejoices at news of Seneca's death, then sleeps as her nurse, Arnalta, sings a lullaby ("Adagiati, Poppea"). Disguised as Drusilla, Ottone enters the garden to commit murder. But Amore blocks him; Poppea awakens to see "Drusilla" poised over her with a knife, and Ottone escapes.

## Act III
Drusilla awaits news of her rival's death. Instead, she is arrested for attempted murder and presented to Nerone. To protect Ottone, she admits to the crime, and is removed for execution. But Ottone

▲ **Jacek Laszczkowski, as Nerone**, and Anna Caterina Antonacci, as Poppea, perform in the coronation scene staged by David Alden at the Opéra Bastille, Paris, 2005.

confesses, explaining that Ottavia ordered the murder. Nerone sends the three plotters into exile, and renews his bond of love with Poppea ("Ne più s'interporrà noia o dimora"). Ottavia touchingly bids Rome farewell ("A Dio, Roma! a Dio, patria!"). In Rome, Consuls and Tribunes crown Poppea empress. And, with the blessing of Venere, goddess of beauty in heaven, Amore crowns Poppea goddess of beauty on earth. Finally, Poppea and Nerone love and idolize one another ("Pur ti miro, pur ti godo").

### Prima prima donna

The original Empress Ottavia was Anna Renzi (right), the first female vocalist to make opera her profession. Women had performed in opera from as early as 1600, when Jacopo Peri's daughters sang in his privately given *Euridice*. But Renzi rose to fame in the public opera houses of Venice, where the Papal Roman decrees preventing women from performing onstage were not enforced. Having created Ottavia as a young woman, Renzi went on to enjoy a long career as the best-loved prima donna of Venice.

# Jean-Baptiste Lully

Born: November 28, 1632, Florence, Italy ▪ Died: March 22, 1687, Paris, France

Jean-Baptiste Lully ruled 17th-century French opera with an authority as absolute as that of his sovereign, Louis XIV. As politically cunning as he was musically gifted, Lully composed regal operas enhanced by dances and *divertissements*. They remained a reference point for French opera through the dawn of the French Revolution.

Born in Florence, Lully arrived in Paris at 13. At age 20, he was a noted violin player in the court ensemble of the young monarch, Louis XIV. As the king flourished, so did Lully. The budding composer rose to prominent posts, and earned acclaim as a musician and exceptional dancer. With Molière in the 1660s, he introduced music to plays to create a new dramatic genre, the *comédie-ballet*. Having insisted that the French language was unsuitable for opera, Lully was taken aback in 1671 by the success of Robert Cambert's *Pomone*, the first opera in French; he began attending plays to study cadences of French speech, and to fashion a recitative style adapted to the language. Cambert's financial problems soon allowed Lully to seize his royal rights to stage operas. After that, virtually no music theater could be staged in the kingdom without Lully's blessing, which from 1672 to 1686 he bestowed almost exclusively on himself. Librettos by long-term collaborator Philippe Quinault treated heroic myths and medieval chivalric exploits; Lully responded with music of refined precision and glorious pomp.

◀ **A costume design** for Lully's *Armide* places typical emphasis on lavish textiles, ornate headwear, and shoes designed for onstage dancing.

## FIRST PERFORMANCES

- 1672 *Les fêtes de l'Amour et de Bacchus*
- 1673 *Cadmus et Hermione*
- 1674 *Alceste, ou Le triomphe d'Alcide*
- 1675 *Thésée*
- 1676 *Atys*
- 1677 *Isis*
- 1678 *Psyché*
- 1679 *Bellérophon*
- 1680 *Proserpine*
- 1682 *Persée*
- 1683 *Phaëton*
- 1684 *Amadis*
- 1685 *Roland*
- 1686 *Armide* · *Acis et Galathée*
- 1687 *A Polixène* (cowritten with Pascal Collasse)

# Armide

*Tragédie en musique* in a prologue and five acts, 2½ hours ▪ Composed: 1685–1686 ▪ First performed: February 15, 1686, Palais-Royal, Paris, France
▪ Libretto: Philippe Quinault, after Cantos II, V, X, and XIV of Torquato Tasso's poem *Gerusalemme liberata* (1575)

*Armide* responded to new developments in the French court. Marie-Thérèse, the fun-loving first wife of Louis XIV, had died in 1683. His new wife, Madame de Maintenon, cast a more pious shadow over royal entertainments. Pyrotechnical stagecraft and fanciful *divertissements* were not banned, but a moralistic tone is established in the prologue. Highlights include *Armide*'s famous Act II solo "Enfin, il est en ma puissance."

### Prologue
Wisdom and Glory exchange views on the triumph of Love.

### Act I
Below an Arch of Triumph, the sorceress Armide and her army celebrate victory over Christian Crusaders. All pay her homage save one: Renaud. Armide is incensed. Her uncle Hidraot urges her to select a husband, but Armide vows to marry only the man who defeats Renaud.

### Act II
On Armide's island, Renaud is held captive, and Armide uses magic music to bring him under her sway ("Enfin, il est en ma puissance"). Unable to kill Renaud, Armide orders spirits to take him to her palace.

### Act III
Renaud and Armide are now in love, but she is unhappy that his love for her is purely the result of magic. She invokes La Haine (Hatred) to expel the love in her heart, then changes her mind.

### Act IV
Ubalde and a Danish knight search for Renaud, their missing companion. Ubalde uses a magic diamond shield to vanquish monsters and block spells cast by Armide.

▼ **Stephanie Novacek** as Armide and Curtis Sullivan as La Haine at Opera Atelier, Toronto, Canada, in 2005.

### PRINCIPAL ROLES

**Armide** *soprano* A sorceress, niece of Hidraot

**Hidraot** *bass* Magician, King of Damascus

**Renaud** *haute-contre* Heroic Christian knight

**Phénice** *soprano* Confidante to Armide

**Sidone** *soprano* Confidante to Armide

**La Haine (Hatred)** *baritone*

### Act V
Renaud's companions arrive with their shield to break Armide's spell on him. She tries many tactics to detain her beloved Renaud ("Le perfide Renaud me fuit"). When he finally leaves, she invokes evil spirits. As she departs in her chariot, her palace crumbles and burns.

Lully and his librettist Philippe Quinault had created 14 operas before this one, their last collaboration. It was the Lully opera most frequently given in Paris in the 18th century, when leading French composer Rameau considered it Lully's masterpiece.

# Henry Purcell

Born: 1659, London, England • Died: November 21, 1695, London, England

Henry Purcell wrote only one true opera, *Dido and Aeneas*. And with this single short work, he became the most important composer of opera in English for a period of over 200 years. Purcell's unsurpassed musical responses to language made him a model for Benjamin Britten and other modern composers setting works in English.

Purcell turned to opera only in the last years of his life. He had studied music in London and his early posts led him to compose mainly for the court. In 1678, he succeeded the celebrated John Blow as organist of Westminster Abbey. But in 1689, when the reign of William and Mary brought hard times for artists, he began accepting commissions. Apart from *Dido and Aeneas* (1689), possibly composed at the request of a schoolmaster, other works were "semi-operas" for the Dorset Garden Theatre in London. The first of these popular plays featuring elaborate musical segments was *The Prophetess, or The History of Dioclesian* (1690), for which the famous Shakespearean actor Thomas Betterton provided the libretto. Purcell's next librettist was the great writer John Dryden, who had worked as a playwright in London before being appointed Poet Laureate of England in 1668. Dryden penned the libretto for Purcell's semi-opera *King Arthur, or The British Worthy* of 1691. To an anonymous

libretto, *The Fairy Queen* followed in 1692, based on Shakespeare's popular comedy *A Midsummer Night's Dream*. In 1695, Purcell was composing *The Indian Queen* to a libretto inspired by John Dryden and Sir Robert Howard's verse tragedy. He died while writing this tragic semi-opera, but his younger brother, Daniel Purcell, completed the score.

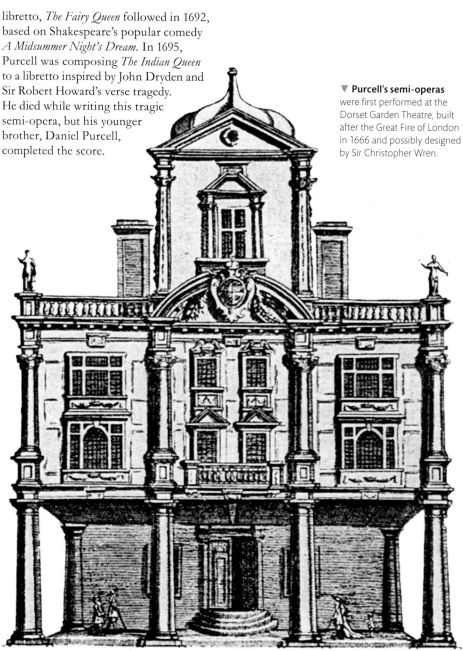

▼ **Purcell's semi-operas** were first performed at the Dorset Garden Theatre, built after the Great Fire of London in 1666 and possibly designed by Sir Christopher Wren.

## Semi-operas

The semi-opera gained popularity in London in the late 17th century, not least through successful works by Purcell. These were essentially plays in which non-singing actors interpreted the lead roles. But dramatic action was rather spare, and shaped to absorb interspersed musical episodes and lively masques, which were performed by singers and dancers. Purcell's semi-operas—*Dioclesian*, *King Arthur*, *The Fairy Queen*, and *The Indian Queen*—premiered in London over the first half of the 1690s. Their colorful plots and mixed casts were popular with the audiences of the day.

# The Fairy Queen

Semi-opera in a prologue and five acts, 3½ hours (2 hours of music) • Composed: 1691–1692 (rev. 1693) • First performed: May 2, 1692, Dorset Garden Theatre, London • Libretto: Anonymous adaptation of Shakespeare's *A Midsummer Night's Dream* (1595–1596)

In this traditional semi-opera, the principal actors carry the story with Shakespeare's spoken dialogue, while Purcell adds unrelated, but enchanting, musical set pieces. Audiences of the period were weary of wordplay and desired spectacle (as in Act V's Chinese Garden of Eden). Purcell's rich yet frolicsome diversions, or masques, do not appear in Shakespeare's text, but they illuminate its personality. The score was first lost, then long neglected before its rediscovery in 1901.

## Act I
Hermia's father attempts to force her engagement to Demetrius despite her love for Lysander (musical scene). In the forest, Titania's fairies pinch and torment three drunken poets, one of whom stutters terribly and confesses to writing doggerel verse.

## Act II
Oberon and Titania quarrel. The fairies entertain Titania until she asks for a lullaby. Oberon sprinkles a love potion over her eyes (musical scene). The fairies Night, Mystery ("I am come to lock all fast"), Secresie, and Sleep sing a cycle of airs to lull Titania into sleep.

## Act III
Puck accidentally makes both Lysander and Demetrius fall in love with Helena. Titania falls in love with Bottom and conjures a bucolic scene to court him (musical scene). Coridon the shepherd pleads with Mopsa, who refuses him kisses.

## Act IV
Oberon corrects Puck's folly and wakes Titania and Bottom from the spells cast on them. He requests music from Titania (musical scene). The fairies present the four seasons.

## Act V
The two pairs of lovers marry (musical scene). Oberon gives entertainments, such as the spectacle of an exquisite garden ("Hark now the Echoing Air").

Focusing on Titania, Purcell eliminated some of the most popular scenes from the Shakespeare play. Instead, he added ravishing if rather arbitrary songs, such as "The Plaint" of Act V.

### PRINCIPAL ROLES

**Oberon** *spoken* King of Fairies

**Titania** *spoken* His wife

**Coridon** *bass baritone* A shepherd

**Fairy** *soprano* Attendant to Titania

▶ **Scottish soprano Janis Kelly** performs in the English National Opera's quirky 1995 production of Purcell's semi-opera directed by David Pountney.

# Dido and Aeneas

Tragic opera in three acts, 1 hour • Composed: c. 1689 • First known performance: Spring 1689, Mr. Josias Priest's Boarding School for Young Gentlewomen, Chelsea, England • Libretto: Nahum Tate, based on his play *Brutus of Alba* (1678), after Virgil's *Aeneid* (c. 30–19 BCE)

*Dido and Aeneas* is England's operatic crowning glory. It is the only major work of music theater in English before the operas of Benjamin Britten, in the 20th century. Purcell integrated the dances favored in French opera, and followed Italian fashion by dwelling on arias. But he broke new ground with his treatment of lyrics and action. The opera was publicly given in 1700, but only entered the repertoire in 1895.

## PRINCIPAL ROLES

**Dido** *soprano* Queen of Carthage

**Belinda** *soprano* Dido's sister

**Aeneas** *tenor* Prince of Troy

**Sorceress** *mezzo-soprano*

**First Witch** *soprano*

**Spirit** *mezzo-soprano*

**Second Woman** *soprano*

**Sailor** *soprano*

---

The earliest known performance of the opera dates from 1689, when girls performed it at their school in Chelsea under headmaster Josias Priest, also choreographer to the Theatre Royal in London.

---

### Dido's lament

Dido's final aria is among the greatest opera laments ever composed. Music alternately caresses and resists lyrics, illustrating their sense, or conveying their expressive limits. As the opera opens, Dido is isolated by inner turmoil. But the action switches to a hurried exterior world, as a storm requires the lovers to seek shelter. Dido's lament finally returns her to emotional turbulence, but this time so strong as to be fatal.

## Act I

In the palace of Carthage, Belinda urges her sister Dido to be joyful, but the lovesick queen suffers because her anguish is concealed ("Ah, Belinda"). Belinda encourages Dido to express her love for the Trojan prince Aeneas, and courtiers praise their political union. As Dido's torment mounts, Belinda is moved to pity. Aeneas asks Dido when he will be blessed with her love. She replies that fate forbids her to love him. He begs Dido to pity him, if not for his own sake, then for the sake of empire-building—he is destined to found a new Troy, and her rejection would spell failure. With fresh energy, Belinda and the people of Carthage encourage Aeneas's bid for love ("To the hills and the vales"). A dance celebrates love's triumph.

## Act II

A sorceress beckons witches to a cave to help her deprive Dido of "fame, of life, and love!" The witches scheme: Aeneas and Dido are hunting, but a conjured storm will lure Aeneas to their cave, where a spirit resembling the god Mercury will order him to leave Carthage. Their voices echoing in the cavern, the witches enjoy their wicked plot in song and dance ("In our deep vaulted cells"). In a remote grove favored by the goddess Diana, Belinda and a second woman recall Actaeon, devoured by his hunting dogs when he happened on Diana bathing naked. The tragic mood endures, and Dido's women dance for their Trojan guest. Aeneas presents the fruits of his hunt, a boar's head. But all scatter when Dido notes a storm's arrival ("Haste, haste to town"). Aeneas is

▶ **Dancers Guillermo Resto as Aeneas** and Mark Morris as Dido in a 2000 production by the Mark Morris Dance Group for the English National Opera, London.

lured to the witches' cave, where the disguised Spirit says Jove orders his departure. Aeneas agrees to obey, but laments his loss of Dido.

## Act III

A sailor with Aeneas's fleet urges preparation for departure. Fellow sailors respond in song and dance. The witches rejoice in Dido's demise with their own song and dance. Dido complains to Belinda that her advice on love matters has failed. Belinda finds comfort in Aeneas's heartfelt sorrow, but Dido does not believe him. She urges him to depart and found the new empire, while she dies. Aeneas proposes to stay instead. But Dido will not hear of his remaining. When Aeneas leaves, Dido welcomes her new guest, death. She then begs Belinda to remember her, but to forget her fate ("When I am laid in earth"). The people of Carthage solemnly invite cupids to watch eternally over Dido's tomb.

▶ **An escape route** can lead as easily to freedom as to further entrapment, just as a welcoming cave can suddenly become threatening.

# Antonio Vivaldi

Born: March 4, 1678, Venice, Italy ▪ Died: July 27 or 28, 1741, Vienna, Austria

Vivaldi is best remembered for his instrumental *Four Seasons*, but the ordained red-headed composer known as "the Red Priest" also wrote some 50 operas. While only 16 complete operas survive, partial scores continue to be discovered. Vivaldi's vibrant opera music is readily recognized by its often maverick instrumentation.

Like his father, Antonio Vivaldi was a celebrated violinist. From his native Venice, he also became the reigning Italian concerto composer. His first opera, *Ottone in villa*, already captures distinctive instrumentation. Like his contemporary, Handel, the prolific Vivaldi also struggled as an impresario. *L'incoronazione di Dario* was his first opera for a theater he managed, the Teatro Sant'Angelo. Following a period in Mantua, he returned to Venice in 1720, but only briefly; his operas were attacked in a satirical essay by Benedetto Marcello. Five years later he was back, but then to contend with the new fervor for Neapolitan opera, in which the orchestra mainly served virtuoso vocalists. *Orlando furioso* and *L'Olimpiade* date from this dynamic period, 1725 to 1728. At the end of the decade, Prague proved more welcoming to the Red Priest. Then, in the 1730s, he donned his impresario hat for the last time, to tour operas through the Italian provinces. Vivaldi traveled in 1740 to Vienna, where he died penniless.

◀ **Vivaldi's room** at the Ospedale della Pietà, a convent orphanage and music conservatory where he taught violin from 1704 to 1740.

## FIRST PERFORMANCES

- 1713 *Ottone in villa*
- 1717 *L'incoronazione di Dario*
- 1719 *Tito Manlio*
- 1720 *La verità in cimento*
- 1724 *Il Giustino*
- 1726 *Dorilla in Tempe*
- 1727 *Farnace • Orlando furioso*
- 1732 *La fida ninfa*
- 1734 *L'Olimpiade*
- 1735 *La Griselda • Il Tamerlano*

# Orlando furioso

ORLANDO ENRAGED *Dramma per musica* in three acts, 4 hours ▪ Composed: c. 1727 ▪ First performed: Fall 1727, Teatro Sant'Angelo, Venice, Italy
▪ Libretto: Grazio Braccioli, loosely taken from part of the epic poem *Orlando furioso* (1516) by Ludovico Ariosto

Vivaldi had contributed to an earlier Venice opera about the wildly jealous Orlando in 1713, but in 1727 he and librettist Grazio Braccioli returned to the material. Exquisite roles, glorious music, and luminous vocal lines form a far-fetched yet coherent drama. Highlights include Alcina's role; Orlando's "mad scene" of Act II; and Ruggiero's velvety aria "Sol da te, mio dolce amore," where voice and flute flutter around one another like magic love birds.

## Act I
The enchantress Alcina promises to unite Angelica with her lost Medoro and to protect her from Orlando, who is violently jealous of Medoro. The female warrior Bradamante counts on a magic ring to block Alcina's powers over her beloved Ruggiero. Alone, Orlando resolves to uncover the source of Alcina's magic: the sorcerer Merlin's ashes. Alcina finds Medoro shipwrecked on the shore. Then, when she uses a potion, Ruggiero falls for her ("Sol da te, mio dolce amore"). Bradamante despairs when Ruggiero fails to recognize her.

## Act II
Bradamante breaks the spell on Ruggiero, but when she deserts him Orlando offers consolation ("Sorge l'irato nembo"). Angelica cruelly sends the worshipful Orlando on a mission that traps him. Bradamante and Ruggiero reunite, and Angelica and Medoro celebrate their wedding. Escaped, Orlando loses his senses when he sees the newlyweds.

## Act III
Bradamante and Ruggiero believe Orlando is dead. They thwart Alcina's magic and, in a temple, find a statue of Merlin. Orlando, demented, arrives to mistake "Merlin" for Angelica. Lifting the statue, he destroys Alcina's power. Her island now deserted, she departs, vowing revenge. Orlando comes to his senses, reconciles with Angelica, and approves her marriage to Medoro.

### PRINCIPAL ROLES

**Orlando** *contralto* A knight jealous of Medoro

**Alcina** *contralto* Enchantress

**Medoro** *contralto* Prince betrothed to Angelica

**Angelica** *soprano* Beloved of Medoro

**Ruggiero** *contralto* A knight following Orlando

**Bradamante** *contralto* Female warrior, beloved of Ruggiero

In 1726, grenadiers threatened to arrest the diva contralto Maria Caterina Negri in her Prague home for breaking a singing contract. She went on to create Bradamante both in this opera and in Handel's *Alcina* (1735).

▼ **Choreographer Zuzana Dostálová** modernized Baroque dance for the Czech premiere of *Orlando Furioso* in 2001 at Prague's State Opera.

# Jean-Philippe Rameau

Baptized: September 25, 1683, Dijon, France ▪ Died: September 12, 1764, Paris, France

The first great composer of French birth, Jean-Philippe Rameau was 50 years old when his first opera, *Hippolyte et Aricie*, shook Paris. Reactions were extreme, but far from harmonious. Some derided Rameau's sound as "baroque," "turbulent," and "a lot of noise." Others, including luminaries of the day, heard his music as ageless, and posterity was to prove them right.

Already before Rameau's birth, Jean-Baptiste Lully was the reigning composer at Louis XIV's court in Versailles. In 1733, when Rameau made his operatic debut in Paris, Lully's ghost still haunted the Paris opera world. War was instantly declared: *Lullistes* attacked Rameau's work, and *Ramistes* hailed it the music of France's new Orpheus. Tension mounted with each successive opera until, in 1739, *Dardanus* so enraged the *Lulliste* librettist Charles-Pierre Roy that he and the composer traded punches. Rameau grew up in Dijon, where he studied under his father, an organist. From 1702, he was also an organist, mainly in provincial cathedrals. But publication in 1722 of his book *A Treatise on Harmony*—which would prove influential even into the 20th century—brought Rameau to settle in Paris. Rameau's new understanding of harmony first and foremost distinguished his own vocal and instrumental writing. Even Voltaire and Jean-Jacques Rousseau collaborated on his librettos, while Louis XV's court extended commissions. The earliest operas, including *Les Indes galantes* and *Castor et Pollux*, premiered at the Paris Opéra. But from 1745, the king requested pieces ranging from the comical *Platée*, which delighted the court, to the sumptuous *Les Boréades*, which, for unknown reasons, was rehearsed but never given in Rameau's lifetime. And, like Lully before him, Rameau composed glorious music for dances, a vital element in French opera.

◀ **French tenor Jean-Paul Fouchécourt** plays the title role of the conceited marsh nymph in *Platée* at the Palais Garnier, Paris, in 2010. The production was directed by Laurent Pelly, who also designed the costumes.

## FIRST PERFORMANCES

- **1733** *Hippolyte et Aricie*
- **1735** *Les Indes galantes*
- **1737** *Castor et Pollux*
- **1739** *Les fêtes d'Hébé, ou Les talens lyriques* · *Dardanus*
- **1745** *La princesse de Navarre* · *Platée* · *Les fêtes de Polymnie* · *Le temple de la gloire*
- **1748** *Zaïs* · *Pygmalion*
- **1749** *Naïs* · *Zoroastre*
- **1751** *La guirlande, ou Les fleurs enchantées* · *Acante et Céphise, ou La sympathie*
- **1763** *Les Boréades* (rehearsal; no performance given)

"True music speaks in the language of the heart."

JEAN-PHILIPPE RAMEAU

# Platée

PLATAEA *Ballet bouffon* in three acts, 2 hours ▪ Composed: c. 1744–1745 ▪ First performed: March 31, 1745, La Grande Écurie, Versailles, France ▪ Libretto: Adrien-Joseph Le Valois d'Orville from Jacques Autreau's play, *Platée, ou Junon jalouse* (1745)

*Platée* is a farcical opera about a hideous and conceited marsh nymph who is ridiculed in a mock marriage to the god Jupiter. It was written for the Dauphin Louis's marriage in 1745 to the Spanish princess Maria Teresa. While a risky venture, the piece was well-received. Revised for the Paris Opéra in 1749, *Platée* enjoyed popular success, and has since been acclaimed a masterwork of French comic opera.

### Prologue

As the inventor of Comedy, Thespis conspires with Cupid (Love), Momus (Ridicule), and Thalie (Comedy's Muse) to present a "new spectacle" demonstrating how Jupiter cured his wife of jealousy.

### Act I

Mercure tells Cithéron, the King of Greece, of his plan to cure the goddess Junon of jealousy: Jupiter, her husband, will feign love for the ugly marsh nymph Platée. When Mercure informs Platée that Jupiter loves her, she swells with pride and impatience ("Quittez, Nymphes, quittez vos demeures profondes").

### Act II

Jupiter and Momus, god of Ridicule, descend from the heavens. While Cithéron and Mercure watch, Jupiter transforms into an ass to enchant Platée. When Jupiter turns into an owl and is frightened off by birds, Platée laments. Jupiter finally reveals himself to his "fiancée," and Platée is fêted with a concert led by Folly.

### Act III

Platée enjoys her "nuptial" festivities ("Chantons, célébrons en ce jour le pouvoir de l'Amour"). Jealous, Junon rips the veil from the face of Jupiter's "bride" and, seeing Platée, she bursts into laughter. The ridiculed Platée vents her anger, and then runs off to fling herself back into her marsh home.

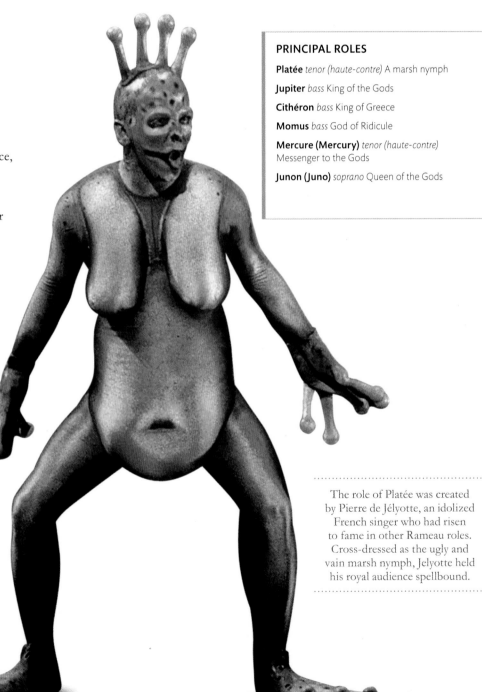

▶ **English tenor** Mark Padmore embodied the creepy and vain marsh nymph at the Edinburgh Festival in Scotland in 1997.

### PRINCIPAL ROLES

**Platée** *tenor (haute-contre)* A marsh nymph

**Jupiter** *bass* King of the Gods

**Cithéron** *bass* King of Greece

**Momus** *bass* God of Ridicule

**Mercure (Mercury)** *tenor (haute-contre)* Messenger to the Gods

**Junon (Juno)** *soprano* Queen of the Gods

The role of Platée was created by Pierre de Jélyotte, an idolized French singer who had risen to fame in other Rameau roles. Cross-dressed as the ugly and vain marsh nymph, Jelyotte held his royal audience spellbound.

# Les Indes galantes

THE AMOROUS INDIES *Opéra-ballet* with a prologue and four *entrées*, 2½ hours ▪ Composed: Year unknown ▪ First performed: August 28, 1735, Paris Opéra, France (complete form) ▪ Libretto: Louis Fuzelier

Such was the success of *Les Indes galantes* in 1735 that it was given in various forms more than 300 times in Paris over the course of four decades. The opera reflects colonial ideas of the time, imagining faraway countries and peoples as entertainingly "exotic" and those enslaved as the "property" of their masters. It opera presents a sequence of four independent lyrical dramas linked by a theme established in its prologue: that love unites distinct cultures. The librettist Louis Fuzelier turned for his stories to documents and eyewitness accounts of "the Indies," by which he understood exotic places: Turkey, Peru, Persia, and North America. Rejecting standard Baroque figures—gods, goddesses, and enchanters—Fuzelier favored "average" people who fall in love. Rameau responded to this libretto with highly varied music for each *entrée*. Melodic lines, rhythms, and his signature wealth of harmonic invention present a mosaic of worlds united by love, and by music.

## PRINCIPAL ROLES

**Osman** *bass* A Turkish pasha

**Émilie** *soprano*
A French girl taken captive by Osman

**Don Carlos** *tenor (haute-contre)*
A Spanish officer

**Phani** *soprano* A Peruvian princess

**Huascar** *bass* An Inca priest

**Tacmas** *tenor (haute-contre)*
A Persian prince

**Fatime** *soprano* An enslaved girl serving Tacmas

**Damon** *tenor (haute-contre)* A French officer

**Don Alvar** *bass* A Spanish officer

◀ **Nothing would seem more exotic** for opera-goers in 18th-century Paris than the rivers, forests, volcanoes, and Indigenous peoples of faraway South America.

### Prologue: In the garden of Hébé

Four men of the allied nations of France, Spain, Italy, and Poland abandon Hébé, god of marriage, to carry out a war campaign. Cupids who are followers of Hébé note that, with Europe having forsaken them, they will depart for "the Indies," exotic lands.

### First *entrée*: Le Turc généreux (The generous Turk)

Emilie, a French girl from Provence, is enslaved by the pasha Osman on his Turkish island. Osman is in love with the Christian girl ("Il faut que l'amour s'envole"), but she remains true to her beloved Valère, an officer in the French marines; she has not seen him since the day of their wedding, when pirates abducted her. By chance, a storm shipwrecks Valère on the pasha's island. There, Osman recognizes the Frenchman as the person who once freed him from enslavement, and releases the lovers from captivity ("Partez! On languit sur le rivage").

### Second *entrée*: Les Incas du Pérou (The Inca of Peru)

Below an active volcano, Don Carlos, a Spanish officer, and Phani, a Peruvian princess, vow mutual love. Huascar, the High Priest of the Sun, is also in love with Phani. When the volcano erupts during a festival worshipping

the sun god, Huascar tries to persuade Phani that the god protests her love for the enemy officer. But Carlos discovers that Huascar cast rocks into the volcano's crater to set off the eruption ("Pour jamais l'amour nous engage"). A real eruption finally engulfs Huascar in lava.

### Third *entrée*: Les Fleurs, Fête Persane (A Persian flower festival)

Tacmas, a Persian prince, is in love with Zaïre, the enslaved girl serving his confidant Ali. Tacmas disguises himself as a woman to sneak into Ali's garden and discover Zaïre's feelings. There, Fatime, the enslaved girl serving Tacmas, also enters the garden, only disguised as a man; she is in love with Zaïre's master, Ali. When Tacmas mistakes Fatime for a rival lover of Zaïre's, he nearly kills her with his dagger before recognizing her. Tacmas and Ali then exchange their favorites to form two contented couples. Love's victory is celebrated with a Festival of Flowers.

### Fourth *entrée*: Les Sauvages (The Savages)

In a North American forest, Zima, daughter of the tribal chief, is wooed by two officers: Don Alvar of Spain is possessive, while Damon of France advocates freer love. Zima finds each too extreme ("Le cœur change à son gré"). Instead, she gives her hand to Adario, an Indigenous man who is head of the tribal armies. The ceremony of the Great Pipe of Peace marks the reconciliation between the Indigenous peoples and the Europeans, and celebrates the union of Zima and Adario.

**Costumes and sets** are used to explore the exotic settings of the "amorous Indies" of Rameau's opera in a visually arresting Zurich production staged in 2004.

In 1725, two Indigenous chiefs from North America demonstrated traditional dances in Paris. Rameau drew from their exhibit to compose *Les Sauvages*, a work for the harpsichord, revised for the fourth *entrée* of this opera.

### Dance

The wild dancing in this opera suited its exotic themes. But from the time of Lully, dance or ballet interludes were essential in French opera. Rameau perpetuated this tradition, which continued well into the 19th century. The Paris Opéra would then insist that even guest composers such as Donizetti and Verdi include ballet segments in French productions of their operas. Lully's legacy remains strong even today in France, where an acclaimed ballet corps forms part of the Opéra National de Paris.

# George Frideric Handel

Born: February 23, 1685, Halle an der Saale, Germany • Died: April 14, 1759, London, England

George Frideric Handel is best known today for the *Messiah, Theodora,* and other oratorios, but he is also the uncontested master of 18th-century *opera seria*. Born and raised in Germanic Saxony, he set operas in Italian for London audiences speaking English. Together, his extraordinary works and vibrant career establish him as the first truly European composer.

▲ **The English mezzo-soprano** Sarah Connolly in the title role of Handel's *Giulio Cesare* for the Glyndebourne production of 2005.

Handel studied under a church organist in Halle and, at age 17, was made organist of the town's Domkirche. At 19, he played violin for the opera in Hamburg, where he became its harpsichordist. His first two operas premiered in Hamburg in 1705, but only the first, *Almira*, set to a libretto in German, survives. The composer then traveled to Florence, which saw the premiere of *Rodrigo*, his first opera in Italian, and Venice, where *Agrippina* brought success. At age 25, he was appointed Kappelmeister to the House of Hanover, whose Elector became George I of England in 1714. By then, Handel was residing in London. His first opera for an English audience, *Rinaldo*, was given in 1711. It was a phenomenal success, and it served to fire up entrepreneurial spirits at the Haymarket Theatre, which was in the risky business of presenting Italian operas to English patrons.

In 1719, Handel helped found the Royal Academy of Music and became its "Master of the Orchestra." The Haymarket was renamed The King's Theatre, and Handel's operatic masterpieces, including *Giulio Cesare, Tamerlano, Rodelinda,* and *Orlando,* then premiered on its stage. Acclaimed casts were led by prima donnas Faustina Bordoni and Francesca Cuzzoni, and by the alto castrato Senesino. In 1728, the Academy went bankrupt (today's Royal Academy was founded in 1822), leaving Handel with the challenge of managing his own company.

### A rival opera company
New problems arose in 1733, when Handel's carefully assembled star singers were lured to a rival company, the Opera of the Nobility, which was run by the influential Italian composer Nicola Porpora. Under these trying circumstances, Handel was forced to cede The King's Theatre to Porpora, and to set up his own company in Covent Garden. Bolstered by newly recruited singers, he then waged a sporadically successful opera war on Porpora. When Porpora gained the upper hand, fresh ideas kept Handel's company in the game of enticing London audiences to attend operas sung in Italian. Two operas from this period, *Ariodante* and *Alcina,* even offered the curiosity of a French ballet troupe.

### Operas and oratorios
The Opera of the Nobility closed in 1737, and audiences began to lose interest in Italian operas. Still, Handel wrote several more, including the magnificent *Serse*. But his last opera, *Deidamia,* was given in London the same year that he composed his *Messiah*: 1741. Handel then abandoned

## FIRST PERFORMANCES
- 1705 *Almira*
- 1711 *Rinaldo*
- 1720 *Radamisto*
- 1724 *Giulio Cesare* • *Tamerlano*
- 1725 *Rodelinda*
- 1733 *Orlando*
- 1735 *Ariodante* • *Alcina*
- 1737 *Berenice*
- 1738 *Serse*
- 1741 *Deidamia*

> "The inspired master of our art."
>
> CHRISTOPH WILLIBALD GLUCK

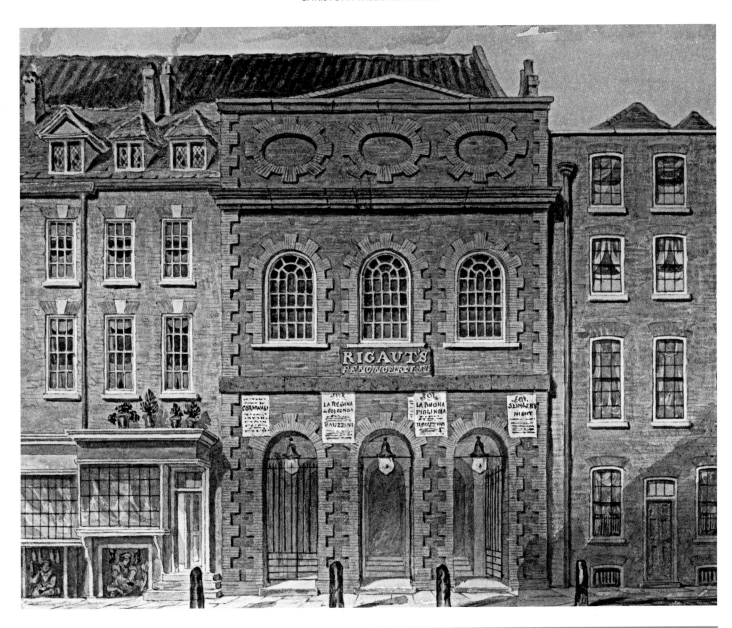

▲ **The King's Theatre**, London, was destroyed by a fire in 1789, although it was later rebuilt. Handel's greatest operas, including *Giulio Cesare* and *Tamerlano*, premiered on its stage.

opera to inject opera-like qualities into the oratorio, a non-dramatic form of vocal music employing religious themes. Indeed, whether closer to opera or oratorio, his great works of this era, including *Samson*, *Semele*, *Judas Maccabaeus*, and *Jephtha*, defied neat classification. Yet through powerful music and storytelling, they continue to win devoted listeners today.

### The Beggar's Opera

In 1728, London audiences applauded *The Beggar's Opera* by John Gay, who was also the librettist for Handel's *Acis and Galatea* (1718). Gay used existing songs—some traditional, some by composers including Purcell and Handel—but added his own lyrics satirizing life and Handel's opera company in London. Spoken dialogue and nearly 70 numbers advance the action. The first of its kind, this "ballad opera" was to set the stage for the French *opéra comique*, the German Singspiel, and the American musical.

▲ **The climactic scene** from *The Beggar's Opera* is set in Newgate Prison, and shown here in a 1729 painting by William Hogarth.

# Giulio Cesare

JULIUS CAESAR *Dramma per musica* in three acts, 3¼ hours ▪ Composed: 1723–1724 ▪ First performed: February 20, 1724, King's Theatre, Haymarket, London, England ▪ Libretto: Nicola Francesco Haym, after a 17th-century libretto by Giacomo Francesco Bussani

*Giulio Cesare* has been called the quintessential *opera seria*. With grand themes of historical warfare and passionate love, of heroic action and inner turmoil, it offers lyric drama on a truly epic scale. Its wide scope is matched by its prodigious number of arias; Cleopatra and Cesare alone are allotted eight each. Along with *Tamerlano*, also premiering in 1724, and *Rodelinda* of 1725, *Giulio Cesare* shows Handel at the height of his powers while leading England's Royal Academy of Music. The opera enjoyed an initial run of 13 performances, and Handel revived it twice in London with continued success. Today, it is the most often-performed Handel opera. And, with its many strongly drawn principal roles, it is also a favorite among singers of Baroque repertoire.

## PRINCIPAL ROLES

**Giulio Cesare** *alto (castrato)* Roman emperor

**Curio** *bass* Roman tribune

**Cornelia** *contralto* Wife of Pompeo, Cesare's foe

**Sesto Pompeo** *soprano* Son of Pompeo

**Cleopatra** *soprano* Queen of Egypt

**Nireno** *alto (castrato)* Eunuch to Cleopatra

**Tolomeo** *alto (castrato)* Half-brother to Cleopatra

**Achilla** *bass* In service to Tolomeo

Handel broke new ground in the opening scene of Act II: Cleopatra arranges a set piece of nine Muses atop Mount Parnassus to help her seduce Cesare, and the Muses are accompanied by onstage musicians.

▶ **Soprano Kathleen Battle** sang Cleopatra in sumptuous costumes for a *Giulio Cesare* of 1988 at the Metropolitan Opera, New York.

### Act I

On a plain near Alexandria, Egyptians praise Cesare, who arrives victorious from battle against Pompeo. Cesare accepts a peace agreement offered by Pompeo's wife and son, Cornelia and Sesto. But Achilla arrives on behalf of Tolomeo, Queen Cleopatra's half-brother, to present Pompeo's severed head. Cornelia curses Tolomeo's barbarity, but Achilla falls in love with her. The Roman tribune Curio offers to make Cornelia his wife and to avenge Pompeo. Alone, Sesto resolves to be the man to avenge his father. In the palace, Cleopatra learns that Tolomeo has decapitated Pompeo, and she angers him by asserting that she alone is Egypt's ruler. Achilla offers to kill Cesare if Tolomeo will give Cornelia as a reward. In his camp, Cesare honors Pompeo, grieving over his coffin ("Alma del gran Pompeo"). Cleopatra arrives disguised as the servant "Lidia," and Cesare falls in love with her. When "Lidia" laments the usurping Tolomeo ("Piangerò la sorte mia"), Cesare vows to exact justice. Cleopatra observes as Cornelia grieves her husband's death. Cornelia takes up a blade to avenge Pompeo, but her son Sesto stops her: this is his task. Still incognito, Cleopatra offers to lead them to Tolomeo. Tolomeo warmly welcomes Cesare, who detects the scheme to murder him. When Cornelia appears with Sesto, Tolomeo also falls in love with her, and plans to betray his promise to Achilla. Meanwhile, Cornelia rejects Achilla's offer of freedom in exchange for marriage, and is heartbroken to be separated from her son ("Ah, sempre piangerò").

### Act II

As "Lidia," Cleopatra seduces Cesare with enchanting music ("V'adoro, pupille"). In the palace harem garden, Achilla and Tolomeo successively fail to seduce Cornelia. Sesto arrives just in time to prevent her suicide. Cleopatra's eunuch, Nireno, summons Cornelia to Tolomeo's harem, promising Sesto a chance to avenge his father at last. Meanwhile, "Lidia" has agreed to be Cesare's wife. But Curio reports that conspirators are calling for Cesare's death. Cleopatra reveals her identity, and as Cesare leaves to confront the conspirators, she prays for him ("Se pietà di me non senti").

### Act III

After Tolomeo's forces defeat Cleopatra, he imprisons her. Sesto and Nireno discover the wounded Achilla, now eager for Tolomeo's downfall. Before dying, Achilla hands over a seal that commands a secret army. Using this seal, Cesare leads the secret army to

▲ **The sensual delight of the opera** is mirrored in this mosaic of Cupid, which dates back to Caesar's reconstruction of Carthage as a Roman city in the 1st century BCE.

rescue Cleopatra, and then to complete the conquest of Egypt. The enamored Cleopatra is ecstatic ("Da tempeste il legno infranto"). In the palace, Tolomeo is about to rape Cornelia when Sesto kills him. In Alexandria, Egyptians rejoice at the tidings of Tolomeo's death. After embracing Sesto and Cornelia in mutual friendship, Cesare and Cleopatra declare their everlasting love for each other.

### Senesino

The charismatic and versatile Italian castrato Francesco Bernardi (right), better known as "Senesino," riveted London audiences in Handel operas for 13 seasons. The composer wrote eight captivating arias for him to deliver as Giulio Cesare, one of Handel's most demanding roles. In 1733, having created the love-struck Medoro in *Orlando*, Senesino moved to the rival Opera of the Nobility. There, composer Nicola Porpora set his contralto voice to maximum effect in operas costarring the younger castrato sensation Farinelli, a soprano.

# Rinaldo

*Dramma per musica* in three acts, 3 hours ▪ Composed: 1710–1711 (rev. 1731) ▪ First performed: February 24, 1711, Queen's Theatre, Haymarket, London, England ▪ Libretto: Giacomo Rossi, after *Gerusalemme liberata* (1575), by Torquato Tasso

*Rinaldo* was the first of Handel's operas for a London audience. With its love story set amid pageantry in magical realms, it calls for elaborate stagecraft. Indeed, the London *Spectator* applauded its "Thunder and Lightning, Illuminations, and Fireworks." Handel scored the opera in mere weeks, but he also borrowed music, including the much-loved march for Crusade forces in the closing act, from some of his earlier work still unknown in London.

### PRINCIPAL ROLES

**Rinaldo** *alto (castrato)* Christian soldier

**Goffredo** *alto (castrato)* Captain of the Christian army

**Eustazio** *alto (castrato)* Brother to Goffredo

**Almirena** *soprano* Daughter to Goffredo

**Argante** *bass* King of Jerusalem

**Armida** *soprano* Enchantress Queen of Damascus

## Act I

The Christian leader Goffredo has offered the hand of his daughter, Almirena, to Rinaldo if he can take Jerusalem from King Argante. But as the sweethearts vow love, the enchantress Armida, Argante's mistress, uses magic to kidnap Almirena. Rinaldo despairs ("Cara sposa, amante cara"). But his spirits lift when Goffredo and Eustazio tell him of a Christian hermit.

## Act II

Journeying to the hermit, Rinaldo is lured into a magic boat, which carries him to Armida's palace. There, Argante tries to seduce the captive Almirena, who rejects him ("Lascia ch'io pianga"). When Rinaldo arrives, Armida falls in love and, using magic to appear as Almirena, woos him. Still seeming to be Almirena, Armida attracts Argante's lust. Furious, she changes out of her disguise to declare war on Argante.

The first Rinaldo was the singer-actor Nicolino (1673–1732), a castrato whose career began in Naples at age 12. Popular in London before Handel first arrived in 1710, his star appearances added to the success of *Rinaldo*.

## Act III

Goffredo and Eustazio visit the hermit, who gives them a magic wand. In the palace, Rinaldo saves Almirena from Armida. Goffredo and Eustazio use the wand to transform Armida's palace into the battle zone before Jerusalem. There, Armida and Argante end their personal quarrel and prepare for battle. But Rinaldo takes them captive. Christians celebrate their victory and welcome the now-married Rinaldo and Almirena.

◀ **Soprano Emma Bell** performs as Almirena in a *Rinaldo* of 2000 directed and codesigned by David Fielding for the Grange Park Opera in Hampshire, England.

# Alcina

*Dramma per musica* in three acts, 3½ hours • Composed: 1735 • First performed: April 16, 1735, Covent Garden, London, England • Libretto: After *L'isola d'Alcina*, set by Riccardo Broschi (1728) from Cantos VI and VII of the epic poem *Orlando furioso* by Ludovico Ariosto (1516)

Handel created the enchanting *Alcina* to lure audiences away from a new rival company in London, the Opera of the Nobility. With its themes of passionate love and spectacular magic, this opera was the fourth and final time Handel drew on Ariosto's epic poem *Orlando furioso*. The other three were *Rinaldo*, *Orlando*, and *Ariodante*. Following *Alcina*, Handel wrote eight more operas, but *Alcina* was the last of his operatic successes.

### Act I

The heartless Alcina transforms men into rocks and beasts on her island. Now, she has fallen in love with Ruggiero, her latest captive. His fiancée, Bradamante, disguised as "Ricciardo" to search for Ruggiero, arrives with Melisso, her beloved's old tutor. Alcina's magic has, however, caused Ruggiero to forget Bradamante's existence. Worse, Alcina's servant Oronte becomes jealous when his own beloved, Morgana, falls in love with "Ricciardo." Then, Oronte persuades Ruggiero that Alcina loves "Ricciardo," hoping this will rid him of the rival. When Morgana learns that Alcina is about to transform "Ricciardo" through magic, she reveals her love to the visitor.

### Act II

Melisso breaks Alcina's spell over Ruggiero, who finally remembers Bradamante. He strategically feigns continued love for Alcina. When Alcina learns that Ruggiero has betrayed her and plots to escape from her island, she is crushed by grief ("Ah, mio cor"). For her part, Morgana is enraged to overhear Ruggiero and Bradamante planning to run off together. Alcina's woe turns to shock when her magic wand appears to have lost its power.

### Act III

With "Ricciardo" unmasked, Morgana turns her affections to Oronte. Alcina threatens revenge on Ruggiero, even as she tries to win him back. While Alcina makes her final appeal, Bradamante warns her lover against Alcina's magic ("Non è amor, né gelosia"). Finally, Ruggiero and Bradamante destroy the source of Alcina's power and ruin her palace. It sinks into the sea, Alcina vanishes, and the men she had transformed regain human form.

Cast as Ruggiero, the castrato Carestini initially rejected "Verdi prati," an Act II aria that he found unflattering to his voice. Handel reputedly cursed the vocalist and threatened not to pay him unless he sang the part as scored.

▶ **Alcina** (right) uses sex as a form of magic to charm her captives in the Stuttgart Staatsoper production of 2000.

# Christoph Willibald Gluck

Born: July 2, 1714, Erasbach, Germany • Died: November 15, 1787, Vienna, Austria

Gluck's name is synonymous with a movement to reform opera that began in the 1750s. Spurred on by Parisian luminary Jean-Jacques Rousseau, reformists advocated putting dramatic action first, eschewing vocal virtuosity for its own sake, and banishing music or dance that failed to serve an opera's dramatic *raison d'être*. Against all odds, Gluck achieved this goal.

Christoph Willibald Gluck, a composer of formidable influence, composed more than 40 works of music theater. Following studies in Prague, Milan, and Venice, he worked in opera capitals across Europe, finally settling in Vienna. His early operas were either in the *opera seria* style, with librettos by Pietro Metastasio, or in the French *opéra comique* vein then fashionable in Vienna's court. But by 1760 change was in the air. Gluck's vision of opera reform called for sharp attention to the libretto and its dramatic fiber, which he saw as opera's heart and soul. Irrelevant dances, diverting music, and the florid da capo arias so cherished by castratos and prima donnas would be sacrificed to opera's chief concern—drama. Indeed, sacrifice was the very theme of Gluck's two masterpieces for the Opéra in Paris, *Iphigénie en Aulide* and *Iphigénie en Tauride*. While their textual sources were drawn from antiquity, Gluck's key works lit the way to opera's future. A pivotal composer, Gluck closed the Baroque era of Monteverdi, Lully, and Handel, and opened the Classical one that flourished in the masterpieces of Mozart and Cherubini. But his impact did not stop there. Richard Wagner and Richard Strauss were deeply influenced by Gluck, and composers contend with his operas even today.

◄ **Jonas Degerfeldt as Achille** protects Verónica Cangemi's Iphigénie in a 2002 production of *Iphigénie en Aulide* at Glyndebourne, England.

## FIRST PERFORMANCES

- 1750 *Ezio*
- 1752 *La clemenza di Tito*
- 1756 *Il re pastore*
- 1758 *L'île de Merlin, ou Le monde renversé*
- 1762 *Orfeo ed Euridice* (rev. 1774 *Orphée et Eurydice*)
- 1764 *La rencontre imprévue*
- 1765 *Telemaco, ossia L'isola di Circe*
- 1767 *Alceste*
- 1770 *Paride ed Elena*
- 1774 *Iphigénie en Aulide*
- 1777 *Armide*
- 1779 *Iphigénie en Tauride* • *Echo et Narcisse*

# Iphigénie en Tauride

IPHIGENIA IN TAURIS *Tragédie lyrique* in four acts, 2 hours ▪ Composed: 1778 ▪ First performed: May 18, 1779, Paris Opéra, France ▪ Libretto: Nicolas-François Guillard, after Euripides and the 1757 tragedy *Iphigénie en Tauride* by Claude Guimond de la Touche

*Iphigénie en Tauride* premiered triumphantly at the Paris Opéra and has since been viewed by many as a masterpiece of 18th century opera. Its stark and unrelenting examination of tormented souls concludes with a rapid succession of glorious recognition, satisfying revenge, and merciful salvation. The opera abounds in stunning arias, but its uncontested jewel is Iphigénie's *"Ô malheureuse Iphigénie"* from Act II, which has lifted star sopranos to new heights of vocal glory from the first performances to modern productions.

### Act I

As a storm fades, Iphigénie laments the storm still raging within her. In Diane's temple, she reveals a nightmare, in which her mother killed her father, and she herself murdered her dear brother, Oreste. She prays to be reunited with Oreste. Thoas, King of Scythia, reports that two strangers have come ashore. The Scythians demand that these Greek captives be sacrificed.

### Act II

Oreste and his friend Pilade lament their fates and object when separated by guards. Alone, Oreste feels curiously serene ("Le calme rentre dans mon coeur"). But Furies and the ghost of his mother torment him. Iphigénie appears, unrecognized. Extracting news from the Greek prisoner, she learns that her father has been murdered by her mother, in turn slain by her brother Oreste, who "found the death he sought." He leaves, and Iphigénie mourns Oreste's death "Ô malheureuse Iphigénie").

### Act III

Iphigénie explains that one prisoner must return to Mycenae, but the other must die. She orders Oreste to leave for Mycenae, but he persuades her to send Pilade instead.

### Act IV

Before Diane's altar, Iphigénie musters courage to complete the dreaded sacrifice. As Oreste is ritually presented, they finally recognize one another. Thoas tries to kill them, but Pilade arrives with Greek guards to slay him. Diane sends Oreste and Iphigénie to Mycenae with her temple statues, and all praise the gods.

> **PRINCIPAL ROLES**
>
> **Iphigénie** *soprano*
> Priestess in the temple of Diane
>
> **Oreste** *baritone* Brother to Iphigénie
>
> **Pilade** *tenor (haute-contre)* Friend to Oreste
>
> **Thoas** *bass* Barbaric King of Scythia
>
> **Diane (Artemis)** *soprano* Goddess

Gluck had nothing against castratos, but French opera-goers did. They found the castrato disturbing. Thus, the role of Pilade was scored for the haute-contre, France's answer to the Italian castrato.

◀ **French diva Rose Caron**
astonished audiences in leading tragic roles for 15 years before singing the part of Iphigénie in Paris in 1900.

# Orfeo ed Euridice

ORPHEUS AND EURYDICE *Azione teatrale per musica* in three acts, 1¾ hours ▪ Composed: 1762 ▪ First performed: October 5, 1762, Burgtheater, Vienna, Austria ▪ Libretto: Ranieri de Calzabigi

*Orfeo ed Euridice* is, with the exception of Mozart's late masterpieces, the most important 18th-century opera. Its theme recalls opera's roots in Jacopo Peri's 1600 work *Euridice* and in Monteverdi's 1607 *L'Orfeo*. But if Gluck appeared to be looking back, this work took opera on a forward path. Laser-sharp focus on dramatic action, instead of virtuoso distraction, exemplifies Gluck's new approach. In 1774, he revised the score for a French version, *Orphée et Euridice*, winning him resounding praise in Paris. The opening captures its unique place in music history: a chorus laments Euridice's death in formal, elegiac manner, while Orfeo cries out for her in a thrilling voice heralding the Romantic era's arrival. This hybrid of two distinct sound-worlds is pure Gluck.

## PRINCIPAL ROLES

**Orfeo** *alto* Shepherd and musician

**Euridice** *soprano* Beloved wife of Orfeo

**Amore** *soprano* God of Love

**Chorus** Shepherds, Nymphs, Furies, Infernal Spirits, Heroes, and Heroines from the Elysian Fields

When Orfeo encounters Cerberus, guard dog of Hades, at the beginning of Act II, masterful scoring for orchestra and chorus produces a terrifying effect, at once evoking the animal's hellish threats and Orfeo's nervous fear.

### The Gluck's dream team

The first performance of *Orfeo ed Euridice* in Vienna in 1762 assembled talents ideally suited to Gluck's music: the reformist librettist Ranieri de Calzabigi; the visionary choreographer Gasparo Angiolini; and the renowned designer Giovanni Maria Quaglio, whose sets mixed formal and natural elements to match the opera's novel sound. Creating the role of Orfeo was castrato Gaetano Guadagni. He had sung oratorios for Handel in London, where he also studied acting with the famous Shakespearean David Garrick. Rare for a castrato, he was noted for avoiding excess.

## Act I

Mourning shepherds and nymphs gather around Euridice's tomb with flowers and incense. As they sing, Orfeo, reclining on a rock, cries out her name through their orderly lament. Orfeo asks to be left alone with his grief ("Ah, se intorno a quest'urna funesta"). He calls to his lost love, Euridice, but in vain, since echoes are the only reply he receives. Suddenly, Orfeo's anger at the gods of the underworld stirs him: with the courage of a hero, he will descend into hell to search for his beloved wife. Amore announces that Jove is moved by Orfeo's grief and will allow him to make the journey to Hades. If his music calms the dark spirits of the underworld, Orfeo may return Euridice to daylight. But he will lose her forever and live in misery if he beholds her before emerging from the caves of the River Styx. And he is forbidden to speak to her of this decree ("Gli sguardi trattieni"). Alone, Orfeo resolves to succeed. When he accepts the challenge that the gods have laid down, thunder sounds and lightning flashes.

## Act II

In a cavern leading to Hades, spirits of the underworld terrify Orfeo, and the barks of Cerberus menace him ("Chi mai dell'Erebo"). But when Orfeo sings of his grief, they are moved and open the gates of the infernal region for "the victor." Orfeo enters the sunny Elysian Fields, home to gods and heroes. Orfeo rejoices in its blissful perfection, but cannot find

▶ **Janet Baker as Orfeo** escorts Elisabeth Spieser's blindfolded Euridice from the Elysian Fields in a 1982 production at Glyndebourne, England.

Euridice. Heroes and Heroines present her, noting Orfeo's superhuman loyalty. Without beholding her, Orfeo escorts Euridice away from the Elysian Fields.

## Act III

Orfeo leads his beloved out through a labyrinth of rocks and wild plants. She asks if he is alive, and if she is. Each question tortures Orfeo, who hurries her along. When he refuses her requests for an embrace or even a glance, she finally calls him a traitor. She asks to remain dead, and he insists he would always come after her ("Vieni, appaga il tuo consorte!"). As Orfeo nearly turns around, Euridice falls fainting to the ground, asking him to remember her.

At last, Orfeo turns around only to see his Euridice die before him. He tries in vain to revive her ("Che farò senza Euridice?"). Orfeo wants to join her in death, but Amore prevents him. Then, as if rising from sleep, Euridice is renewed to life. The lovers reunited, Amore beckons them to return to earth. In a temple dedicated to Amore, Shepherds join in the dance in joyful celebration of Euridice's return, and sing of the triumph of love and faith.

▶ **A watercolor set design** from 1911 presents the vision of Russian designer Alexdandr Jakovlevic Golovin for an Art Nouveau staging of the opera.

# Wolfgang Amadeus Mozart

Born: January 27, 1756, Salzburg, Austria ▪ Died: December 5, 1791, Vienna, Austria

Wolfgang Amadeus Mozart stands alone in the history of opera. Other great opera composers, including Verdi and Wagner, made their mark only in opera, but Mozart's genius embraced every kind of music. Nonetheless, he always had a special passion and a unique gift for opera. During the last decade of his life, he transformed the genre beyond all recognition.

Like no composer before him, Mozart understood that, by exploiting the emotional power of the singing voice, he could give flesh and blood to the *serio* and *buffo* heroes of traditional opera. With his operatic masterpieces, *Le nozze di Figaro*, *Don Giovanni*, *Così fan tutte*, and *Die Zauberflöte*, he went still further. Inspired by challenging librettos, he painted fully fledged characters through subtle orchestration, harmonically ambitious recitatives, memorable arias, and intricate ensembles. It took Mozart 25 years to reach this pinnacle.

His precocious talent was immediately recognized by his father, Leopold, a respected Salzburg musician, who even helped the boy with his early compositions. But it was as a performer that Mozart first astonished. He was only five when he and his gifted sister, Maria Anna, played the harpsichord at the Bavarian court in Munich. And he was eight when a three-year "prodigy tour" took him to Europe's major cities. With opera flourishing as never before outside Italy, young Mozart was soon drawn to the genre. Returning to Salzburg in 1767, he wrote his first opera, *Apollo et Hyacinthus*, a three-act *intermezzo* in Latin. The next year, he composed *La finta semplice*, an *opera buffa* in Italian, for the archbishop's palace in Salzburg. And a few months later, he presented *Bastien und Bastiennne*, a German Singspiel, in Vienna. Before he was 13, he had written operas in three distinct styles and languages.

## Learning in Italy

Italy, however, remained the true home of opera, and Mozart felt a need both to complete his education and to make his mark there. From late 1769, he spent 15 months in Italy.

▲ **Matthias Görne as the bird catcher Papageno** displays his caged wares in a vibrant scene from Achim Freyer's production of *Die Zauberflöte* staged at the annual Salzburg Festival in 1999.

◄ **Constanze Weber**, Mozart's wife, helped preserve the composer's musical legacy after his premature death.

He began by learning the art of counterpoint, the harmonious juxtaposition of two or more musical parts. Then, having proved himself in private recitals, he was commissioned to write *Mitridate, rè di Ponto*, an *opera seria*, for Milan's royal theatre. Acclaimed as a "little master," he went back there in 1772 to present *Lucio Silla*.

### The Salzburg years

However, the next nine years presented fewer opportunities, and he wrote only two operas, *La finta giardiniera* and *Il rè pastore*, both in 1775. In contrast to instrumental music, opera

### Lorenzo da Ponte

Starting with *Le nozze di Figaro* in 1785, Lorenzo da Ponte wrote librettos for three of Mozart's late masterpieces. Born into an Italian-Jewish family in 1749, da Ponte became a priest and a poet before legal troubles forced him to flee Venice. In Vienna, where he was befriended by Emperor Joseph II, he worked closely with Mozart between 1784 and 1789. He then resumed his wanderings as a down-at-heel poet, playwright, and librettist, eventually reaching the United States, where he died in 1838.

"I have an inexpressible longing to write another opera ... I envy anyone who is composing one."

WOLFGANG AMADEUS MOZART

▶ **An engraving of the spectacular** celestial decor used for the entrance of the Queen of the Night, designed by Karl Friedrich Schinkel for a Berlin production of *Die Zauberflöte* in 1816.

required not only a commission, but also a libretto and singers—and Salzburg had neither a proper theater nor an opera house. Mozart was also kept busy as court and cathedral organist. Gradually, though, he became desperate to leave the city. "You know how hateful Salzburg is to me," he wrote to a friend. Finally, in 1781, thanks to a commission from Munich, Mozart composed *Idomeneo*, his first mature stage work. By now, he had mastered the musical legacy of the past and was ready to create a new future. Later that year, he left Salzburg forever, breaking his ties with the city's formidable Prince-Archbishop Colloredo at the same time as escaping the loving but controlling embrace of his father.

## Operatic greatness

The next decade would enshrine him as the Mozart of legend, but it would also prove tumultuous. In 1782, he married the young soprano Constanze Weber, whose sister he had previously wooed. She was frequently ill, and bills for her health care often led to Mozart being swamped in debt. The job he coveted as court composer was also firmly held by Antonio Salieri. But Mozart worked hard, composing prolifically and taking exhausting

road trips to other cities. In July 1782, he made his grand entrance into Vienna's opera world with a farcical Singspiel, *Die Entführung aus dem Serail*, which was an immediate success. But the turning-point came in 1784 when he met the Italian poet and librettist Lorenzo da Ponte. Now Mozart could not only pick the subject of his operas, but could also draw strength from da Ponte's daring librettos: *Le nozze di Figaro*, with its rebellious servants, hints at class warfare; *Don Giovanni* celebrates— and eventually punishes—a philandering noble; and *Così fan tutte* suggests women can be as fickle as men. What has put these works at the heart of every opera repertory, however, is their music: beautiful, disturbing, and at times almost painfully intimate.

## A life cut short

In 1791, the last year of his life, Mozart added a fourth jewel to opera's crown, *Die Zauberflöte*. While working on it, he hurriedly wrote *La clemenza di Tito* for the coronation of the Emperor Leopold II in Prague. Following the premiere of this *opera seria*, Mozart then rushed back to Vienna to complete *Die Zauberflöte*, which opened on September 30. But only weeks later he was struck down

with fever, perhaps brought on by infection. He died on December 5, 1791, just seven weeks short of his 36th birthday. His last great choral work, *Requiem*, was left unfinished.

▼ **Leopold Mozart** accompanies the young Wolfgang and his sister, Maria Anna, performing in Paris in 1763.

# Idomeneo, re di Creta

IDOMENEUS, KING OF CRETE *Dramma per musica* in three acts, 3½ hours ▪ Composed: 1780–1781 ▪ First performed: January 29, 1781, Cuvilliés-Theater, Munich, Germany ▪ Libretto: Giambattista Varesco, after Antoine Danchet's 1731 libretto, *Idoménée*, scored by André Campra

*Idomeneo*, Mozart's third and greatest *opera seria*, anticipates his later masterpieces. Written after a long period in which he concentrated on instrumental music, it stands out for its arias of great beauty and passion, a remarkable quartet, powerful choruses, and rich orchestration. Initially, it was presented only three times, and it did not reach Britain and the United States until the mid-20th century. Today, it is considered a major work.

▼ **Norman Shankle** as Idomeneo and Alexandra Reinprecht as Ilia, at the Stuttgart Staatsoper, Germany, in 2005.

## PRINCIPAL ROLES

**Idomeneo** *tenor* King of Crete

**Idamante** *mezzo-soprano or tenor* Idomeneo's son and heir

**Ilia** *soprano* Trojan princess

**Elettra** *soprano* Greek princess

**Arbace** *tenor* Idomeneo's aide

**High Priest** *tenor*

## Act I

The Trojan princess Ilia is held captive in Crete, where, to prove his love, Prince Idamante releases all Trojan prisoners. Meanwhile, returning home after many years, King Idomeneo is feared drowned. To save himself, he promises Neptune to sacrifice the first person he meets on shore. He is received by a young man whom he at last recognizes as his son, Idamante. The Cretan people celebrate Idomeneo's return, but he is plunged into despair.

## Act II

Idomeneo orders Idamante to leave for Argos with Elettra, a Greek princess who is in love with the prince. Heartbroken, Ilia tells Idomeneo of her love for Idamante ("Se il padre perdei"). To punish Idomeneo's betrayal, Neptune sends a monster in a storm to assail the island. The king offers himself as a sacrifice, but Neptune angrily intensifies the storm. The people of Crete flee in terror.

## Act III

As Idamante prepares to fight the monster, Ilia finally confesses her love for him, but Idomeneo again orders Idamante to flee ("Andrò ramingo e solo"). With the people growing restive, the king realizes he must sacrifice his son to Neptune. Idamante kills the monster and is ready to die. But when Ilia offers to take his place, Neptune instead orders Idomeneo to abdicate, naming Idamante and Ilia as the new rulers of Crete.

At 25, Mozart still lacked the power to pick his cast. In the case of *Idomeneo*'s premiere, he described the men who sang Idomeneo and Idamante as "the two worst actors any stage has ever borne."

# Die Entführung aus dem Serail

THE ABDUCTION FROM THE SERAGLIO Singspiel in three acts, 2¼ hours ▪ Composed: 1781–1782 ▪ First performed: July 16, 1782, Hofburgtheater, Vienna, Austria ▪ Libretto: Gottlieb Stephanie, after a 1781 libretto by Christoph Friedrich Bretzner

*Die Entführung aus dem Serail* was Mozart's first opera for Vienna and his first full-length Singspiel, the name given to Germanic opera with spoken dialogue. It is no coincidence that the heroine is called Konstanze: a month after the opera's premiere, Mozart married Constanze Weber. Designed to appeal to the fashion for all things Turkish, the story's frivolity is more than compensated by musical fireworks, with 21 arias, duets, or ensembles.

### Act I

Belmonte is looking for his kidnapped love, Konstanze, at Selim's palace. He is chased away by Osmin, Selim's vizier, but he meets Pedrillo, his servant, who is also a hostage. Through Pedrillo, he learns that Konstanze is Selim's favorite and that Blonde, her English maid (who Pedrillo is in love with), has been handed to Osmin. Belmonte yearns to be reunited with Konstanze ("Konstanze, Konstanze"). He then overhears Selim demanding her love. Selim is rebuffed and gives Konstanze a day to change her mind. Pedrillo presents Belmonte to the court as an "architect."

### Act II

Blonde skilfully parries Osmin's advances, while Konstanze laments her plight ("Martern aller Arten"). Blonde is thrilled to hear of Belmonte's escape plan, which is set in motion when Pedrillo gives Osmin a sleeping draft. As Belmonte falls into Konstanze's arms, he and Pedrillo are chastised for doubting their lovers' fidelity.

### Act III

The women are given the signal to escape, but they are spotted and taken to Osmin, who promises terrible punishment. Selim is all the more furious when he learns that Belmonte's father is his sworn enemy. Then, as Belmonte and Konstanze prepare to die, Selim decides to free the two couples, and all but Osmin celebrate.

◀ **Erol Sander as the Turkish pasha** Bassa Selim tries to win over Simona Šaturová's Konstanze at the Semperoper, Dresden, Germany, in 2017.

Modern audiences may be tested by this opera's lengthy German-language dialogue, but Emperor Joseph II was more impressed by the score. "An awful lot of notes, my dear Mozart," he is said to have remarked.

### PRINCIPAL ROLES

**Bassa Selim** *speaking part*
A Turkish pasha in North Africa

**Konstanze** *soprano* A Spanish noblewoman

**Blonde** *soprano* Konstanze's English maid

**Belmonte** *tenor* Konstanze's betrothed

**Pedrillo** *tenor* Belmonte's servant

**Osmin** *baritone* Selim's vizier

# Le nozze di Figaro

THE MARRIAGE OF FIGARO *Opera buffa* in four acts, 3 hours ▪ Composed: 1785–1786 ▪ First performed: May 1, 1786, Hofburgtheater, Vienna, Austria ▪ Libretto: Lorenzo da Ponte, after Beaumarchais's 1784 play, *La folle journée, ou Le mariage de Figaro*

*Le nozze di Figaro* is considered by many to be Mozart's greatest opera and, arguably, the most perfect opera ever written. Uniting Mozart and librettist Lorenzo da Ponte for the first time, it combines breathtaking arias and ensembles with a strong, highly entertaining plot. The music also plays a central role in revealing the psychology and temper of the main characters: the count's arrogance, the countess's melancholy, Figaro's fury, and Susanna's mischief. Amid all the humor and confusion, Mozart's score expresses raw emotional truths. Further, he blends arias and recitatives so seamlessly that much of the narrative recitative is as melodic as the set pieces. Today, *Le nozze di Figaro* is a cornerstone of the opera repertoire.

## PRINCIPAL ROLES

**Count Almaviva** *baritone* A rakish Spanish noble

**Countess Almaviva** *soprano* His long-suffering wife

**Figaro** *baritone* Count Almaviva's valet

**Susanna** *soprano* The countess's chambermaid and Figaro's betrothed

**Cherubino** *soprano* or *mezzo-soprano* A housekeeper

**Marcellina** *soprano* or *mezzo-soprano* A housekeeper

**Bartolo** *bass* A doctor

**Basilio** *tenor* A music teacher

### Act I

Figaro is to marry Susanna, the countess's maid, but the philandering Count Almaviva wants to exercise his feudal right to the first night with the bride. Susanna reassures Figaro, but he is furious. Marcellina in turn says Figaro promised to marry her in exchange for a loan. Cherubino, a young page who loves the countess above all women, is banished for chasing Barbarina, the gardener's daughter. Cherubino begs Susanna for help ("Non so più cosa son, cosa faccio"). When the count arrives, Cherubino hides. Basilio, the music teacher, then appears and the count also hides. The count then hears of Cherubino's passion for his wife and orders the page to join the army. Figaro cheers him on ("Non più andrai").

### Act II

As the countess laments her unloving husband ("Porgi, amor, qualche ristoro"), Figaro unveils a scheme. He will warn the count that his wife has a tryst. Meanwhile, Susanna will arrange to meet the count, but Cherubino will take her place, dressed as a woman. When the count appears, Cherubino hides in a dressing room.

Beaumarchais's play *Le Mariage de Figaro* was banned as subversive. But by eliminating political satire and replacing class resentment with sexual rivalry, Mozart and da Ponte won permission for their *opera buffa*.

▶ **As Alison Hagley as Susanna hides** under her bed, Renée Fleming's countess challenges Andreas Schmidt's Count Almaviva about his infidelity in Stephen Medcalf's 1994 production at Glyndebourne, England.

The countess pretends Susanna is trying on her wedding dress. Suspicious, the count leaves to get a hammer, letting Cherubino escape. When the count returns, Susanna emerges. Antonio, the gardener, says someone leaped out of the window, but Figaro "confesses" it was he. Marcellina marches in to claim Figaro.

## Act III

The count has ordered Figaro to marry Marcellina, but Figaro says he needs the consent of his parents, whom he does not know. Marcellina asks if he has a birthmark on his arm. When he so admits, she swoons. Bartolo the doctor says Marcellina is Figaro's mother and he is his father ("Riconosci in questo amplesso"). Seeing Figaro hugging Marcellina, Susanna slaps him. Marcellina explains; the count is lost for words. The countess still hopes to win back her husband ("Dove sono"). As Figaro's wedding celebrations begin, Susanna slips the count a note arranging their rendezvous.

▲ **Giorgio Strehler's** classic 1980 production has been frequently revived by the Paris Opéra, with Dmitri Hvorostovsky seen here as Count Almaviva and Patrizia Ciofi as Susanna at the Opéra Bastille in 2003.

## Act IV

Figaro hides in the garden, as Susanna and the countess arrive in disguise. Susanna is overjoyed to see Figaro ("Deh vieni, non tardar"), but he does not recognize her. Cherubino takes the countess for Susanna and tries to kiss her. The count steps forward and receives the kiss; Figaro rushes out and the count strikes him. As "Susanna" slips away, Figaro spots "the countess," then hears Susanna's voice. With the count now looking for "Susanna," Figaro proclaims his love for "the countess." The count is outraged until "Susanna" unmasks as the real countess. Humbled, the count begs forgiveness. "I am kinder," she says. "I will say yes." Everyone is happy.

### Bryn Terfel

In recent years, no singer has become more identified with Figaro than the charismatic Welsh bass-baritone Bryn Terfel. As his first lead role at the major opera houses of Santa Fe, London, New York, Vienna, and Milan, Figaro not only made Terfel's name internationally, but also led him to two other great Mozartian bass-baritone roles, Leporello and Don Giovanni. With a stage presence to match his fine voice, Terfel has since also expanded his repertoire to include such roles as Scarpia in *Tosca*, Falstaff, and Wotan in Wagner's monumental *Ring* cycle.

# Don Giovanni

*Dramma giocoso* in two acts, 2¾ hours ▪ Composed: 1787 ▪ First performed: October 29, 1787, Gräflich Nostitzsches Nationaltheater, Prague, Czech Republic ▪ Libretto: Lorenzo da Ponte, after Giovanni Bertati's libretto for Giuseppe Gazzaniga's 1787 opera, best known as *Don Giovanni Tenorio*

*Don Giovanni* was commissioned for Prague after the city acclaimed *Le nozze di Figaro*. Mozart turned anew to Lorenzo da Ponte, who took his story from another Don Giovanni opera recently presented in Venice. Da Ponte's wit and poetry inspired Mozart's brilliant score, which brings humor and tragedy— as well as memorable arias and complex ensembles—to the essentially grim story of a serial seducer who escapes all retribution except death. Throughout, the deep humanity of the music reinforces the drama: it can even be argued that the music does half the acting.

## PRINCIPAL ROLES

**Don Giovanni** *bass* or *baritone*
A licentious young noble

**Il Commendatore** *bass*
Killed by Don Giovanni

**Donna Anna** *soprano*
Il Commendatore's daughter

**Don Ottavio** *tenor*
A gentleman, Anna's betrothed

**Donna Elvira** *soprano*
A noble lady abandoned by Don Giovanni

**Leporello** *bass* Don Giovanni's rascal servant

**Zerlina** *soprano* A peasant girl

**Masetto** *bass* Zerlina's betrothed

### Act I

Leporello waits while his master, Don Giovanni, seduces yet another woman. Don Giovanni runs out masked, with Anna in pursuit. Her father, the Commendatore, challenges Don Giovanni. As Anna flees, the Commendatore is slain. Anna finds his body and demands that Ottavio, her fiancé, avenge the murder. Elvira laments her love for Don Giovanni, saying he seduced her with the promise of marriage. As Don Giovanni walks off impatiently, Leporello adds up his master's conquests ("Madamina, il catalago è questo").

Don Giovanni takes a fancy to Zerlina and invites her betrothed, Masetto, to a party at his villa. Alone with Zerlina, he begins flirting ("Là ci darem la mano"). Elvira rushes in to warn Zerlina against the rake. Anna is now sure that Don Giovanni is the masked killer of her father, while Ottavio vows to discover the truth ("Dalla sua pace"). Leporello reports that Elvira disrupted the party, but Don Giovanni wants to enjoy himself with new conquests ("Finch'han dal vino"). As Elvira, Anna, and Ottavio arrive wearing masks, Don Giovanni leads Zerlina away, but she cries for help. Don Giovanni finds Ottavio waving a pistol. The trio take off their masks and threaten him. Don Giovanni is shaken, but defiant.

◄ **English soprano** Emma Albertazzi (1814-1847) as Zerlina in a contemporary illustration of the opera.

### Act II

Don Giovanni exchanges clothes with Leporello so he can seduce Elvira's maid. Elvira hears Don Giovanni begging her forgiveness and wants to believe him. Leporello, now dressed as his master, embraces Elvira, while Don Giovanni, dressed as Leporello, serenades Elvira's maid ("Deh, vieni alla finestra"). Masetto comes looking for Don Giovanni and is promptly punched by "Leporello." As "Don Giovanni" flees Elvira, Anna and Ottavio spot him and he immediately reveals he is Leporello. Ottavio vows to kill Don Giovanni. But Elvira still loves the noble ("Mi tradì, quell'alma ingrata"). At the cemetery, Don Giovanni jokes about a woman who took him for Leporello. Suddenly, a voice is

heard warning that his laughter will soon end. Seeing the Commendatore's statue, Don Giovanni mocks its threat.

Leporello invites the statue to dine with his master, and it nods. Don Giovanni is unperturbed. He summons musicians to accompany his dinner. Elvira appears, but is insulted. As she leaves, she screams. The statue of the Commendatore appears. Don Giovanni offers him dinner, but the statue instead invites Don Giovanni to dine with him. Leporello begs his master to refuse, but he agrees. Taking the noble's hand, the statue tells him to repent. "No!" "Repent!" "No!" Then, with a final cry, Don Giovanni is consumed by flames. His enemies arrive and each one decides to start life afresh, now satisfied that Don Giovanni has finally paid for his sins.

### Don Juan

The legend of Don Juan was born as a morality tale designed to warn against loose living. It was brought to the stage in 1630 in Tirso de Molina's play, *El burlador de Sevilla*, which inspired Molière's better-known *Dom Juan, ou le festin de Pierre* in 1665. More than a century later, Mozart's operatic version was viewed more lightly. This, after all, was the age of Giacomo Casanova, who probably even attended the premiere of *Don Giovanni* in Prague.

▶ **John Brownlee**, the great Australian baritone, was a popular Don Giovanni and also sang lead roles in other operas by Mozart, Verdi, and Wagner.

▲ **Robert Lloyd** as the Commendatore and Gerald Finley as Don Giovanni in the opera's dramatic final scene at the Royal Opera House, London, in 2003.

Mozart displays mischief during Don Giovanni's final supper scene by "quoting" from three contemporary operas, including *Le nozze di Figaro*. Recognizing *Figaro*, Leporello remarks: "I know this piece a little too well."

# Così fan tutte

THUS DO ALL WOMEN *Dramma giocoso* in two acts, 3 hours • Composed: 1789 • First performed: January 26, 1790, Burgtheater, Vienna, Austria
• Libretto: Lorenzo da Ponte

*Così fan tutte, ossia La scuola degli amanti* (*Thus Do All Women, or The School of Lovers*) was not recognized as a masterpiece until the 20th century. Although it has sublime arias and duets and two remarkable 19-minute ensembles, its plot was long considered decadent. It was acceptable for *Don Giovanni* to portray men as philanderers, but not for *Così fan tutte* to show women as fickle. Today, the opera stands on its own, rightly celebrated for its lively plot and beguiling score. Yet it is more than simple *divertimento*. Mozart's music gives the story a poignantly realistic dimension by exploring both the universal fear of betrayal and the thrill of unexpected love. At the same time, for all the work's slapstick and humor, *Così fan tutte*'s temper is melancholic: unusually, this *opera buffa* ends without joy or laughter.

## PRINCIPAL ROLES

**Don Alfonso** *bass* A town philosopher

**Fiordiligi** *soprano* A lady of Ferraro

**Dorabella** *mezzo-soprano* Fiordiligi's sister

**Ferrando** *tenor* Dorabella's betrothed

**Guglielmo** *baritone* Fiordiligi's betrothed

**Despina** *soprano* A scheming chambermaid

◄ **A contemporary engraving** of Herrn Gunbaum as Ferrando, in Albanian disguise. With the women absent, some tenors remove the customary mustache to sing "Un'aura amorosa" in Act I.

### Act I

Don Alfonso warns two young army officers, Ferrando and Guglielmo, that no woman can be trusted. Outraged, they boast of the constancy of their fiancées, the sisters Dorabella and Fiordiligi. Don Alfonso suggests a wager to test the women's fidelity. The officers accept his conditions: to say nothing to their fiancées and, for 24 hours, to obey his orders. Dreaming of their weddings, Fiordiligi and Dorabella admire their lovers' portraits in lockets ("Ah, guarda sorella"). Don Alfonso brings word that the men have been mobilized. The women join him in bidding the soldiers farewell ("Soave sia il vento"). The sisters are heartbroken, but the chambermaid Despina assures them that men are easy to find.

As part of the test, Don Alfonso bribes Despina to introduce two men to the girls. Disguised as Albanians, Ferrando and Guglielmo throw themselves at the astonished sisters' feet. As Fiordiligi proclaims her unwavering faithfulness ("Come scoglio immoto resta"), the men feel confident of winning the wager. But when Don Alfonso orders the men to feign drinking poison, the sisters show concern. A doctor—Despina in disguise—pretends to cure them. To help their recovery, the men ask for a kiss, but are rebuffed.

*Così fan tutte* echoes elements in Mozart's own life: he married the sister of a woman he had once loved; and his wife, Constanze, frequently away on health cures, left him to his own devices.

## Act II

When Dorabella welcomes the idea of some fun, her sister suggests she pick between the two men. To complicate matters, they swap lovers, Dorabella preferring the "dark-haired" fellow (Guglielmo), and Fiordiligi, the "blonde" (Ferrando). Don Alfonso and Despina lead the women to their "Albanian" suitors. Guglielmo claims to be ill—from love—and Dorabella surrenders ("Il coro vi dono"). Fiordiligi rejects Ferrando, then seems to waver ("Per pietà, ben mio, perdona"). Guglielmo is proud Fiordiligi has remained faithful to him, while Ferrando is upset to learn that Dorabella has even given away his portrait. At last, Fiordiligi admits she loves a second man, but decides to join her lover at the front.

Hearing this, Ferrando demands that she plunge a sword into his heart—and she is won over. Despina announces that the sisters are ready to marry. The officers complain to Don Alfonso, who explains that "thus do all women"—*così fan tutte* ("Tutti accusan le donne").

The notary—again Despina—reads out the marriage contract, and, as the women sign, Don Alfonso announces their lovers' return. The "Albanians" vanish and reappear in their own guises. When they show the signed marriage contracts, the women admit their guilt. When they display their "Albanian" disguises, the humbled sisters beg forgiveness. Don Alfonso tells the couples to make up, and all conclude that it is better to laugh than to weep.

### Perhaps not so funny

Mozart's music is as magical as ever, but opera-lovers have long been disturbed by *Così fan tutte*'s cynical undertone. On one level, it offers an amusing new twist to a familiar story: this time, women, not men, are tempted to be unfaithful. But on another level, it presents a deeply jaded view of romantic love. As a result, while it is relatively easy to stage this opera as a farce, rare is the production that successfully conveys its comic-serious duality.

▼ **Lillian Watson as Despina** watches Wendy Dawn Thompson's Dorabella and Sarah-Jane Davies' Fiordiligi nurse the "Albanians," Garsington Opera, 2004.

# VIENNA STATE
## OPERA

By creating his most popular operas for Vienna, Mozart sealed its reputation as one of the world's great musical capitals, a stature it has enjoyed ever since. Mozart wrote principally for the royal court and earned his keep in the city's many popular theaters, although not at the Vienna State Opera, or Wiener Staatsoper, which opened only in 1869. Nonetheless, Mozart was not overlooked when Emperor Franz Josef inaugurated the new 1,709-seat Italianate opera house: the work performed for the occasion was *Don Giovanni*.

The opera house survived the collapse of the Austro-Hungarian Empire after World War I, with Gustav Mahler among its interwar general managers, Richard Strauss one of its music directors, and the tenor Richard Tauber its star attraction. The theater was badly damaged by aerial bombardment in March 1945, and because for the next decade Austria was under the joint occupation of the victorious Allied powers, the reconstructed Staatsoper could only reopen in November 1955, this time with Beethoven's *Fidelio*.

The Vienna State Opera is best known for the so-called "Vienna sound" of the Vienna Philharmonic, which doubles as the in-house orchestra. It is an unusual arrangement in that, while the opera house has had numerous prestigious music directors, among them Claudio Abbado, Seiji Ozawa, and Philippe Jordan, the Vienna Philharmonic operates independently with a tradition of retaining no permanent conductor.

Nowhere is the city's conservative tradition more apparent than in the annual Vienna Opera Ball, an occasion seemingly plucked out of the 19th century. Stalls are removed and a new dance floor laid for an evening that includes the presentation of scores of debutantes and their partners (including, in 2020, a same sex couple), along with dancers and singers from the opera house. All this takes place in front of Austria's President and political and business elite, and their bejeweled spouses.

> "In the coming years, the Vienna State Opera has to open itself to a bigger audience. One has a very faithful audience, and a tourist audience, but more young people have to be drawn in."

PHILIPPE JORDAN, MUSIC DIRECTOR, VIENNA STATE OPERA

▶ **At the heart of Vienna's social life** since the mid-19th century, the Vienna State Opera is a model of imperial elegance.

# Die Zauberflöte

THE MAGIC FLUTE *Eine Deutsch Oper* in two acts, 2½ hours ▪ Composed: 1791 ▪ First performed: September 30, 1791, Freihaustheater auf der Wieden, Vienna, Austria ▪ Libretto: Emanuel Schikaneder

*Die Zauberflöte*, Mozart's only opera written specifically for a popular audience, is as delightful as it is complex. It can be enjoyed as a fairy tale, with its magic flute and bells, its animals, its clown, and its romantic couple. But it is also rife with symbols of Freemasonry and, as such, promotes the ideals of virtue, love, and wisdom. The work is best known for its stream of catchy melodies, the most famous being the Queen of the Night's two show-stopping soprano arias, with their furious high Fs. Mozart wrote this opera at the same time as composing *La clemenza di Tito* and much of his *Requiem*. They left him exhausted. He conducted *Die Zauberflöte*'s premiere, but it would be his last. He died nine weeks later.

## PRINCIPAL ROLES

**Sarastro** *bass* A mystic lord

**Tamino** *tenor* A prince

**Pamina** *soprano* An imprisoned princess

**Queen of the Night** *soprano* Pamina's fearsome mother

**Papageno** *baritone* A bird catcher

**Papagena** *soprano* His beloved

**Monostatos** *tenor* A Moor in the service of Sarastro

**Speaker of the Temple** *bass*

**Three Ladies** *sopranos*

 **Mozart and his librettist** cleverly named the flute-playing bird catcher after the German word for parrot, *Papagei*, thus setting the stage for Papageno to use song to woo his lovebird, Papagena.

### Act I

Three Ladies save Tamino from a serpent. Impressed by his beauty, they inform the Queen of the Night. Papageno is dreaming of trapping maidens in his bird net ("Der Vogelfänger bin ich, ja") when he hears about the serpent. He claims to have strangled it, but the Ladies padlock his lips for lying. Tamino falls for a picture of Pamina, the queen's daughter. The queen tells him he can win Pamina if he rescues her from the monster Sarastro ("O zittre nicht, mein lieber Sohn"). Tamino is given a magic flute, and Papageno, silver bells.

At Sarastro's castle, the Moor Monostatos is enraged to be rebuffed by Pamina. Recognizing Pamina, Papageno reveals Tamino's passion for her. Together, Papageno and Pamina dream of finding love. Meanwhile, entering a temple, Tamino is ready to fight Sarastro. As voices tell him Pamina is alive, his flute-playing attracts friendly animals ("Wie stark ist nicht dein Zauberton"). Papageno and Pamina are caught by Monostatos, but Papageno's bells set the Moor and his enslaved people dancing. Sarastro arrives in a chariot drawn by lions. Pamina complains of the brutish Moor, but Sarastro cannot allow her to return to her evil mother. Monostatos drags in Tamino, and the lovers recognize each other. Sarastro decides to test Tamino and Pamina's fitness for membership in his brotherhood.

### Act II

Tamino is ready to fight for friendship and love, although he is not allowed to speak to Pamina. The Queen of the Night reappears, telling Pamina to kill Sarastro with a dagger ("Der Hölle Rache kocht in meinem Herzen"). After the queen vanishes, Monostatos again tries to woo Pamina. As Papageno ignores Tamino's orders to remain silent, an old hag offers him water. She gives her age as 18 years and two minutes and names Papageno as her sweetheart. She then disappears. Tamino and Papageno are brought food and their magic flute and bells. As Papageno cheerfully digs into the feast, Tamino's flute summons Pamina, but she is heartbroken when he refuses to speak ("Ach, ich fühl's"). Papageno's only wish is for some wine and a "little wife." The old hag reappears to offer him marriage or eternal captivity. When he reluctantly accepts her, she turns into Papagena. But he is still unworthy of her.

Ready to kill herself, Pamina learns that Tamino still loves her. Together, they triumph over flames and floods. In vain, Papageno plays his pipe to call Papagena, but when he rings his bells, she appears ("Pa, pa, pa ... Papagena! Papageno!"). Monostatos joins forces with the Queen of the Night, but they vanish at sunrise. Finally, with Tamino and Pamina in priestly gowns beside him, Sarastro gives thanks to Iris and Osiris for the reward of beauty and wisdom.

### Freemasonry

Mozart joined the Freemasons in 1784 and wrote several cantatas for their ceremonies. With *Die Zauberflöte*, he created a majestic operatic homage to the movement's ideals of wisdom, friendship, nature, and sacrifice. In the libretto, written by a fellow Mason, Emanuel Schikaneder, Sarastro's mystical sect represents a Masonic lodge (right) and is guided by symbols and rituals of the brotherhood.

Wagner viewed *Die Zauberflöte* as the cornerstone of German opera, describing it as "a masterpiece of almost unsurpassable perfection, one which virtually ruled out further expansion of the genre."

▼ **Stéphane Degout as Papageno** and Claire Ormshaw as Papagena in a 2005 production at the Opéra Bastille, Paris, directed by Àlex Ollé and Carlus Padrissa and designed by the artist Jaume Plensa.

# 3

# ITALIAN OPERA
## (c. 1800–1925)

# Italian opera c. 1800–1925

Having dominated opera since the birth of the art form, Italian musicians again demonstrated their extraordinary inventiveness in the 19th century. By then, they faced competition from Germanic, French, Russian, and Czech opera, yet they held their own, thanks to the remarkable gifts of five composers. In quick succession, Rossini, Bellini, Donizetti, Verdi, and Puccini swept the world with their operas.

Today, the term "Italian opera" refers to these and a handful of other 19th-century composers. Yet this burst of creativity did not take place in a vacuum. From the mid-18th century, leading Italian composers took up posts in northern Europe, where they absorbed non-Italian influences from Christoph Willibald Gluck and, notably, from Mozart, who blurred the line between *opera seria* and *opera buffa*, and created "real life" characters on stage.

## Mozart's influence

Johann Simon Mayr, a Bavarian-born admirer of Mozart and Haydn, is usually mentioned only as Gaetano Donizetti's teacher yet, in his prime, he was Italy's most influential composer and served as a musical bridge between Mozart and Gioachino Rossini. Rossini, who referred admiringly to him as "papa Mayr," is also the reason that he is forgotten. Only 21 when he burst onto the scene in Venice, Rossini is best remembered for two comic operas, *Il barbiere di Siviglia* and *La Cenerentola*. He was, above all, a writer of dazzling vocal parts, a style that became known as *bel canto*, or "beautiful singing." Rossini demonstrated another crucial talent—that of steering clear of politics in an era of national disarray, with Napoleon's defeat in 1815 returning Italy's traditional kingdoms and duchies to oppressive conservative rule.

## Watched by the censor

For the opera world, this meant that every new libretto required approval, with the authorities ever alert to anything minimally critical of the monarchy, the Roman Catholic Church, or foreign occupation. Vincenzo Bellini, who with *Il pirata* in 1827 was

◀ **An early 19th-century painting by a French artist** shows the stage and auditorium of Naples' Teatro di San Carlo, considered by many to be Italy's most elegant opera house.

proclaimed Rossini's *bel canto* successor, escaped these problems by carefully avoiding political or religious pitfalls. He had written 10 operas when he died at 33 in 1835.

After Bellini's death, with Rossini now retired in Paris, Donizetti was hailed the greatest Italian composer of his day, notably for *L'elisir d'amore* and *Lucia di Lammermoor*. Plagued by censorship, Donizetti tried to avert trouble by setting historical operas in Protestant England, as with *Anna Bolena* and *Roberto Devereux*. But *Maria Stuarda* was banned by the King of Naples in 1834 because its tragic heroine, Mary Queen of Scots, was Catholic. Tired of squabbling with censors, Donizetti decided to follow Rossini to Paris.

By the 1830s, the Teatro alla Scala in Milan, the most prosperous Italian city, had become the ultimate Italian *palazzo* of opera. And just as Bellini and Donizetti won international recognition only after they triumphed at La Scala, so it was with Giuseppe Verdi: his first opera, *Oberto*, and his last opera, *Falstaff*, both premiered at La Scala.

## Verdi the magnificent

The popularity enjoyed by Verdi has been matched by no other Italian composer. He quickly broke free from *bel canto* and took opera into an entirely new orbit of music drama. Like his immediate predecessors, he had a natural talent for haunting melodies. But he also had a unique ability to create memorable characters who personified the universal themes of love, honor, power, greed, betrayal, and death. Unsurprisingly, all but two of his operas were tragedies, ranging from the poignancy of *La traviata* to the grandeur of *Don Carlos*. Verdi was also loved as a nationalist symbol, a status thrust upon him in 1842 after he wrote *Nabucco*, a story about the Jewish captivity in Babylon that appeared to mirror the plight of Italians under Austrian occupation. And beyond *Nabucco*, works such as *La battaglia di Legnano*, or *The Battle of Legnano*, reinforced Verdi's identity with the *Risorgimento* ("Rising again") independence movement. After the Kingdom of Italy was proclaimed in 1861, Verdi served briefly as a member of the new parliament. By the 1890s, a more realistic style known as *verismo* was introduced by Pietro Mascagni and Ruggero Leoncavallo, but only Giacomo Puccini could fairly claim to be Verdi's successor.

# Gioachino Rossini

Born: February 29, 1792, Pesaro, Italy · Died: November 13, 1868, Paris, France

Gioachino Rossini emerged in the early 19th century as the "savior" of Italian opera. Best remembered for *Il barbiere di Siviglia*, his importance goes far beyond this charming and beloved comedy. He not only rejuvenated *opera buffa* and *opera seria*; with his love for the virtuoso vocal style known as *bel canto*, or "beautiful singing," he also returned the voice to the center of Italian opera.

## FIRST PERFORMANCES

- 1810 *La cambiale di matrimonio*
- 1813 *Tancredi* • *L'italiana in Algeri*
- 1814 *Il turco in Italia*
- 1815 *Elisabetta, regina d'Inghilterra*
- 1816 *Il barbiere di Siviglia* • *Otello*
- 1817 *La Cenerentola* • *La gazza ladra*
- 1819 *La donna del lago*
- 1820 *Maometto II*
- 1822 *Zelmira*
- 1823 *Semiramide*
- 1825 *Il viaggio a Reims*
- 1828 *Le Comte Ory*
- 1829 *Guillaume Tell*

◄ **Lucia Cirillo** as Cenerentola's jealous stepsister, Tisbe, at the masked ball in Act II of *La Cenerentola*. This 2005 Glyndebourne Festival production was directed by Peter Hall and conducted by Vladimir Jurowski.

◄ **Isabella Colbran** (1785–1845), a Spanish soprano of note, married Rossini in 1822 and went on to sing the lead role in several of the composer's late operas.

What most distinguishes Rossini is the sheer exuberance of his music. His deep admiration for Mozart—"my idol and my master," as he once put it—led some early critics to consider him "too German." But such reservations were soon swept away by his strong rhythms, richly colored orchestration, catchy tunes, and florid arias, which made him sound Italian. In all, Rossini wrote 35 operas over two decades, although only a few of his comedies are regularly produced today, notably *Il barbiere di Siviglia*, *L'italiana in Algeri*, *Il turco in Italia*, and *La Cenerentola*. Even so, he bequeathed a sound so recognizable that it is known simply as "Rossinian."

Like many great composers, Rossini was born into a family of musicians. From an early age, he was both a performer—pianist, cellist, and singer—and a composer. In fact, by the time he was 21, he had written ten operas which were, in the main, comedies. Then,

> "Give me a laundry list and I will set it to music."
>
> GIOACHINO ROSSINI

with *Tancredi*, he made his entrance into *opera seria*. Hailed as Italy's leading young composer, he was equally at ease with tragedy and with comedy. But he evidently relished *opera buffa*, creating his four most famous comedies in quick succession by the time he was 25. In great demand in Italy, with *bel canto* all the rage, he wrote for opera houses in Venice, Milan, Rome, and Naples. In 1815, Rossini became the artistic director of Naples's Teatro di San Carlo, managed by the talented and famously corrupt impresario Domenico Barbaia. Although Naples was the cradle of *opera buffa*, its public now expected *opera seria*. And in the years that followed, Rossini created ten musical tragedies, starting with *Elisabetta, regina d'Inghilterra* and ending seven years later with *Zelmira*. Stimulating him were excellent soloists who could handle his coloratura arias, complex ensembles, fast tempos, high notes, and sudden crescendos. Indeed, he often wrote for their voices, not only for Spanish soprano Isabella Colbran, who became his

first wife, but also for Giovanni Battista Velluti, the last operatic castrato. However, he did not allow improvised ornamentation: his soloists were expected to sing precisely what he had written.

### An early retirement

In 1824, now renowned across Europe, Rossini moved to Paris, a city with a rich musical life sustained mainly by foreign composers. He became artistic director of the Théâtre-Italien, where in 1825 he presented *Il viaggio a Reims*, his last Italian-language work. From then, he wrote to French-language librettos, climaxing in 1829 with *Guillaume Tell*, a massive four-act opera. It would be his last. In 1836, still only 37, Rossini moved to Bologna and abandoned opera. His reason for doing so, though, is not known. He was certainly wealthy enough to retire. But with opera undergoing radical changes in France, Italy, and Germany, he may also have simply concluded that the Rossini era was over.

▲ **Rossini first made his name in Italy**, but Paris became his second home. After his death in Paris on November 13, 1868, thousands of mourners accompanied his funeral cortege.

### A happy legacy

But Rossini's comedies continued to work their charm. As the librettist Felice Romani noted in 1840: "They fill the coffers of all the impresarios in the peninsula, exhilarate the ponderous Germans, inflame the frigid Britons, and make even the pensive Quakers of Pennsylvania dance with joy." Almost two centuries after they were written, more or less the same can still be said of them today. Finally, in 1855, Rossini returned to Paris, where he held court as the music world's elder statesman. He died there at the age of 76 in 1868.

# L'italiana in Algeri

THE ITALIAN GIRL IN ALGIERS *Dramma giocoso per musica* in two acts, 2¼ hours • Composed: 1813 • First performed: May 22, 1813, Teatro San Benedetto, Venice, Italy • Libretto: Angelo Anelli, first set by Luigi Mosca

*L'italiana in Algeri* is Rossini's most farcical opera. Completing the work in just 27 days, the young composer was forced to use an existing libretto, but he poured his talent into the music. The overture is one of Rossini's most popular, while the sparkling score is rich in testing coloratura arias as well as complex and humorous ensembles. The patriotic aria "Pensa alla patria" may also have contributed to the opera's success.

## PRINCIPAL ROLES

**Mustafà** *bass* The Turkish Bey of Algiers

**Elvira** *soprano* His wife

**Haly** *bass* Captain of the Bey's corsairs

**Lindoro** *tenor* Italian enslaved to the Bey

**Isabella** *contralto* Lindoro's lover and savior

**Taddeo** *bass* Isabella's aged suitor

This *opera buffa* shamelessly exploited the prevailing fashion for all things Turkish, but with a feminist twist: usually a man is the hero, but here a woman rescues her lover from enslavement.

### Act I

Bored with his wife Elvira, Mustafà the Bey decides to marry her off to his enslaved Italian Lindoro. Lindoro in turn yearns for Isabella, but Mustafà assures him that Elvira will serve him well. Meanwhile, Isabella, who is looking for Lindoro, is captured and sent to Mustafà's harem. The Bey is delighted by her, but she manipulates him with words of love. Seeing Lindoro about to embark for Italy with Elvira, she declares that Mustafà must keep Elvira, while Lindoro becomes her servant. Mustafà objects, but Isabella overrules him.

### Act II

Lindoro is able to persuade Isabella that he was fleeing only to be reunited with her, and they agree to escape together. Aware that Mustafà is eavesdropping, Isabella muses aloud on how to please the man she loves ("Per lui che adoro"). Mustafà believes that she has made herself beautiful for him, but when he meets with Isabella, she annoyingly invites Elvira to join them. Isabella decides to honor Mustafà as her *Pappataci*—slang for a tamed husband. For this, he must eat, drink, and sleep. While she vows to free other enslaved Italians and stirs their patriotism ("Pensa alla patria"), Lindoro plies the Bey with drink. When Mustafà finally realizes that the Italians are escaping, everyone is too drunk to stop them. Recognizing defeat, he turns to Elvira and begs her forgiveness, and bestows his blessing upon the departing lovers.

▼ **Ildar Abdrazakov as Mustafà** appears to trap Daniela Barcellona's Isabella in a 2003 production of the opera at the Teatro dell'Opera in Rome, but in practice the clever and spirited Isabella constantly outsmarts her captor.

# Il turco in Italia

THE TURK IN ITALY *Dramma buffo per musica* in two acts, 2¼ hours ▪ Composed: 1814 ▪ First performed: August 14, 1814, La Scala, Milan, Italy ▪ Libretto: Felice Romani, after the libretto by Caterino Mazzolà for Joseph Seydelmann's 1788 opera *Il turco in Italia*

Before its premiere, *Il turco in Italia* seemed doomed because Milan's opera-goers suspected Rossini of taking much of the story and music from *L'italiana in Algeri*, the previous year's oriental *divertimento*. In reality, the story is different and the music all original. The score offers Fiorilla some fine arias and feisty duets, but it relies heavily on ensembles to convey the plotting and misunderstandings that provide much of the comedy.

## Act I

Preparing a comedy about Geronio's capricious wife, Fiorilla, Prosdocimo the poet hears the Gypsy Zaida predict Geronio's misfortune. She reveals she was to marry a Turkish noble until he wrongly believed her unfaithful. The poet says a visiting Turkish prince will intercede on her behalf. Fiorilla falls for the prince, angering her former lover, Narciso. Learning that the prince is called Selim Damelec, the poet recognizes Zaida's beloved. When Selim and Fiorilla are interrupted by Geronio, they arrange to meet secretly. Instead, Zaida is reunited with Selim. Fiorilla discovers them and a fight erupts between "rivals in love" ("Ah! Che il cor non m'ingannava").

## Act II

After Geronio refuses to sell Fiorilla, Selim decides to steal her. Summoning Zaida, Fiorilla tells him to pick between them. When he hesitates, Zaida storms out. But after Fiorilla also threatens to leave, Selim chooses her. Selim plans to abduct Fiorilla at a masked ball, but Fiorilla confuses Narciso for Selim, while Selim follows Zaida, thinking she is Fiorilla. Geronio is perplexed to see two Fiorillas and two Selims ("Oh! Guardate che accidente"). The poet tells Geronio he can win back his wife by filing for divorce. When Fiorilla learns she has lost Selim and Geronio wants a divorce, she is suddenly remorseful. Finally, Geronio forgives her and everyone agrees to forget mistakes born of love.

## PRINCIPAL ROLES

**Selim** *bass* A Turkish prince

**Fiorilla** *soprano* Geronio's flighty wife

**Geronio** *bass* Fiorilla's hapless husband

**Narciso** *tenor* Fiorilla's former lover

**Prosdocimo** *bass* A poet in search of material

**Zaida** *soprano* A Gypsy, Selim's former lover

◀ **Inga Kalna** attends a masked ball as the flighty Fiorilla at the Hamburg Staatsoper's 2005 staging.

Echoes of Mozart are not coincidental. Not only was *Così fan tutte* being staged in Milan when Rossini was writing *Il turco in Italia,* but both operas also borrowed from the same libretto.

# Il barbiere di Siviglia

THE BARBER OF SEVILLE *Commedia* in two acts, 2¾ hours • Composed: 1816 • First performed: February 20, 1816, Teatro Argentina, Rome, Italy • Libretto: Cesare Sterbini, after Beaumarchais's 1775 play and Giuseppe Petrosellini's libretto for Giovanni Paisiello's 1782 opera

*Il barbiere di Siviglia* is one of the greatest comic operas ever written. Composed in barely two weeks, it is a delightful romp packed with wonderful coloratura arias and ensembles, high speed "patter songs," splendid *buffo* characters, and successive laugh-aloud scenes. Like Mozart's great opera *Le nozze di Figaro*, it was adapted from a Beaumarchais play—*Le Barbier de Séville*—with a strong and clever plot. Indeed, it demands virtuoso singers who are also exceptional comic actors. Nonetheless, its premiere was a flop because the young composer was thought arrogant for daring to tread the same path as Paisiello's ever-popular opera with the same name. Aware of the problem, Rossini initially called his opera *Almaviva, ossia L'inutile precauzione* (*Almaviva, or The Useless Precaution*). But after a few performances, his version caught on as *Il barbiere di Siviglia*, and its appeal has never faltered.

## PRINCIPAL ROLES

**Count Almaviva** *tenor* Rosina's suitor

**Dr. Bartolo** *bass* Rosina's guardian and suitor

**Rosina** *contralto* or *mezzo-soprano* Bartolo's ward

**Figaro** *bass* A barber and rascal

**Basilio** *bass* A music teacher

### Act I

Count Almaviva's musicians serenade the beautiful Rosina. Figaro the barber wanders by, singing his own praises ("Largo al factotum"), and informs the count that Rosina is the ward of Bartolo. Rosina drops a letter from her balcony, asking her suitor's name and vowing to escape her guardian, who wants to marry her for her money. Eager to be loved for himself, the count gives his name as "Lindoro." Figaro suggests he enter Bartolo's house disguised as a drunken soldier.

▼ **Antonino Siragusa as Count Almaviva** in Dario Fo's colorful production, which has toured Europe since 1987, is seen here at the Nederlandse Opera in 2006.

### Figaro

Figaro was to Beaumarchais what Falstaff was to Shakespeare, a character so mischievously appealing that he appeared in three of his plays. Mozart adapted the second Figaro play as *Le nozze di Figaro*, leaving Rossini to compose *Il barbiere di Siviglia*. Here, Giorgio Ronconi's Figaro wears traditional Andalusian dress and holds a guitar for an 1844 production at the Théâtre-Italien, Paris. Curiously, the "Figaro operas" are now better known than the original plays.

While Rosina writes to "Lindoro" ("Una voce poco fa"), Basilio the music teacher warns Bartolo that her secret suitor is Count Almaviva. But Figaro tells Rosina that his cousin "Lindoro" is hopelessly in love with her and awaits a letter. She has one ready. Pretending to be drunk, the count says he has been billeted in Bartolo's house. As Bartolo protests, the "soldier" confides to Rosina that he is "Lindoro." Summoned by Bartolo, an officer comes to arrest the "soldier," who quietly identifies himself as the count. No one else has much idea of what is going on ("Mi par d'esser colla testa").

### Act II

The count reappears as "Don Alonso," replacing the ailing Basilio, and repeatedly blesses the house ("Pace e gioia sia con voi"). He then reveals that, while visiting the count, he found a letter from Rosina. Bartolo pockets the letter and calls Rosina to her singing lesson. She recognizes "Lindoro" and, when Bartolo falls asleep, they plan to elope. Basilio arrives in good health, but "Alonso" bribes him to leave ("Buona sera, mio signore").

As Figaro starts shaving Bartolo, "Lindoro" apologizes for using Rosina's letter, but Bartolo overhears him and sends him packing. Summoned by Bartolo, Basilio says he suspects "Alonso" is really the count. With that, Bartolo decides to marry Rosina immediately. He persuades Rosina that "Alonso" and Figaro intend to kidnap her for Count Almaviva. Feeling betrayed by "Lindoro," she agrees to marry Bartolo. As "Alonso" and Figaro climb into the house, Rosina accuses them of treachery, saying she loves "Lindoro." But all is forgiven when "Alonso" reveals that he is the count ("Ah! Qual colpo inaspettato").

A notary arrives, believing that Figaro's niece will marry the count. By the time Bartolo returns with soldiers, he discovers the count and Rosina are married. Finally, after more commotion, Bartolo accepts his fate and joins with the company in a celebration of love.

In his famous Barber's Song, "Largo al factotum," with its "Figaro here, Figaro there, Figaro up, Figaro down," Figaro boasts of his multiple talents.

▶ **Roberto Frontali as Figaro** tries to confuse Ildebrando D'Arcangelo's Bartolo while shaving him in a 1997 production at the Teatro dell'Opera in Rome.

# La Cenerentola

CINDERELLA *Dramma giocoso* in two acts, 2½ hours ▪ Composed: 1816–1817 ▪ First performed: January 25, 1817, Teatro Valle, Rome, Italy ▪ Libretto: Giacomo (Jacapo) Ferretti, after Charles Perrault's *Cendrillon*, and earlier librettos after the same tale

Inspired by the Cinderella fairy tale, *La Cenerentola* is Rossini's most popular opera after *Il barbiere di Siviglia*. Once again, the composer demands a contralto or mezzo-soprano able to handle extended coloratura passages. The title role also calls for lyricism, not least in the first love duet, while ensembles test other singers with their rapid patter and exquisite ornamentation. The opera includes the *buffo* Don Magnifico, but dark undertones suggest an *opera semi-seria*.

## PRINCIPAL ROLES

**Angiolina (La Cenerentola)** *contralto* or *mezzo-soprano* Don Magnifico's stepdaughter

**Don Ramiro** *tenor* Prince of Salerno

**Dandini** *bass* The prince's valet

**Don Magnifico** *bass*
A baron and La Cenerentola's stepfather

**Clorinda** *soprano* & **Tisbe** *mezzo-soprano*
Don Magnifico's daughters

### Act I

Angiolina, known as Cenerentola, dreams of a king who chooses a wife for her innocence and goodness ("Una volta c'era un re"), but the half-sisters Clorinda and Tisbe mock her. When Alidoro, a philosopher disguised as a beggar, knocks at their door, the sisters abuse him, but Cenerentola offers him bread and coffee. Learning that Prince Ramiro has decided to pick a bride, the sisters order Cenerentola to prepare their gowns. Awakened from a siesta, Don Magnifico interprets a dream to mean his daughters will become queens. When told Ramiro is to choose a bride, he believes that his dream will come true. Ramiro arrives disguised as his valet and sees Cenerentola. For both, it is love at first sight ("Un soave non so che"). As

Cenerentola explains her sad life, Ramiro is touched by her innocence. His valet, Dandini, then arrives disguised as the prince. As the sisters court him, Dandini inspects them with distaste. He then reveals that he risks losing his inheritance if he does not marry. Cenerentola begs Don Magnifico to take her to the palace, but instead he threatens to beat her ("Signora, una parola"). Alidoro invites Cenerentola to the ball and changes her rags for jewels. At the palace, Clorinda and Tisbe fight over Dandini in his role as the prince, but he warns Ramiro that they are vain and bad-tempered. Alidoro then introduces a mysterious veiled lady. When she shows her face, Don Magnifico notices that she resembles Cenerentola.

In Rossini's version of Cinderella, a bracelet replaces the glass slipper of the original tale, probably because it was considered improper for a woman's foot to be shown "naked" on stage.

◀ **Jonathan Veira** as Don Magnifico harasses Tuva Semmingsen's Cenerentola, at the Royal Danish Theatre in 2005.

**A girl left to her dreams** might easily imagine entering this opulent Baroque Spanish ballroom at the Royal Casino of Murcia and being swept off her feet by her Prince Charming.

## Act II

Although disturbed by the Cenerentola lookalike, Don Magnifico hopes one of his daughters will become powerful ("Sia qualunque delle figlie"). Dandini, still disguised as the prince, declares his love for Cenerentola, but she says she loves his valet. When Ramiro "the valet" steps forward, Cenerentola gives him a bracelet and tells him to find the other. Don Magnifico urges Dandini to pick one of his daughters—until Dandini admits that he is only a valet. While Alidoro arranges for Ramiro's carriage to break down outside Cenerentola's home, she is back sweeping floors. She again dreams that a king will pick her, then remembers she prefers the prince's valet. Dandini announces that the prince's carriage has overturned in a

storm. As Ramiro enters, he sees a bracelet on Cenerentola's arm and declares his love. Don Magnifico and the sisters start insulting Cenerentola ("Siete voi?"), who begs Ramiro to pardon them. Alidoro warns the sisters that they face misery if they do not seek Cenerentola's mercy. Finally, Don Magnifico kneels before Cenerentola and she also forgives the sisters. As everyone praises her goodness, she recalls her long years of heartache as nothing more than a dream ("Non più mesta accanto al fuoco").

### Rossini's contraltos

Rossini wrote Angiolina in *La Cenerentola* and Rosina in *Il barbiere di Siviglia* for his favorite voice, the contralto. Indeed, the roles are authentic gifts to a voice—now usually the mezzo-soprano—that all too often plays a supporting role to sopranos. Helping sustain the Rossini revival since the 1950s has been a succession of fine coloratura mezzo-sopranos who displayed a great feeling for comic opera, among them Giulietta Simionato, Teresa Berganza (right), and Cecilia Bartoli.

# Vincenzo Bellini

Born: November 3, 1801, Catania, Sicily, Italy • Died: September 23, 1835, Puteaux, near Paris, France

Vincenzo Bellini is the master of *bel canto*, the art of using "beautiful singing" to express high drama. In this, he both followed and improved on Rossini. He stripped arias and ensembles of florid embellishments and turned the voice into something resembling a laser of light cutting through darkness. He wanted to stir the emotions at the same time as pleasing the ear.

▲ **The Russian soprano** Galina Gorchakova takes on the title role of Norma, the most dramatic part in Bellini's repertoire, in a 2003 production at the San Diego Opera.

To achieve this, he worked slowly, writing only ten operas before his death at 33—one-third as many as Rossini had composed by the same age. Still, between 1827 and 1835, "Bellini, the divine Bellini," in the words of one fellow composer, was the brightest star of Italian opera, acclaimed above all for his ability to match melody with powerful poetry. "I want something that is at the same time a prayer, an invocation, a threat, a delirium," he told Felice Romani, his principal librettist. His best-known aria, "Casta diva" from *Norma*, is all of those things.

Born in Sicily in 1801, Bellini learned music from his father and grandfather and, by age 10, had composed church music. At 18, he entered the Real Collegio di Musica in Naples, where Niccolò Zingarelli, an *opera seria* composer of note, shielded him from what he considered to be Rossini's corrupting avant-garde influence. In practice, Bellini looked up to Rossini as he did to Mozart. However, he did heed his old teacher's advice in one important way. "The public want melodies, melodies, always melodies," Zingarelli told him. Legend has it that, years later, while attending *Il pirata*, the opera that made Bellini's name, tears rolled down Zingarelli's face.

Bellini's first break, though, came two years earlier in 1825, when he was the student chosen to compose an opera—*Adelson e Salvini*—for the Teatro di San Carlo in Naples. The San Carlo also presented his next, *Bianca e Fernando*, which led La Scala in Milan to commission *Il pirata* in 1827. The acclaim was immediate: Bellini was Rossini's heir! Critics noted that he had purified *bel canto* by simplifying melodies and orchestration to the point where their sole purpose was to convey emotion.

## FIRST PERFORMANCES

- 1825 *Adelson e Salvini*
- 1826 *Bianca e Fernando*
- 1827 *Il pirata*
- 1829 *La straniera* • *Zaira*
- 1830 *I Capuleti e i Montecchi*
- 1831 *La sonnambula* • *Norma*
- 1833 *Beatrice di Tenda*

### Greatness beckons

*Il pirata* was especially important for Bellini because it established his relationship with Romani, the admired theater-poet who also wrote librettos for both Rossini and Donizetti. They followed with *La straniera*, which was well received at La Scala, and *Zaira*, which flopped at the inauguration of Parma's new opera house. Then, in a burst of creativity, they created Bellini's three most popular operas, *I Capuleti e i Montecchi*, *La sonnambula*, and the monumental *Norma*, which was arguably the high point of the *bel canto* tradition. In their dramatic intensity, these works pointed the way for Verdi and Puccini.

### A premature death

In early 1833, Bellini fell out with his librettist over *Beatrice di Tenda*, and with the unraveling of an illicit love affair, Bellini fled to London to oversee the premiere of *Norma*. He then went to Paris, where Rossini arranged for the Théâtre-Italien to present his only Paris opera, *I puritani*. Its January 1835 premiere was a success, but Bellini was unhappy with

> "The music drama must make people
> weep, shudder, die by means of singing."

VINCENZO BELLINI

▲ **The San Carlo Theatre** in Naples, Italy, where *bel canto* was born and where works by Rossini, Bellini, and Donizetti premiered.

the libretto and, more than ever, missed working with Romani. Hopes for a reconciliation grew when La Scala asked Bellini for a new opera for Italy's reigning diva, Maria Malibran. He hurriedly adapted *I puritani* to her mezzo-soprano voice, but the score was completed too late for the new season and, in fact, was not performed until 1985. In the summer of 1835, while planning his return to Italy, Bellini fell ill with acute gastroenteritis and died in Puteaux, outside Paris, on September 23, 1835. A brilliant life had been tragically cut short.

# I Capuleti e i Montecchi

▲ **Denis Krief's production** for the 2005 Festival della Valle d'Itria sets the opera in the immediate post-war period to emphasize the group conflict of the title.

**THE CAPULETS AND THE MONTAGUES** *Tragedia lirica* in two acts, 2¼ hours ▪ Composed: 1830 ▪ First performed: March 11, 1830, Theatro La Fenice, Venice ▪ Libretto: Felice Romani, after a 16th-century novella by Matteo Bandello and an 1818 play by Luigi Scevola

*I Capuleti e i Montecchi* recounts the familiar story of Romeo and Juliet, but uses original Italian Renaissance sources and eliminates many of the characters who appear in Shakespeare's play. As befits a tragic love story, it is a powerfully lyrical work, with Bellini giving the role of Romeo to a mezzo-soprano. Adding drama, the yearning arias by Romeo and Giulietta contrast with the stormy confrontations of the warring clans.

Bellini was so angered by *Zaira*'s poor reception in Parma the year before that he adapted eight movements from that opera to be used in this different story of *I Capuleti e i Montecchi*.

## PRINCIPAL ROLES

**Capellio** *bass* Head of the Capuleti clan

**Giulietta** *soprano* Capellio's daughter

**Romeo** *mezzo-soprano* Head of the Montecchi clan and Giulietta's lover

**Tebaldo** *tenor* Giulietta's husband-to-be

**Lorenzo** *baritone* Capellio's adviser and Romeo's friend

### Act I
In the Capuleti's palace, Capellio ignores calls for peace from Lorenzo and vows to kill Romeo, the Montecchi leader. Romeo arrives disguised as a Montecchi envoy and proposes reconciliation through Romeo's marriage to Capellio's daughter, Giulietta. When Capellio announces that she will marry Tebaldo, Romeo prepares for combat. Giulietta is resigned to her fate, but Romeo arrives with Lorenzo and begs her to flee with him ("Si, fuggire: a noi non resta"). Unwilling to dishonor her family, she refuses. With Giulietta's marriage about to take place, Romeo comes dressed as a Capuleti. As he pleads with his beloved, he is unmasked ("Soccorso, sostengo accordagli") and a fight erupts between the clans.

### Act II
Assuring Giulietta that Romeo has escaped, Lorenzo proposes she drink a potion that will make her appear dead. Once in the Capuleti's tomb, he says, Romeo will awaken her. As Capellio arrives, she drinks the potion and begs his forgiveness. When Romeo receives no word from his beloved, he approaches the Capuleti's palace, where he meets Tebaldo. As they duel, they hear a choir lamenting Giulietta's death. Romeo enters the tomb and, seeing Giulietta's inert body, takes poison. Waking, she is horrified to see her dying lover and kills herself. As their bodies are found, the two clans blame one another.

# La sonnambula

THE SLEEPWALKER *Melodramma* in two acts, 3 hours ▪ Composed: 1831 ▪ First performed: March 6, 1831, Teatro Carcano, Milan, Italy ▪ Libretto: Felice Romani, after Eugéne Scribe's scenario for the ballet *La somnambule, ou L'arrivée d'un nouveau seigneur*

*La sonnambula* is a charming pastoral idyll, with a succession of sweet arias and duets compensating for its lack of dramatic punch. The plot is built around unwarranted jealousy: the heroine climbs into the wrong bed while sleepwalking. As the misunderstandings are being cleared up, Bellini offers his most lyrical score to date, so melodic that some critics considered it too lush. Several arias are firm favorites in soprano recitals.

### Act I

Amina, an orphan raised by Teresa, is to marry Elvino. She thanks Teresa for her care and dreams of love ("Come per me sereno"). After the marriage contract is signed and rings exchanged, a handsome stranger arrives and, to Elvino's annoyance, flirts with Amina. Teresa sends everyone home, warning them of the village ghost. At the inn, Lisa takes a fancy to the stranger, whom she recognizes as Count Rodolfo. Suddenly, Amina enters his room through a window and Lisa hurries away, leaving a handkerchief. Rodolfo realizes Amina is sleepwalking and leaves her asleep on his bed. Shown the sleeping Amina, Elvino angrily cancels his wedding.

### Act II

Convinced that he has been betrayed, Elvino snatches his ring from Amina's finger. Lisa persuades Elvino to marry her, but Rodolfo swears to Amina's innocence. Meanwhile, Teresa asks for silence as Amina is asleep. She displays Lisa's handkerchief, which she found in Rodolfo's room. Elvino now believes Lisa has also betrayed him. Amina appears in her nightdress and, asleep, walks toward a fragile bridge. As the villagers pray for her safety, she crosses the bridge and, kneeling, prays for Elvino. Realizing his error, Elvino places his ring again on her finger. When she awakens, she is surrounded by joy and, forgiving Elvino, is led to the altar ("Ah! non giunge uman pensiero").

### PRINCIPAL ROLES

**Amina** *soprano* A peasant girl who sleepwalks

**Elvino** *tenor* Amina's betrothed

**Count Rodolfo** *bass* A benign feudal lord

**Teresa** *mezzo-soprano* Amina's foster mother

**Lisa** *soprano* Owner of the inn

**Alessio** *bass* Lisa's suitor

Such was Bellini's perfectionism that he asked his librettist, Felice Romani, to rewrite Amina's final aria, *"Ah! non giunge uman pensiero,"* no fewer than ten times before he was satisfied.

▶ **The Kazakh-born Greek** soprano Elena Kelessidi as the ever-sleeping Amina at the Royal Opera House, London, in 2002.

# Norma

*Tragedia lirica* in two acts, 2¾ hours • Composed: 1831 • First performed: December 26, 1831, La Scala, Milan, Italy • Libretto: Felice Romani, after Alexandre Soumet's 1831 verse tragedy *Norma*

In *Norma*, Bellini's finest and most popular opera, the music reinforces the drama to create a deeply moving work. Felice Romani's libretto is excellent, but it is the score that lifts the work to greatness. Surprisingly simple orchestration sustains long and complex ensembles and richly melodic arias, notably the spine-tingling "Casta diva," or "Chaste goddess." The role of Norma is particularly testing, requiring a coloratura soprano with a voice of immense power, range, stamina, and virtuosity as well as a talent for conveying tragedy on stage. As it happens, the premiere of *Norma* was sabotaged by friends of a rival composer, Giacomo Pacini, prompting Bellini to describe the occasion as "a fiasco, a total fiasco." But within a few years, the opera had conquered Europe and the United States.

## PRINCIPAL ROLES

**Pollione** *tenor*
Roman proconsul and father of Norma's children

**Oroveso** *bass* Archdruid and Norma's father

**Norma** *soprano* Druid high priestess

**Adalgisa** *soprano* Druid priestess

**Clotilde** *soprano* Norma's attendant

**Flavio** *tenor* A centurion

**Two children of Norma and Pollione** *silent*

---

Wagner never hid his distaste for most Italian opera, but he made an exception for *Norma*. After hearing Bellini's masterpiece, he said: "We must not be ashamed to shed a tear and express emotion."

---

### Act I

In a sacred forest, Archdruid Oroveso and his followers hope the high priestess Norma will lead a revolt against the Roman occupiers. Nearby, the Roman proconsul Pollione, the father of Norma's two secret children, reveals he loves another priestess, Adalgisa. But he fears Norma's wrath. Expecting an uprising, he hears Norma proclaim that the Gods alone will decide the moment. The Druids obey her as a chaste goddess ("Casta diva"), while she yearns to recover Pollione's love. As the Druids disperse, Adalgisa feels guilty for betraying her vows of chastity. When Pollione reiterates his love for her, she rejects him ("Va crudele, al Dio spietato"). He invites her to Rome, and she first refuses, then yields. Norma is torn between love and hate for her children. Adalgisa arrives to confess she has fallen in love with someone. As she describes how she was won, Norma recalls

Pollione using the same words. Norma asks the name of her lover, and, as Pollione approaches, Adalgisa points to him. Turning on Pollione in fury, Norma tells Adalgisa she has been deceived ("Oh! di qual sei tu vittima"). Adalgisa suddenly realizes that she has taken Norma's lover and vows to take steps to reunite them.

### Act II

Watching over her sleeping children, Norma imagines they might be better dead, but she draws back from killing them. Summoning Adalgisa, she demands obedience. She then discloses her decision to die and tells Adalgisa to care for her children in Rome. But Adalgisa refuses to leave Gaul and vows to reawaken Pollione's love for Norma ("Mira, o Norma").

Oroveso tells the Druid warriors that a commander worse than Pollione is coming, but that Norma wants her army to disband. Oroveso urges the warriors to hide their hatred until it can explode. Learning Pollione has sworn to abduct Adalgisa, Norma summons her warriors to battle. As they sing to their victory, a Roman is found violating the sacred cloister of the virgins and is captured. When Pollione is brought in, Norma ignores cries to kill him and orders him to leave without Adalgisa and never to return ("In mia man"). Pollione prefers to die, but Norma decides Adalgisa will be sacrificed in his stead. Pollione pleads for Adalgisa's life and asks for Norma's dagger to kill himself. Norma then says a different

◀ **Nothing better prefaces** an opera rich in mysticism than a dark forest beneath a stormy sky, where light struggles to penetrate the clouds.

▲ **The Spanish soprano** Montserrat Caballé
played a part in the revival of *bel canto* with
Norma, one of her preferred roles.

victim will be sacrificed. As the pyre is
prepared, she reveals that she is the traitress
who must die ("Qual cor tradisti"). Suddenly
remorseful, Pollione now wants to die with
her. The Druids are shocked to learn of
Norma's unchaste relationship with a
Roman, but Norma begs her father to
protect her children. Then, weeping, she
ascends the pyre with Pollione.

### Maria Callas as Norma

Of the many *bel canto* heroines revived by Maria Callas,
none matched her powerful voice and fragile personality
more perfectly than Norma. As her own life became more
tragic, she embraced the role with ever greater passion.
"In a lifetime, one can see many great things in the theater,"
Mirto Picchi, her first Pollione, recalled, "but to see Maria
Callas in *Norma*, what is there to compare to it? As Norma,
Maria created the maximum of what opera can be."

▶ **Maria Callas** as Norma, her most performed role, at the Paris Opéra in 1964.

# SYDNEY OPERA
## HOUSE

From the moment the Sydney Opera House opened, in October 1973, its striking appearance and dramatic position overlooking Sydney's harbor made it as much a symbol of Australia as the Eiffel Tower is of France. Its innovative design, with numerous sail-shaped concrete shells giving it the appearance of an angry armadillo, was the focus of intense debate during the 14 years of construction, with the project's Danish architect, Jørn Utzon, resigning well before completion.

Yet such was the worldwide acclaim the building earned that it posed a challenge to architects of future opera houses to show comparable daring. In that sense, the Sydney Opera House became the precursor for the ultra-modern opera houses that have since appeared in places such as Oslo, Copenhagen, Valencia, Dubai, and Guangzhou—at times raising the question of whether their purpose is to exhibit a city's architecture or to promote lyrical music.

The Sydney Opera House is in fact a cultural complex, with a 1,500–seat opera hall, a 2,700-seat concert hall, a 544-seat drama theater, and several other small performance spaces. It is therefore home to Australian Ballet and Bell Shakespeare as well as to Opera Australia. With the winter opera season in the southern hemisphere coinciding with summer in Europe, Sydney can also draw singers from afar to bolster its homegrown talent in major productions.

The notion that a country devoted to outdoor sports would struggle to respond to opera was forever negated by Australia's greatest soprano, Joan Sutherland, who, during a 30-year career, conquered opera lovers from London and Milan to Paris and New York. Indeed, one of her last stage appearances was at the Sydney Opera House in the auditorium that now carries her name. And since her death in 2010, she has become the guardian angel of all aspiring Australian opera singers.

Jørn Utzon found inspiration for the Sydney Opera House in pre-Columbian Aztec and Maya designs, later describing his travels to Mexico and Guatemala as among the most transforming architectural experiences of his life.

◄ **At dawn, the Sydney Opera House** seems to suggest a flock of seagulls preparing for flight.

# Gaetano Donizetti

Born: November 29, 1797, Bergamo, Italy • Died: April 8, 1848, Bergamo, Italy

Gaetano Donizetti is in many ways the overlooked master of early Italian Romantic opera. Even today, long after the post-1950s revival of the florid style known as *bel canto*, or "beautiful singing," only a half-dozen of his 75 or so operas are regularly performed. Yet for more than a decade from 1830, this modest and gregarious melody-maker was the dominant Italian composer of his day.

Although Donizetti stands in the shadow of Rossini and Verdi, he in fact served as a bridge between these two opera giants: like Rossini, he believed in *bel canto*; and like Verdi, he believed that music should reinforce the drama. But he was an innovator, too: he eliminated Rossini's excesses—crescendos, double-arias, and the finale aria—and rejected the traditional separation between recitatives and arias, moving toward continuous music. Most of all, he was a hard-working craftsman who wrote splendid tunes.

Born into a poor family, Donizetti was given free music tuition by Johann Simon Mayr, a Bavarian-born priest who was music director at Bergamo's main church as well as an accomplished opera composer. Donizetti then gained entry to Bologna's music academy, where he wrote mainly sacred music. But he was drawn to opera, not least because, as a hard-up young composer, he found that 19th-century Italy had an almost insatiable demand for opera. Adept in both *opera seria* and *opera buffa*, over a 12-year period he wrote 31 works, mostly for Naples. Finally, in 1830, he was commissioned to write a *tragedia lirica* for La Scala in Milan. The success of *Anna Bolena* made him a household name, even beyond Italy. Then, 18 months—and four operas—later, he was again acclaimed in Milan, this time for *L'elisir d'amore*, one of his most popular works. Like *Anna Bolena*, it benefited from a libretto by Felice Romani, a theater poet who also wrote for Rossini and Bellini. Working at an extraordinary pace, Donizetti wrote four more operas before La Scala applauded him for *Lucrezia Borgia* in 1833.

## FIRST PERFORMANCES

- 1822 *Zoraida di Granata*
- 1830 *Anna Bolena*
- 1832 *L'elisir d'amore*
- 1833 *Lucrezia Borgia*
- 1835 *Maria Stuarda* • *Lucia di Lammermoor*
- 1837 *Roberto Devereux*
- 1840 *La fille du régiment* • *La favorite*
- 1843 *Don Pasquale* • *Dom Sébastien*

▲ **Violina Anguelov as Queen Elizabeth I** berates Noluvuyiso Mpofu's Mary Queen of Scots in a 2015 production of *Maria Stuarda* at the Artscape Theatre in Cape Town, South Africa.

## Struggles with censors

Donizetti often set operas in Protestant Britain in the hope of appeasing Catholic censors. But *Maria Stuarda* was nonetheless banned in Naples in 1834 because of its underlying Protestant-versus-Catholic theme. He reused some of its score for an opera called *Buondelmonte* and finally presented *Maria Stuarda* at La Scala in 1835. But it was again in Naples, that same year, that he created his most memorable tragedy, *Lucia di Lammermoor*. Donizetti's own life was also marked by tragedy: his wife died in 1837 at the age of 29 after giving birth to their third stillborn child. His response to her death was an intense tragedy set in Britain, *Roberto Devereux*, a fictional account of Elizabeth I's love for the Earl of Essex. But the next year, after *Poliuto* was banned in Naples, he moved to Paris where, with Rossini retired and Bellini dead, he had no Italian competitor.

## Triumph in France

From this period, three operas stand out: *La fille du régiment*, *La favorite*, and *Don Pasquale*, all originally performed in French. But by

> "I want love, violent love, because
> without it subjects are cold."

GAETANO DONIZETTI

1843, when he created his final work, *Dom Sébastien*, a five-act grand opera, the syphilis he had contracted years earlier was rapidly undermining his physical and mental health. A man known for his patience and charm suddenly grew irascible. And worse was to follow. In 1846, he was interned in a private asylum. Finally, his family took him home to Bergamo where, now totally insane, he died in 1848.

▲ **The figure of Donizetti** emerges from an asylum at Ivry, outside Paris, where he spent his final years before being repatriated to Italy to die.

# L'elisir d'amore

THE LOVE POTION *Opera comica* in two acts, 2 hours ▪ Composed: 1832 ▪ First performed: May 12, 1832, Teatro della Canobbiana, Milan, Italy ▪ Libretto: Felice Romani after Eugène Scribe's text for Daniel Auber's 1831 opera *Le philtre*, itself after Silvio Malaperta's play, *Il filtro*

*L'elisir d'amore* has long been one of Donizetti's most popular operas, memorable above all for its almost uninterrupted flow of enchanting melodies. Classified as an *opera buffa*, it boasts the required *buffo* character in the quack Dr. Dulcamara, who entertains with the inevitable "patter song." But *L'elisir d'amore*'s story also invites lyricism as Nemorino resorts to magic—an elixir of love—in the hope of winning over Adina, the rich and fickle object of his passion. With the score bringing rich colors to the narrative, Nemorino's pining tenor arias and Adina's mischievous coloratura soprano arias pave the way to the couple's happiness. As it happens, the story had been told before, in fact just one year earlier, also in Paris, in Daniel Auber's opera, *Le philtre*. But only Donizetti's version is now remembered.

## PRINCIPAL ROLES

**Adina** *soprano* A rich young landowner

**Nemorino** *tenor* A farmer in love with Adina

**Sergeant Belcore** *baritone* A visiting soldier

**Dr. Dulcamara** *buffo* A charlatan doctor

**Giannetta** *soprano* A village girl

▼ **In this painting** by Giacomo Mantegazza, Dulcamara can be seen rehearsing his sales pitch to Donizetti on the piano.

### Act I

As Adina reads the story of Tristan and Isolde, Nemorino recognizes the impossibility of his love for such a wonderful woman ("Quanto è bella, quanto è cara!"). Suddenly bursting into laughter, Adina reads out to the harvesters on her farm how Isolde conquered Tristan with a love potion. Sgt. Belcore arrives with his platoon and, struck by Adina's beauty, promptly proposes to her, suggesting they marry immediately. But Adina is in no hurry and, when Nemorino finally tells her of his love, she declares she is as fickle as the wind and urges him to find another woman ("Chiedi all' aura lusinghiera").

A trumpet announces the arrival of Dr. Dulcamara, a traveling quack, who boasts he can cure every ill. Nemorino discloses that he is love-struck and asks the charlatan about Isolde's love potion. Claiming he has just the thing, Dulcamara gives the naive young man a bottle of cheap red wine, assuring him it will work within 24 hours. Nemorino drains the bottle and is soon tipsy. Meanwhile, when Belcore renews his proposal, Adina agrees to marry him in a week. Belcore then receives orders to leave town. Adina, puzzled by Nemorino's apparent indifference ("Esulti pur la barbara"), moves her wedding to the following day. As Belcore and Adina visit the notary, Nemorino sobers up and goes in search of Dulcamara.

### Act II

The wedding party is in full swing, although Adina has not yet signed the marriage contract. She joins Dulcamara in a popular Venetian song about a girl who chooses to marry a poor gondolier rather than a rich senator. As the notary arrives to formalize the marriage, Nemorino needs money to buy more love potion. Seeing no alternative, he enlists, collects a payment from Belcore, and goes looking for Dulcamara. A village

girl announces that Nemorino's uncle has died and left him a fortune. When the young farmer returns, his spirits lifted by more wine, the village girls surround him excitedly. And since he knows nothing about his bequest, he believes the potion is at last working. Dulcamara explains Nemorino's odd behavior to Adina and, realizing she loves the young man, he offers her some wine. She responds that she has no need for magic potion ("Quanto amore!"). Seeing a tell-tale tear in Adina's eye, Nemorino now also realizes that she loves him ("Una furtiva lagrima"). Adina then finally confesses her love to him, telling Nemorino that she has purchased his freedom from the army. With Belcore resigned to losing Adina, Dulcamara points to Nemorino's good fortune as proof that his potion brings wealth as well as love. Dulcamara sells the remainder of his stock of cheap wine to the crowd and rides away.

▲ **Riccardo Novaro**, as the charlatan Dr. Dulcamara, hawks his love potion at Glyndebourne, in 2013.

In December 1920, Enrico Caruso coughed up blood while singing the role of Nemorino in New York. Despite appeals from the audience, he finished the performance, but he died nine months later.

# Lucia di Lammermoor

LUCY OF LAMMERMOOR *Dramma tragico* in three acts, 2½ hours ▪ Composed: 1835 (rev. in French 1839) ▪ First performed: September 26, 1835, Teatro di San Carlo, Naples, Italy ▪ Libretto: Salvatore Cammarano, after the 1819 novel *The Bride of Lammermoor* by Sir Walter Scott

*Lucia di Lammermoor*, Donizetti's most exquisitely realized work, represents the climax of Italian Romantic opera and features in two great Romantic novels, Flaubert's *Madame Bovary* and Tolstoy's *Anna Karenina*. A poignant story of family feuds crushing love and life, it also inevitably recalls *Romeo and Juliet*. Best known for Lucia's "mad scene" in Act III, it is packed with other haunting melodies. Lucia and her lover, Edgardo, have stirring arias, as well as a touching duet. The richly woven sextet that ends Act II, with each voice expressing a different emotion, is considered one of the finest ensembles in the opera canon.

## Act I

Enrico Ashton is lamenting his misfortunes and the delight they must give his mortal enemy, Edgardo Ravenswood. He concludes that the only solution is for his sister, Lucia, to marry into money. Raimondo, the chaplain, says she is too sad over her mother's death to wed, but Normanno, Enrico's friend, says she is already aflame with love. He has witnessed her secret meetings with a man believed to be Edgardo Ravenswood. Enrico is wild with anger. In the castle gardens, Lucia recalls "seeing" the stabbing of the lover of a Ravenswood ancestor ("Regnava nel silenzio"). Lucia's friend, Alisa, begs her to abandon this dangerous love, but she cannot. Edgardo brings word that he must leave for France to seek allies for Scotland and will first ask for Lucia's hand. But Lucia insists their love must remain secret, and, exchanging rings, they bid farewell ("Ah! Verrano a te sull'aure").

## Act II

With Enrico nervously awaiting Lucia, Normanno boasts that he has forged a letter from Edgardo to another woman. Lucia arrives looking sad, and Enrico tells her he has chosen a husband for her, one whose help he needs. When she says she is already pledged, he gives her the forged love letter. Shattered by Edgardo's betrayal, she awaits the arrival of Arturo, her future husband ("Se tradirmi tu potrai"). Arturo has heard rumors about Lucia's secret love for Edgardo, but Enrico dismisses them and joins him in signing the marriage contract. Lucia, too, then signs her

"death warrant." At that moment, Edgardo bursts in ("Chi me frena in tal momento"), insisting he still loves her. He and Enrico draw their swords, but he is then shown Lucia's signature on the marriage contract. Stunned, he returns his ring to Lucia.

## Act III

Raimondo interrupts the wedding party to announce that, hearing cries from Lucia's apartment, he entered and found Arturo dead, with Lucia still holding his dagger. As the crowd gasps in horror, Lucia enters, clearly deranged and "hearing" Edgardo's voice ("Il dolce suono"). Faced with her mad ravings, Enrico is full of remorse. At the tomb of the Ravenswoods, Edgardo sees lights in Lammermoor Castle and imagines Lucia celebrating her new love. He hears people leaving the castle regretting the "horrendous fate" of a "wretched girl." They tell him that Lucia is dying and with her last breath is calling for him. Raimondo then brings news that she has expired. Devastated ("Tu che a Dio spiegasti l'ali"), Edgardo stabs himself to death in order to be reunited with Lucia.

---

### PRINCIPAL ROLES

**Lucia di Lammermoor** *soprano*

**Edgardo Ravenswood** *tenor* Lucia's beloved

**Enrico Ashton** *baritone* Lucia's brother

**Raimondo** *bass* The chaplain

**Arturo** *tenor* Lucia's husband

**Alisa** *mezzo-soprano* Lucia's confidante

---

During the Austrian occupation, an 1837 production in Parma was disrupted by police when the female chorus wore white dresses with green and red ribbons, colors representing Italy's independence movement.

---

◀ **The Korean coloratura** soprano Sumi Jo, seen here at the Opéra Bastille, Paris, in 1999, has made Lucia di Lammermoor one of her favorite roles.

---

### Sir Walter Scott

Personifying Gothic Romanticism, Sir Walter Scott was enormously popular in 19th-century Europe, with 16 of his novels adapted as operas. Although the best known, Donizetti's *Lucia di Lammermoor* was only one of six operatic versions of *The Bride of Lammermoor*. Bellini's final opera, *I puritani*, was inspired by *Old Mortality*; Rossini turned *The Lady of the Lake* into *La donna del lago*; and Bizet's opera *La jolie fille de Perth* is based entirely on *The Fair Maid of Perth*.

# Anna Bolena

ANNE BOLEYN *Tragedia lirica* in two acts, 3¼ hours ▪ Composed: 1830 ▪ First performed: December 26, 1830, Teatro Carcano, Milan, Italy ▪ Libretto: Felice Romani, after the plays *Henri VIII* by Marie-Joseph Chénier and *Anna Bolena* by Alessandro Pepoli

*Anna Bolena*, Donizetti's 30th opera, was his first great triumph and his passport to international fame. While this rendering of Anne Boleyn's execution is historically unreliable, the opera is above all a feast of *bel canto*: it has glorious soprano and tenor arias, a poignant duet between the ill-fated queen and her chosen successor, and masterful finales to both acts. Nonetheless, due to its length, it is usually performed with significant cuts.

## PRINCIPAL ROLES

**Enrico VIII** *bass* King Henry VIII

**Anna Bolena** *soprano* The king's second wife

**Giovanna (Jane) Seymour** *mezzo-soprano* The king's third wife

**Smeton** *mezzo-soprano* A court musician

**Percy** *tenor* Anna's former lover

### Act I

At Windsor, Giovanna Seymour feels guilty about her love affair with the king. Anna Bolena asks Smeton, her musician, for a song, but it reminds her of her first love, Percy. When Giovanna tells the king she feels shame, he says they will soon be married. He has recalled Percy from exile, intent on proving he is still Anna's lover. Smeton, who adores the queen, overhears her telling Percy the king hates her. When Percy declares his love, she orders him to leave. He tries to stab himself, but Smeton stops him. As Anna faints, the king enters. When Smeton's miniature of Anna falls to the ground, the king has proof of her betrayal and orders her arrest ("In quegli sguardi impresso").

### Act II

In the Tower of London, after urging Anna to admit her guilt, Giovanna confesses she will become the new queen. Horrified, Anna curses her, then pardons her, blaming only the king. To save her life, Smeton "confesses" to adultery with Anna, but the king instead uses it against her. Lord Percy declares that he was once married to Anna and now reclaims her. Stunned, the king dismisses Giovanna's plea for mercy. Awaiting death, Anna recalls her first love ("Al dolce guidami"). Then, as a cannon announces the king's marriage, she is led to the scaffold.

Giuditta Pasta was the diva who made *Anna Bolena* famous. It would take another diva, Maria Callas, to revive this long-forgotten opera in a memorable production at La Scala, Milan, in 1957.

◀ **Anna Netrebko** as Anna Bolena, with Stephen Costello as Percy, in David McVicar's 2011 production at the Metropolitan Opera in New York.

# La fille du régiment

THE DAUGHTER OF THE REGIMENT *Opéra comique* in two acts, 1½ hours • Composed: 1839 (*opera buffa* version with recitatives, 1840) • First performed: February 14, 1840, Opéra-Comique, Paris, France • Libretto: Jean-François Alfred Bayard and Jules-Henri Vernoy de Saint-Georges

With *La fille du régiment*, Donizetti's first *opéra comique*, the composer went out of his way to charm Paris audiences with a love story that ends with a rousingly patriotic "Salute to France." The score is rich in lyrical arias and duets but, in keeping with the plot, its choruses also echo military music. Donizetti later adapted the opera into Italian, replacing spoken dialogue with sung recitative. Today, the French version is usually preferred.

### Act I

Marie, an orphan raised by soldiers, follows her French regiment to the Tyrol. When her guardian, Sgt. Sulpice, sees her with a young man, she recounts how he saved her from a precipice. Soldiers then enter with a Tyrolean suspected of spying, but Marie identifies him as her rescuer. Alone, she and Tonio declare their love ("Quoi! Vous m'aimez"). In order to marry the regiment's "daughter," Tonio even enlists. The Marquise de Birkenfield arrives seeking safe conduct. But when Sulpice recalls that her name was on a letter found with the baby Marie, he discovers that she is Marie's aunt. The Marquise decides that the baby should live in her chateau.

### Act II

The Marquise sets out to turn Marie into a lady, with dancing and singing lessons. Marie is briefly cheered when Sulpice joins her in the song of the regiment, but she is not happy about marrying a rich heir. Sulpice urges the Marquise to allow Marie to marry her true love. Marie and Tonio even plan to elope. The Marquise then reveals she is in fact Marie's mother. As Marie prepares to marry the heir, she recounts her happy life with the regiment. The guests are horrified, but the Marquise is touched by her gratitude to the regiment, and decides she can marry Tonio. Led by Marie, all cheer France ("Salut à la France").

> PRINCIPAL ROLES
>
> **Marie** *soprano*
> An orphan adopted by the regiment
>
> **Tonio** *tenor* A Tyrolean peasant in love with Marie
>
> **Sergeant Sulpice** *bass* Marie's guardian
>
> **Marquise de Birkenfield** *mezzo-soprano*
>
> **Hortensius** *bass* The Marquise's steward

With its nine high Cs, the aria "Pour mon âme" earned the tenor Luciano Pavarotti the title "King of the High Cs" in 1972, just as it made Juan Diego Flórez's name 35 years later.

◄ **The American Lily Pons**, seen here as Marie in 1940, was a coloratura soprano with legions of admirers at the Metropolitan Opera in New York.

# La favorite

THE FAVORITE Grand opera in four acts, 2½ hours • Composed: 1840 • First performed: December 2, 1840, Paris Opéra, France • Libretto: Alphonse Royer, Gustave Vaëz, and Eugène Scribe, after Baculard d'Arnaud's 1764 play *Le Comte de Comminge*

*La favorite*, Donizetti's second French language work for the Paris Opéra, recounts the implausible story of a monarch ceding his mistress to a war hero. But, as so often with this composer, the plot is mere excuse for a glittering score that stands out for its contrasting colors. While a succession of fine arias illustrate the love triangle of Léonor, Fernand, and Alphonse, threats of divorce and excommunication add darker undertones.

## PRINCIPAL ROLES

**Alphonse** *baritone* King of Castile

**Léonor** *mezzo-soprano* The king's mistress

**Ines** *soprano* Léonor's confidante

**Fernand** *tenor* A young novice

**Balthazar** *bass* Father Superior

**Don Gaspard** *tenor* The king's minister

### Act I
Fernand, a novice in the monastery at Santiago de Compostela, confesses to Balthazar, his Superior, that he is haunted by a beautiful woman whom he saw praying in church. When Balthazar sends

▼ **Giacomo Prestia as Balthazar** chastises Carlos Álvarez's Alphonse and his mistress Léonor, sung by Violeta Urmana, in the Vienna Staatsoper production in 2003.

him away, Fernand traces the woman, Léonor, to an island. She loves him, too, but she dare not reveal that she is the king's mistress.

### Act II
Having defeated the Moors, King Alphonse plans to divorce his wife and marry Léonor. Yearning for Fernand, Léonor begs the king to release her. He refuses, but is upset to read an intercepted love letter to her. Balthazar, also the queen's father, then threatens the king with excommunication if he decides on divorce.

### Act III
Alphonse receives Fernand as a war hero and offers him any wish. When he asks to marry Léonor, the king agrees ("Pour tant d'amour"). Léonor tries to inform Fernand about her past before they marry, but the message never reaches him. When he learns the truth from Balthazar, he breaks his sword before the king and returns to the monastery in Santiago.

### Act IV
The queen has died of sorrow, and, at her funeral in Santiago, Fernand remembers his former love ("Ange si pur"). Suddenly, Léonor appears in disguise as a novice, weak and ill. Fernand tells her to leave, but his passion is rekindled. He prepares to flee with her, but she dies in his arms.

Donizetti wrote *La favorite* in a rush, even borrowing some of the music from *L'ange de Nisida*, his earlier opera about a royal mistress, which was never staged because the theater went bankrupt.

# Don Pasquale

*Opera buffa* in three acts, 2 hours ▪ Composed: 1842 ▪ First performed: January 3, 1843, Théâtre-Italien, Paris, France ▪ Libretto: Giovanni Ruffini and Gaetano Donizetti, after Angelo Anelli's libretto for Pavesi's opera *Ser Marc'Antonio*

*Don Pasquale* is Donizetti's comic masterpiece. In the opera, a love story somehow triumphs over absurd characters, unlikely disguises, and much confusion. With a dazzling score keeping the plot moving apace, farcical scenes lead to sweet soprano and tenor arias and love duets. At the heart of the opera, though, is the great *buffo* character of Don Pasquale. His Act III duet with Malatesta is acknowledged to be one of the high points of the entire work.

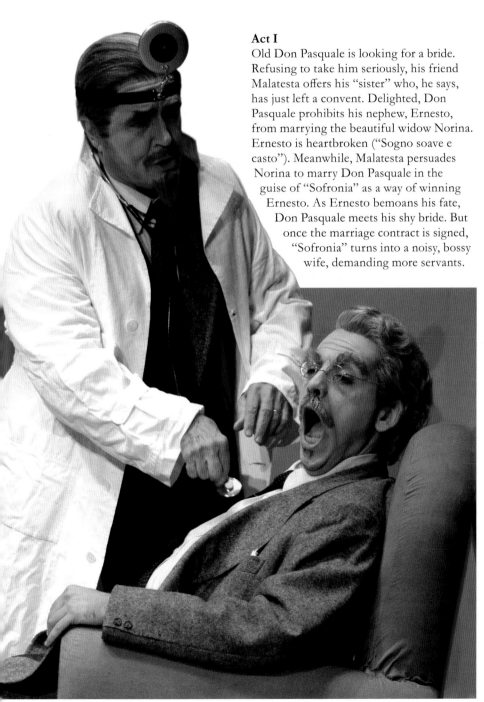

### Act I

Old Don Pasquale is looking for a bride. Refusing to take him seriously, his friend Malatesta offers his "sister" who, he says, has just left a convent. Delighted, Don Pasquale prohibits his nephew, Ernesto, from marrying the beautiful widow Norina. Ernesto is heartbroken ("Sogno soave e casto"). Meanwhile, Malatesta persuades Norina to marry Don Pasquale in the guise of "Sofronia" as a way of winning Ernesto. As Ernesto bemoans his fate, Don Pasquale meets his shy bride. But once the marriage contract is signed, "Sofronia" turns into a noisy, bossy wife, demanding more servants.

> **PRINCIPAL ROLES**
>
> **Don Pasquale** *bass* A foolish old bachelor
>
> **Ernesto** *tenor* Don Pasquale's nephew
>
> **Norina** *soprano* A young widow
>
> **Dr. Malatesta** *baritone* Don Pasquale's friend

By now, informed about Malatesta's plan, Ernesto is again confident of Norina's love. Don Pasquale realizes he has made a terrible mistake.

### Act II

Don Pasquale is horrified by his wife's wild spending and is shocked to see her leaving for the theater without him. They argue and she strikes him, persuading him it is time to flee his marriage. As Norina leaves, she drops a note, purportedly from Ernesto setting a late-night rendezvous. Don Pasquale summons Malatesta for help. Ernesto is serenading Norina, but hides when Don Pasquale rushes in to eject "Sofronia" from his house. Malatesta announces that a new wife will soon arrive—Norina. When "Sofronia" protests, even Don Pasquale agrees to his nephew's marriage. Finally, realizing he has been tricked, Don Pasquale forgives everyone.

◀ **Alberto Rinaldi** as Dr. Malatesta looks after Alfonso Antoniozzi's Don Pasquale at the Teatro dell'Opera, Rome, in 2003.

> *Don Pasquale*'s plot is an old standby borrowed from Ben Jonson's 1609 play, *Epicœne or The Silent Woman*. This play has also inspired other operas, including *Die schweigsame Frau* by Richard Strauss.

# Giuseppe Verdi

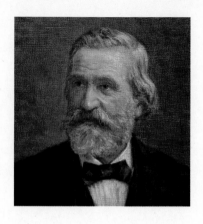

Born: October 9 or 10, 1813, Le Roncole, near Busseto, Italy • Died: January 27, 1901, Milan, Italy

Giuseppe Verdi is the most successful and widely performed composer in opera history. He was not a musical pioneer in the manner of Mozart or Wagner. Yet, more than any other composer, through the sheer number of immortal works he created, he made opera what it is today. No opera season in the world is complete without the inclusion of at least two of his major pieces.

▲ **The American soprano** Renée Fleming captures the innocence of Desdemona in her last hours in the final scene of Verdi's opera *Otello* in a Paris Opéra production of 2011, directed by Andrei Șerban.

The intense melodrama of Verdi's works has become synonymous with the word "operatic." And even when the plots of his operas seem implausible, they still address universal themes of love, betrayal, violence, power, and death. Verdi was also a man of his times and, with several of his works interpreted as allegories for Italy's struggle for freedom and unification, he was credited with helping to forge a national identity. But it was above all his talent for matching unforgettable melodies to moments of high drama that carried his name around the world. Indeed, for half a century, Verdi dominated Italian opera and shared the limelight with only one other composer, Richard Wagner. While Wagner's work is often admired for its German intensity, it is the very universality of Verdi's operas that sustains their enduring popularity.

Born in the village of Le Roncole near Busseto in northern Italy, Verdi had church organists as his first teachers, and he was gifted enough for a local merchant, Antonio Barezzi, to finance his studies. But, at 18, Verdi was too old to enter the Milan Conservatory, and instead learned the art of counterpoint and fugue from a private teacher. In April 1836, he was named Busseto's music master and, weeks later, married his teenage sweetheart, Barezzi's daughter, Margherita. By then, he was working on his first opera, *Oberto*, which was presented at La Scala in Milan in November 1839. Then tragedy struck. After his two children had died in infancy, Verdi's wife died in June 1840. Not surprisingly, his next work, *Un giorno di regno*, was a flop; he would not write another *opera buffa* until *Falstaff*, more than 50 years later.

## Recognition

In 1842, with *Nabucco*, his fortune changed. It was with this production, Verdi later remarked, that his career truly began. With its chilling soprano arias and the melancholic—and catchy—chorus, "Va, pensiero," *Nabucco's* portrayal of the Jews' captivity in Babylon rang true to northern Italians living under Austria's stern rule. The opera's success placed Verdi on the throne of Italian opera, one previously occupied by Rossini (now retired), Bellini (now dead), and Donizetti (settled in Paris). Suddenly, everyone wanted him and, in what he would later describe as the life of "a galley slave," Verdi responded: over the next 17 years, he wrote 20 operas for theaters in Italy, London, and Paris. It was also in Paris, in 1847, that he again met the soprano

### Risorgimento

Although Verdi was hardly a political activist, the patriotic tone of several of his operas, starting with *Nabucco*, turned him into a symbol of the *Risorgimento*, or "Rising again," the 19th-century movement (below) that climaxed in Italy's unification as a kingdom in 1861. Famously, cries of "Viva Verdi" were understood to be an acronym for "Viva Vittorio Emanuele Re D'Italia"— "Long Live Victor Emmanuel, King of Italy." But for decades after unification, Verdi himself continued to be viewed as the personification of Italian nationhood. His death marked the end of an era.

> **Verdi's death**, at the age of 87, prompted national mourning, with thousands of people accompanying his funeral cortege through Milan on January 30, 1901.

"When I am alone with my notes, my heart pounds and the tears stream from my eyes."

GIUSEPPE VERDI

Giuseppina Strepponi, who had sung in *Nabucco* five years earlier and whom he finally married in 1859.

### The popular touch

While not all his works after *Nabucco* were equally successful, *Macbeth* and *Luisa Miller* were well received. But then a trio of operas, which premiered between March 1851 and March 1853, placed Verdi in a class of his own. *Rigoletto*, with its ever-popular tenor aria "La donna è mobile," was soon staged around the world. *Il trovatore*, an intense melodrama with some of Verdi's greatest melodies, was a still bigger hit. *La traviata*, his most popular opera today, had an unhappy premiere in Venice in March 1853, but a revised version a year later was acclaimed. Even so, through the 1850s, Verdi did not slow down, presenting *Les vêpres siciliennes* in Paris, *Simon Boccanegra* in Venice, and *Un ballo in maschera* in Rome.

By now, Verdi was considered a national treasure. Having supported Italy's fight for liberation, he agreed to serve as a deputy in the Turin parliament after Italy's unification in 1861. He also devoted more time to a large farm he had bought years earlier outside Busseto. Immensely wealthy and already contemplating retirement, he nonetheless accepted three foreign commissions: for the Imperial Theatre in St. Petersburg in 1862, he wrote *La forza del destino*; for the Paris Opéra in 1867, he created the five-act grand opera *Don Carlos*, later to become *Don Carlo* in a four-act Italian version; and for the Cairo Opera in 1871, he wrote his incomparable Pharaonic epic, *Aïda*. And, with that, Verdi returned to life as a country gentleman.

Only a few years passed before his music publisher, Giulio Ricordi, persuaded the composer to rework *Simon Boccanegra* and hired a young composer and librettist, Arrigo Boito, to revise the original libretto. The partnership flourished and *Simon Boccanegra II*, the version performed today, had its premiere in 1881. Ricordi then guided the duo toward Verdi's final masterpieces, *Otello* in 1887 and *Falstaff* in 1893, adaptations, respectively, of Shakespeare's *Othello* and *The Merry Wives of Windsor*. They provided a fitting climax to Verdi's career because he had always loved Shakespeare and, after *Macbeth*, had hoped to adapt *King Lear*. They also drew from him powerfully expressive scores of almost continuous music.

Nearly 80 years old when *Falstaff* was presented, Verdi spent his final years revered like a secular deity. After his death, on January 27, 1901, the 20,000 mourners at his funeral spontaneously burst out singing "Va, pensiero" from *Nabucco* as his cortege passed through the streets of Milan.

> **The piano score** for the opera *Nabucco*, Verdi's first popular hit, was issued by the composer's music publisher, Edizioni Ricordi.

# Nabucco

*Dramma lirico* in four parts, 2¼ hours • Composed: 1841 (rev. 1842) • First performed: March 9, 1842, La Scala, Milan, Italy • Libretto: Temistocle Solera, after the 1836 play *Nabucodonosor* by Auguste Anicet-Bourgeois and Francis Cornu

*Nabucco*, Verdi's first major success, won him immediate acclaim. Daringly, he takes on the Biblical story of the Israelites held captive in Babylon, using a large cast of soloists and a chorus. Unusually, the opera's most memorable song, "Va, pensiero," is a chorus sung almost entirely in unison. But the opera also includes fine soprano, tenor, and bass arias as well as a remarkable duet in which Abigaille and Nabucco wrestle for power.

## PRINCIPAL ROLES

**Nabucco** *baritone* King of Babylon

**Abigaille** *soprano*
A former enslaved woman thought to be Nabucco's daughter

**Fenena** *soprano* Nabucco's daughter

**Ismaele** *tenor* King of Jerusalem's nephew

**Zaccaria** *bass* High Priest of Jerusalem

**High Priest of Babylon** *bass*

### Part I: Jerusalem
Babylon's King Nabucco advances on Jerusalem, where his daughter, Fenena, is held hostage. Zaccaria, the high priest, leaves her with Ismaele, her secret Israelite lover. Abigaille, Nabucco's other daughter, offers to spare the Israelites if Ismaele returns her love, but he rejects her.

▼ **Matteo Manuguerra** cuts an impressive, regal figure as Nabucco, King of Babylon, in a San Francisco Opera production staged in 1982.

When Nabucco appears, Ismaele saves Fenena from Zaccaria's dagger, but the Temple is destroyed.

### Part II: The Unbeliever
In Babylon, Abigaille discovers she was born enslaved ("Anch'io dischiuso un giorno"). Believing Nabucco dead, the Babylonians beg Abigaille to seize power. As Zaccaria announces Fenena's conversion, Nabucco returns, proclaiming he is a god, but he is struck by lightning.

### Part III: The Prophecy
Learning that Abigaille is planning Fenena's death, Nabucco denounces her as an enslaved woman, but she tears up the incriminating document. When he offers her the throne in exchange for Fenena's life, he is rebuffed. On the banks of the Euphrates, the captive Israelites sing a lament of yearning for their homeland ("Va, pensiero"), but Zaccaria prophesies the fall of Babylon.

### Part IV: The Broken Idol
As Fenena is led away in chains, Nabucco begs the God of the Israelites for forgiveness. Fenena and other Israelites are standing before the sacrificial altar when cries of "Viva Nabucco" are heard. Nabucco then destroys the false idol and frees the Israelites. Remorseful, Abigaille takes poison and dies as Nabucco is proclaimed king of kings.

*Nabucco* is best known for the lilting melody of "Va, pensiero," but Italians also embraced the chorus as an allegory for their own struggle for freedom against Austrian occupation.

# Macbeth

Opera in four acts, 2¾ hours • Composed: 1846–1847 (rev. 1864–1865) • First performed: March 14, 1847, Teatro della Pergola, Florence, Italy • Libretto: Francesco Maria Piave, after Shakespeare's *Macbeth* (1605–1606)

Verdi took immense care in recreating *Macbeth* as opera, determining the shape of the libretto, and capturing the tormented psychology of the protagonists with his music. The result was his most inventive and idealistic opera so far. Even more than in Shakespeare, the drama centers on Macbeth and Lady Macbeth: their Act I duet and her Act IV "sleepwalking scene" are highlights.

## Act I

Witches predict that Macbeth will become Thane of Cawdor and King of Scotland and that Banquo will father future kings. When the first prophecy comes true, Lady Macbeth sets in motion the prophecy of kingship ("Vieni! T'affretta!"). With King Duncan asleep in Macbeth's castle, she forces her reluctant husband to kill him. Macduff comes to wake Duncan and finds him murdered.

## Act II

Now king, Macbeth decides that Banquo and his children must die. But although Banquo is killed, his son escapes. As Banquo's ghost appears during a banquet, Macbeth panics, crying out at the specter, which he alone can see. His wife tries to distract the guests, but Macduff decides to flee Scotland for England.

## Act III

The witches assure Macbeth that "no man of woman born" will harm him, while another apparition tells him he is safe until Birnam Wood moves toward him. Alarmed to see a vision of eight kings passing before him, the last of whom is in the form of Banquo, Macbeth decides to kill Banquo's son as well as Macduff's wife and children.

## Act IV

As Macduff vows to avenge his family, Lady Macbeth imagines blood on her hands while sleepwalking ("Una macchia è qui tuttora"). Macbeth sees Birnam Wood approaching, but boasts that "no man of woman born" can hurt him. Macduff responds that he was "ripped" from his mother's womb and slays Macbeth in single combat.

| PRINCIPAL ROLES |
| --- |
| **Macbeth** *baritone* A general and future king |
| **Lady Macbeth** *soprano* |
| **Duncan** *silent* King of Scotland |
| **Banquo** *bass* A general |
| **Macduff** *tenor* A Scottish noble |
| **Malcolm** *tenor* Duncan's son |

▼ **Kathleen Broderick** in the disturbing role of Lady Macbeth at the Theater an der Wien, Austria, in 2000.

The curse often associated with productions of Shakespeare's *Macbeth* also affected opera in 1988, when a man jumped to his death from the balcony of the Metropolitan Opera in New York during a performance of Verdi's *Macbeth*.

# TEATRO ALLA
## SCALA

No theater can speak for opera more than the Teatro alla Scala, known to the world simply as La Scala. As the cradle of the art form, Italy had many opera houses before La Scala opened in Milan in 1778, but it soon became the stage where the likes of Donizetti, Bellini, Verdi, and Puccini came to win the ultimate approval of demanding Italian audiences.

Performers, too, have always been tested, notably by the low-price ticket holders in the upper galleries, known as *I loggionisti*, who not only have strong opinions but may also have been paid to cheer or heckle singers. Still, it was the sheer magic of Maria Callas's voice that won her La Scala's embrace as its favorite prima donna in the early 1950s.

One sign of La Scala's central place in Milan's life is that its season always opens on the feast day of the city's patron saint—December 7, Saint Ambrose's Day—with a glittering occasion attended by Italy's President. In fact, politics have always been inseparable from La Scala. Thanks notably to Verdi, starting with his opera *Nabucco*, created at the theater in 1842, La Scala became a key player in Italy's struggle for unification. Verdi's name even became an acronym for Vittorio Emanuele Re D'Italia, after Italy's newly crowned king in 1861.

The theater was damaged by Allied bombing in August 1943, but, such was its symbolic importance to Milan, its classically Italian horseshoe auditorium was rebuilt long before most other buildings: on May 11, 1946, La Scala reopened with a concert conducted by the inimitable Arturo Toscanini. Today, La Scala lacks the budget to compete for the biggest names in opera, but it is still where many of them are first noticed. A triumph at La Scala will always be a watershed for any young singer.

> "If tomorrow we talk about music before
> we talk about politics in this theater,
> I think we will have carried out
> a historic change."

STÉPHANE LISSNER, FORMER DIRECTOR OF LA SCALA

▶ **Home to Italian opera** for more than two centuries, Milan's Teatro alla Scala is famous—and feared—for its demanding and judgmental audiences.

# Rigoletto

*Melodramma* in three acts, 2 hours ▪ Composed: 1850–1851 ▪ First performed: March 11, 1851, Teatro La Fenice, Venice, Italy ▪ Libretto: Francesco Maria Piave, after Victor Hugo's tragedy *Le Roi s'amuse* (1832)

*Rigoletto* was the opera that founded Verdi's international reputation: within ten years, it had been staged in some 250 opera houses around the world. The catchy tenor aria "La donna è mobile" certainly helped spread its fame, but it is also sustained by a daring plot, one that Venetian censors only accepted after two revisions. Musically, *Rigoletto* represented a clear break with the past: Verdi eliminated entrance arias and finale ensembles and added pace through Rigoletto's *recitativo cantando*, or melodic sung recitative. In fact, the lead soprano, Gilda, has only one aria, although she shares several poignant duets and joins a sensational quartet in the final act. Most unusually, though, this is an opera dominated, both theatrically and musically, by the baritone voice of the almost-Shakespearean tragi-comic figure of Rigoletto.

## PRINCIPAL ROLES

**Duke of Mantua** *tenor* A rakish noble

**Rigoletto** *baritone* The duke's hunchback jester

**Gilda** *soprano* Rigoletto's daughter

**Sparafucile** *bass* A hired assassin

**Maddalena** *contralto* Sparafucile's sister

**Giovanna** *mezzo-soprano* Gilda's chaperone

**Count Monterone** *bass* The duke's enemy

**Count Ceprano** *bass*

**Countess Ceprano** *mezzo-soprano*

▶ **The cover of the** Italian magazine *Musica e Musicisti* (*Music and Musicians*) shows Rigoletto being comforted by a conductor.

Verdi was so certain that he had written a hit song in "La donna è mobile" that he instructed orchestra members not to whistle or sing it outside rehearsals in the theater before the premiere.

### Act I

At a palace ball, the Duke of Mantua is musing on a young woman he plans to win. But first he decides to conquer Countess Ceprano ("Questa o quella per me pari sono"). His hunchbacked jester, Rigoletto, ridicules her husband, but when he mocks Count Monterone, whose daughter has been seduced by the duke, he is shocked when Monterone curses him. Rigoletto is stopped by Sparafucile, who offers his services as a killer. Sending him away, he embraces his daughter Gilda. He pledges his love for her and, telling her to let no one into the house, he leaves ("Figlia"). Now realizing that Gilda is Rigoletto's daughter, the duke enters and, posing as a student, declares his love for her. She is swept off her feet ("Caro nome"). A group of men plan to kidnap Rigoletto's mistress, but they tell the jester that they have come to capture Ceprano's wife. In the dark, they blindfold Rigoletto and have him hold up a ladder against his own house. When he hears Gilda's cries, he remembers Monterone's curse.

### Act II

The duke is upset that Gilda has been stolen from him, but then is delighted to learn she is in the palace. Rigoletto arrives, feigning nonchalance until he realizes that Gilda is with the duke. As the courtiers scoff at him, he shouts that she is his daughter. Gilda appears and, alone with her father, she confesses she fell for a young student, but was then seized and brought to the palace ("Tutte le feste al tempio"). On his way to jail, seeing the duke's portrait, Monterone admits defeat. Rigoletto also dwells on his own ill fate and vows revenge.

### Act III

While Gilda still loves the duke, Rigoletto wants her to know he is worthless. Peeping into Sparafucile's house, she recognizes the duke in disguise and hears him call for wine, proclaiming that no woman can be trusted ("La donna è mobile"). As the duke woos Maddalena, Sparafucile's sister, Rigoletto points him out to Sparafucile as the man to be killed ("Bella figlia d'amore"). He then pays off the assassin, saying he will return to collect the body. When Maddalena understands her new lover is to die, she pleads for his life. Finally Sparafucile agrees

▲ **The Duke of Mantua's courtiers** abandon the noble's most recent conquest in David Pountney's production at the New Israel Opera in 2000.

to kill the next visitor to arrive. Overhearing the plan, Gilda decides to save the duke. She knocks on the door and is stabbed. Rigoletto takes the body in a sack, but then suddenly hears the duke's voice. In panic, he cuts open the sack and finds Gilda. She begs his forgiveness and, as she dies, Rigoletto realizes the curse has come true.

### Tito Gobbi

Tito Gobbi, one of the finest baritones of the mid-20th century, is perhaps best known for singing Scarpia opposite Maria Callas in Puccini's *Tosca*, but the role that he made his own was Rigoletto (right). It not only suited his mid-range voice, but it also enabled him to display his great acting talent, one that required him to be an odious and sadistic jester to the cynical duke as well as a protective and loving father to the ill-fated Gilda. During a long career, Gobbi also sang other major Verdi characters, including Iago in *Otello* and the title role in *Simon Boccanegra*.

# Il trovatore

THE TROUBADOUR *Dramma* in four parts, 2¼ hours ▪ Composed: 1851–1853 (rev. 1856) ▪ First performed: January 19, 1853, Teatro Apollo, Rome, Italy ▪ Libretto: Salvatore Cammarano and Leone Emanuele Bardare, after the 1836 play *El trovador* by Antonio García Gutiérrez

*Il trovatore* is an immensely popular opera, in which a convoluted and implausible plot is transformed by a dizzying succession of magnificent melodies. Along with *Rigoletto* and *La traviata*, it forms part of the great trilogy of Verdi's middle years, but it is the most traditional of the three: a melodrama about chivalry, honor, valor, and tragic love powered by unremittingly high-voltage music. Verdi was most drawn to Azucena, the Gypsy "outsider," whose burning desire for revenge is finally rewarded by the opera's tragic denouement, although fine arias and duets are fairly distributed.

## PRINCIPAL ROLES

**Il Conte di Luna** *baritone*
Commander in the army of Aragon

**Leonora** *soprano*
Lady-in-waiting to the Princess of Aragon

**Manrico** *tenor* A Gypsy and rebel

**Azucena** *mezzo-soprano* A Gypsy

**Ferrando** *bass* A captain in di Luna's guard

**Ines** *soprano* Leonora's confidante

**Ruiz** *tenor* A soldier in Manrico's band

### Part I

Captain Ferrando recounts the tragic story of Count di Luna's brother: the baby's nurse awoke to find a Gypsy peering at him with an evil eye. When the boy fell ill, the Gypsy was burned at the stake. But her daughter killed the baby. Now the count has sworn revenge. Leonora eagerly awaits her troubadour lover ("Tacea la notte placida"), but the count, who also loves her, lurks nearby. Hearing singing, she recognizes her lover but in the dark embraces the count in error. The troubadour steps out and identifies himself as Manrico, a rebel. The two men leave to duel.

Lovers of Italian opera never miss a chance to relive *Il trovatore*'s soul-drenching story and music, but music critics have long expressed doubts about its music as too "easy" to enjoy.

▶ **The Italian tenor** Salvatore Licitra as Manrico protects Barbara Frittoli's Leonora at La Scala in 2000.

## Part II

At a Gypsy camp, Azucena describes a woman's horrible death at the stake ("Stride la vampa"). She tells her son Manrico how his grandmother was killed by the old count. Hearing her cries, Azucena seized the count's son and threw him into the flames, only to discover she had murdered her own baby. When Manrico is shocked, she insists he is her son, but is angry he did not kill the count in their duel. He says he heard a cry from heaven. Believing Manrico dead, Leonora has entered a convent. The count, also sure of Manrico's death, enters the convent to abduct her ("Il balen del suo sorriso"). At first, hearing the nuns praying, he loses his nerve. But as he comes forward to claim her, Manrico also appears, and his men surround and disarm the count.

## Part III

The count is besieging Castellor castle, where Manrico has taken Leonora. When a Gypsy is captured near the count's camp, he interrogates her about the child stolen years earlier. She denies all knowledge, but Ferrando recognizes her. As she is tied up, she cries out for Manrico, revealing she is the mother of the count's rival. He orders her burned at the stake. Manrico comforts Leonora ("Ah sì, ben mio, coll'essere") while they await an attack, but, as they prepare to marry, Manrico sees that a pyre has been prepared for Azucena. Summoning his troops, he leaves to rescue his mother.

## Part IV

Outside a prison, Leonora pines for Manrico ("D'amor sull'ali rosee"). As monks sing a *Miserere*, she vows to save his life. She offers herself to the count in exchange for Manrico's life, then sucks poison from her ring. Leonora comes to free Manrico, but when she tells him to leave alone, he accuses her of selling her love. Again begging him to flee, she reveals she is dying. Realizing that he has been deceived, the count orders Manrico's execution. Almost gleefully, Azucena tells the count that he has killed his brother.

### Azucena

Divas are invariably sopranos, the voice favored by opera-lovers and composers for its ability to suggest drama through high notes. But the "darker" sound of mezzo-sopranos is in many ways more emotional. This is certainly true with Azucena, one of the finest mezzo-soprano roles in opera. It is an immensely challenging part and the most difficult to cast in *Il trovatore*. Even the role's great arias are introspective, but Azucena is still the character around which the entire opera revolves.

▶ **Irina Mishura** as Azucena at the Royal Opera House, London, in 2004.

# La traviata

THE FALLEN WOMAN *Melodramma* in three acts, 2 hours ▪ Composed: 1853 (rev. 1854) ▪ First performed: March 6, 1853, Teatro La Fenice, Venice, Italy ▪ Libretto: Francesco Maria Piave, after the 1852 play *La Dame aux camélias* by Alexandre Dumas *fils*

*La traviata* is among the world's favorite operas, yet it flopped at its Venice premiere. The music cannot be faulted: lyrical and dramatic arias of great beauty; opera's most famous "drinking song" or *brindisi*; the extended duet between Violetta and Giorgio Germont; the richly scored ensemble that ends Act II; and Violetta's poignant last testament. *La traviata* was evidently beyond the talents of the first cast. But soon afterward its qualities were widely acclaimed.

## PRINCIPAL ROLES

**Violetta Valéry** *soprano* A courtesan

**Alfredo Germont** *tenor* Violetta's lover

**Giorgio Germont** *baritone* Alfredo's father

**Baron Douphol** *baritone* Violetta's suitor

**Flora** *mezzo-soprano* Violetta's friend

**Annina** *soprano* Violetta's maid

▼ **At a party**, Violetta's guests turn eagerly as Marcelo Álvarez's Alfredo raises a toast to his beautiful hostess at La Scala, Milan, in 2002.

### Act I

Violetta Valéry, a Paris courtesan, is receiving guests when Alfredo Germont is introduced as an admirer. Violetta invites him to make a toast and Alfredo leads the crowd in a drinking song ("Libiamo ne' lieti calici"). Alfredo tells Violetta he has loved her for a year, but she says she has only friendship to offer him. As the party breaks up, Violetta feels disturbed, realizing she has never truly loved or been loved, yet concluding it is her destiny to "flutter from pleasure to pleasure" ("Sempre libera"). Suddenly, hearing Alfredo serenading her, she again contemplates love before dismissing it as madness.

### Act II

Now living happily with Violetta outside Paris, Alfredo learns from a maid that Violetta has sold her horses and carriages to pay for their upkeep. Embarrassed to be living off her, Alfredo leaves for Paris ("O mio remorso!"). Violetta, puzzled by his absence, is distracted by an invitation to a party at Flora's that night. Giorgio Germont, Alfredo's father, arrives to accuse Violetta of ruining his son. When she shows that she has been keeping them, Germont remarks nastily about exploiting the fruits of her past. He then explains that if his daughter is to marry, Alfredo must end his shameful affair with Violetta ("Pura siccome un angelo"). Violetta at first objects, but finally agrees to his demand. Germont suggests she leave unannounced, but she begs him to tell his daughter of her sacrifice. In tears, Violetta is writing to Alfredo when he returns. She entreats him to love her forever and runs out. Moments later, a messenger brings her letter. When Alfredo sees Flora's invitation, he

### Plácido Domingo

Plácido Domingo, one of the finest opera singers of the late 20th century, has performed all of Verdi's major tenor roles in a career lasting decades. One of his many triumphs was as the dashing Alfredo Germont in Franco Zeffirelli's 1982 film version of *La traviata*, a role he first sang in 1961 at the age of twenty. More recently, now as a baritone, he has appeared in the same opera as Giorgio Germont. An all-around musician, he resigned as general manager of the Los Angeles Opera in 2019 after he was accused of sexual harassment. Now unwelcome in the United States as a consequence, he continues to perform across Europe, to the delight of his devoted followers.

vows revenge. At Flora's party, Alfredo is winning at cards when Violetta arrives with Baron Douphol. After Alfredo angers Douphol by winning money from him gambling, Violetta begs him to leave for his own safety, but refuses to follow him. Shocked and angered, Alfredo calls the guests together and throws his winnings at her. As she swoons, Germont rebukes his son, who is now full of remorse. Slowly coming round, Violetta tells him that one day he will understand.

▶ **Rolando Villazón** as Alfredo admires Anna Netrebko's Violetta at the Salzburg Festival, 2005.

## Act III

Terminally ill, Violetta rereads a letter from Germont recounting that, after wounding the baron in a duel, Alfredo left the country, but will soon return. She knows it is too late ("Addio del passato"). Then, as carnival music streams through the window, Annina announces Alfredo's arrival. Falling into each other's arms, Violetta and Alfredo vow never again to be apart. Excitedly, Violetta promises to get well, but she knows she is dying ("Ah! Gran Dio!").

As Germont and the doctor arrive, she gives a miniature portrait to Alfredo. Suddenly, crying out that she feels better, she dies.

### The real *traviata*

Marie Duplessis was a famous Paris courtesan long before Alexandre Dumas *fils* relived their affair in his 1848 novel and play *La Dame aux camélias*. Born into poverty but with ample wit and beauty, she rose quickly to host salons attended by *le tout Paris*. In 1847, only 23, she died of tuberculosis. Dumas never forgot her, writing years later of "her cherry red lips." In *La traviata*, Verdi shows he, too, was charmed by this "fallen woman."

Although the courtesan was a fixture of European society, until the 1890s it was thought proper to set *La traviata* in an earlier era.

# Un ballo in maschera

A MASKED BALL *Melodramma* in three acts, 2¼ hours ▪ Composed: 1857–1858 ▪ First performed: February 17, 1859, Teatro Apollo, Rome, Italy ▪ Libretto: Antonio Somma, after Eugène Scribe's libretto *Gustave III*, set by Daniel Auber in 1833

*Un ballo in maschera* is often called Verdi's love poem, his *Tristan und Isolde*. While not among his most performed operas, it is a work of great sophistication. It not only combines dramatic and lyrical music but, with almost Shakespearean panache, it also switches seamlessly between the humorous and the tragic. In all, it is a profoundly romantic opera, with Riccardo's clandestine meeting with Amelia in Act II offering what is arguably Verdi's finest love duet.

## PRINCIPAL ROLES

**Riccardo, Earl of Warwick** *tenor*
English colonial governor

**Renato** *baritone* Riccardo's secretary

**Amelia** *soprano* Renato's wife

**Ulrica** *contralto* A fortune-teller

**Oscar** *soprano* A page

**Samuel and Tom** *bass* Conspirators

## Act I

Riccardo, the governor, loves Amelia, the wife of Renato, his secretary. When Renato warns him of a plot to kill him, he decides to consult Ulrica, the fortune-teller. Meanwhile, Amelia asks Ulrica for help in fighting her love for Riccardo and is told to pick an herb at midnight. Ulrica then warns Riccardo he will die by the next hand he shakes. As two conspirators, Samuel and Tom, turn away from him, Riccardo seizes Renato's hand.

## Act II

Riccardo and Amelia finally confess their love ("Non saitu che se l'anima mia"). Renato appears and warns Riccardo that a gang awaits him. The governor tells Renato to escort Amelia without seeing her face. Tom and Samuel arrive, and Amelia's face is bared in the confusion. Renato vows revenge.

## Act III

Renato joins Samuel and Tom in their plot. Riccardo decides to send Renato and Amelia to England, but yearns to see Amelia one last time ("Ma se m'è forza perderti") and ignores a warning not to attend the masked ball. Amelia recognizes Riccardo and begs him to flee, but Renato appears and stabs Riccardo. Telling Renato that his love for Amelia was chaste, Riccardo pardons the conspirators and dies.

▲ **Alberto Cupido as Riccardo** interrogates Oscar, a page sung by Ofelia Sala, in a 2002 production at the Deutsche Oper in Berlin.

*Un ballo in maschera* originally portrayed the murder of Sweden's Gustave III. But since no king could be killed on an Italian stage, the victim became the governor of an English colony in the Americas.

# La forza del destino

THE FORCE OF DESTINY Opera in four acts, 3¼ hours • Composed: 1861 (rev. 1867–1869) • First performed: November 10, 1862, Imperial Theatre, St. Petersburg, Russia • Libretto: Francesco Maria Piave, after the 1835 play *Don Álvaro, o La fuerza del sino*, by Ángel de Saavedra.

Commissioned by the Imperial Theatre in St. Petersburg, *La forza del destino* is a powerful and passionate work that helped inspire Mussorgsky's monumental *Boris Godunov*. Rich in choruses designed to appeal to the Russian sense of spectacle, it also boasts extraordinary set pieces, among them the opening love duet of Alvaro and Leonora; Leonora's penitence arias in Acts II and IV; and the pre-duel duet between Alvaro and Carlo.

## Act I
Leonora is torn between eloping with Alvaro, her South American lover, and staying loyal to her father, the Marchese di Calatrava. When she agrees to leave, the Marchese appears and challenges Alvaro, who throws down his pistol, accidentally killing him.

## Act II
The Marchese's son, Carlo, tells guests at an inn that he is pursuing a foreigner who murdered a close friend's father and abducted his sister. A gypsy predicts a terrible future for him. Meanwhile, Leonora, disguised as a man, is given refuge in a monastery ("La Vergine degli angeli"), where no one will know her identity.

## Act III
Having joined the Spanish army in Italy, Alvaro rescues Carlo in battle, but they do not recognize each other and pledge friendship. When Alvaro is wounded, Carlo finds a picture of Leonora in his belongings. Challenged to a duel, Alvaro insists he never seduced Leonora, but Carlo says she must also die. Their duel is interrupted and Alvaro decides to enter a monastery.

## Act IV
Carlo tracks down Alvaro and demands a fresh duel ("Invano Alvaro"). Wounded, Carlo cries out for a priest, and Alvaro runs

to Leonora's cave. They recognize each other, but Leonora hurries to help Carlo. Moments later, she reappears bleeding, mortally wounded by Carlo in a final act of revenge. Dying, she pardons Alvaro.

▼ **The legendary tenor** Enrico Caruso as Alvaro holds the dying Leonora, sung by Rosa Ponselle, in this opera's final scene in a 1918 production in New York.

> Verdi always insisted on approving the singers for his premieres. In this case, when he arrived in St. Petersburg, he vetoed the unfortunate soprano cast as Leonora and refused to rehearse until she was replaced.

---

**PRINCIPAL ROLES**

**Marchese di Calatrava** *bass*

**Leonora** *soprano* Calatrava's daughter

**Don Carlo** *baritone* Calatrava's son

**Don Alvaro** *tenor*
Leonora's lover, an Inca prince

**Preziosilla** *mezzo-soprano* A Gypsy

**Father Superior** *bass*

# Don Carlos

Grand opera in five acts, 3½ hours (four-act version, 3 hours) ▪ Composed: 1866–1867 (rev. 1872); Italian version 1882–1883 ▪ First performed: March 11, 1867, Paris Opéra, France ▪ Libretto: Joseph Méry and Camille du Locle, after Schiller's 1787 dramatic poem *Don Carlos, Infant von Spanien*

*Don Carlos*, Verdi's most ambitious opera, has long been burdened by its very size. Verdi dropped Act I for the Italian version, *Don Carlo*, but he later restored it to create the now preferred "Modena version." Both in its paean to freedom and its musical grandeur, *Don Carlos* is a *tour de force*. Among its many highlights are the duets between Carlos and Elisabeth and the confrontation between Philip and the Grand Inquisitor.

## PRINCIPAL ROLES

**Philip II** *bass* King of Spain

**Don Carlos** *tenor* The Spanish heir

**Elisabeth de Valois** *soprano* Philip's bride

**Rodrigo, Marquis de Posa** *baritone* Don Carlos's friend

**Eboli** *mezzo-soprano* Lady-in-waiting

**Grand Inquisitor** *bass*

Although Paris demanded lengthy five-act operas, the first version of *Don Carlos* still had to be cut by half an hour because the last train left Paris for the suburbs at 12:25 am.

### Act I
Don Carlos travels incognito to France to meet Elisabeth and gives her a casket with his likeness. When she recognizes him, they celebrate their union ("De quels transports poignants"). But they learn she must wed his father, King Philip.

### Act II
Upset by Spain's occupation of Flanders, Carlos urges Elisabeth to have the king send him there. She admits that she loves him, while King Philip harbors suspicions about her loyalty.

### Act III
Carlos mistakes Eboli for the queen. When Eboli realizes his love is not for her, she vows revenge. As the king watches heretics burning in an *auto-da-fé*, Carlos demands

to be made regent of Flanders. Rebuffed, he draws his sword, but his friend Rodrigo disarms him.

### Act IV
The Grand Inquisitor approves Philip's plan to kill his son and declares Rodrigo a heretic. Philip finds Carlos's portrait in Elisabeth's casket and accuses her of adultery. When Rodrigo visits Carlos in prison, he is murdered. Eboli helps Carlos escape.

### Act V
Elisabeth urges Carlos to forget her and to save Flanders. As they bid each other a tender farewell ("Au revoir dans un monde"), King Philip arrives to arrest them. Carlos retreats toward the tomb of his grandfather, and the specter of Charles V pulls him to safety.

# Simon Boccanegra

*Melodramma* in a prologue and three acts, 2¼ hours ▪ Composed: 1880–1881 (a radical revision of the 1857 score) ▪ First performed: March 24, 1881, La Scala, Milan, Italy ▪ Libretto: Francesco Maria Piave and Arrigo Boito, after Antonio García Gutiérrez's 1843 play, *Simón Bocanegra*.

*Simon Boccanegra* is a father–daughter love story enclosed within a weighty political drama. Although rarely performed, even in its final 1881 form, it is a stirring opera, dominated by low male voices: two baritones and two basses. It has few arias, but instead evokes the mood of conspiracy through a wealth of rich duets and ensembles. The great novelty of the 1881 revised version is the chamber council scene in Act I, one of Verdi's finest finales.

## Prologue
Nominated to succeed Fiesco, a hated patrician, as Doge, the corsair Simon Boccanegra hopes to be reunited with Fiesco's daughter, Maria. Fiesco, knowing that Maria has died, says he will forgive Simon only when he gives up Amelia, Maria's missing daughter with Simon. As Simon discovers Maria's body, cheers announce his election as Doge.

## Act I
Twenty-five years later, Amelia's lover Gabriele and her guardian Andrea (Fiesco) are conspiring against Simon. Suspecting the Doge wants her to marry Paolo, she says she loves another. When she also reveals she is an orphan, Simon recognizes his lost daughter ("Figlia! … a tal nome"). Gabriele tries to kill Simon, but Amelia stops him.

## Act II
Paolo has poisoned Simon's water and convinced Gabriele that Amelia is Simon's mistress. Amelia denies betrayal. When Simon drinks the poisoned water and falls asleep, Gabriele prepares to kill him. Learning that Simon is Amelia's father, he pledges loyalty to the Doge.

## Act III
As bells from the wedding of Amelia and Gabriele ring out, Simon recognizes Andrea as Fiesco. Reconciled with his enemy at last ("Piango, perchè mi parla"), Simon dies in the arms of Fiesco, proclaiming Gabriele his successor with his last breath.

### PRINCIPAL ROLES

**Simon Boccanegra** *baritone*
A corsair and later Doge

**Amelia Boccanegra (Grimaldi)** *soprano*
Boccanegra's "lost" daughter

**Gabriele Adorno** *tenor* Amelia's lover

**Jacopo Fiesco** *bass* A former Doge

**Paolo Albiani** *bass*
A plebeian and advisor to Boccanegra

**Pietro** *baritone* A plebeian

Even Verdi considered his 1857 version of *Simon Boccanegra* to be depressing, cold, and monotonous. He was therefore all too happy to rework it with the librettist Arrigo Boito more than 20 years later.

▼ **Gabriele** (Plácido Domingo, left) is reunited with Amelia (Kallen Esperian), Royal Opera House, London, 1997.

# Aïda

Opera in four acts, 2¼ hours • Composed: 1870 (rev. 1871) • First performed: December 24, 1871, Opera House, Cairo, Egypt • Libretto: Antonio Ghislanzoni, after Camille du Locle's French version of Auguste Mariette's proposed storyline

*Aïda*, Verdi's most spectacular work, is an exotic Italian opera with authentic Egyptian roots. Cairo's Opera House opened in November 1869 with *Rigoletto*, but the archaeologist Auguste Mariette persuaded the Turkish governor of Egypt to commission an "Egyptian opera" from Verdi. Mariette then invented the story which became *Aïda*. In creating the triumphal march of Act II, Verdi took his inspiration from French grand opera. Hugely dramatic and musically exciting, *Aïda* was an immediate success and, within ten years, had been performed in 155 opera houses around the world.

## PRINCIPAL ROLES

**The King of Egypt** bass

**Amneris** mezzo-soprano The Egyptian king's daughter

**Aïda** soprano An enslaved Ethiopian princess

**Radamès** tenor An Egyptian captain

**Ramfis** bass High Priest of Isis

**Amonasro** baritone Aïda's father, King of Ethiopia

---

Having had its premiere in Cairo's opera house in 1871, *Aïda* returned to Egypt in 1987 with a dramatic outdoor production before the 3,000-year-old Temple of Amenhotep III beside the Nile in today's Luxor.

---

### Luciano Pavarotti

Luciano Pavarotti, who died in 2007 aged 71, was the leading tenor divo of the late 20th century, albeit hailed more for the remarkable timbre of his voice than for his stage performances. He covered the entire 19th-century Italian repertoire, from the *bel canto* of Rossini and Donizetti to the dramatic operas of Verdi and Puccini, with Radamès in *Aïda* one of his best-known roles. By singing before vast crowds in stadiums around the world, he helped carry opera to new audiences.

## Act I

At the royal palace in Memphis, Radamès hopes to lead the Egyptian army against the invading Ethiopians, inspired by his love for Aïda, a captured Ethiopian princess ("Celeste Aïda, forma divina"). But Radamès is also loved by Amneris, the Egyptian princess. When the king enters, Ramfis, the High Priest, names Radamès as Egyptian commander. As Radamès is led away to be blessed, Aïda worries he will fight her father, Amonasro, the Ethiopian king ("Ritorna vincitor").

## Act II

As enslaved Moors dance, Aïda enters looking forlorn. Amneris feigns sympathy and tests her by announcing that Radamès has been killed. Seeing Aïda's distress, Amneris accuses her of loving Radamès. She then reveals that Radamès lives and, as Aïda thanks the gods, announces that she is Aïda's rival. Aïda begs for mercy, but Amneris vows revenge. Radamès returns to Thebes victorious, leading a triumphal march. Suddenly, Aïda recognizes her father among the prisoners. Disguised as a soldier, he tells the Egyptian king of Amonasro's death and asks him to free the Ethiopian prisoners. When Radamès supports the appeal, the king concurs and offers Amneris to Radamès. Aïda is heartbroken.

## Act III

Awaiting Radamès on the banks of the Nile, Aïda laments she will never again see Ethiopia ("O patria mia"). Her father appears, again ready to attack Egypt. He says he knows Radamès loves her and demands that she discover Egypt's military secrets. Seeing Aïda, Radamès promises to tell the king of his love for her. Warning of Amneris's wrath, she insists they flee now ("Fuggiam gli ardori inospiti") and asks how they can avoid the Egyptian legions. He then reveals the army's

route. As Amonasro steps forward, Radamès realizes with horror that he has betrayed Egypt and waits to be arrested. In the confusion, the Ethiopians escape.

## Act IV

Amneris begs Radamès to justify his action so she can plead for his life ("Già i sacerdoti adunansi"), but he refuses, saying he will not exchange his life for Aïda's death. Amneris responds that Aïda has not died, but he must promise never to see her again. He again refuses. As Ramfis orders Radamès buried in a sealed tomb, Amneris collapses in despair. Inside the dark tomb, Radamès is awaiting his death when Aïda suddenly appears, saying she has come to die with him. Seeing there is no escape, they fall into each other's arms and bid the world farewell ("O terra, addio; addio, valle di pianti"). As Aïda dies, Amneris can be heard imploring peace.

▲ **While Aïda was premiered** almost on-location in Cairo, almost in its actual setting, the opera's appeal comes from its power to transport the mystery of Egypt to Western stages.

▶ **Fiorenza Cedolins as Aïda** deceives Walter Fraccaro's Radamès into betraying his country in a pivotal scene from Act III of this exotic production of Verdi's well-loved opera, staged at the Teatro Regio in Turin, Italy, in 2005.

**Cairo Opera** marked the tenth anniversary of its new theater and the silver jubilee of the 1973 October War by presenting *Aida* at the Giza pyramids in October 1998.

# Otello

OTHELLO *Dramma lirico* in four acts, 2¼ hours ▪ Composed: 1884–1886 (rev. 1887) ▪ First performed: February 5, 1887, La Scala, Milan, Italy ▪ Libretto: Arrigo Boito, after Shakespeare's *Otello*

*Otello* is considered to be the finest of the more than 200 operas based on Shakespeare's plays. For operatic purposes, Arrigo Boito's fast-paced libretto may even have improved on *Othello* by eliminating Act I and focusing immediately on Iago's evil machinations. Verdi in turn devoted enormous energy to writing, revising, and polishing what some experts consider his greatest opera. It includes one of the most demanding tenor parts in the entire opera repertoire, though there are few arias. Instead, Verdi uses deeply expressive orchestral writing to create near-continuous music. As a musical drama, it evokes Richard Wagner; melodically, though, it remains thoroughly Italian.

## PRINCIPAL ROLES

**Otello** *tenor*
A Venetian general of Moorish extraction, now governor of Cyprus

**Desdemona** *soprano* Otello's wife

**Iago** *baritone* Otello's ensign

**Emilia** *mezzo-soprano*
Iago's wife and Desdemona's companion

**Cassio** *tenor* A Venetian officer

**Roderigo** *tenor* A Venetian gentleman

**Ludovico** *bass* A Venetian ambassador

**Montano** *bass* A The former governor of Cyprus

◀ **An elegant poster** for a new production of *Otello* staged at the Teatro Sociale in Como, Italy, in 1899.

At the premiere of *Otello*, Verdi was called to take a bow 15 times during the performance, and, at the final curtain, the entire audience rose to its feet, shouting, "Viva Verdi!"

## Act I

Surviving a fierce storm, Otello arrives in Cyprus as the island's new governor. His perfidious ensign, Iago, pretends to help Roderigo win Otello's wife, Desdemona, but his real intent is to avenge Cassio's promotion over him. He persuades Cassio to drink, and then warns Roderigo that Cassio is his rival for Desdemona's love. Roderigo provokes a fight, in the course of which Cassio wounds the island's retiring governor. Otello is furious at the disturbance and demotes Cassio. Eventually Otello is left alone with Desdemona and together they reminisce over how they fell in love ("Già nella notte densa").

## Act II

Iago assures Cassio that Desdemona will persuade Otello to reinstate him. Iago then celebrates his own evil in a blasphemous Credo ("Credo in un Dio crudel"). Observing Cassio with Desdemona, Iago asks Otello if he trusts Cassio. Otello's reaction is immediate, but Iago warns him against jealousy. Desdemona seeks pardon for Cassio. Otello complains of a burning head and, when Desdemona wipes his brow with a handkerchief, he throws it to the ground. Emilia picks it up, but Iago, her husband, grabs it. He pretends to calm Otello, who angrily demands proof of his wife's impurity. Iago recounts hearing Cassio talk in his sleep of making love to Desdemona and seeing Cassio carrying Desdemona's handkerchief. As Otello falls to his knees, they swear vengeance ("Si, pel ciel marmoreo giuro").

## Act III

Otello says his head hurts again and he asks Desdemona for her handkerchief. She offers one, but he demands the one he gave her. He then accuses her of being false, but she swears that she is faithful. Pushing her from the room, he plunges into despair ("Dio! Mi potevi scagliar"). With Otello observing them, Iago asks Cassio in a soft voice about his mistress. Otello sees Cassio laugh and display to Iago an embroidered handkerchief left in his lodgings. With Otello now convinced of Desdemona's betrayal, Iago suggests strangling her in her bed of sin. Venetian ambassadors bring word that Otello has been recalled to Venice and Cassio will succeed him. Forcing Desdemona to her knees, Otello tells her to weep. Everyone is shocked by Otello's inexplicable behavior, except Iago, who urges him to complete the task. Iago then tells Roderigo that it is time to murder Cassio.

## Act IV

Sitting with Emilia, Desdemona sings the "Willow Song" taught to her as a child ("Mia madre aveva"). After a heartfelt farewell, Emilia then leaves her alone to pray ("Ave Maria"). Otello bursts in, enraged. Desdemona begs for her life,

▲ **Tenor Ronald Samm's** Otello embraces soprano Stephanie Corley's Desdemona before the Moor becomes crazed by jealousy in this 2009 production by the Birmingham Opera Company, England.

protesting her innocence, but he strangles her. Emilia brings word that Cassio has killed Roderigo, and then sees Desdemona. She calls for help and, as others arrive, reveals Iago's treachery. Destroyed by what he has done, Otello stabs himself and, giving Desdemona a final kiss, he dies.

### Not for everyone

Otello is widely recognized as one of the most difficult tenor roles in the canon. Unlike most Verdi operas, acclaimed for their powerful arias, this late masterpiece offers no such respite as the Moor is carried on an uninterrupted psychological voyage from heralded war hero to mindless murderer. The role also demands a dramatic tenor with a baritone color to his voice. Many leading tenors, among them Luciano Pavarotti, have steered clear of *Otello*, leaving a handful of outstanding singers to dominate the role over the years, from Mario del Monaco and Jon Vickers in the mid-20th century to Plácido Domingo and, most recently, Jonas Kaufmann (right).

# Falstaff

*Commedia lirica* in three acts, 2¼ hours ▪ Composed: 1889–1892 (rev. 1893–1894) ▪ First performed: February 9, 1893, La Scala, Milan, Italy ▪ Libretto: Arrigo Boito, after Shakespeare's *The Merry Wives of Windsor*

*Falstaff*, Verdi's final opera, was also his first comic opera since the disaster of *Un giorno di regno* 53 years earlier. Written almost secretly because Verdi was not sure he would live to finish it, the opera showed that, at 79, he was still full of surprises. As in *Otello*, *Falstaff* abandons set-piece arias for the Wagnerian model of continuous music. But unlike *Otello*'s familiar territory of tragedy, *Falstaff* reveals Verdi's humor through its almost talkative orchestration, "comic fugues," and riotous ensembles— one with 12 voice parts. He parodies not only Rossini's comic operas, but also some of his own dramatic works. La Scala's audiences were puzzled at first, but *Falstaff*'s overwhelming charm soon won them over.

## PRINCIPAL ROLES

**Sir John Falstaff** *baritone*
A paunchy dissolute knight

**Ford** *baritone* A wealthy local

**Fenton** *tenor* A young gentleman

**Dr. Caius** *tenor* The local physician

**Bardolph** *tenor* & **Pistol** *baritone*
Falstaff's henchmen

**Alice Ford** *soprano* Ford's wife

**Nannetta** *soprano* Ford's daughter

**Mistress Quickly** *contralto* The innkeeper

**Meg Page** *mezzo-soprano* Alice Ford's friend

▼ **An ornate Italian** edition of *Falstaff* depicts the fat knight in contemplation of a jug of ale.

### Act I

Dr. Caius storms into the Garter Inn, protesting that Falstaff's men, Bardolph and Pistol, stole his money. Falstaff also wants money—for wine. He has a solution: he has fallen for two Windsor wives, Alice Ford and Meg Page, and has love letters for each. His sidekicks refuse to deliver them out of honor, but Falstaff has his own idea of honor: "Can honor fill your belly?" ("L'onore! Ladri!"). Alice and Meg receive identical letters from Falstaff and, with Mistress Quickly, the innkeeper, they decide to teach him a lesson. Meanwhile, Ford hatches his own plan after learning of Falstaff's plan to seduce his wife. As the women resume their plotting, Nannetta, Alice's daughter, and Fenton steal hidden kisses ("Torno all'assalto").

### Act II

Mistress Quickly tells Falstaff that Alice can receive him that afternoon. As Falstaff beams, Ford arrives disguised as "Fontana," complaining that his love for Alice Ford is not returned. He offers Falstaff money to seduce her, so he can follow. Falstaff agrees, boasting that he will soon be cuckolding Alice's husband. Alone, Ford gives way to jealousy ("È sogno? O realtà"). At Ford's house, Falstaff declares his love for Alice, but she notes that he already loves Meg Page. When Meg is announced, Falstaff hides behind a screen.

Rossini thought Verdi "too melancholy and serious" to write *opera buffa*, while Verdi feared appearing "frivolous." But *Falstaff* rejuvenated him. At the end of the score, he scribbled: "On your way, old John!"

Ford and others rush in, empty a laundry basket, and search the house. Alice moves Falstaff to the laundry basket, but sounds of kissing behind the screen convince Ford that Falstaff has been found. Instead, he discovers Fenton and Nannetta. Amid much confusion, Alice has her servants tip the laundry basket—and Falstaff—into the Thames.

## Act III

Falstaff is consoling himself with wine ("Mondo ladro") when Mistress Quickly tells him to meet Alice at midnight in Windsor Park, where he must dress as the "Black Huntsman." The others take note that the huntsman's ghost sometimes appears, wearing long horns and accompanied by fairies. While Alice tells Nannetta to come as a bride, Ford orders Dr. Caius

to don a friar's hood and be ready to marry Nannetta. Fenton is dreaming of love ("Dal labbro il canto"), when Alice gives him a friar's hood. At midnight, Falstaff arrives and tries to embrace Alice but, hearing witches approach, he throws himself on the ground. Dressed as fairies, satyrs, and witches, everyone pinches and insults the prostrate knight until he repents. It is then time for Dr. Caius to marry Nannetta, but another masked couple joins them. When the ceremony is over, Dr. Caius has wed Bardolph by mistake. With Falstaff happy not to be the only fool, everyone leaves for a feast.

▼ **At the English National Opera** in 1997, Alan Opie as Falstaff wears the horns of the "Black Huntsman" and is mocked by "fairies."

### Falstaff

From the moment Falstaff appeared in Shakespeare's *Henry IV Part I*, he became one of theater's most beloved rascals. Even Elizabeth I was charmed and reportedly asked for a play about Falstaff in love. Shakespeare swiftly penned *The Merry Wives of Windsor* (the inspiration for Verdi's opera), then brought Falstaff back for *Henry IV Part II* and killed him off in *Henry V.* Yet somehow the fat knight lived on, inspiring at least four operas, although only Verdi's *Falstaff* is now still performed.

▶ **Tito Gobbi**, the Italian baritone, as Falstaff in Budapest, 1968.

# Pietro Mascagni

Born: December 7, 1863, Livorno, Italy • Died: August 2, 1945, Rome, Italy

Mascagni won instant fame almost accidentally: unbeknown to him, his wife sent the score of *Cavalleria rusticana* to a competition for one-act operas—and it won. The work's immediate worldwide popularity prompted others to write operas in the same *verismo* style, but Mascagni himself never matched its success.

# Cavalleria rusticana

RUSTIC CHIVALRY • *Melodramma* in one act, 1¼ hours • Composed: 1889 • First performed: May 17, 1890, Teatro Constanzi, Rome, Italy • Libretto: Giovanni Targioni-Tozzetti and Guido Menasci, after Giovanni Verga's play *Cavalleria rusticana*

*Cavalleria rusticana* vividly depicts life in a Sicilian village, where love, betrayal, and honor become the ingredients of a tragedy foretold. The score sets the mood with a chorus and an Easter hymn, but soon arias and duets come to drive the drama. The best-known solo is Santuzza's "Voi lo sapete, o mamma."

◀ **Plácido Domingo's Turridu** tries to reassure Santuzza, played by American mezzo-soprano Tatiana Troyanos, who begs him not to abandon her, in a 1976 production at the San Francisco Opera.

Turridu returns from military service to discover that his fiancée, Lola, has married a local cart-driver, Alfio. When Turridu seduces another girl, Santuzza, leaving her pregnant, Lola decides to win him back. On Easter Sunday, Santuzza hopes to see Turridu in church. Lucia, his mother, says he has left on an errand. Santuzza tells Lucia that she fears Lola has again conquered Turridu ("Voi lo sapete, o mamma"). Turridu tries to reassure Santuzza, then pushes her away when he sees Lola. Burning with jealousy, Santuzza tells Alfio of Lola's betrayal. Alfio challenges Turridu to a duel. Turridu seeks his mother's blessing ("Mamma, quel vino è generoso") and begs her to care for Santuzza should he not return. A terrible scream announces Turridu's death. Lucia and Santuzza collapse in grief.

## Mascagni and Leoncavallo

The names of Pietro Mascagni and Ruggero Leoncavallo are invariably linked. They carried the late-19th-century Italian literary movement called *verismo*, or "realism," into opera, each with a single memorable work: *Cavalleria rusticana* for Mascagni and *Pagliacci* for Leoncavallo. These short operas are often presented together.

# Ruggero Leoncavallo

Born: April 23, 1857, Naples, Italy • Died: August 9, 1919, Montecatini, Italy

Leoncavallo was a struggling composer when Mascagni's *Cavalleria rusticana* inspired him to try *verismo* in opera. The result, *Pagliacci*, was a triumph. But, like Mascagni, Leoncavallo left little mark with his later works. He wrote a version of *La bohème*, but it was overshadowed by Puccini's opera, which had premiered 18 months earlier.

# Pagliacci

THE CLOWNS • *Dramma* in a prologue and two acts, 1¼ hours • Composed: 1891–1892 • First performed: May 21, 1892, Teatro dal Verme, Milan, Italy • Libretto: Ruggero Leoncavallo

*Pagliacci* shows a *commedia dell'arte* play repeating itself tragically in real life. Its setting among villagers and strolling players placed it squarely in the *verismo* movement, contributing to its success. The best-known aria, "Vesti la giubba," with its plaintive cries of "Pagliaccio," is also a favorite for tenor recitals.

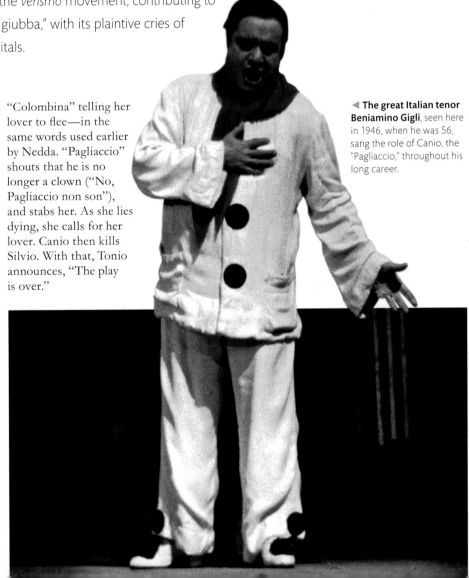

◀ **The great Italian tenor Beniamino Gigli**, seen here in 1946, when he was 56, sang the role of Canio, the "Pagliaccio," throughout his long career.

**Prologue**

Tonio, the clown, announces to the audience that the perils of love will be presented on stage.

**Act I**

As strolling players prepare their show, Canio, their leader, says he expects the crowd to laugh at his wife's infidelity in the play. But in real life, he warns, he would avenge such treachery. His wife, Nedda, is alarmed. When Tonio tries to kiss her, she strikes him. But she is in love with Silvio, a villager, and agrees to run away with him. Overhearing them, Tonio summons Canio, but Nedda urges Silvio to flee. When she refuses to identify her lover, Canio realizes he has become the jealous husband he will enact in the play ("Vesti la giubba").

**Act II**

On stage, "Colombina" (Nedda) awaits her lover, "Arlecchino" (Beppe). When "Taddeo" (Tonio) arrives first, she throws him out. She then welcomes "Arlecchino," and they prepare to elope. Returning unexpectedly, "Pagliaccio" (Canio) hears

"Colombina" telling her lover to flee—in the same words used earlier by Nedda. "Pagliaccio" shouts that he is no longer a clown ("No, Pagliaccio non son"), and stabs her. As she lies dying, she calls for her lover. Canio then kills Silvio. With that, Tonio announces, "The play is over."

# Umberto Giordano

Born: August 27, 1867, Foggia, Italy ▪ Died: November 12, 1948, Milan, Italy

Umberto Giordano was swept up by the operatic fashion for *verismo*, or "realism," initiated by Mascagni's *Cavalleria rusticana*. But while Giordano wrote a dozen operas, he is remembered only for *Andrea Chénier*. Set during the French Revolution, this opera benefited from an excellent libretto by Luigi Illica, who also helped to create Puccini's most popular works. After *Andrea Chénier*, Giordano wrote *Fedora*, which is occasionally performed today, but his other operas fared poorly even during his lifetime. However, apart from the high drama of *Andrea Chénier*, Giordano bequeathed a number of melodic arias for both tenor and soprano, which have remained popular as recital pieces.

# Andrea Chénier

*Dramma di ambiente storico* in four acts, 2¼ hours ▪ Composed: 1894–1896 ▪ First performed: March 28, 1896, La Scala, Milan, Italy ▪ Libretto: Luigi Illica

*Andrea Chénier* is inspired by the French Romantic poet André Chénier, whose courageous stand against the excesses of the French Revolution cost him his life. Built around Illica's strong libretto, the opera evokes the turbulent mood of Paris through revolutionary songs like "Ça Ira" and "La Carmagnole." While giving Chénier opportunity to defend his ill-fated idealism, Giordano and Illica also add romance to the political mix: Chénier competes with a servant-turned-revolutionary for the love of an aristocratic woman. Through these three major roles, Giordano displays his talent for lyrical intensity. The work's best-known melody is Maddalena's aria "La mamma morta," mourning her mother, slain by a revolutionary mob. No less poignant is the final duet, "Vicino a te," when Maddalena chooses to die with Chénier.

## Act I
Before a party at the Coigny's château, one servant, Gérard, curses the "gilded house." But when he sees the contessa's beautiful daughter, Maddalena, his anger melts. Guests decide to ignore news of unrest in Paris. The poet Chénier dedicates an ode to love to Maddalena, but guests are scandalized when the poem denounces poverty ("Un dì all'azzurro spazio"). Gérard returns with a crowd of beggars and, tearing off his uniform, announces he is resigning. The contessa blithely calls for dancing to resume.

## Act II
Five years later, in a Paris café, Chénier is being watched by a spy, Incredibile. His friend, Roucher, urges him to flee. But the poet refuses, saying he awaits a mysterious woman who says she is in danger and signs her letters as "Hope." Gérard, now a revolutionary, is looking for the same woman. A maid leads Chénier to her mistress, Maddalena. Recognizing Maddalena, Chénier is overwhelmed by love and vows to protect her with his life. Summoned by the spy, Gérard arrives

and is wounded in a fight with Chénier. Nonetheless, he warns Chénier that he is being sought as a counterrevolutionary.

## Act III
At a Revolutionary Tribunal, Gérard calls for donations to help France against its enemies. As the crowd sings "La Carmagnole," Incredibile reports Chénier's capture and urges Gérard to sign the poet's indictment. Gérard hesitates, ashamed that he has betrayed his principles and is now driven only by hate and love ("Nemico della patria?!"). But he signs the paper. Maddalena begs Gérard to save Chénier. When Gérard recalls his lifelong love for her, she offers her body in exchange for Chénier's life. Gérard is moved by Maddalena's account of her mother's death in a fire set by revolutionaries ("La mamma morta"). At his trial, Chénier is denounced as dangerous. He defends his fight against hypocrisy, and even Gérard speaks up for him, but the judge orders his death.

## Act IV
While Chénier writes a final poem, Gérard arrives with Maddalena. Bribing the jailer, she takes the place of a condemned woman. Finally, alone, Chénier and Maddalena fall into each other arms, swearing eternal love. Then, summoned to their execution, they cry out, "We welcome death together!"

◀ **Katarzyna Suska** as the contessa (center) urges her guests to ignore the approaching revolution and continue dancing, in a 2005 staging at the Polish National Opera.

---

**PRINCIPAL ROLES**

**Andrea Chénier** *tenor* A poet

**Maddalena di Coigny** *soprano*
An aristocrat and Chénier's beloved

**Contessa di Coigny** *mezzo-soprano*
Maddalena's mother

**Carlo Gérard** *baritone*
A servant in the Coigny family

**Roucher** *bass* Chénier's friend

**Incredibile** *tenor*
A dandy spying for the revolutionaries

▶ **A costume design** for Maddalena di Coigny in a 19th-century production of Giordano's opera staged at the Paris Opéra, France.

---

During his final weeks, André Chénier's muse was an aristocrat called Aimée de Coigny, but his infatuation was not reciprocated: de Coigny neither died at his side nor even mentioned him in her memoirs.

# Giacomo Puccini

Born: December 22, 1858, Lucca, Italy • Died: November 11, 1924, Brussels, Belgium

Giacomo Puccini enjoys a unique place in the history of opera thanks to *La bohème*: For over a century, this tragic love story set among down-at-heel Parisians has been the most performed work in the entire canon. It was not, however, an isolated triumph. Although Puccini created only ten operas in a 40-year career, *Tosca*, *Madama Butterfly*, and *Turandot* are beloved for their beauty and passion.

P uccini was born into a family of Tuscan musicians, taking his first lessons from his father and uncle. But it was a performance of Verdi's *Aïda* in Pisa in 1876 that won him over to opera. Years later, he explained: "God touched me with His little finger and said, 'Write for the theater, only for the theater." When he entered the Milan Conservatory in 1880, he then had the good fortune to have an opera composer, Amilcare Ponchielli (*La Gioconda*), among his teachers. In 1884, his first opera, *Le villi*, was a huge success, but his second, *Edgar*, flopped, prompting the music publisher Giulio Ricordi to send him to Bayreuth to hear Wagner's *Die Meistersinger von Nürnberg*. Upon his return, he wrote *Manon Lescaut*, the first work to bring him international recognition. Then, over the next 12 years, with *La bohème*, *Tosca*, and *Madama Butterfly*, he was unchallenged as Verdi's heir.

What these operas have in common is the power of their melodies and melodrama to move audiences, even to tears: in each, a beautiful heroine—Manon, Mimi, Tosca, and Cio-Cio-San—dies tragically. The shocking and violent reality they portrayed also placed them inside a turn-of-the-century Italian movement called *verismo*.

As it happens, Puccini's off-stage life was also not short of drama. In his twenties, he provoked a scandal by running away with a married woman, Elvira Gemignani, with whom he had a son long before they finally married in 1904. Even then, his eye would wander, and another scandal erupted in 1908 when a young maid in his household took her own life: ever jealous, Elvira had wrongly accused her of carrying Puccini's child.

## FIRST PERFORMANCES

- 1884 *Le villi*
- 1889 *Edgar*
- 1893 *Manon Lescaut*
- 1896 *La bohème*
- 1900 *Tosca*
- 1904 *Madama Butterfly*
- 1910 *La fanciulla del West*
- 1917 *La rondine*
- 1918 *Il trittico*
- 1926 *Turandot*

▲ *Tosca*, an opera in which the heroine is herself a diva, is Puccini's most dramatic. Act II (above) climaxes with Tosca's daring murder of the evil police chief Scarpia.

◄ **An Italian poster** evokes the scene in Act II of *Tosca* where Tosca murders Scarpia.

> "If I could only find my subject, a subject full
> of passion and pain."

GIACOMO PUCCINI

▲ **Puccini, who loved fast cars**, is shown in this 1909 photograph with an Isotta Fraschini. In the back seat on the left is his wife, Elvira Gemignani.

## Distractions

Still, other factors account for his slow pace of writing. Wealthy at an early age, he enjoyed traveling and had a passion for cars. Indeed, a serious car accident stopped him from working for eight months in 1903. But he also wavered before choosing a subject, combing plays and books for exotic tales. He would then become fully engaged with his writers in shaping the libretto, often adding his own characters and scenes. After *Madama Butterfly*, he was distracted when a group of (now forgotten) young composers accused him of writing "petit bourgeois" operas. This criticism may well have led the ever-sensitive Puccini to write his next opera, *La fanciulla del West*, around an American theme for an American audience. But it also signaled a change in Puccini's music, with greater emphasis on narrative composition and less on catchy tunes. In this opera, non-Italian influence was evident: of Wagner, and also Debussy, Richard Strauss, and Stravinsky.

All came together in the marvelous inventiveness of Puccini's final—unfinished— opera, *Turandot*, first performed in 1926, two years after his death. Yet even with the unquestioned virtuosity of *Turandot*, Puccini's music has continued to divide opera lovers, some happy to be embraced by its melodic warmth, others put off by its unabashed sentimentality. Still, Puccini's place in operatic history is secure. Although he wrote more than half his operas in the 20th century, he was in spirit a 19th-century composer and, as such, brought three centuries of Italian-dominated opera to a brilliant close.

# La bohème

THE BOHEMIAN Opera in four scenes, 1¾ hours ▪ Composed: 1893–1895 (rev. 1896) ▪ First performed: February 1, 1896, Teatro Regio, Turin, Italy
▪ Libretto: Giuseppe Giacosa and Luigi Illica, based on episodes from Henri Murger's 1845 play, *Scènes de la vie de bohème*

*La bohème*, arguably the world's favorite opera, had a stormy birth: another composer, Ruggero Leoncavallo, was already working on the story and accused Puccini of stealing his idea. Both versions were staged, but only Puccini's is remembered. Its strength lies in the perfect marriage of intensely poignant story and wonderfully melodic score. The best-known arias show Rodolfo and Mimì falling in love in Act I, but the Act III quartet is also remarkable for blending duets of tenderness and wrath. Puccini plainly cared deeply for the story, which stirred nostalgia for his student days in Milan. After composing the final scene, he recalled, "I began to weep like a child." Today, Mimì's death still brings on tears.

## PRINCIPAL ROLES

**Mimì** *soprano* A poor seamstress

**Rodolfo** *tenor* A poet

**Marcello** *baritone* A painter

**Musetta** *soprano* Marcello's mistress

**Schaunard** *baritone* A musician

**Colline** *bass* A philosopher

**Parpignol** *tenor* The toy seller

**Benoît** *bass* Landlord of the artists

### Act I

Spending Christmas Eve in a Paris garret, Rodolfo, a poet, and Marcello, a painter, fight the cold by burning Rodolfo's manuscript in a stove. As Colline, a philosopher, joins them, two boys bring food, drink, and cigars. Ready for a feast, Schaunard, a musician, enters waving money and announces they must eat out. The landlord Benoît wants his rent, but the men distract him with wine and talk of women. When he admits philandering, the men feign shock and chase him away. As they head for Café Momus, Rodolfo says he must finish an article. Hearing a knock, Rodolfo finds a young woman needing a light for her candle. Coughing violently, she faints and Rodolfo revives her with some wine. She loses her key, and he helps look for it on the floor. Suddenly her cold hand touches his and, moved, he introduces himself ("Che gelida manina"). Hesitatingly, Mimì gives her name and says she lives alone. As Rodolfo's friends call, urging him to make haste, he and Mimì realize they have fallen in love.

### Act II

In a crowded Left Bank street, Rodolfo buys Mimì a red bonnet before joining his friends at Café Momus. Everyone seems happy until Marcello sees his former mistress, Musetta, arriving with her aged suitor, Alcindoro. Treating Alcindoro with disdain, she plays up to Marcello ("Quando me'n vo"). Pretending her feet hurt, she

sends Alcindoro to buy her new shoes and falls into Marcello's arms. The waiter brings the bill to the revelers, who slip away and leave Alcindoro to pay for their fun.

### Act III

Two months later, Mimì tells Marcello that, because of Rodolfo's constant jealousy, she must leave him even though they still love each other. Marcello promises to intercede and, with Mimì nearby, Rodolfo confesses that he still loves her but fears she is terminally ill. Mimì's coughs and sobs reveal her presence. Full of remorse, Rodolfo leads her into the warmth of the tavern, where she sadly bids farewell to him ("Addio. Donde lieta uscì"). Meanwhile, as a furious fight erupts between Marcello and Musetta, Rodolfo and Mimì decide that they will remain together until the spring.

### Act IV

Months later in the garret, as Rodolfo and Marcello try to forget their lost loves, Musetta arrives with Mimì, who can barely walk. Rodolfo carries her to bed and, to pay for a doctor, Musetta decides to sell her earrings, while Colline says goodbye to his overcoat. Between coughs, Mimì tells Rodolfo that she always loved him and they remember their meeting. Gradually, Mimì falls asleep and, as the others return, they notice she has died. Finally Rodolfo, too, understands and collapses in tears.

◀ **The title page** of the first edition of *La bohème*, published by Giulio Ricordi, emphasizes the carefree lifestyle enjoyed by the bohemians.

### Caruso and Melba

Enrico Caruso, the most admired tenor of the early 20th century and the first to become a recording star, made his debut at La Scala as Rodolfo in *La bohème*. When Puccini first heard him, he exclaimed: "Who has sent you to me? God?" Caruso was also famous for his practical jokes. One victim was the Australian soprano Nellie Melba. During a London performance of *La bohème*, as he grasped Melba's "frozen hands" in Act I, Caruso slipped her a warm sausage.

▲ **Luciano Pavarotti** sings Rodolfo opposite Kallen Esperian's Mimì in a production at the Exhibition Hall Theatre, Beijing, in 1986.

After the premiere of *La bohème*, a Turin newspaper wrote: "Even as it leaves little impression in the minds of the audience, *La bohème* will leave no great trace on the history of opera."

# Manon Lescaut

Lyric drama in four acts, 2 hours ▪ Composed: 1889–1892 (rev. 1893 and 1922) ▪ First performed: February 1, 1893, Teatro Regio, Turin, Italy ▪ Libretto: Ruggero Leoncavallo and others, based on the Abbé Prévost's 1731 novel, *L'histoire du chevalier des Grieux et de Manon Lescaut*

*Manon Lescaut*, Puccini's first international success, established his reputation for life. He took a risk by returning to a story that had already been set by Auber and Massenet, but he plagued no fewer than seven librettists until he was happy. The result is a deeply lyrical opera, with memorable arias and duets tracking Manon's ill-fated passage through love, frivolity, exile, and finally her miserable death in a distant desert.

## PRINCIPAL ROLES

**Manon Lescaut** *soprano*

**Il Cavaliere Renato des Grieux** *tenor* Manon's lover

**Lescaut** *baritone* Manon's brother

**Geronte di Ravoir** *bass* Manon's wealthy suitor

**Edmondo** *tenor* Des Grieux's friend

### Act I
Outside an inn in Amiens, des Grieux is flirting with girls when a coach arrives with an elderly official, Geronte, accompanied by Manon and her brother Lescaut, a soldier. Des Grieux promptly falls for Manon ("Donna non vidi mai"), but she is bound for a convent. Learning that Geronte plans to abduct Manon, des Grieux persuades her to come with him to Paris.

### Act II
In Paris, Geronte's wealth has won over Manon, but she still yearns for des Grieux ("In quelle trine morbide"). When he appears, her love is reawakened. They prepare to escape, but she is reluctant to leave her jewels. Her brother warns that Geronte has denounced her as immoral and, when she delays once more, police arrest her.

### Act III
Des Grieux and Lescaut hope to free Manon before she is deported from Le Havre to America. Through a cell window, des Grieux tries to reassure her, but soon the jailed women are led toward the prison ship. As Manon is pushed aboard, des Grieux persuades the captain to hire him as a deckhand.

### Act IV
Lost in a Louisiana desert, Manon faints. Des Grieux revives her, then sets off to look for water. Manon remembers her "horrible past." When des Grieux returns empty-handed, she expires, vowing her love will never die.

Puccini was unworried that Massenet had written *Manon* nine years earlier. "He feels it as a Frenchman, with powder and minuets," he said. "I shall feel it as an Italian, with a desperate passion."

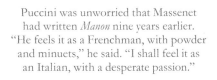

◀ **The Italian soprano** Daniela Dessì as a briefly wealthy Manon Lescaut in Act II of a 2003 production of Puccini's opera in Seville, Spain.

# La Fanciulla del West

THE GIRL OF THE GOLDEN WEST Opera in three acts, 2 hours ▪ Composed: 1908–1910 ▪ First performed: December 10, 1910, Metropolitan Opera, New York, US ▪ Libretto: Guelfo Civinini and Carlo Zangarini, after David Belasco's 1905 play *The Girl of the Golden West*

*La fanciulla del West* has long been considered an oddity in Puccini's work, a lyrical opera set among roughneck gold miners in the American West. But he wrote it only partly to please his American fans. As *Madama Butterfly* and *Turandot* testify, he liked stories about faraway places. Musically, it also represented a change of direction, with the fast-paced narrative accompanied by continuous music, which is only rarely interrupted for arias. Its New York premiere, conducted by Arturo Toscanini, was a triumph.

### Act I

After breaking up a fight among miners, Sheriff Rance reminds Minnie, the saloon's straightlaced owner, that he loves her. As talk turns to the bandit Ramerrez, a man enters, giving his name as Johnson. He and Minnie have met and their warmth angers Rance. A captured bandit whispers to Johnson that the gang is ready to rob the saloon, but he has fallen for Minnie, who invites him to visit her.

### Act II

Minnie receives Johnson in her mountain home and, after describing her happy life alone there ("Oh, se sapeste"), she allows herself to be kissed, her first kiss. As a snow storm rages, Rance arrives, forcing Johnson to hide. Warning Minnie that Johnson is really Ramerrez, Rance leaves. Furious,

Minnie expels Johnson, but he is shot on her doorstep. She hides him in the loft, but Rance returns to find fresh blood. Minnie challenges him to poker: Johnson's life against her love. She cheats and Rance accepts defeat, leaving Johnson unconscious in Minnie's arms.

### Act III

Miners catch Johnson, and Rance authorizes summary justice. Accepting death, Johnson's sole request is that Minnie believe him to be free ("Ch'ella mi creda libero"). Suddenly Minnie arrives, draws a pistol, and reminds the miners of everything she had done for them. Finally, they decide they cannot refuse her, and Minnie and Johnson ride away.

---

**PRINCIPAL ROLES**

**Minnie** *soprano* Owner of the Polka Saloon

**Dick Johnson (Ramerrez)** *tenor* A bandit

**Jack Rance** *baritone* A sheriff

**Ashby** *bass* Wells Fargo agent

---

The Royal Opera House, in London, described *La fanciulla del West* as "opera's very own spaghetti western," not only because it boasts a gun-toting outlaw, but also because it includes nods to American folk music and ragtime.

◀ **The Argentine tenor** José Cura as the fugitive outlaw Dick Johnson woos Minnie, the prim saloon-keeper, sung by the American soprano Andrea Gruber, in a production at the Royal Opera House in 2005.

# METROPOLITAN OPERA,
## NEW YORK

Unlike Europe's major government-subsidized opera houses, the Metropolitan Opera has always depended on private financing to operate. As a result, while escaping the ravages of war, its state of health has tended to rise and fall with economic activity. That said, since the Met, as it is known, opened on Broadway and 39th Street with Gounod's *Faust* in October 1883, its opera company has gone out of its way to draw the biggest stars of the day, some making the theater their second home—among them the great soprano Renata Tebaldi. From 1931, the public at large could also enjoy opera through live radio broadcasts from the Met.

A "new" Met opened at Lincoln Center in September 1966 and, like its predecessor, it was vast: with seating for a 3,800-strong audience, it is the largest opera house in the world. This poses a major challenge to singers, with weaker voices easily lost in the giant hall. It also influences the opera house's programming, since, in order to fill the auditorium, management must frequently present the most popular operas and best-known voices. In doing so, it bends to the taste of older and more conservative opera-goers, who can best afford the high price of tickets and who rarely welcome modern productions by European theater directors.

Since 2006, the Met has nonetheless played a key role in making opera more accessible through its live transmissions of performances shown in cinemas across the world. During the Covid-19 lockdowns, it also offered a rich variety of productions online at no charge. Several opera houses in Europe are now following this example. Along with offering the best voices, the Met boasts an orchestra of the highest standard, thanks, in good measure, to James Levine, who was its brilliant music director from 1976 until 2016. His relationship with the opera house ended in 2018 after he was accused of sexual misconduct, a charge he denied.

> "At the Met, we are masters of illusion.
> When we want to create the illusion
> of a 60-foot staircase, we build a
> 60-foot staircase."

CLEMENTE D'ALESSIO, OPERA PRODUCER

▶ **The Metropolitan Opera, New York**, which opened this "new" theater at Lincoln Center in 1966, is famed for drawing the biggest names in opera to its stage.

# Tosca

Opera in three acts, 2 hours ▪ Composed: 1896–1899 ▪ First performed: January 14, 1900, Teatro Constanzi, Rome, Italy ▪ Libretto: Giuseppe Giacosa and Luigi Illica, after Victorien Sardou's 1887 play *La Tosca*

Puccini's most plot-driven opera, *Tosca* is a feverish drama of love, jealousy, courage, and death. Inspired by seeing Sarah Bernhardt on stage in Sardou's *La Tosca*, Puccini quickly recognized the play's operatic potential. Working with Giacosa and Illica, his librettists for *Manon Lescaut* and *La bohème*, he then extracted the play's dramatic core. Driven by Tosca's fiery temperament, the score is packed with stirring arias and duets. At the heart of the work is one of opera's most powerful scenes, the Act II confrontation between Tosca and Rome's police chief, Scarpia, where each uses sex as a weapon until Scarpia lies dead at Tosca's feet. To keep pace with the action, Puccini's orchestration is stormier than anything he had written before. For poetry, he noted, he substituted passion.

## PRINCIPAL ROLES

**Floria Tosca** *soprano* A prima donna

**Mario Cavaradossi** *tenor* Her lover

**Baron Scarpia** *baritone* Police chief of Rome

**Cesare Angelotti** *bass* A fugitive rebel

**Sacristan** *baritone*

**Spoletta** *tenor* Scarpia's henchman

◀ **Emilio de Marchi** (1851–1901), one of the greatest tenors of Puccini's time, created the role of Cavaradossi in Rome in 1900.

## Act I

Angelotti, a fugitive republican, is hiding in the church of Sant'Andrea della Valle, where Mario Cavaradossi is completing a painting of Mary Magdalene. The sacristan says the portrait resembles a woman who prays in the church, but Cavaradossi muses that, while painting the "unknown beauty," he thinks only of Tosca ("Recondita armonia"). As the sacristan leaves, Angelotti emerges and Cavaradossi offers his help. When Tosca arrives, Angelotti again hides. Dreaming of love, she tells Cavaradossi to meet her after her evening concert. But then she recognizes the portrait of the Marchesa Attavanti, Angelotti's sister, and explodes with jealousy. Cavaradossi reassures her of his love ("Mia gelosa") and finally persuades her to leave. Angelotti reappears and, as a cannon shot announces his escape, Cavaradossi offers his villa as a hideout. Hunting for the fugitive, Scarpia, the police chief, only finds a fan forgotten in the church by Angelotti's sister. When Tosca returns, Scarpia provokes her by saying the portrait is of a loose woman and displaying the fan as evidence. Furious, Tosca heads for Cavaradossi's villa, followed by Scarpia's agents. As a Te Deum celebrates a royalist victory over Napoleon, Scarpia dreams of winning Tosca.

## Act II

In the Palazzo Farnese, Scarpia is yearning for Tosca ("Ha più forte sapore"). The escaped prisoner has not been found, but Cavaradossi is dragged in. Interrogated about Angelotti, he says he knows nothing. As Tosca arrives, he is taken away. She hears his groans and Scarpia says she can end the torture. She refuses to cooperate but, as the torture intensifies, she finally reveals Angelotti's hiding place. Cavaradossi feels betrayed by Tosca, but is elated by news of a royalist defeat and cries "Victory!" Scarpia angrily orders his execution. But he then tells Tosca that, if she gives herself to him, she can still save her lover's life. Distraught, Tosca asks if she deserves this fate ("Vissi d'arte"). As word arrives of Angelotti's suicide, she finally accepts Scarpia's condition, but insists on her lover's freedom. Scarpia says that, after a mock execution, they can flee. As he signs a safe-conduct, Tosca stabs him in the heart, crying "Die, you fiend! Die! Die!"

## Act III

Awaiting death in the Castel Sant'Angelo, Cavaradossi dreams of Tosca ("E lucevan le stelle"). To Cavaradossi's disbelief ("O dolci mani"), Tosca explains how she killed Scarpia and tells her lover that a carriage awaits them. But first he must undergo a mock execution. Cavaradossi is led to the roof of the castle and shots ring out. As he falls, Tosca tells him to lie still until the soldiers have left. Then, in horror, she realizes he is dead. As officers return to arrest her for murdering Scarpia, she leaps to her death.

*Tosca* is famous for its production mishaps. On one occasion, poorly briefed extras in the firing squad shot Tosca instead of Cavaradossi; on another, Tosca leaped to her death, landed on a trampoline and bounced back into view.

▶ **Catherine Malfitano**, playing Tosca, appears to leap off the Castel Sant'Angelo in a 1992 production televised live from the opera's original settings.

## Maria Callas

One of the most charismatic sopranos of the 20th century, Maria Callas—herself a temperamental opera singer—was best known for high-voltage roles like Tosca. Callas's formidable voice was not beautiful in a conventional way, yet it pulsated with personality and had an electrifying effect on audiences. Offstage, too, she played the role of the ultimate diva. And while her operatic career was brief and she was only 53 when she died, recordings have kept alive the legend of "La Callas."

▲ **In Anthony Minghella's** 2006 production at the Met, Cio-Cio-San (Cristina Gallardo-Domâs) bids adieu to her son, unusually played here by a puppet.

The premiere of *Madama Butterfly*, conducted by Arturo Toscanini, was a rowdy affair. With heckl the outset, laughter, and even animal sounds from the audience, the production was withdrawn. reworked the piece and presented a revised version at the Teatro Grande, in Brescia three mont

# Madama Butterfly

A Japanese tragedy in three acts, 2 hours ▪ Composed: 1902–1903 (rev. 1904–1906) ▪ First performed: February 17, 1904, La Scala, Milan, Italy ▪ Libretto: Giuseppe Giacosa and Luigi Illica, after David Belasco's 1900 play *Madame Butterfly*, from a short story by John Luther Long

*Madama Butterfly* is a hauntingly lyrical opera which, in its day, mirrored the West's new interest in Japan. Puccini himself studied Japanese folk songs and manners in a bid for authenticity. But while he borrows some Japanese motifs and imitates some Japanese melodies, the music remains Italian. Unusually, though, this is a tragedy laced with cruelty. Cio-Cio-San is only 15 and already a geisha when she meets Pinkerton, the purity of her love contrasting fiercely with the American's predatory cynicism. This innocence is conveyed in the sumptuous duet closing Act I, the ever-hopeful "One Fine Day," and even in Butterfly's farewell to her child. Puccini described it as his most "deeply felt and imaginative" opera.

## Act I

Goro, the marriage broker, shows Lt. Pinkerton of the US Navy his new home and introduces his future wife's maid, Suzuki. The American consul Sharpless arrives and warns Pinkerton against the marriage. Boasting of a different love on every shore ("Dovunque al mondo"), Pinkerton says he is delighted by his pretty Japanese bride, who flutters "like a butterfly," but adds that one day he will marry "a real American bride." Butterfly (Cio-Cio-San) arrives, beaming with happiness. Butterfly says she is 15 and became a geisha after her family fell on hard times. As her relatives gather for the wedding, she shows Pinkerton the dagger used by her father to take his own life. After they are married, her uncle, a Buddhist priest, chastises her for becoming a Christian. Butterfly's shocked family leaves and the newly married couple at last celebrate their love ("Viene la sera").

### History repeated

The cultural misunderstanding that shapes *Madama Butterfly* has its roots in the American decision to force an end to Japan's isolation in 1854. This resulted not only in the gradual Westernization of Japanese public life, but also in the frequent visits of US Navy warships to Japanese ports, including Nagasaki. By the turn of the century, a love affair between an American officer and a geisha was not only plausible, but also common.

▶ **Matthew Perry**, the American naval commander of the fleet that "opened" Japan, is depicted at Yokohama in this print.

## Act II

Butterfly has heard nothing from Pinkerton in three years, but she is convinced he will return, even imagining his first words to his "dear little wife" ("Un bel dì, vedremo"). Sharpless brings a letter from Pinkerton, but Butterfly gives him no chance to read it. She tells a wealthy suitor, Prince Yamadori, that she is still married. Finally Sharpless begins the letter, but Butterfly keeps interrupting him. When he asks what she would do if Pinkerton never returned, she replies she would again become a geisha or, better, die. He urges her to accept Yamadori's proposal, but she surprises him by bringing out a blue-eyed child ("Che tua madre"). As he leaves, Sharpless asks the boy's name; she says he is Sorrow but will become Joy when his father returns. The harbor gun heralds a ship and, peering through a telescope, Butterfly cries out that it is Pinkerton's. She mocks Suzuki's lack of faith, telling her to scatter the house with flower petals. She dons her bridal gown.

## Act III

After waiting all night, Butterfly falls asleep just as Pinkerton arrives with Sharpless. Suzuki sees a woman with them and realizes it is Pinkerton's wife. Suzuki is devastated, but Sharpless and Pinkerton ask her to persuade Butterfly to give up her child. Seeing the flowers, Pinkerton is upset and, feeling forever haunted by Butterfly's "sweet face," he flees ("Addio, fiorito asil"). As Butterfly looks for Pinkerton, she instead finds the American woman who is now his wife. Reluctantly, she agrees to give up her son, but only if Pinkerton comes for him. Alone, Butterfly gives their son an American flag and bids him farewell ("Tu? tu? tu? tu? Piccolo Iddio!"), then stabs herself with her father's dagger. As Pinkerton returns, she collapses and dies.

### PRINCIPAL ROLES

**Cio-Cio-San (Madama Butterfly)** *soprano*
A geisha

**Suzuki** *mezzo-soprano* Cio-Cio-San's maid

**B. F. Pinkerton** *tenor* An American naval lieutenant

**Sharpless** *baritone* The American consul

**Kate Pinkerton** *mezzo-soprano*
Pinkerton's American wife

**Goro** *tenor* A marriage broker

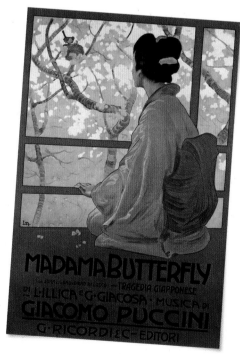

▲ **An Italian poster** for the 1904 premiere of Puccini's opera *Madama Butterfly*.

# Turandot

Opera in three acts, 1¾ hours • Composed: 1920–1924 (completed by Franco Alfano 1925–1926) • First performed: April 25, 1926, La Scala, Milan, Italy • Libretto: Giuseppe Adami and Renato Simoni, after Carlo Gozzi's 1762 play *Turandot*

*Turandot* has never enjoyed the popularity of *La bohème* or *Tosca*, but in many ways it represents the zenith of Puccini's career, an extraordinary spectacle of high drama and musical invention. It has several fine arias, including "Nessun dorma," popularized by Luciano Pavarotti during the 1990 World Cup. While dominated by Calàf's high-risk love for Turandot, the opera gives a pivotal role to the loyal enslaved girl Liù, a tragic heroine in the mold of Mimì. Many of *Turandot*'s melodies, woven seamlessly into the flowing narrative of the score, suggest the influence of Wagner and Debussy, though Puccini adds a distinctly Chinese color.

## PRINCIPAL ROLES

**Princess Turandot** *soprano*

**Emperor Altoum** *tenor* Turandot's father

**The Unknown Prince, Calàf** *tenor* Turandot's suitor

**Timur** *bass* Exiled King of Tartary and Calàf's father

**Liù** *soprano* An enslaved girl

**Ping** *baritone* Grand Chancellor of China

**Pang** *tenor* Lord of provisions

**Pong** *tenor* Lord of the Imperial Kitchen

**A Mandarin** *baritone*

A 1998 staging of *Turandot* in its original setting of Beijing's Forbidden City signaled China's growing interest in Western opera. Acted before a 14th-century Ming dynasty temple, hundreds of Chinese soldiers were used as extras.

### Unfinished work

When Puccini died in 1924, he left *Turandot*'s final love duet unfinished. It was completed by Franco Alfano, a minor Italian composer, but a mystery remains about how Puccini intended it to sound. The conductor Arturo Toscanini interrupted the premiere to announce: "Here the opera ends, because at this point the Maestro died." After that, Alfano's finale was included.

▶ **Gwyneth Jones** as Turandot opposite Plácido Domingo's Calàf at the Royal Opera House, London, 1984.

## Act I

A crowd awaits the execution of the Prince of Persia, the latest suitor to fail Princess Turandot's test of love: those who cannot answer three riddles must die. Amid the jostling, a young woman, Liù, cries out as an old man stumbles. Rushing to help, Calàf, who is hiding his identity from his enemies, recognizes his father, Timur, deposed King of Tartary. He asks Liù why she is risking her life to help. She says it is because one day Prince Calàf smiled at her. Finally, amid great pomp, Turandot confirms the execution. Calàf is overwhelmed by the Princess's beauty and resolves to win her. The emperor's ministers, Ping, Pang, and Pong, discourage him, telling him Turandot is just like any other woman. When Calàf shouts that only he loves her, Liù begs him to give up ("Signore ascolta!"). He urges Liù to look after his father ("Non piangere, Liù"), then strikes the ceremonial gong.

## Act II

Ping, Pang, and Pong recall executions they have witnessed. They hear trumpets announce Turandot's grand entrance. She explains that her cruelty and chastity are to avenge the suffering of an ancient Chinese princess ("In questa reggia"). She then warns her unnamed suitor that there are three riddles but one death. Calàf answers the first two riddles. Turandot then poses the last: "Ice that burns, and with your flame, it freezes you still more; bright and dark, in wanting you free, it further enslaves you; in accepting you as a slave, it makes you king." Calàf answers, "Turandot." The devastated princess begs to be released from her pledge. Wanting her love, the "unknown" prince offers a way out: if she discovers his name before dawn, he agrees to die.

## Act III

No one can sleep in Beijing, but Calàf feels safe with his secret ("Nessun dorma"). The ministers warn that Turandot will massacre the population if he is not identified. The people even threaten to kill Calàf. When Turandot appears, Liù says only she knows the prince's name, but even under torture she will not reveal it. Turandot asks what is the source of her strength. She replies, "Love," saying the princess will also love the prince ("Tu, che di gel sei cinta"). She then grabs a dagger and stabs herself. As shock spreads through the crowd, Calàf rips off Turandot's veil and kisses her passionately ("Principessa di morte!"). Feeling humiliation and defeat, she tells him to leave without revealing his name. But he says that he has no interest in remaining mysterious and offers her both his name and his life. Triumphant at last, Turandot turns to the emperor, courtiers, and people and announces the prince's name: Love.

▶ **The soprano Christine Goerke** is a stirring Turandot in Franco Zeffirelli's production at the Metropolitan Opera, New York, in 2016.

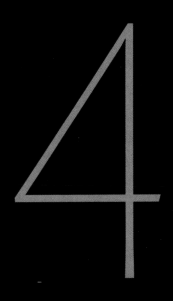

# GERMANIC OPERA

## (c. 1800–1950)

# Germanic opera c. 1800–1950

Romantic opera found its German voice at the start of the 19th century, and reached its apex in Richard Wagner's mammoth *Ring* cycle of 1876. In the interim, new theaters in dozens of German-speaking cities staged popular Romantic operas. Germanic lore provided stories, and large symphonic orchestras wed densely textured music to powerful singing.

## German operas before Beethoven

Operas in German had been written since the 17th century as Singspiels, which included speaking as well as singing. The earliest were based on sacred subjects, as with Johann Thiele's *Adam und Eva* of 1678, which inaugurated Hamburg's Oper am Gänsemarkt, the first public opera house outside Venice. Yet, while Hamburg became the Singspiel capital, Germanic cities from Hanover to Vienna also welcomed Italian composers and librettists. Even the German-speaking Gluck and Mozart were influenced chiefly by Italian music. Indeed, Mozart's best operas were in Italian, not least *Le nozze di Figaro* and *Don Giovanni*.

## *Sturm und Drang*: German Romanticism

After the French Revolution, as Europe was engulfed by Romanticism, German Romanticism became known as *Sturm und Drang*, or "Storm and Stress." This intensity permeated the works of writers such as Schiller and Goethe and led the brothers Jacob and Wilhelm Grimm to collect traditional German fairy tales and myths. This new body of literature prepared the ground for a new kind of German opera. Premiering in 1805, Beethoven's *Fidelio* was the first Singspiel to embrace Romantic humanism. Sung in German, it was nonetheless based on a French play.

## Native lore for German operas

Carl Maria von Weber wrote the first major Romantic German opera, *Der Freischütz*, in which a man enters into a pact with the devil to win the woman he adores. Set in a mythical forest, this Singspiel was replete with hunting, folkloric dancing and singing, supernatural

figures, and a satanic thunderstorm. A huge success, *Der Freischütz* triggered an upsurge of operas based on native sources. Among them was *Hans Heiling* of 1833, by the Hanover-based Heinrich Marschner, whose Singspiel, like Weber's, intertwined folk music with thrilling symphonic music to tell a traditional story of love and supernatural forces. Richard Wagner was just nine when he attended *Der Freischütz*; he, too, fell under its spell.

## Wagnerian opera

German Romantic opera reached its pinnacle with Wagner. Following Prussia's revolutionary period between 1848 and 1849, Wagner melded mythical stories to seamless, powerful symphonic music. New voice types, brilliant and forceful, emerged in the Heldentenor, or "heroic tenor," and the Germanic soprano. Wagner also merged naturalistic stage action and scenery with intense music and heartfelt words, aiming to serve the dramatic essence of the opera or, as he would redefine it, the "total art form," or *Gesamtkunstwerk*. In building a theater north of Munich, the Bayreuth Festspielhaus, Wagner also introduced new ways to stage and attend opera. In an era increasingly bereft of sacred experience, he believed that music dramas should overwhelm audiences with mystical truths. This was unquestionably the approach he took in such masterpieces as *Parsifal*, *Tannhäuser*, *Die Meistersinger von Nürnberg*, and the four-part *Ring* cycle. Such was Wagner's sway that no major composer in his wake remained untouched.

Wagner's rightful heir was arguably the Bavarian Richard Strauss, whose first opera, the 1894 *Guntram*, was thoroughly Wagnerian. Then, with the startling *Salome* in 1905 and *Elektra* in 1909, Strauss stretched tonality far beyond the frontiers Wagner had charted in *Tristan und Isolde*, so that, with this modern approach, he effectively deserted Romantic opera territory. Strauss's operas thereafter continued to range in style, but each explored the rhythms, spoken and poetic, of the German language. Viennese waltzes and Mozartian sound enveloped *Der Rosenkavalier* and *Arabella*, premiered in 1911 and 1933 respectively, while his final work, the 1942 *Capriccio*, recalled even earlier music by Rameau and Gluck. In contrast, after Strauss, German opera took its cue less from Wagner and Mozart than from the 20th century's most avant-garde composers: Arnold Schoenberg and Alban Berg of the so-called Second Viennese School.

◀ **Richard Wagner**, in his signature beret, is pictured in Bayreuth, Germany, amid family members and artists who created his *Ring* cycle of 1876, which premiered in the opera house Wagner had built, the Festspielhaus.

# Ludwig van Beethoven

Born: December 16, 1770, Bonn, Germany • March 26, 1827, Vienna, Austria

No name in music history evokes greater drama or more sublime lyricism than that of Ludwig van Beethoven. Nor has any composer left opera fans so mystified by his limited output, for while his nearly 400 works include symphonies, concertos, ballets, and songs, they boast only one opera: *Fidelio*.

The young Beethoven studied under his father, and at the age of 8 was performing publicly. He then took up the organ and composition under the celebrated Christian Gottlob Neefe. With his first work composed at age 12, Beethoven's talents eventually landed him in Vienna, first in 1787 to meet Mozart,

and again in 1792, to study with Franz Joseph Haydn and Antonio Salieri. The lively Viennese opera scene eventually stirred the composer's interest, and in 1804 he turned to his own opera score. By this time, Beethoven was complaining of hearing problems that would leave him deaf. But even as he struggled to

complete *Fidelio* to his satisfaction, he pursued other opera projects, including a *Macbeth* based on Shakespeare's tragedy. At the end of his life, he was at work on an opera based on *Faust*, the lyrical narrative fiction by Johann Wolfgang von Goethe. Beethoven believed this would be his masterpiece.

### The rescue opera

As a young violist in his native Bonn, Beethoven performed in operas by Mozart and Gluck. But inspiration to compose his own opera came from Luigi Cherubini's *Lodoïska*, a "rescue opera" that riveted Paris before it triumphed in 1802 Vienna. Rescue operas, about an innocent person heroically freed from wrongful captivity by human endeavor, were popular in Paris after the French Revolution. Dialogue advanced these action-packed *opéras comiques*. Because it is spoken as well as sung, *Fidelio* is referred to as a Singspiel.

◀ **The piano** Beethoven used when working at Brunswick Mansion in Martonvásár, Hungary, remains on display.

# Fidelio

Opera in two acts, unknown duration • Composed: 1804–1805 (rev. 1806 and 1814) • First performed: November 20, 1805, Theater an der Wein, Vienna, Austria • Libretto: Joseph Sonnleithner and Georg Friedrich Treitschke, from Jean-Nicolas Bouilly's libretto

First performed in 1805, *Fidelio* was twice revised before the opera was successfully given in 1814. The opera offers a dual challenge to its performers: lead roles require powerful vocalists able to sing over the large German orchestra, but important spoken exchanges favor singers who also shine as actors. *Fidelio* bears Beethoven's unmistakable musical signature and offers glorious music, particularly for the prisoners' chorus at the end of Act I, and Florestan's exquisite aria opening Act II.

## Act I

In the courtyard of the state prison, Marzelline dreams of marrying the new employee, Fidelio. Marzelline's father, Rocco, approves of the match. But "Fidelio" is in fact Leonore, a loving wife disguised as a man to free her wrongfully jailed husband, Florestan. The governor Don Pizarro plots to murder Florestan, and instructs Rocco to dig a grave for him in the prison's dungeon. Leonore is horrified but affirms her "faith in wedded love." She persuades Rocco to defy Pizarro's orders and allow the prisoners to take the air in the courtyard. All prisoners save Florestan emerge to discover light, air, and a taste of liberty ("O welche Lust"). Furious, Pizarro orders the inmates back to their cells.

## Act II

Florestan suffers in his dungeon cell but imagines an angel liberating him ("Gott! Welch Dunkel hier!"). Rocco and "Fidelio" arrive to dig Florestan's grave. But when Pizarro prepares to slay Florestan, "Fidelio" reveals her true identity. The minister Don Fernando, Florestan's old friend, arrives at the last moment to save the day. All prisoners are released, and Don Fernando is amazed to see Florestan, whom he believed long dead. Marzelline is no less surprised to discover that her beloved "Fidelio" is Florestan's wife. Once Pizarro is arrested and led off to be executed, Leonore celebrates the courage love gave her to free her husband.

### PRINCIPAL ROLES

**Don Fernando** *bass-baritone*
Minister

**Don Pizarro** *baritone*
Governor

**Florestan** *tenor* A prisoner

**Leonore (Fidelio)** *soprano*
Florestan's wife

**Rocco** *bass* Jailer

**Marzelline** *soprano*
Rocco's daughter

*Fidelio*'s premiere is among the most disastrous dates in opera history: November 20, 1805, mere days after Napoleon Bonaparte occupied Vienna. Theater patrons had evacuated the city, leaving an audience that consisted mainly of rowdy French officers.

▼ **Set design** by Stéphane Braunschweig and Giorgio Barberio Corsetti suggests freedom beyond imprisonment at Berlin's Staatsoper Unter den Linden in 1995.

# Carl Maria von Weber

Born: November 18, 1786, Eutin, Germany ▪ Died: June 5, 1826, London, England

Carl Maria von Weber catapulted Germanic opera into the new aesthetic of the day: Romanticism. Mozart and Beethoven had already scored operas in German, but Weber also made use of German stories. Fusing the folkloric to the classical, his greatest work, *Der Freischütz*, sent German opera on a path toward Wagner.

Dramatic, intense, colorful—words capturing Weberian opera also describe Weber. He grew up in an itinerant theater troupe led by his father. Musical studies were interrupted as the family decamped for another town. Still, Weber scored his first opera (now lost) in Munich at age 13. In Freiburg, he composed a second, of which fragments survive. *Peter Schmoll und seine Nachbarn* was scored in Salzburg and staged in Augsburg in 1803. Pursuing his craft, he arrived in Vienna, where he was posted to Breslau as the theater's Kappellmeister. Still only 17, Weber began a two-year struggle to reform the theater's repertoire. Then, in a bizarre turn of events, he accidentally drank acid used for engraving scores. Following his recovery, he accepted posts first in Prague and later in Dresden, where he scored the groundbreaking *Der Freischütz*. A commission from Vienna yielded *Euryanthe*, and another from London, *Oberon*. For this last opera, Weber ignored doctor's orders and traveled to London, where he died at the age of 40.

## FIRST PERFORMANCES

- 1803 *Peter Schmoll und seine Nachbarn*
- 1810 *Silvana*
- 1811 *Abu Hassan*
- 1821 *Der Freischütz*
- 1823 *Euryanthe*
- 1826 *Oberon, or The Elf King's Oath*

 **From 1818 to 1824**, the composer summered in Dresden. Weber's former home (left) is now the Carl Maria von Weber Museum, dedicated to his life and work.

# Oberon, or The Elf King's Oath

Romantic opera in three acts, 2 hours • Composed: 1825–1826 • First performed: April 12, 1826, Covent Garden, London, England • Libretto: James Robinson Planché, after the epic poem *Oberon* by Christoph Martin Wieland (1780)

Weber wrote this opera while dying of tuberculosis. His libretto was in English, and based on a poem that drew on characters from Shakespeare's *A Midsummer Night's Dream*. But the opera's story is different. It is framed by a popular overture—with its inaugural horn call, impish woodwinds, and expressive strings—and a "Turkish" finale. Despite its uneven score, the music won plaudits from the likes of Richard Wagner.

## Act I

Oberon, the Elf King, and his wife argue over which is the more loyal gender, and refuse to agree until they meet equally loyal human lovers. Puck, Oberon's servant, has found a potential couple: Sir Huon has been charged by King Charlemagne to travel to Baghdad and seize the Caliph's daughter, Reiza, for his bride. To inspire the pair, Oberon presents a vision of Reiza to Huon and vice versa. Huon lauds love and the glory of combat ("From boyhood trained in battlefield"). Reiza awaits her knight.

## Act II

Under the protection of Oberon's magic horn, Huon storms the Caliph's banquet hall, claiming Reiza and killing her betrothed. As Huon, Reiza, and their two servants escape, Puck conjures elemental spirits to shipwreck their boat. Reiza curses the ocean ("Ocean! Thou mighty monster!") but, spotting a boat, hopes for rescue. Pirates disembark and move to kill Huon, but Reiza throws herself upon him. Both are carried off.

Planché blamed criticism of the libretto on the public, which he said could handle only "Ballads, duets, choruses, and glees, provided they occupy no more than the fewest number of minutes possible."

## Act III

In Tunis, the two servants Sherasmin and Fatima comfort one another. Huon finds them and discovers Reiza is in the Emir's harem. He steals into the harem and resists the temptation of the women. The Emir condemns the intruder. When Reiza begs for Huon's life, she is also condemned to death. Oberon appears, saves them, and praises their mutual fidelity.

### PRINCIPAL ROLES

**Oberon** *tenor* King of the Elves

**Puck** *contralto* His servant

**Sir Huon** *tenor* Duke of Guienne

**Sherasmin** *baritone* His squire

**Reiza** *soprano* The Caliph's daughter

**Fatima** *mezzo-soprano* Reiza's attendant

▶ **In a painting of a scene** from Act II, Huon claims Reiza and slays her betrothed. Weber complained that too much of the libretto's action is spoken rather than sung.

# Der Freischütz

THE FREESHOOTER Romantic opera in three acts, 2½ hours • Composed: 1817–1821 • First performed: June 18, 1821, Schauspielhaus, Berlin
 • Libretto: Johann Friedrich Kind, after the German folk story retold by Johann August Apel and Friedrich Laun in *Gespensterbuch* (1811)

*Der Freischütz*, from a folk song about a man driven to sell his soul for the love of a woman, premiered to immediate success in 1821. It was soon translated into a host of languages, including English, Dutch, French, Hungarian, Polish, and Russian. Weber's intrepid masterpiece captured the diabolical force of human passions and fears. Composers, notably Wagner, were deeply influenced by its German themes and brilliant orchestration. Cosmic struggles—between good and evil, providence and hazard, dreams and reality, love and death—provide the dramatic core of *Der Freischütz*. The work also delivers charming solos, traditional songs, and rousing choruses. But some of its most astounding music, including the overture, is instrumental.

## PRINCIPAL ROLES

**Ottokar** *baritone* Prince of Bohemia

**Kuno** *bass* Head forester

**Kaspar** *bass* First huntsman

**Max** *tenor* Second huntsman

**Kilian** *baritone* Rich villager

**Agathe** *soprano* Daughter to Kuno

**Ännchen** *soprano* Cousin to Agathe

**Eremit (Hermit)** *bass* A religious man of the forest

**Samiel** *speaking part* The Black Huntsman

### Act I

In the forest, Kilian celebrates victory in a shooting match. Kuno, head forester, arrives just in time to prevent violence between Kilian and the jealous huntsman, Max. Kuno warns Max that if he aims to win the hand of his daughter, Agathe, he must succeed in an ancient shooting contest at dawn. Alone, Max bemoans his bad luck ("Durch die Wälder"). But, feigning friendship, the huntsman Kaspar distracts Max with wine-drinking ("Hier im ird'schen Jammertal"). Kaspar, who has sold his soul to the devil, has magic bullets that guarantee success but must be fetched at midnight in the haunted Wolf's Glen. Out of love for Agathe, Max agrees to meet there. Kaspar is thrilled to have ensnared Max ("Schweig,' schweig'!").

### Act II

At home, the lovesick Agathe tells her cousin, Ännchen, that she was warned of danger by the religious hermit living in the forest. Alone, sleepless Agathe admires the night sky and seeks God's protection, until Max's arrival brings joy ("Leise, leise, fromme Weise"). When Max reports that he must venture into the Wolf's Glen, Agathe is terrified. At midnight in the Wolf's Glen, Kaspar seals a bargain with the demonic Samiel: six bullets will hit their marks; the seventh will hit a target of Samiel's choosing. Max discovers Kaspar alone, practicing his dark arts. When a hellish storm erupts, Max calls out for Samiel. The Black Huntsman appears, riveting Kaspar and Max with fear.

### Act III

The next morning, Max and Kaspar have spent six bullets. Max still has the seventh bullet, fated to kill his beloved Agathe. At home in her bridal gown, Agathe believes that God watches over her ("Und ob die Wolke"). She tells Ännchen of her bad dream: that she was a white dove, shot down by Max. All gather in the forest for the wedding feast. At a distance, Kaspar climbs a tree to spy on the party. Max prepares to take his final shot: Ottokar selects a white dove, and Max follows it to a tree with his rifle. He fires just as Agathe rushes toward him, begging him not to shoot. The dove escapes as Agathe and Kaspar fall. Agathe has fainted, but Kaspar, hit by his own magic bullet, dies in agony. Upon confessing his deeds to Ottokar, Max is exiled. But the venerable hermit intervenes: Max's weakness was human and should be forgiven. Ottokar decrees that Max may marry Agathe after a year of virtuous conduct. All join the hermit in prayer, vowing faith in divine providence.

▶ **Like a solid oak tree**, love that stands firm when challenged by storms of doubt, jealousy, and threats emerges stronger for the trial.

▲ **Carola Höhn** sings the role of Agathe at the Staatsoper Unter den Linden in Berlin in 2006.

## A Romantic German opera

*Der Freischütz* marked the arrival of Romantic German opera. Throughout the 19th century, operas by Heinrich Marschner, Richard Wagner, and Engelbert Humperdinck would recall elements that Weber was the first to integrate in his operatic masterpiece. Chief among them were supernatural powers; the dark forest setting; powerful forces of nature, such as the thunderstorm; rural life in the form of hunting or festivities; and folkloric elements.

▶ **A watercolor from the late 1930s** by Nuremberg-based set designer Heinz Grete depicts the hellish world of the Wolf's Glen in the opera's second act.

Satanic storm music for the Wolf's Glen scene that concludes Act II unsettled early audience members. German doctors treating these patients referred to the unique medical condition as *Freischütz fieber* ("Freischütz Fever").

# Richard Wagner

Born: May 22, 1813, Leipzig, Germany ▪ Died: February 13, 1883, Venice, Italy

Richard Wagner pushed opera to unsurpassed heights of musical intensity and revolutionized the entire opera-going experience. Unlike Mozart and Verdi, Wagner took charge of every aspect of his operas. He wrote the librettos, scouted for singers, conducted, and even created a unique opera house. His monumental *Ring* cycle, comprising four operas, holds a place of its own in Western culture.

Wagner was a man of extremes in every aspect of his life, from opera to politics and from theoretical writings to intimate affairs, but above all in his music and its wide-ranging influence. Wagner's strident positions on virtually every subject have also made it difficult to separate personal failings from creative achievements. His biological father was reputedly Ludwig Geyer, his mother's lover and her second husband after Friedrich Wagner. A prominent actor, Geyer sparked the boy's passion for theater and even put him on stage.

Growing up in Dresden, and harboring ambitions to be a playwright, Richard, who then went by the possibly Jewish name Geyer, devoured works by Shakespeare and Goethe. Tellingly, he was at first interested in music for its dramatic uses. Although he had not completed high school, Wagner studied at the University of Leipzig, where he immersed himself in Beethoven. His first opera, *Die Feen*, or *The Fairies*, came at age 20 under the influence of Weber's *Der Freischütz*. He was soon invited to direct regional opera houses, including that of Magdeburg, which premiered his second opera, *Das Liebesverbot*, or *The Ban on Love*, based on Shakespeare's *Measure for Measure*. But it closed on its opening night, when a backstage love triangle resulted in violence.

### Dresden and Minna

Following trying times in Riga and Paris, Wagner welcomed a return to Dresden for the successful 1842 premiere of *Rienzi*. He soon settled there with his actress wife Christine Wilhelmine Planer, known as Minna. *Der fliegende Holländer* premiered in Dresden the following year and, while the opera initially confused audiences

### King Ludwig II of Bavaria

Soon after he was crowned King of Bavaria in 1864 at the age of 18, Ludwig II (1845–1886) became Wagner's patron. Known as the Mad King, Ludwig was, like Wagner, devoted to realizing extravagant dreams. One building project was the fairy tale–like castle, Neuschwanstein (below), which he had decorated with Wagnerian opera scenes. In 1886, Ludwig was declared insane and relieved of his kingly duties. On June 13, he drowned himself. Trying to save him, his doctor drowned as well.

expecting an Italianate work like *Rienzi*, it has since been recognized as the first to convey Wagner's peerless musical signature. A gifted conductor, Wagner was then employed to lead the court opera in Dresden, where his *Tannhäuser* fared better in 1845. *Lohengrin* followed, but by then Wagner's radical politics prevented a production in the court's opera house. In 1848, a new French uprising kindled rebellion in most German territories and, embracing the new ideas, Wagner joined the Dresden uprising of 1849. When the uprising was crushed, Wagner was forced to flee, and some of his comrades were jailed.

▲ **Rhinemaidens in the opening moments** of *Das Rheingold*, staged and lit by Robert Wilson at the Théâtre du Châtelet in Paris, 2005.

## "I write music with an exclamation point!"

RICHARD WAGNER

▶ **Richard Wagner** (center) presents his work to his wife Cosima, her father Franz Liszt, and the German writer Hans von Wolzogen at his Bayreuth home, Wahnfried House, 1882.

### Exile and Mathilde

While in political exile, Wagner was unable to stage his operas in German theaters. Residing in Zurich, he devoted himself instead to conducting, composing, reading the philosopher Arthur Schopenhauer, and writing. Key essays included "The Artwork of the Future," which articulated Wagner's famous idea of opera as a subsuming *Gesamtkunstwerk*, or "total artwork." It pictured music drama as a kind of art able to fuse distinct forms of expression, from poetry, music, and movement to stagecraft and scenery. Under the pseudonym Freigedank, or "Free Thought," he also wrote "Judaism in Music," his infamous attack on Jewish composers; the tract would later endear him to Hitler and Nazi Germany.

At the same time, Wagner mined medieval German and Nordic poetry for opera material to capture his mystical ideas about the power of love and German identity. By 1852, he had completed the libretto for his four-opera cycle *Der Ring des Nibelungen*, and by 1857 he had composed its first two operas—*Das Rheingold* and *Die Walküre*—as well as part of the third, *Siegfried*. But 1857 also brought a wild passion for the married Mathilde Wesendonck, Wagner's adoring muse for the sizzling eroticism coursing through *Tristan und Isolde*. After Minna intercepted a love letter to

Mathilde, Wagner left Zurich. But in 1861, with the German ban on him repealed, he moved from Paris, where he was then based, to Prussia, where he began to score his only comic opera: *Die Meistersinger von Nürnberg*.

### Bavaria and Cosima

The sudden patronage of Bavaria's King Ludwig II brought Wagner to Munich in 1864. Royal support brought relief from debt, and returned Wagnerian opera to the stage after a break of 15 years. In 1865, *Tristan und Isolde* premiered victoriously under the baton of Wagner's friend Hans von Bülow. However, that same year also brought the birth of another Isolde: Wagner's daughter by von Bülow's wife, Cosima. Ensuing scandal caused Ludwig to move Wagner to Switzerland, where the composer inspired and befriended—but later fell out with—the philosopher Friedrich Nietzsche. Although he now lived outside Bavaria, Wagner still fathered two more children with Cosima. When she finally divorced von Bülow, another name was added for a time to Wagner's list of estranged friends: Cosima's father, the composer and conductor Franz Liszt. Wagner married Cosima in 1870 and settled on Bayreuth as the location for the theater he had long envisaged. Residing in

Wahnfried, a Bayreuth villa, and touring widely to raise funds to realize his gigantic plan, Wagner oversaw the construction of the Festspielhaus and completed the final operas of his *Ring* cycle: *Siegfried* and *Götterdämmerung*. Finally, in 1876, 28 years after he had first imagined it, the *Ring* premiered. His last opera, *Parsifal*, was written especially for the Festspielhaus. Following its summer premiere in 1882, Wagner wintered in Venice, where a heart attack ended his life in February 1883. He was buried in the garden at Wahnfried.

▼ **Wagner conducted** Beethoven's Symphony No. 9 at the Margravial Opera House in Bayreuth, Germany on May 22, 1872.

# Der fliegende Holländer

THE FLYING DUTCHMAN *Romantische Oper* in three acts, 2¼ hours ▪ Composed: 1840–1842 (rev. 1846; 1852; 1860) ▪ First performed: January 2, 1843, Hoftheater, Dresden, Germany ▪ Libretto: Richard Wagner

*Der fliegende Holländer* is arguably the opera in which Wagner found his voice. Inspired by the story of a man condemned to sail the seas forever, the opera's Romantic elements include a nocturnal storm, supernatural forces, and tragic love. Act II offers the heroine Senta's ballad and her love duet with the Flying Dutchman. The Norwegian sailors' rousing song, "Steuermann! Lass die Wacht," cheerfully opens Act III. Even greater music comes when the Dutchman's crew delivers a terrifying song in response.

## PRINCIPAL ROLES

**Der Holländer (The Dutchman)** *baritone*
He is doomed to wander

**Daland** *bass* A Norwegian sea captain

**Senta** *soprano*
His daughter, devoted to the Dutchman

**Mary** *mezzo-soprano* Her nurse

**Erik** *tenor* A poor huntsman in love with Senta

**Der Steuermann (The Steersman)** *tenor*

In 1839, Wagner fled debtors' prison in Riga. He escaped across the Russian border at night to board a boat for London. A violent storm held the vessel on Norway's coast. The sounds of the storm served him in this opera.

### Act I
The Norwegian captain Daland and his sailors pause in a violent storm. As they sleep, the Dutchman anchors his own ship and yearns to end his cursed existence: every seven years, he is cast ashore to seek a beloved; when she proves unfaithful, he returns to sea ("Die Frist ist um"). Daland agrees to give his daughter's hand to the Dutchman in exchange for riches.

### Act II
Girls at spinning wheels sing of love in Daland's home. His daughter, Senta, counters with a ballad about the legendary

▼ **In this Berlin Staatsoper Unter den Linden** production of 2001, the opera unfolds as Senta's fantasy of a demon saved by her love.

Flying Dutchman, whom she longs to save. Erik, a man who loves her, warns her that he dreamed she was ensnared by the satanic Dutchman. Her father returns with her betrothed. The Dutchman is smitten by the angelic Senta, and she vows fidelity.

### Act III
Aboard the Norwegian ship, sailors and girls celebrate. But they are terrified by ghostly sailors singing of their unlucky captain aboard the Flying Dutchman's ship ("Johohoe! Johohoe!"). On land, Erik reminds Senta of her former vow to love him. Hearing them, the Dutchman reveals his identity and returns to sea, where his boat sinks. Senta leaps from a cliff to join her beloved, and the lovers' spirits soar into the heavens.

# Tannhäuser

*Grosse romantische Oper* in three acts, 3 hours • Composed: 1843–1845 (rev. 1847–1852, 1861, and 1875) • First performed: Dresden version on October 19, 1845, Hoftheater, Dresden, Germany; Paris version on March 13, 1861, Théâtre Impérial de l'Opéra, Paris, France • Libretto: Richard Wagner

The opera centers around the singers' contest at Wartburg Castle and Tannhäuser's behavior there. Featuring arias, ensembles, and recitatives, it is in the "number opera" form. But the opera also shows Wagner beginning to move toward the through-composed approach that would characterize his subsequent operas. The evocative Act III prelude presents a musical narrative of Tannhäuser's pilgrimage and hints at Wagner's growing interest in continuous music to portray dramatic action.

### Act I

Having spent months in Venus's embrace, Tannhäuser begs his leave. She tries to retain him but shrinks away when he invokes the Virgin Mary. Minstrel knights discover Tannhäuser, but he is reluctant to join them. He only relents when they mention his beloved, Elisabeth.

### Act II

Elisabeth jubilantly greets the Hall of Song ("Dich, teure Halle"). She and Tannhäuser reunite, while Hermann announces that love is the theme of the singers' contest. Wolfram offers an air about the virtue of chastity, and Tannhäuser counters by praising sensual desire. To the audience's horror, he responds similarly to the others' songs. Elisabeth protects him from the mob, and Tannhäuser vows to seek pardon from the pope in Rome.

### Act III

Wolfram observes Elisabeth as she awaits Tannhäuser. Failing to see him among returning pilgrims, she beseeches the Virgin Mary to take her life, and leaves to die at the Wartburg. Wolfram discovers Tannhäuser, who bitterly recounts his travels and the pope's verdict: his staff would sooner flower than he can be absolved ("Hör an, Wolfram, hör an!"). In despair, the former knight calls Venus to receive him. Wolfram frantically advises him to repent and tells him Elisabeth prays for him as an angel in heaven. Tannhäuser, redeemed, falls dead. The pilgrims express awe that the papal staff has bloomed.

> PRINCIPAL ROLES
>
> **Tannhäuser** *tenor* A former minstrel knight
>
> **Elisabeth** *soprano* A chaste princess, his beloved
>
> **Hermann** *bass* Landgrave of Thuringia, her uncle
>
> **Wolfram** *baritone* A minstrel knight
>
> **Walther** *tenor* A minstrel knight
>
> **Venus** *soprano* Goddess of love

Wagner described Wolfram as "a poet and artist," making Dietrich Fischer-Dieskau, the renowned interpreter of German art songs, a perfect fit for the role, and Act III's "Ode to the Evening Star" ideal for his Bayreuth debut in 1954.

▶ **At Bayreuth** in the 1970s, Gwyneth Jones famously sang as both Venus (right) and Elisabeth.

# Lohengrin

*Romantische Oper* in three acts, 3½ hours ▪ Composed: 1845–1848 ▪ First performed: August 28, 1850, Grand Ducal Court Theatre, Weimar, Germany ▪ Libretto: Richard Wagner

*Lohengrin* places supernatural Arthurian romance elements in the historical reign of King Heinrich I of Saxony (876–936) to form a hybrid opera. Characters are sharply etched—the Lady Macbeth-like Ortrud, for example—while the chorus, responding to action as the plot unfolds, often resembles one from Ancient Greek drama. The most frequently played excerpt was always the beloved "Bridal Chorus" ("Treulich geführt,") which opens Act III, although Wagner complained that it lost its dramatic sense when amputated from the opera. *Lohengrin*, shaped throughout by symphonic music, has been interpreted both as an early masterpiece and as a major stepping stone toward Wagner's *Ring* cycle.

### PRINCIPAL ROLES

**Lohengrin** *tenor* Knight of the Grail, son of Parsifal

**Elsa von Brabant** *soprano*
She rejects Friedrich's marriage bid

**Count Friedrich von Telramund** *baritone*
He accuses Elsa of fratricide

**Ortrud** *soprano*
Wife of Count Friedrich, a sorceress

**König Heinrich der Vogler (King Heinrich the Fowler)** *bass* He prepares for war

**Der Heerrufer des Königs (The King's Herald)** *baritone*

Wagner was in political exile in Switzerland when *Lohengrin* premiered in Weimar. He had hoped to be present and even planned to sneak across the border to attend the opera in disguise. Instead, he spent the evening in a pub in Lucerne called The Swan.

▲ **The swan is ever present in folklore**, from Greek mythology, where Zeus assumes its form to seduce Leda, to the German fairy tale where a swan averts being shot by revealing she is a princess.

### Act I

On a river bank, König Heinrich unifies his people to defend Germany. But discord surrounds Count Friedrich, who accuses Elsa von Brabant of murdering her brother. He adds that when she also rejected his marriage bid, he married Ortrud instead. Summoned, Elsa says that a certain knight will be her champion ("Einsam in trüben Tagen"). The king calls for combat before God to settle the murder accusation. All marvel when a glorious knight arrives on a boat led by a swan. Elsa agrees to the knight's terms: if he wins, she must marry him, but never inquire about his identity. The knight vanquishes Friedrich, and spares his life. All but Friedrich and Ortrud rejoice.

### Act II

In Antwerp's fortress, the court celebrates. Outside, the resentful Ortrud persuades Friedrich to seek revenge ("Der Rache Werk sei nun beschworen"). When Elsa steps onto a balcony to confess her joy to the evening breezes, Ortrud cunningly elicits her pity. In a moment of privacy, Ortrud relishes her scheme ("Entweihte Götter!"). Ortrud warns Elsa not to trust the knight. But Elsa feels sorry for Ortrud, who lacks faith in trust. In the morning, the king's herald proclaims the knight "Protector of Brabant." Elsa arrives in her wedding procession, but Ortrud interferes, accusing the knight of sorcery. When the king and knight parade by, Friedrich calls out for the knight to reveal his name. The knight refuses to tell him, and notes Elsa's trembling. Ortrud and Friedrich savor her distress. The couple enter the Minster to be married.

## Act III

The wedding party blesses the couple in the bridal chamber. Alone, they celebrate their love ("Das süsse Lied verhallt"). But Elsa, troubled by doubt, asks the knight to reveal his name. Friedrich suddenly attacks, but falls to the knight. The knight instructs Elsa to go to join the king. On the riverbank, Heinrich greets warriors preparing to be led by the knight in shining armor, and is surprised to see Elsa. The knight arrives. He presents Friedrich's body, and accuses his wife of breaking her vow. He reveals that he is Lohengrin, son of Parsifal. As a knight of the Grail, he may serve the world, but must return to the Grail's seat at Monsalvat if his identity is discovered ("In fernem Land"). As all bitterly despair at the loss of their hero, the swan and boat reappear ("Mein lieber Schwan!"). Ortrud boasts that her magic transformed Elsa's brother into the swan. Lohengrin prays, then rejoices when a dove arrives in response. Removing a chain from the swan, he transforms the bird back into Elsa's brother, Gottfried. Lohengrin's boat, led now by the dove, departs. Calling out to her husband, Elsa dies in her brother Gottfried's arms.

▼ **Tenor Jonas Kaufmann** played the title role for the Bayerische Staatsoper at the Nationaltheater, Munich. The production was directed by Richard Jones as part of the Munich Opera Festival of 2009.

### Premiere of 1850

Wagner was composing *Lohengrin* when Europe was rocked by France's 1848 Revolution. He had hoped to premiere the opera in Dresden. But following his participation in the Dresden uprising of 1849, his works were banned in German principalities. From Zurich, where he was living in exile, Wagner petitioned his friend and fellow composer—conductor Franz Liszt (right), who finally succeeded in arranging a premiere in Weimar. *Lohengrin* was given there in 1850, with Liszt relying on Wagner's notes to lead the orchestra.

# Tristan und Isolde

TRISTAN AND ISOLDE *Handlung* in three acts, 3¾ hours • Composed: 1856–1859 • First performed: June 10, 1865, Königliches Hof-und Nationaltheater, Munich, Bavaria , Germany • Libretto: Richard Wagner

*Tristan und Isolde* is about romantic love so transcendent that it may only achieve perfection in the eternity of death. This tragic tale had been told in the 13th century by Gottfried von Strassburg, whose *Tristan* inspired the composer to set aside the *Ring* cycle. Wagner had been engrossed in Arthur Schopenhauer's writings about sexual desire and death, the opera's key subjects. But, like Tristan, he was also in love with a forbidden woman. Mathilde Wesendonck was the married muse for Wagner's expression of erotic love too great for the physical world to contain. Striking harmonic textures seem to make the lovers' suffering ache with beauty. And by testing the absolute limits of tonality, the opera was a crucial step toward atonal modern operas.

## PRINCIPAL ROLES

**Marke** *bass* King of Cornwall

**Tristan** *tenor* His nephew, a knight

**Kurwenal** *baritone* Tristan's loyal companion

**Isolde** *soprano* Irish princess, and a sorceress

**Brangäne** *mezzo-soprano* She attends on Isolde

**Melot** *tenor* A courtier who betrays Tristan

**Shepherd** *tenor*

▶ **The storyline** of Wagner's *Tristan und Isolde* is based on a popular romance of medieval Celtic origin.

In 1857–1858, Wagner set five poems by Mathilde Wesendonck for female voice and piano. One of the *Wesendonck Songs*, *Träume* (*Dreams*), spawned music that Wagner used for Act II of *Tristan und Isolde*.

### Act I

Aboard Tristan's ship, Isolde rages. They love each other, but Tristan is obliged to ignore her as he escorts her to Cornwall to marry his uncle, King Marke. Isolde's attendant, Brangäne, appeals to Tristan, whose companion, Kurwenal, insists that Lord Tristan is not in Isolde's thrall. And yet, Isolde's fury mounts as she recalls Tristan's debt to her: he first came to Ireland on the verge of death, wounded by the Irish Lord Morold. Isolde was duty-bound to slay Tristan, who had killed Morold, but instead she saved him ("Wie lachend sie mir Lieder singen"). Suicidal, Isolde asks Brangäne to fetch a death potion. Her gaze then meets Tristan's. When she seeks vengeance for the death of Morold, to whom she was betrothed, Tristan offers her his sword and invites her to slay him. In response to his request, Isolde gives Tristan a drink of "reconciliation." Both quaff the potion. Then, expecting to die, they instead embrace in passionate love ("Wie sich die Herzen wogend erheben!"). As the boat moors, Brangäne reveals to Isolde that she replaced the death potion with an elixir of love. In despair, Isolde falls unconscious.

### Act II

As night descends in the garden of Cornwall's castle, Brangäne warns Isolde against Tristan's "friend" Melot, who is hunting with King Marke. But Isolde asks Brangäne to beckon Tristan by putting out the torchlight. Reunited, Tristan and Isolde wish for an oblivion in which they may love forever, released from the world ("O sink hernieder, Nacht der Liebe"). Brangäne warns that daylight approaches. But Tristan assures Isolde that their love is unconquerable, even by death. When Brangäne again warns them, the lovers hope for an eternal night ("O ew'ge Nacht, süsse Nacht!"). Returning from the hunt to discover the lovers, Marke is devastated, and Melot is exposed as a traitor. Tristan challenges Melot, then lowers his sword as Melot strikes him.

### Act III

Tristan lies near death at his family castle in Brittany. He is awakened by the music of a shepherd's reed pipe. Kurwenal assures Tristan that he will heal in his old home.

## "Impossible" roles

*Tristan und Isolde* was to premiere in Vienna in 1861, but was canceled after 77 rehearsals left Wagner defeated. Indeed, the title roles are among the most physically taxing of the repertoire, and were musically unlike anything heard at the time. Finally, in 1865, the husband and wife singers Ludwig and Malwine Schnorr von Carolsfeld created Tristan and Isolde (below). Ludwig gave four legendary performances, only to die a month later. Some accused the monstrous opera role of killing its Heldentenor (a strong-voiced tenor playing a heroic role).

But Tristan corrects his friend to insist that he awakens in a mysterious place and longs for death. Kurwenal explains that Isolde has been summoned to heal him. Tristan senses her ship approaching. The boat indeed arrives, sending Tristan into a blissful delirium ("O diese Sonne!"). Isolde appears. Tristan rises and goes to her, only to die in her arms. A second ship brings Marke, Melot, and Brangäne, who has told Marke of the love potion. Kurwenal slays Melot. Marke laments; he had intended for Tristan and Isolde to marry. But Isolde cannot hear him; she is enraptured by the love she shared with Tristan ("Mild und leise wie er lächelt"). Isolde, as if exalted, sinks onto Tristan's corpse. Finally, Marke blesses the lovers' bodies.

▶ **At the Opéra Bastille** in 2005, Peter Sellars staged characters before immense videos by Bill Viola to engulf audiences in Wagner's majestic music.

# Die Meistersinger von Nürnberg

**THE MASTERSINGERS OF NUREMBERG** Music drama in three acts, 4¼ hours • Composed: 1862–1864; 1866–1867 • First performed: June 21, 1868, Königliches Hof-und Nationaltheater, Munich, Bavaria, Germany • Libretto: Richard Wagner

*Die Meistersinger von Nürnberg*, Wagner's only comical opera, was written during a pause in the composition of the *Ring* cycle. It is unique among Wagner's mature operas for including a string of standalone numbers. These are built into Wagner's libretto, the only one for which the composer invented an original storyline. A goldsmith's daughter and a knight fall in love, but may not marry until they have navigated their way through the esoteric world of Nuremberg's Mastersingers. The opera belongs to Hans Sachs, a lovable cobbler, inspired poet, and wise Mastersinger. Folksy and funny, the opera offers great entertainment, then shifts gear to conclude with a paean to German culture.

## PRINCIPAL ROLES

### MASTERSINGERS

**Hans Sachs** *bass* A cobbler

**Veit Pogner** *bass* A goldsmith

**Sixtus Beckmesser** *baritone* Town clerk

**Fritz Kothner** *bass* A baker

**Walther von Stolzing** *tenor*
A young Franconian knight

**Eva** *soprano* Daughter of Veit Pogner

**Magdalene** *mezzo-soprano* Her nurse

**David** *tenor* Apprentice to Hans Sachs

*Die Meistersinger von Nürnberg*, Hitler's favorite opera, was used to enliven Nazi Party congresses in Nuremberg. In Berlin, in 1995, director Götz Friedrich succeeded with a risky production set in post-war Nuremberg.

### Act I

Walther von Stolzing, a knight newly arrived in Nuremberg, has fallen for the goldsmith's daughter, Eva, who returns his love. In church, Walther learns that Eva's hand in marriage will be the prize of a Mastersinger contest the next day, and he suddenly wishes to become a Master in order to compete. David, apprentice to the Mastersinger and cobbler Hans Sachs, outlines for Walther the bewildering basics of the art form ("Der Meister Tön' und Weisen"). As their Song School commences in the church, fellow Masters are introduced to Walther by Pogner, Eva's father. Sachs is welcoming, but Beckmesser frowns on Walther's inclusion, and Kothner eagerly consults the guild's rule book. Walther sings rapturously of spring's arrival while Beckmesser interrupts and, as the marker of errors, notes many faults. Sachs tries to defend Walther's song while others attack it ("Halt, Meister! Nicht so geeilt!"). Amid the rude commotion, Walther completes his song and departs angrily.

### Act II

On the eve of the contest, Eva learns that her beloved Walther failed to impress the Masters. In his workshop, Sachs ponders Walther's sweet singing ("Was duftet doch der Flieder"). When Eva discovers that Beckmesser intends to serenade her that night, she proposes that her nurse Magdalene appear in her place. Walther persuades Eva to elope with him. As they run down an alley, they are forced to hide. Beckmesser comes up the alley

 **Robert Dean Smith** (left) played Walther to Jan-Hendrik Rootering's Hans Sachs in Graham Vick's production at the Royal Opera House, London, in 2002.

with his lute to serenade "Eva," in fact Magdalene. Walther and Eva observe as Sachs disrupts Beckmesser's music by hammering loudly over it. Neighbors are awakened, while David, who loves Magdalene, explodes in jealousy only to knock the lute from Beckmesser's grip. A fight breaks out. A Night Watchman finally returns quiet to the streets.

## Act III

On the day of the competition, Walther reports a dream and Sachs notes it down as poetry. Beckmesser, delighted by prospects of winning Eva with poetry by the great Sachs, pockets the lyrics and limps off, still sore from the previous night's events. Walther praises Eva in a song. When Sachs calls it a Master melody, Eva rejoices ("Selig, wie die Sonne meines Glückes lacht"). Guilds parade into a meadow for the festival. Sachs greets the townspeople and praises art, while Beckmesser sweats over the lyrics he has yet to memorize. A strange performance is given by Beckmesser, the first to compete ("Morgen ich leuchte in rosigem Schein"). But Walther's singing dazzles everyone ("Morgenlich leuchtend im rosigen Schein"). Eva then crowns Walther the winner, and Sachs welcomes him among the Mastersingers, the keepers of "a holy German art."

▼ **Allied bombs destroyed** the Berlin Staatsoper, which reopened with *Die Meistersinger* in 1955. Harry Kupfer's 2005 staging (below) marked the event 50 years later.

### Hans Sachs

In about 1520, the Lutheran cobbler Hans Sachs became a Mastersinger in Nuremberg, home to one of the region's famously strict Song Schools that traced their origins to refined medieval courts. Creating thousands of Master Songs, Sachs gained popularity in his lifetime. The writer J. W. von Goethe rediscovered Sachs' works, and in 1776 paid tribute to the cobbler-poet in a poem that inspired Albert Lortzing's opera of 1840, *Hans Sachs*, and Wagner's *Die Meistersinger von Nürnberg*.

# Der Ring des Nibelungen

THE NIBELUNG'S RING Richard Wagner's *Der Ring des Nibelungen* encompasses four operas: *Das Rheingold*, *Die Walküre*, *Siegfried*, and *Götterdämmerung*. The cycle was intended for presentation over four consecutive evenings. Wagner labored for 28 years to complete the *Ring*, which requires more than 15 hours to perform and is arguably the greatest single operatic work of all time. In 1876, it premiered in Bayreuth at the Festspielhaus, and has since been given around the world.

## The *Ring*: from idea to opera

France's 1848 Revolution sparked the *Ring* cycle. Following events in France, Wagner began to picture a "theater of Revolution," portraying the dramatic upheaval of established orders. He was also absorbed in the traditional literature favored by Romantic thinkers and artists of his day. His mystical political visions and fecund imagination were galvanized as he read the Norse myths recounted in the *Eitr* and other Scandinavian narratives, such as the *Völsunga Saga*; the German folklore and mythical tales collected and published by the Brothers Grimm; and *Das Nibelungenlied*, a major medieval German epic. By 1848, Wagner had already written "Siegfried's Death," the text for a heroic opera to express his new-found passions. Captivated by the hero, he wove Siegfried's story into a web of themes and threads suggestive of a cosmos unto itself. He then set out to create that world. He peopled it with his own mix of Germanic heroes and gods who would, in the end, be engulfed in sacrificial, revolutionary flames. Wagner began composing the preliminary opera in 1853, and finished the final one only in 1874. King Ludwig II of Bavaria, Wagner's patron, provided financial and political backing for the *Ring* premiere of 1876. Wagner also raised funds for the project, but the first Festival at Bayreuth proved a financial disaster.

## Motifs in the *Ring*

The *Ring* forms its own musical and dramatic world. Among its innovations is the use of some 200 musical themes known as "motifs." Wagner tied these to characters, objects, and ideas, which evolve as the operas unfold. For example, the motif for the sword called Nothung takes the sharp and gleaming shape of the weapon, while that of the character Hunding rumbles with crude foreboding to announce his disposition and his place in the cycle's story. Even used for less tangible matters, such as the curse placed on the Ring, motifs are subtly deployed to look forwards or backwards to the moments when they are most strikingly expressed. They are introduced, altered, expanded, and interwoven to shape storied layers of evocative musical textures.

### THE ROLES IN THE *RING* CYCLE

The *Ring* evokes mythic proportions but is built around surprisingly few soloists, who appear in clear groupings. Its story pits love against power and greed, with love ultimately proving to be the greatest force of all. Major roles include Wotan, Brünnhilde, Siegfried, and the Nibelung Alberich.

**Rhinemaidens** Seductive nymphs of the river Rhine; **Woglinde, Wellgunde, Flosshilde**

**Nibelungs** Gnomes of Nibelheim, a subterranean realm; **Alberich, Mime, Hagen**

**Giants** Builders of Valhalla, the fortress of the gods; **Fasolt, Fafner** (in *Siegfried*, Fafner appears as a dragon)

**Gods** Residents of Valhalla; they are doomed to perish; **Wotan** (disguised as "the Wanderer" in *Siegfried*), **Fricka, Loge, Freia, Donner, Froh, Erda**

**Wälsungs** Descendants of Wälse, a pseudonym for Wotan; **Siegmund, Sieglinde, Siegfried**

**Valkyries** Chaste warriors, daughters of Wotan; **Brünnhilde, Gerhilde, Ortlinde, Waltraute, Schwertleite, Helmwige, Siegrune, Grimgerde, Rossweisse**

**Norns** Daughters of Erda who spin fates on golden rope; **First Norn, Second Norn, Third Norn**

**Gibichungs** Royals residing in a palace near the Rhine; **Gunther, Gutrune**

**Others** Hunding, Woodbird

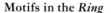

◀ **Siegfried slays the dragon** Fafner in this mural in Ludwig II's famous Neuschwanstein Castle in Germany.

▶ **"The Death of Siegfried,"** a theme from Germanic lore, inspired countless works of art. It was Wagner's starting point for what was to become the *Ring* cycle.

## Possessors of the magic Ring

The Nibelung Alberich forswears love to win the Ring from the Rhinemaidens. The Ring, which is called the Nibelung's even though Alberich stole it, brings its owner limitless riches and power. But in the opening opera, Alberich puts a curse on the Ring: anyone other than himself who touches it, and is aware of its magic, is doomed. In the final opera, Brünnhilde sacrifices herself to remove the curse, and the Ring ends up where it began: in the Rhine River, to be guarded by the seductive Rhinemaidens.

| DAS RHEINGOLD | DIE WALKÜRE | SIEGFRIED | GÖTTERDÄMMERUNG |

1. The Rhinemaidens
3. Wotan, lord of the gods
6. Fafner, now a dragon
9. Siegfried
10. Brünnhilde

2. Alberich, a Nibelung
4. Fasolt, a Giant
5. Fafner, his brother
Remains with Fafner
7. Siegfried, a Wälsung
8. Brünnhilde, Siegfried's wife
11. The Rhinemaidens

# Das Rheingold

THE RHINEGOLD In one act, 2½ hours • Composed: 1853–1854 • First performed: September 22, 1869, Königliches Hof-und Nationaltheater, Munich, Bavaria, Germany • Libretto: Richard Wagner

*Das Rheingold*, the first of four operas forming Wagner's *Ring* cycle, is subtitled A *Preliminary Evening*. This opera was written to set the stage for the trilogy of operas to follow on subsequent evenings: *Die Walküre*, *Siegfried*, and *Götterdämmerung*. Even before the curtain rises, the music pulls the audience into a mystical realm populated by gods and otherworldly creatures. Scene three is set below the earth, in Nibelheim, the domain of the Nibelungs, or gnomes. The opera is about one of them, Alberich, who upsets the cosmic balance of the world by stealing the magic gold of the Rhine River. Highlights abound in the opera's fourth and final scene, which includes the fantastic solo of the god Donner as he unleashes thunderbolts.

## PRINCIPAL ROLES

**Wotan (Odin)** *high bass* Lord of the gods

**Loge** *tenor* The wily god of fire

**Freia** *high soprano* The goddess of love and beauty

**Erda** *contralto* The primeval mother

**Donner** *high bass* God of strength

**Alberich** *high bass* Lord of the Nibelungs

**Mime** *tenor*
His brother, a smith who forges a magic helmet

**Fasolt** *high bass;* **Fafner** *low bass*
Giants, they built Valhalla for Wotan

**Woglinde** *high soprano;* **Wellgunde** *high soprano;*
**Flosshilde** *low soprano* Rhinemaidens

### Scene I
Three sensuous nymphs frolic in the Rhine as they guard the river's precious gold. Alberich, a Nibelung, emerges from a chasm and lusts after them. The nymphs reject him, but explain that whoever wears a ring made from the Rhine's gold possesses absolute wealth and power; to take the gold, one must forswear love. Alberich curses love, seizes the gold, and escapes.

### Scene II
Below a mountain top fortress, the goddess Fricka complains to her husband, Wotan: he has promised her sister Freia, goddess of beauty, to the Giants in exchange for building his fortress. Wotan insists that he

▶ In the *Ring* production of 1976 in Bayreuth, directed by Patrice Chéreau and designed by Richard Peduzzi, the Rhine "river" took the form of a hydroelectric dam.

will not give them Freia. The Giants Fasolt and Fafner arrive, seeking Freia. The god Loge reports that Alberich has stolen the Rhinegold. Fasolt seizes Freia, and refuses to return her unless the Rhinegold is handed to the Giants by evening. The Giants depart with Freia, whose absence spells death for the gods. Wotan and Loge resolve to recover the Rhinegold from the Nibelung.

### Scene III
In a subterranean cavern, Alberich tests the Tarnhelm, a magic helmet forged by his brother, Mime; it renders him invisible. Alberich departs. Mime tells Wotan and Loge that Alberich terrorizes the Nibelungs with a ring made of the Rhinegold. Loge promises freedom. Alberich forces the Nibelungs to pile up gold, and boasts that he will rule the world. Loge tricks Alberich into transforming himself into a toad. Loge and Wotan capture Alberich and climb up from the depths of the earth.

### Scene IV
Wotan receives the Nibelung treasure in exchange for Alberich's release. Alberich whispers a spell into the Ring. When Wotan takes the Ring, Alberich warns that it will bring death, then disappears. The Giants arrive with Freia. Wotan gives them the treasure and

◀ **For the 1876 premiere** of the *Ring* in Bayreuth, a special contraption with hand-maneuvered dollies and poles was constructed to provide the illusion that the Rhinemaidens were swimming in the river.

helmet, but not the Ring. Erda, mother of the gods, rises from below to command the Ring's surrender ("Wie alles war, weiss ich"). Freia is returned. Fasolt grabs the Ring but is clubbed by Fafner, who takes the Ring. Wotan notes the power of the Ring's curse. Donner climbs a peak to make a thunderstorm ("Heda! Heda! Hedo!"). During the storm, Fafner hauls off his treasure. When a rainbow bridge appears, Wotan invites Fricka to step along it to the hall of the gods, Valhalla ("Abendlich strahlt der Sonne Auge"). The gods follow, save Loge. In the valley, the Rhinemaidens lament the lost Rhinegold ("Rheingold! Rheingold!").

The opera begins with a chord in E flat, which continues for 136 bars. Wagner noted that the pitch and drone-like effect, meant to capture the unceasing flow of the Rhine River, came to him as he was half asleep.

### An opera house ahead of its time

The Bayreuth Festspielhaus, which was inaugurated in 1876 with the first *Ring* cycle, was a theater unlike any built before it. The orchestra pit (below) was sunken and concealed from the audience so that music seemed to emerge organically from the staged drama. Breaking further with tradition, Wagner eliminated hierarchical loges and boxes in which the wealthy had long enjoyed privileged sight lines and acoustics in theaters. In the democratic Festspielhaus, all could view and hear the opera equally. But perhaps Wagner's most radical step was the

least architectural: he was the first to darken the house in order to direct audience attention to the only source of light: the stage. And with no aisles between seats, audiences were prevented from circulating during performances. Through these simple yet striking innovations, those attending the opera were to be absorbed not in mere entertainment, but in a mystical, even sacred, event.

# Die Walküre

THE VALKYRIE In three acts, 3¾ hours ▪ Composed: 1856–1857; 1864–1865; 1869–1871 ▪ First performed: June 26, 1870, Königliches Hof-und Nationaltheater, Munich, Bavaria, Germany ▪ Libretto: Richard Wagner (written 1851–1852)

*Die Walküre*, the second opera of Wagner's *Ring* cycle, follows *Das Rheingold* and precedes *Siegfried* and *Götterdämmerung*. In productions of the *Ring*, audiences often prefer *Die Walküre* to other operas in the cycle. It introduces many of Wagner's most memorable motifs, or musical themes. The most famous is for the extraordinary Valkyries, immortal female warriors. But as with all Wagner operas, love is the main subject. Act I is about the passionate yet forbidden romance between a brother and sister. Their offspring, Siegfried, is the subject of the next opera in the *Ring* cycle. Act III deals with Wotan's tragic love for his disobedient Valkyrie daughter, Brünnhilde.

## PRINCIPAL ROLES

**Brünnhilde** *soprano*
A Valkyrie, Wotan's favorite daughter

**Gerhilde, Ortlinde, Waltraute, Schwertleite, Helmwige, Siegrune, Grimgerde, Rossweisse** *sopranos and contraltos*
Valkyrie daughters of Wotan

**Wotan (Odin)** *high bass* Lord of the gods

**Fricka** *mezzo-soprano* His wife

**Siegmund** *tenor*
A Wälsung separated from his twin in infancy

**Sieglinde** *soprano* His twin sister

**Hunding** *bass* Husband to Sieglinde

### Act I
Fleeing attackers in a storm, a man takes refuge in a hut. Sieglinde discovers him in her hut, and they fall in love. Her husband, Hunding, arrives. The guest explains that, as a baby, he was separated from his twin. Recognizing the visitor as his kin's enemy, Hunding warns that they must fight to the death come daylight. Alone with the man, Sieglinde informs him of a sword hidden there. They embrace, and Siegmund celebrates their union ("Winterstürme wichen dem Wonnemond"). Realizing that he is her twin, Sieglinde tells him his name: Siegmund. He retrieves the sword and names it "Nothung." Sieglinde throws herself into his arms as he calls her sister and wife.

### Act II
In the mountains, Wotan orders his Valkyrie daughter Brünnhilde to protect his mortal son Siegmund, who must retrieve the Ring from the Giant Fafner.

▶ **Hildegard Behrens**, a Brünnhilde legend, sang the role at the Metropolitan Opera in 1986.

Wotan's wife, Fricka, argues that Siegmund will fail because the magic sword prevents him from acting freely. Wotan finally agrees. He tells Brünnhilde the story of the Ring and how, having touched it, he is cursed to forswear love. Wotan orders her to ensure that Siegmund falls to Hunding in their battle. Sieglinde urges Siegmund to flee without her. When he refuses, she sleeps in his arms. Brünnhilde warns Siegmund of his death ("Siegmund! Sieh auf mich!"), but then, moved by his devotion to Sieglinde, vows to protect him. Yet, during the battle, Wotan uses his divine spear to shatter Siegmund's sword, Nothung. Hunding slays Siegmund, Brünnhilde sweeps Sieglinde away on horseback, and Wotan kills Hunding.

### Act III
In the mountains, Valkyries collect slain battle heroes who will gain new life serving the gods in their fortress, Valhalla ("Hojotoho! Hojotoho!"). Fleeing Wotan's rage, Brünnhilde arrives with Sieglinde. To save Sieglinde, Brünnhilde directs her to the east, where Fafner hoards the Ring, and where Wotan will not follow. She gives the pregnant Sieglinde fragments of Nothung, for her future son. Wotan delivers his punishment to Brünnhilde: banishment, and a sleep that will last until a man claims her. Brünnhilde pleads fruitlessly that she acted for love, and to express Wotan's deepest wishes. She asks for her body to be ringed in fire so that only a courageous man may win her. Wotan tenderly bids her farewell ("Leb' wohl, du kühnes, herrliches Kind!"). He encircles his daughter in a wall of magic fire, and decrees that no one who fears his spear will ever penetrate its flames.

"The Ride of the Valkyries," which opens Act III, can produce strong responses, even outside the opera house. It tops Britain's Royal Automobile Club's list of the most dangerous music to play while driving.

▼ **Jonas Kaufmann** plays Siegmund to Eva-Maria Westbroek's Sieglinde in Robert Lepage's production at the Metropolitan Opera, New York in 2011.

### Heroic vocalists

The singers who created principal roles in the 1876 premiere of the *Ring* were nearly as heroic as the characters they depicted. The remarkable German soprano Amalie Materna (right) sang Brünnhilde in each of the operas in which the favorite Valkyrie appears: *Die Walküre, Siegfried, and Götterdämmerung*. Today, lead singers are given rest days between performances, but Materna took on the notoriously demanding role in three different operas over three consecutive evenings. Albert Niemann was the celebrated Heldentenor who interpreted Siegmund in *Die Walküre*. He hoped to create the character of Siegfried in the *Ring* cycle's final two operas, but Wagner felt that Niemann's voice and bearing were too mature to portray the younger, friskier hero. Instead, the part went to tenor Georg Unger, who had also sung Froh in *Das Rheingold* for the Bayreuth premiere. The entire cycle was conducted by the Hungarian Hans Richter.

# Siegfried

In three acts, 4¼ hours ▪ Composed: 1856–1857; 1864–1865; 1869–1871 ▪ First performed: August 16, 1876, Festspielhaus, Bayreuth, Bavaria, Germany ▪ Libretto: Richard Wagner (written 1851–1852)

*Siegfried*, the third opera in Wagner's *Ring* cycle, is preceded by *Das Rheingold* and *Die Walküre*, and followed by *Götterdämmerung*. *Die Walküre* ended with the pregnant heroine Sieglinde fleeing into the woods, and with the Valkyrie Brünnhilde condemned to sleep in a ring of fire until rescued. This opera skips ahead: Sieglinde's child is now a young man, Siegfried. Since Sieglinde died in childbirth, Siegfried was raised by a Nibelung, Mime. Siegfried is defiant, boastful, and even arrogant. But these are not negative traits. Instead, they reflect his unconquerable nature and innate heroism. Act III features exceptional music, when Wotan as "the Wanderer" bares his soul to the goddess Erda, and when Siegfried and Brünnhilde fall in love.

## PRINCIPAL ROLES

**Wotan (Odin)** *bass* Lord of the gods, he travels as "the Wanderer"

**Erda** *contralto* Primeval goddess of wisdom

**Brünnhilde** *soprano* Daughter of Wotan and Erda

**Siegfried** *tenor*
Grandson of Wotan, he wins the Ring

**Mime** *tenor* A Nibelung, he raised Siegfried and hopes to seize the Ring

**Alberich** *bass*
His brother, who aims to regain the Ring

**Fafner** *bass*
In the form of a dragon, he hoards the Ring

**Woodbird** *soprano* A bird who guides Siegfried

▶ **Wieland Wagner**, the composer's grandson, revolutionized Bayreuth's *Ring* stagings in the 1950s, including this 1951 production of *Siegfried*.

After composing Act II in 1857, Wagner dropped the opera in order to devote himself to *Tristan und Isolde*. When he returned to *Siegfried* years later, his style had evolved. Act III therefore sounds unlike the earlier acts.

### Act I
Before his cave in the woods, Mime, a Nibelung blacksmith, schemes: if his foster child Siegfried could wield the sword Nothung to slay the dragon Fafner, Mime could take the Ring from the dragon's cave. Mime informs Siegfried that his mother was Sieglinde, and that Nothung was his father's sword. Alone, Mime fails to repair the shattered sword. Wotan, disguised as "the Wanderer," informs him that it must be forged by a man who has never known fear. When Siegfried hopes to learn about fear, Mime explains that Fafner

can teach him. Siegfried joyously forges his father's sword on an anvil ("Nothung! Nothung! Neidliches Schwert!"). The task completed, he celebrates by using Nothung to sever the anvil.

## Act II

At night, near Fafner's cave, the Nibelung Alberich awaits a chance to grab the Ring. Wotan also observes. By daylight, Mime deposits Siegfried there. Lonely and hoping to communicate with a bird, Siegfried blows his horn. This awakens Fafner, whom Siegfried first mocks then slays with his sword. An accidental taste of dragon blood allows Siegfried to understand the bird, who instructs him to fetch the Ring and a helmet, the magic Tarnhelm, from Fafner's treasures. Since Siegfried can also hear Mime's unspoken plans to decapitate him, he slays the Nibelung. The bird informs Siegfried of a sleeping maid: if he walks through a ring of fire, he can make her his bride. The bird leads him to Brünnhilde, Wotan's daughter.

## Act III

By a cave at the base of a mountain, "the Wanderer" awakens the earth goddess Erda, Brünnhilde's mother ("Wache, Wala! Wala! Erwach!"). When she has no wisdom to offer, he urges her to envision his downfall: he will now yield power to his mortal son, the redeeming Siegfried. He encounters Siegfried, armed with Nothung, and warns that his spear has broken the sword before. Happy to meet his father's enemy, Siegfried destroys Wotan's spear with his sword. Lightning strikes, and Siegfried is plunged into a sea of fire.

Brünnhilde is asleep under a tree, where Siegfried discovers her. He kisses her, and she awakens joyfully ("Heil dir, Sonne!"). She instantly falls in love, but hesitates upon recalling her vows of chastity for the purity of Valhalla, fortress of the gods. Siegfried urges her to wake up her spirit, too, and accept his love. Finally, Brünnhilde blissfully accepts love and bids Valhalla goodbye ("Fahr' hin, Walhall's, leuchtende Welt!").

▲ **Walther Kirchhoff** was one of many prewar Heldentenors who portrayed the character of Siegfried in realistic stagings.

## The 1876 *Ring* premiere in Bayreuth

The *Ring* premiere of 1876 was a momentous occasion. It inaugurated Wagner's singular opera house in Bayreuth, the Festspielhaus, and offered music theater of unprecedented scope and depth: a sequence of four operas whose interlinked musical and mythical elements formed an independent aesthetic sphere. The cycle was given three times over the course of a festival initiated in high pomp on August 13. For the opening ceremony, Emperor Kaiser Wilhelm led a full royal cortege. Notable festival guests included the composer Tchaikovsky and the philosopher Friedrich Nietzsche. On stage, audiences beheld naturalistic stage decor realized from artwork by the Viennese landscape painter Josef Hoffmann. Special effects included flying Valkyries in full medieval battle garb. Deemed a major work of art, the *Ring* was also a major expense. So much so that the cycle was not staged again in Bayreuth's Festspielhaus until 1896.

▲ **Wagner and Liszt** meet Kaiser Wilhelm I at the opening of the Festspielhaus in Bayreuth.

# Götterdämmerung

THE TWILIGHT OF THE GODS Prologue and three acts, 4¼ hours ▪ Composed: 1869–1874 ▪ First performed: August 17, 1876, Festspielhaus, Bayreuth, Bavaria, Germany ▪ Libretto: Richard Wagner (written 1848–1852)

*Götterdämmerung* completes Wagner's *Ring* cycle. It follows *Das Rheingold*, *Die Walküre*, and *Siegfried*, which ended with Siegfried and Brünnhilde falling in love. In *Götterdämmerung*, they live in a forest cavern, until Siegfried leaves to seek heroic adventures. The opera introduces Hagen, whose fanatical desire to win the Ring sets in motion the cycle's tragic conclusion. Also new are Hagen's half-brother, King Gunther, and Gunther's sister Gutrune, both pawns in Hagen's plot. Unlike the other *Ring* operas, this one employs a chorus, for which Wagner scored mainly rousing but also solemn passages. Highlights include Act III's "Funeral March" and Brünnhilde's final solo.

## PRINCIPAL ROLES

**First Norn, Second Norn, Third Norn** *soprano*
Spinners of fate

**Siegfried** *tenor* Grandson of the god Wotan

**Brünnhilde** *soprano* His wife, formerly a Valkyrie

**Gunther** *high baritone* King of the Gibichungs

**Gutrune** *soprano* His sister

**Waltraute** *mezzo-soprano*
A Valkyrie, Brünnhilde's sister

**Woglinde** *soprano*; **Wellgunde** *soprano*;
**Flosshilde** *contralto* Rhinemaidens

**Hagen** *bass* A Nibelung

**Alberich** *bass* Hagen's father

### Prologue
The three Norns, who spin gold into fate, foresee the twilight of the gods. But when their rope of destiny is severed, they vanish forever. Brünnhilde bids her beloved Siegfried farewell before their cave dwelling ("Zu neuen Taten, teurer Helde"). Before he departs to gain glory, they exchange love tokens: he gives her the Ring he won upon slaying the dragon Fafner, and she gives him her horse, Grane.

### Act I
In a palace on the Rhine, Hagen advises his half-brother, King Gunther, to marry the wondrous Brünnhilde, who is guarded by a wall of fire. Hagen believes that Siegfried can win her, and a love potion could then secure Siegfried for Gunther's sister, Gutrune. Siegfried arrives and drinks the potion. He falls in love with Gutrune and forgets Brünnhilde. In a ritual pact, Siegfried vows to seize Brünnhilde for Gunther. Hagen watches Siegfried depart on his mission ("Hier sitz' ich zur Wacht"). At home, Brünnhilde receives her Valkyrie sister, Waltraute, but rejects her

request to save the gods by surrendering the Ring, which Siegfried gave her. Using his magic helmet to resemble Gunther, Siegfried arrives at dusk. He grabs the Ring from Brünnhilde and forces her into the cave, where they sleep chastely on either side of his sword.

### Act II
Asleep by the Rhine, Hagen hears his Nibelung father, Alberich, urging him to own the Ring. At dawn, Siegfried returns to Gutrune. When Gunther arrives with Brünnhilde, she goes unrecognized by Siegfried. Noticing the Ring on Siegfried's finger, Brünnhilde accuses him of betrayal. But Siegfried vows loyalty to Gunther, and denies being Brünnhilde's husband. Apart, Hagen persuades Brünnhilde and Gunther that Siegfried must die. Brünnhilde reluctantly joins the dual marriage procession with Gunther.

### Act III
While out hunting, Siegfried meets the Rhinemaidens, who warn of his imminent death. Found by Gunther and Hagen, Siegfried recounts his youth to them.

## The *Ring* cycle after Wagner

The *Ring*'s premiere in 1876 was so costly that it was not given again until 1896, when Bayreuth was headed by the composer's widow, Cosima Wagner. After World War II, their grandsons Wieland and Wolfgang Wagner (right) changed the course of the cycle's production history by supplanting realism with abstraction. But the most legendary production since Wagner's day was arguably the 1976 centennial *Ring* directed by Patrice Chéreau. Costuming gods in Edwardian suits, he imbued the cycle with modern resonances. While some directors have preserved traditional Wagnerian staging, others have brought fresh visions of the work. A notable 21st-century example is by Robert Wilson, whose minimalist *Ring* for Zurich and Paris employed radical lighting effects to explore the themes of darkness and illumination. Wagner's *Ring* is considered difficult, even intimidating, to stage, yet it is produced with increasing frequency on opera stages around the world.

After Hagen's latest potion reminds Siegfried of Brünnhilde ("Brünnhilde! Heilige Braut!"), Hagen slays Siegfried. Aggrieved, Gunther and his men return Siegfried's body to the palace. There,

▼ **Robert Wilson used color** to weave visual motifs in his staging of *Götterdämmerung* at the Théâtre du Châtelet, Paris, France, in January 2006.

hoping to take the Ring from Siegfried's finger, Hagen slays Gunther. However, Brünnhilde captures the Ring and, to cleanse it of the curse, she wears it as she sacrifices herself in Siegfried's funeral pyre ("Starke Scheite schichtet mir dort"). The Rhinemaidens recover the Ring and drown Hagen. As foretold, flames consume the gods and their celestial fortress, Valhalla.

In the final scene, Brünnhilde rides her horse, Grane, into the flames of Siegfried's funeral pyre. For the Bayreuth premiere of 1876, Grane was played by King Ludwig II of Bavaria's black stallion, Cocotte.

**▲ The German mezzo-soprano**
Waltraud Meier is famous for her fierce yet sympathetic Kundry. Others celebrated in the role include Martha Mödl, Christa Ludwig, and Olive Fremstad.

*Parsifal* has produced vehement reactions. In his 1887 *On the Genealogy of Morals*, Wagner's former friend Friedrich Nietzsche attacked its Christianity and moralizing, qualities that invited Nazi praise in the 1930s.

# Parsifal

*Bühnenweihfestspiel* in three acts, 4–4½ hours ▪ Composed: 1877–1882 ▪ First performed: July 26, 1882, Festspielhaus, Bayreuth, Bavaria, Germany ▪ Libretto: Richard Wagner

*Parsifal*, Wagner's final opera, has troubled some scholars with its depiction of religious fervor, purity of caste, and women as sexually depraved heathens. More frequently, audiences and conductors rank it as Wagner's most exquisite opera. It creates a mysterious effect in which, as one Grail knight puts it, "time becomes space." Medieval romance, Buddhism, Christianity, and philosophy inform a sacred operatic idiom built of ceremonial tableaux. Indeed, the opera's structure resembles a ladder into divine rapture. Compassion translates states of agony or sin into sources of redemption and salvation, and the final scene is lifted by glorious harp music.

## Act I

The knight Gurnemanz awakens at Monsalvat to prepare a bath for the suffering Amfortas. The angry magician Klingsor has stolen Monsalvat's Holy Spear and used it to pierce Amfortas's side. Gurnemanz recalls a prophecy: "an innocent fool enlightened through compassion" will save Amfortas. When a "sacred swan" falls dead, its killer, a young man (Parsifal), is presented to Gurnemanz. The man, unaware of his own identity, is shocked when Kundry, a pagan woman, knows his past. Gurnemanz escorts him into the hall, where Grail knights parade ceremonially. In torment, Amfortas laments serving as the Grail's sinful guardian ("Nein! Lass ihn unhenthüllt!"). The knights take communion, while the visitor marvels at the power of pity and love. Amfortas's wound reopens. The guest is moved but, when he fails to articulate what he feels, Gurnemanz ejects him.

### Wolfram von Eschenbach

A major poet of the German Middle Ages, Wolfram von Eschenbach wrote *Parzival* around 1200. It was a lively epic narrative recounting the adventures of a foolish man whose sufferings bring wisdom and the honor of guarding the Holy Grail. In playful and rhythmic poetry, Wolfram was the first to bring the Grail theme from French into German literature. Wagner portrayed the poet in his opera *Tannhäuser*.

▶ **Medieval** illumination of Wolfram's *Parzival*.

## Act II

Klingsor conjures Kundry. She is enraged to be cursed to seduce knights, even though the one who spurns her will remove the curse. A man marvels at Flower Maidens in the castle's magic garden ("Hier war das Tosen!"), but he rejects their tantalizing advances. Kundry surprises him by calling him Parsifal, as his mother did; she claims that his mother died of sorrow over him. Compassion for Amfortas floods the aggrieved Parsifal ("Amfortas! Die Wunde! Die Wunde!"). Resisting Kundry's sexual advances, he encourages her to receive Grace. Her erotic energy rises as she tries anew to lure him ("So war es mein Kuss"). Finally, she curses him and releases him to Klingsor. The magician hurls the Holy Spear at Parsifal. When it hovers over him, Parsifal grasps it from the air to form the sign of the Cross. The castle sinks into quaking earth, and Kundry collapses screaming as Parsifal departs.

## Act III

Gurnemanz, more aged than before, emerges from a hut at Monsalvat. He discovers Kundry lifeless, but soon revives her. He then notes a knight in black armor, improperly outfitted for a Good Friday. Questioned, the man thrusts the Holy Spear into the ground; he disarms and removes his helmet. Gurnemanz is astonished to behold Parsifal, who says he brings salvation for Amfortas ("Nur eine Waffe taugt"). Gurnemanz anoints Parsifal with holy water, while Kundry washes his feet. Parsifal baptizes a weeping Kundry. Hailed the King of Knights by Gurnemanz, Parsifal gazes serenely at blossoming Nature. In the hall, knights bear Amfortas on his litter, and the body of his father,

## PRINCIPAL ROLES

**Titurel** *bass* Founder of the Knights of the Grail

**Amfortas** *baritone*
His son, tainted guardian of the Grail

**Gurnemanz** *bass* An elderly Knight of the Grail

**Parsifal** *tenor* An "innocent fool"

**Klingsor** *bass* A vengeful magician

**Kundry** *soprano*
A heathen healer, cursed to be a seductress

▲ **Plácido Domingo's Parsifal**, seen here at the Metropolitan Opera in New York in 1992, is among the great tenor's noted Wagner roles.

Titurel, in a coffin. They also carry the Grail shrine. Displaying his wound, Amfortas begs the knights to take his life. Parsifal presents the Holy Spear. Miraculously healed, Amfortas staggers in ecstasy. A white dove hovers over Parsifal's head as Kundry and others kneel before him.

# J. Strauss the Younger

Born: October 25, 1825, Vienna, Austria • Died: June 3, 1899, Vienna, Austria

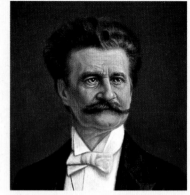

The Waltz King of Vienna was meant to become a banker. But he defied the wishes of his father, composer Johann Strauss the Elder, and in 1845 took up musical studies. In 1863, he was appointed Royal Court Ball Music Director under Emperor Franz Joseph I. French operettas by Jacques Offenbach were then all the rage in Vienna, and Strauss found that the light form, combining speech and self-contained songs, was ideally suited to his effervescent music. He scored more than a dozen operettas, beginning with *Indigo und die vierzig Raüber*, for which he created the immortal "Blue Danube" waltz. But none would rival *Die Fledermaus* for enchanting music and indestructible popularity.

# Die Fledermaus

THE BAT *Comic operetta* in three acts, 2¼ hours ▪ Composed: 1873–1874 ▪ First performed: April 5, 1874, Theater an der Wien, Vienna, Austria ▪ Libretto: Karl Haffner and Richard Genée, after the French play *Le réveillon* (1872), by Henri Meilhac and Ludovic Halévy

*Die Fledermaus*, now held to be the quintessential Viennese operetta, premiered in 1874 to no special enthusiasm. Yet, within a few years, it gained enormous popularity in German-language opera houses, and by the end of the century achieved the international success it has enjoyed since. Its plot was taken from a satirical French comedy by Jacques Offenbach's librettists, but Strauss's work treats the story with a lighter and sweeter touch that would come to define Vienna's "Golden Age" operetta. Endearing pranks drive the action forward, and the cast of lovable schemers delights audiences. Throughout, richly orchestrated music sounds weightless and free from artifice. There are memorable solo vocal parts, but the consistent showstoppers are ensembles, where Strauss's vocal music is just as refined and sparkling as the champagne that flows so copiously in Act II.

## PRINCIPAL ROLES

**Gabriel von Eisenstein** *tenor*
Husband to Rosalinde

**Rosalinde von Eisenstein** *soprano*
Wife to Gabriel

**Alfred** *tenor*
A singing teacher in love with Rosalinde

**Dr. Falke** *baritone* Gabriel's doctor

**Frank** *baritone* Prison warden

**Prince Orlofsky** *mezzo-soprano*
Bored, wealthy Russian prince

**Adele** *soprano* Rosalinde's maid

◀ **Bass-baritone Angelo Gobbato** parties as Frank, the prison warden, in the Cape Town Opera's 2004 production in South Africa.

### Act I

An irresistible tenor named Alfred serenades Rosalinde in the street below her home. Inside, her maid Adele, eager to attend Prince Orlofsky's masked ball, requests the night off, but her timing is bad: Rosalinde's husband is about to serve a jail sentence. Alfred urges Rosalinde to receive him that evening while her husband, Gabriel von Eisenstein, is in prison. Eisenstein returns home in a fury with his inept lawyer, Dr. Blind. His doctor, Falke, proposes a "healthful" plan: delay jail until 6 am, and instead attend Orlofsky's party disguised as "Marquis Renard." Rosalinde grants Adele the night off, while Eisenstein (heading to the party) and Rosalinde (awaiting Alfred) feign separation anxiety ("So muss allein ich bleiben"). Alfred is drinking copiously at Rosalinde's, when Warden Frank arrives to fetch his prisoner. Rosalinde persuades him that Alfred is Eisenstein, and, pleased to be taken for "Rosalinde's husband," Alfred is carted off to jail.

### Act II

Prince Orlofsky receives his disguised guests ("Ich lade gern mir Gäste ein"). Falke confides in the prince that amusement is in store: the "Marquis" (Eisenstein) flirts with a "Hungarian countess" (Rosalinde), who pockets his fancy watch as a love token before delivering a Hungarian song "from her country" ("Klänge der Heimat!"). Falke explains his nickname, Dr. Bat: after a night of masked partying, the "Marquis" left him to pass out in his bat costume. Falke was ridiculed the next day as he made his way home and now hopes to avenge himself with a practical joke on the Marquis. Orlofsky proposes a champagne toast, and the revelers waltz ("Im Feuerstrom der Reben"). As the clock strikes six, Eisenstein rushes off to the jailhouse.

### Act III

Frosch, a drunk jailer, copes with the hyperactive tenor mistaken for Eisenstein, and Frank, the warden, wakes with a hangover in his prison office. The "Marquis" arrives to learn "Eisenstein" was arrested dining with his wife. Posing as their lawyer, Eisenstein counsels Alfred and Rosalinde and, appalled by details of their tryst, finally unmasks. Yet, when Rosalinde produces his watch, he is suitably humiliated. Falke reveals his prank—"the Bat's revenge"—to all who have gathered at the prison ("O Fledermaus, o Fledermaus"). Eisenstein learns that everyone was in on the joke from the outset, although in an aside Alfred leaves some doubt about just how much of his seduction was merely staged. Blame for any misconduct is placed on "King Champagne."

For the 2001 festival in Salzburg, Austria, director Hans Neuenfels turned waltzing revelers into orgiastic cocaine fiends. Many Strauss fans were offended, and one audience member even sued the Salzburg Festival.

# Franz Lehár

Born: April 30, 1870, Komrom, Hungary • Died: October 24, 1948, Bad Ischl, Austria

Franz Lehár, master of the 20th-century operetta, composed 38 operatic works that premiered in an era of European turbulence, from 1893 to 1938. The most enduring of these, the 1905 work *Die lustige Witwe*, was also the first to win Lehár international renown. Later works, including *Das Land des Lächelns*, enjoy periodic revivals.

Franz Lehár learned violin and piano from his father, a military bandmaster. Franz senior's frequent postings exposed young Franz to a wide variety of music all over Central Europe. His first composition, a song, came at age 11, and a year later he studied music in Prague. By age 20, Lehár proudly served as the youngest-ever military bandmaster of the Austro-Hungarian Empire; German Emperor Wilhelm II decorated him for his conducting in 1894. Operetta scores soon followed, as did new postings. In Vienna, the empire's capital, the 29-year-old Lehár composed for grand ceremonial parades and concerts, and by 1902 was known Europe-wide as creator of the much-loved "Gold and Silver Waltz." After his masterpiece, *Die lustige Witwe*, Lehár had little success until the charismatic star-tenor Richard Tauber attracted attention to Lehár's operettas of the 1920s. Later, *Die lustige Witwe* was touted as Hitler's favorite operetta but Lehár's marriage to a Jewish woman meant his life in Austria under Nazi rule was troubled.

### FIRST PERFORMANCES

- 1893 *Rodrigo*
- 1896 *Kukuška*
- 1905 *Die lustige Witwe*
- 1909 *Der Graf von Luxemburg*
- 1910 *Zigeunerliebe*
- 1925 *Paganini*
- 1927 *Der Zarewitsch*
- 1928 *Friederike*
- 1929 *Das Land des Lächelns*
- 1934 *Giuditta*

◀ **Bandmaster Lehár** leading the 26th Hungarian Infantry Regiment band in Vienna in 1900.

# Die lustige Witwe

THE MERRY WIDOW *Operetta* in two acts, 2½ hours ▪ Composed: 1905 ▪ First performed: December 30, 1905, Theater an der Wien, Vienna, Austria ▪ Libretto: Viktor Léon and Leo Stein, from Henri Meilhac's 1861 play *L'attaché d'ambassade*

*Die lustige Witwe* premiered triumphantly in 1905, and soon shattered attendance records well beyond Europe. Lehár had concocted just the right musical cocktail for the day: one part shimmering imperial festivity in the old Viennese style, to one part warm nostalgia. With the new century, audiences craved the idea of a sweeter, less troubled era. Little could compete with such heart-grabbers as the "Lippen schweigen" waltz in Act II of *Die lustige Witwe*.

## Act I

Baron Zeta, Ambassador from Pontevedro, honors his sovereign's birthday with a gala. The arrival of newly widowed, hugely wealthy compatriot Hanna Glawari stirs eligible bachelors. For the benefit of "the Fatherland," Zeta wants Hanna's wealth to remain in Pontevedro and urges countryman Danilo to woo her. By chance, Danilo was Hanna's first love, but his aristocratic family had rejected her, a mere commoner. Danilo, fond of can-can dancers and dinners at Maxim's, shows no interest in Hanna. The ambassador's wife, Valencienne, quietly nudges Camille de Roussillon in the widow's direction, even though he has fallen for Valencienne.

## Act II

The following day, Hanna entertains in high Pontevedrian style in her garden, recounting the story of Vilja, a forest sprite, and flirting with Danilo ("Vilja, o Vilja"). As they dance, Danilo's old feelings for Hanna return. Meanwhile, Camille insists on a kiss, which Valencienne will only give him in the garden pavilion. Baron Zeta is alerted. By the time he and Danilo check the pavilion, Hanna has replaced his wife. Zeta is relieved. And when Danilo departs for Maxim's in a jealous rage, Hanna knows he loves her. At Hanna's home, can-can girls celebrate flirting on the boulevards of Paris. Hanna explains her pavilion trick to Danilo, and differences are mended by a romantic waltz. The Baron is reassured of his wife's fidelity. In a finale, all agree that women are difficult to understand.

> **PRINCIPAL ROLES**
>
> **Baron Zeta** *tenor*
> Ambassador to France from Pontevedro*
>
> **Valencienne** *soprano*
> Wife of the Baron
>
> **Count Danilo Danilowitsch** *tenor*
> Lazy playboy from Pontevedro*
>
> **Camille de Roussillon** *tenor*
> In love with Valencienne
>
> **Hanna Glawari** *soprano*
> Rich young widow from Pontevedro*
>
> * A fictional Balkan country

Mania for *Die lustige Witwe* swept the New World in 1907: more than 5,000 performances were given in the United States; in Buenos Aires, Argentina, the operetta was staged in five theaters at the same time.

▶ **The legendary Australian** soprano Joan Sutherland sings the title role at the San Francisco Opera, 1981.

# Richard Strauss

Born: June 11 ,1864, Munich, Bavaria, Germany • Died: September 8, 1949, Garmisch-Partenkirchen, Bavaria, Germany

Richard Strauss is often described as the last German Romantic composer. But his operatic influences cannot be relegated to any one style. Strauss composed 15 operas, and they range from the astonishing and dissonant *Salome*, arguably the first modern opera, to his waltz-studded homage to Mozart, *Der Rosenkavalier*.

▲ **American soprano Renée Fleming** appears at London's Royal Opera House in 2000 as the incomparable Marschallin in *Der Rosenkavalier*, the most popular opera Richard Strauss created with librettist Hugo von Hofmannsthal.

Richard Strauss has earned a peerless place in opera history. In 1905, his intensely modern *Salome* broke all rules dear to Romantic opera. But, beginning with *Der Rosenkavalier* in 1911, many Strauss operas were profoundly Romantic. And by the time of his final opera, *Capriccio*, in 1942, Strauss was drawn to the earlier music of Rameau and Gluck. Many have tried to explain why Strauss would abandon the avant-garde for less innovative, even nostalgic approaches to opera. Interestingly, though, no matter how his music is classified, Strauss is now viewed as perhaps the most important opera composer of the 20th century, with the only other viable contender being Benjamin Britten.

Like many innovators, Strauss was sharply criticized, but he never doubted his own talent. Some of his success can be attributed to the remarkable synergies he found working with poet-playwright Hugo von Hofmannsthal. The young librettist's approach was dense, symbolic, and reflective. He preferred story lines of primordial drama and philosophical depth, even as Strauss pressed him for lighter material. They could easily have been incompatible; instead they created opera magic.

## A child prodigy

Like his revered Mozart, Strauss was a child prodigy. His father played horn for the Bavarian Court Orchestra in Munich, where Strauss first composed at age four. At five, he was scoring songs. Orchestral works and chamber pieces were soon to follow, and his Symphony No. 1 was performed when he was 16. Strauss lived for music; he composed his Violin Concerto during a mathematics class that bored him, and left school with nearly 150 completed works. At age 20, he led an orchestra in the premiere of his first major

commission, sparking a meteoric career that would take him to top conducting posts in Munich, Berlin, and Vienna. He also conducted his first opera, the Wagnerian *Guntram*, in 1894. Although his father had disliked Wagner, Strauss eventually embraced him as a major influence alongside Mozart. Still, while *Guntram* was a critical failure, it brought Strauss personal success: its principal soprano, Pauline de Ahna, became his devoted, lifelong wife. A turn in his career came in 1905 with the shocking *Salome*. Based on the play by Oscar Wilde, it was variously censored and canceled. But, with its daring story, new symphonic sound, and dazzling vocal parts, it galvanized opera houses wherever it was staged.

A second atonal opera followed in 1909: *Elektra*, the first fruit of Strauss's legendary collaboration with Hofmannsthal. No pair

### Strauss sopranos

Strauss's distinctive scoring for soprano voices has produced specialized "Strauss sopranos." In operas and other works, the voices of Strauss sopranos seem to soar on divine ribbons of breath lifted further by the orchestra. In the composer's day, these rare vocalists included his wife, Pauline de Ahna, and Lotte Lehmann, who sang nine lead Strauss roles. Later specialists include Lisa Della Casa, Renée Fleming, Jessye Norman, Maria Reining, Elisabeth Schwarzkopf, Cheryl Studer, and Deborah Voigt.

▶ **Lotte Lehmann**, one of Strauss's favorite sopranos, as the Marschallin in his opera *Der Rosenkavalier*.

## FIRST PERFORMANCES

- 1894 *Guntram*
- 1901 *Feuersnot*
- 1905 *Salome*
- 1909 *Elektra*
- 1911 *Der Rosenkavalier*
- 1916 *Ariadne auf Naxos*
- 1919 *Die Frau ohne Schatten*
- 1924 *Intermezzo*
- 1928 *Die ägyptische Helena*
- 1933 *Arabella*
- 1935 *Die schweigsame Frau*
- 1938 *Daphne*
- 1942 *Capriccio*
- 1952 *Die Liebe der Danae* (composed 1937–1940)

> "I have always paid the greatest possible attention to natural diction."

RICHARD STRAUSS

▲ **Richard Strauss**, seated at the piano, is joined by cast and crew members of a silent film adaptation of *Der Rosenkavalier*, released in 1926. It was accompanied by recorded music scored by Strauss for the project.

had been so perfectly matched in opera history since Lorenzo da Ponte fired Mozart's imagination in 1780s Vienna. Indeed, they inspired pioneering works: *Der Rosenkavalier* was the first and *Arabella* was the last Mozartian Strauss opera. Between these came *Ariadne auf Naxos*, in which Mozartian and Wagnerian spirits are said to vie for Strauss's musical soul, and *Die Frau ohne Schatten*, again echoing Mozart. Strauss then penned his own conversational libretto for *Intermezzo*, based on everyday exchanges in his home. *Die ägyptische Helena* followed, its Homeric libretto by Hofmannsthal. Strauss described the opera as "Greek Wagner." July 1929 then brought double tragedy: minutes before the funeral for Hofmannsthal's son Franz, who had died by suicide, the librettist suffered a stroke and died.

In 1932, Strauss began working with Austrian librettist Stefan Zweig on *Die schweigsame Frau*. Books by "the Jew Zweig" were soon publicly burned in Munich. Nazi Germany's annexation of Austria in 1934 occurred while Zweig was visiting London; he never returned home. When *Die schweigsame Frau* premiered in Dresden in 1935, Zweig's name was omitted from the program until Strauss, then head of the music department in the Nazi Ministry of Propaganda, intervened. But a letter

from Strauss to Zweig was intercepted and presented to Hitler. Its anti-Nazi tone forced Strauss to resign from his post. In 1941, he moved his family from Bavaria to Vienna. Once there, Strauss used his sway and influence as a cultural icon to shield his Jewish daughter-in-law and grandchildren from persecution, or worse.

### The war years

Zweig, meanwhile, worked behind the scenes revising Josef Gregor's librettos for Strauss's *Friedenstag*, an antiwar opera, and *Daphne*, based on Greek myth. Then, in 1942, Zweig and his wife, now émigrés in Brazil, both took their own lives by taking poison. *Capriccio*, whose story had been Zweig's idea, premiered that year. This, Strauss's last opera, held audience attention in Munich until the opera house was bombed by Allied forces in 1943. Following Germany's defeat in 1945, Strauss took shelter in Switzerland, fearing punishment for his earlier associations with

the Nazis. After the Allied Denazification Board cleared his name in 1948, he returned to his home in Bavaria a few months before his death in 1949. In 1952, at the Salzburg Festival that Strauss had helped create, *Die Liebe der Danae* premiered posthumously. A "cheerful mythology in three acts," its libretto had been sketched by Hofmannsthal in 1920. Allied air raids, and then postwar politics, prevented an earlier premiere, although Strauss had attended a wartime reading of the work in Salzburg in 1944, on his 80th birthday. Always vying with the dominant musical trends during his lifetime, Strauss came to be seen as the greatest opera composer of the first half of the 20th century.

# Salome

Drama in one act, 1¾ hours · Composed: 1904–1905 · First performed: December 9, 1905, Königliches Opernhaus, Dresden, Saxony, Germany · Libretto: Richard Strauss, from Oscar Wilde's play *Salomé* (1893)

The opening night of *Salome* in Dresden brought 38 curtain calls but mixed reactions from the critics. Today, *Salome* stands as a masterpiece, and is arguably the first modern opera. It delves into linked obsessions—Herod's with Salome; Salome's with Jokanaan; and Jokanaan's with God. By turns illustrating and probing the libretto, the orchestra produces exquisite effects, notably in the string section, where Strauss called for new bowing and fingering techniques. Cruelty, perversion, and fixation pervade this work, much as moonlight bathes the palace terrace where its action is set. But however troubling its themes, the opera's velvety, high-tension music grips audiences. And interpretations of Salome and Herod are rarely forgotten.

## PRINCIPAL ROLES

**Herod** *tenor* King of Judea

**Herodias** *mezzo-soprano* Lover to Herod

**Salome** *soprano* Herodias's daughter

**Jokanaan (John the Baptist)** *baritone*
Prophet and prisoner

**Narraboth** *tenor*
Young Syrian captain of the guard

Others: **Nazarenes** view Jokanaan as a prophet of the Messiah, but **Jews** bitterly disagree

▲ **The title page** of a score from 1905 Berlin offering piano and vocal parts for a scene from Strauss's opera *Salome*, created in that year.

Herod arranged his brother's murder because he was in love with his brother's wife, Herodias. Now Herod craves her young daughter, Salome. But the popular prophet Jokanaan (John the Baptist) predicts the ruin of Herod's court. Herod has imprisoned him, forbidding Narraboth, captain of the prison guard, to release him. As the opera begins, Herod celebrates his birthday within his palace. From a moonlit terrace, Narraboth is captivated by Salome's beauty. As she escapes Herod's lustful staring, a voice holds her spellbound. It is the imprisoned Jokanaan, who invokes the Messiah and curses Herodias. Salome persuades Narraboth to defy orders and fetch the prisoner. Jokanaan appears ("Wo ist sie, die den Hauptleuten Assyriens sich gab?"). Salome is first repulsed, then magnetized ("Jokanaan! Ich bin verliebt in deinen Leib").

### Lust and death

As Salome lusts for Jokanaan, in despair, Narraboth stabs himself and dies. The prophet rejects Salome's advances, urging her to seek the Lord's forgiveness. But she fixates on his mouth, pleading for a kiss. Jokanaan is returned to his cell in a cistern, swearing Salome is cursed. Salome also swears: that she will kiss his mouth. Herod bursts onto the terrace and attempts to lure Salome. Herodias begs Herod to hand over the prisoner to the Jews, but Herod refuses to endanger the "holy man." A group of Jews argues that Jokanaan is no prophet ("In Wahrheit weiss niemand"), but the Nazarenes disagree, reminding all of the Messiah's miracles. Herod frets to learn that this man is able to raise the dead, and asks where he is. A Nazarene offers unsettling

### Dance of the Seven Veils

"But when Herod's birthday was kept, the daughter of Herodias danced before them, and pleased Herod" *The Gospel According to St. Matthew* (14.6). The first Salome, Marie Wittich, refused to perform the Dance of the Seven Veils. "I won't do it. I'm a decent woman," Strauss recalled her objecting. A ballerina served as the soprano's body double. Many Salomes have since yielded the scene to a dancer, but intrepid performers, such as Ljuba Welitsch (right), show off their seduction skills in the famous dance.

news: he is everywhere. With new force, the voice from below terrifies Herodias with warnings. Herod begs Salome to dance for him. In exchange, he promises her anything she wishes. Ignoring her mother's objections, Salome dances the Dance of the Seven Veils. Delighted, Herod asks what Salome desires. She wants Jokanaan's head, on a silver platter. Herod offers her anything else he has ("Ah! Du willst nicht auf mich hören"). But Salome insists. "Let her have what she asks for," Herod finally consents. Salome listens for Jokanaan's cries ("Es ist kein Laut zu vernehmen") and is tortured to hear no suffering. When the head is delivered, Herod recoils; Herodias is pleased; and the Nazarenes kneel to pray.

Triumphantly, Salome kisses Jokanaan's mouth ("Ah! Du wolltest mich nicht deinen Mund küssen lassen"). As Herod departs, a black cloud hides the moon. In darkness, Salome notes the bitter taste of Jokanaan's mouth, "perhaps the taste of love." Suddenly, with Salome flooded in light, Herod commands her death. Soldiers rush forward and crush her with their shields.

▲ **Salome (Karita Mattila)** yearns to kiss the mouth of the decapitated Jokanaan in a production directed by Lev Dodin at the Opéra Bastille, Paris, in 2003.

The opera was to be given in Vienna under the baton of Gustav Mahler, but the Catholic Archbishop deemed it immoral. He was not alone. In London, the opera was banned until 1910. And in New York in 1907, *Salome* was canceled after only one performance at the Met due to pressure from its patron J. P. Morgan.

# Elektra

ELECTRA Tragedy in one act, 1¾ hours ▪ Composed: 1906–1908 ▪ First performed: January 25, 1909, Königliches Opernhaus, Dresden, Saxony, Germany ▪ Libretto: Hugo von Hofmannsthal, based on his play *Elektra* (1903), after the tragedy *Electra* by Sophocles, 5th century BCE

*Elektra* is an opera of raw and startling emotions. Strauss was reluctant to compose it so soon after the disturbing *Salome*. But Hugo von Hofmannsthal, initiating their legendary collaboration, encouraged him to set the libretto. Primeval desires for wrongs to be righted propel the unforgiving action of this dissonant opera, as shocking today as it was in 1909. Elektra, a gigantic and riveting role, attracts dramatic sopranos of huge stamina.

## PRINCIPAL ROLES

**Elektra** *soprano*
Daughter to Klytämnestra and slain Agamemnon

**Klytämnestra** *mezzo-soprano*
Mother to Elektra

**Chrysothemis** *soprano*
Younger sister to Elektra

**Orest** *baritone*
Brother to Elektra

**Aegisth** *tenor* Lover to Klytämnestra

Alone, Elektra invokes her father, slain by her mother ("Agamemnon! Agamemnon! Wo bist du, Vater?"). Asking for his help, she promises to dance before his tomb when his murder has been avenged. Elektra seeks allies in her quest for revenge, but her sister Chrysothemis would rather live normally, and not be entwined in vengeance. Their mother, Klytämnestra, burdened by horrid nightmares, asks Elektra what ritual sacrifice will purge her of them. She is terrified when Elektra names

Klytämnestra herself as the sacrificial victim. Elektra wonders why her mother's shock turns to frenzied laughter upon receiving a message, then refuses to believe the news: that her brother, Orest, is dead. Elektra proceeds with her plan. Like a beast, she digs the ground, searching for the buried hatchet used to slay her father. A man arrives, and tension mounts until Elektra recognizes Orest ("Was willst du, fremder Mensch?"). She hears her mother's screams within the palace, and rejoices that Orest has begun to avenge their father. Orest then kills his mother's lover, Aegisth. The palace erupts: some celebrate vengeance; others grieve for the victims. As she promised her father, Elektra dances "a dance without name." When her dance reaches its apex, she dies.

Strauss found an ingenious way to conjure the spirit of Agamemnon, slain by his wife and avenged by his daughter, Elektra: in the opening bars, the orchestra alone heaves up the sound of the name "Ag-a-mem-non."

◀ **Deborah Polaski** (seen here at the Royal Opera, London, in 1997) has sung Elektra more than 300 times, filling the gap left by Birgit Nilsson and Astrid Varnay.

# Der Rosenkavalier

THE KNIGHT OF THE ROSE Comedy for music in three acts, 3¼ hours ▪ Composed: 1909–1910 ▪ First performed: January 26, 1911, Königliches Operhaus, Dresden, Saxony, Germany ▪ Libretto: Hugo von Hofmannsthal

*Der Rosenkavalier* has enthralled audiences since its 1911 premiere. Sensuous symphonic music manages to exude fizzier Viennese pleasures, from prank-playing to waltzing. Strauss's librettist, Hugo von Hofmannsthal, concocted a Mozartian story of modern yet timeless sensibilities. The poetry of his libretto inspired extraordinary music. Indeed, the vocal trio toward the end of Act III is held by many to be among the most exquisite vocal ensembles in opera.

## Act I
The Marschallin breakfasts with Count Octavian, her lover. When Baron Ochs surprises them, Octavian is rapidly disguised as a maid, "Mariandel." Ochs seeks someone to present the traditional silver rose to his fiancée, Sophie. Distracted by the charms of "Mariandel", he accepts the Marschallin's proposal that Octavian should be his *Rosenkavalier*. The Marschallin laments the passing of her youth ("Da geht er hin"). She enjoys a bittersweet moment with her lover, sensing their affair will soon end.

## Act II
Octavian delivers the silver rose to Sophie ("Mir ist die Ehre widerfahren"), and they fall in love. Sophie's love deepens when Octavian defends her honor in a sword fight with Ochs. But her father ejects Octavian from their home. Ochs' mood lifts when a letter from "Mariandel" proposes meeting "tomorrow night."

## Act III
In an inn, Ochs is tormented by Octavian's coconspirators as he tries to seduce "Mariandel." When Ochs tells police he dines with his fiancée, Sophie's father erupts. Octavian is unmasked and Ochs humbled. Finally, the Marschallin endorses Octavian's love for Sophie ("Marie Theres'!").

### PRINCIPAL ROLES

**Marschallin, Princess Werdenberg** *soprano*
Lover to young Octavian

**Octavian, Count Rofrano** *mezzo-soprano*
Selected as rose-bearer

**Baron Ochs auf Lerchenau** *bass*
Betrothed to Sophie for her dowry

**Herr von Faninal** *baritone* Rich father to Sophie

**Sophie** *soprano* Falls in love with Octavian

*Der Rosenkavalier* caused such a sensation that, following its premiere in 1911, railroad operators ran additional trains from German-speaking Europe to take unprecedented throngs of opera-goers to Dresden.

▼ **Adrianne Pieczonka** as the Marschallin enjoys a last morning with the Octavian of Angelika Kirchschlager, Salzburg, 2004.

# Ariadne auf Naxos

ARIADNE ON NAXOS Opera in a prologue and one act, 2 hours • Composed: 1911–1912 (rev. 1916) • First performed: October 4, 1916, Hofoper, Vienna, Austria (2nd version) • Libretto: Hugo von Hofmannsthal

In 1912, *Ariadne auf Naxos* was given as an opera attached to a play that librettist Hofmannsthal had based on Molière's *Le Bourgeois gentilhomme*. But it was the revised version of 1916, an opera-within-an-opera, that would enter the repertory. Intertwining threads from *opera seria* and *commedia dell'arte*, the work is a striking exploration of the divine power of music. Among the little miracles is Ariadne's brief solo "Gibt es kein Hinüber?"

### PRINCIPAL ROLES

**Prima Donna** & **Ariadne** *soprano*

**Tenor** & **Bacchus** *tenor*

**Composer** *soprano or mezzo-soprano*

**Zerbinetta** *soprano* A comedienne

**Harlequin** *baritone* A member of her troupe

Legendary soprano Lotte Lehmann rose to instant fame singing the Composer in the 1916 premiere. Strauss turned the part over to her at the first rehearsal, when the originally cast soprano was unwell.

### Prologue
In the home of Vienna's richest man, post-supper festivities are in preparation. The Music Master complains about the program. A new opera by his student, the Composer, is to be followed by fireworks and then an *opera buffa* presented by Italians. The situation becomes worse when the Major-Domo announces minutes before the performance that his master has changed the program: the tragic opera and the Italian piece will be performed at the same time, followed by fireworks at precisely 9 pm. The furious Composer is pressed to revise his

▼ **Natalie Dessay as Zerbinetta** sings to Sophie Koch as the Composer in Laurent Pelly's 2003 production at the Paris Opéra.

*Ariadne auf Naxos* so that it integrates the alien Italian opera. His mood softens when he starts a conversation with Zerbinetta, the Italian soprano. She understands his work.

### Opera
Ariadne, abandoned on the isle of Naxos, awaits eternal peace in death ("Es gibt ein Reich"). Italians sing and dance to cheer her. Ariadne retreats further into the grotto, even as Zerbinetta attempts to lift her spirits, drawing on her own experiences ("Grossmächtige Prinzessin"). Nymphs announce the arrival of the youthful god Bacchus, whose voice draws Ariadne from her cave. As she emerges, Ariadne falls breathless, and Bacchus's love gives her new life. As a canopy is gently lowered, the passionate lovers are magically transformed.

# Die Frau ohne Schatten

THE WOMAN WITHOUT A SHADOW Opera in three acts, 3¼ hours ▪ Composed: 1914–1917 ▪ First performed: October 10, 1919, Hofoper, Vienna, Austria ▪ Libretto: Hugo von Hofmannsthal

Strauss's underperformed masterpiece, *Die Frau ohne Schatten* follows two pairs of lovers to emotional and spiritual salvation. As a daughter of the King of Spirits, the Empress lacks that crucial symbol of humanity, a shadow, and spends the opera considering whether or not to steal one from a human woman. Strauss's music—driven, opulent, and cataclysmic—matches Hofmannsthal's searching, abstract libretto.

### Act I
The Empress has no shadow, and learns that the Emperor will turn to stone if she does not obtain one. She and the Nurse resolve to find a shadow among humans. In their home, Barak the Dyer is mocked by his Wife. The Empress and Nurse offer themselves as servants to the Wife, and promise her luxury if she casts off her shadow and renounces her marriage bed. She does so, but is disturbed to hear the voices of her unborn children beckoning her.

### Act II
The Nurse conjures a Young Man to tempt the Wife. The Wife anxiously awakens her husband, whom the Nurse drugged, only to gloat over her near infidelity. When she vows to forfeit her shadow and fertility, he is enraged. Suddenly finding him manly and worthy of respect, she pleads for his mercy before they are both swallowed into the earth.

### Act III
Barak and his Wife, now penitent and separated into two cells in the bowels of the earth, long for one another ("Mir anvertraut"). The Nurse is condemned to wander the mortal realm. Refusing to accept a shadow that comes at the cost of Barak's happiness with his Wife, the Empress is rewarded with a shadow of her own. Her action frees the Emperor, and both couples are reunited ("Nun will ich jubeln").

---

## PRINCIPAL ROLES

**Empress** *soprano*
Daughter of Keikobad, King of Spirits

**Emperor** *tenor* Her husband

**Nurse** *mezzo-soprano*
Her protector in the world of spirits

**Barak** *baritone*
A dyer and good-hearted man

**Dyer's Wife** *soprano* His unhappy wife

---

Lotte Lehmann, who created the Dyer's Wife, claimed not to mind the Empress's musical preeminence: "I was perfectly content to sing myself into a state of near prostration and then gradually fade toward the end."

▶ **Beloved Strauss soprano** Inge Borkh (right) is the Dyer's Wife, and Wagnerian powerhouse Martha Mödl is the Nurse, at the Bayerische Staatsoper in 1963.

# Arabella

Lyric comedy in three acts, 2½ hours ▪ Composed: 1930–1932 ▪ First performed: July 1, 1933, Sächsisches Staatstheater Opernhaus, Dresden, Germany ▪ Libretto: Hugo von Hofmannsthal, based in part on his own short story, *Lucidor* (1910)

Strauss saw Arabella as "a second *Rosenkavalier*," a light romantic opera set in early Vienna, and marked by the uplifting tempos of the waltz. The premiere of *Arabella* was not so successful, but over time the opera has gained popularity. It is now often called Strauss's most romantic work. Vocal parts offer strong and gratifying roles for virtuoso singers, and the theme of love at first sight triggers gorgeous music.

### Act I

In their hotel residence, Adelaide Waldner hopes that her daughter, Arabella, will marry a wealthy suitor. Arabella's sister, Zdenka, who passes for a boy to save the family from financial ruin, plots to help Matteo, an officer, win Arabella. But Arabella has other ideas. She has fallen for a mysterious foreigner she saw in the street ("Aber der Richtige, wenn's einen gibt für mich auf dieser Welt"). Count Waldner explains to his wife that, to attract a suitor, he sent a picture of Arabella to a rich old friend. Mandryka, the friend's nephew, suddenly appears. He explains: his uncle died, so he opened the letter, and came to woo Arabella himself. Arabella has no interest in Count Elemer, a Viennese suitor, but he whisks her off to a grand Carnival ball.

### Act II

In a magnificent public ballroom, Arabella's parents introduce her to Mandryka, her mysterious foreigner. She promises to love him forever ("Und du wirst mein Gebieter sein")—after the Carnival dance. As Arabella waltzes with her former suitors, Zdenka passes Matteo a room key supposedly "from Arabella." Mandryka, overhearing, is outraged.

### Act III

Arabella returns to the hotel alone, puzzling Matteo as she is unaware of any key. Discovering them, Mandryka threatens to leave Vienna. Zdenka reveals the plot and her true identity as a girl, and is then betrothed to Matteo. All are humbled and forgiven, and Arabella and Mandryka fall into each other's arms.

PRINCIPAL ROLES

**Count Waldner** *bass* Retired cavalry officer

**Adelaide** *mezzo-soprano* Wife of Waldner

**Arabella** *soprano* Daughter to the Waldners

**Zdenka** *soprano* Sister to Arabella

**Mandryka** *baritone* A mysterious, rich foreigner

**Matteo** *tenor* An officer in love with Arabella

Strauss found the text for Arabella's solo *"Mein Elemer!"* inspiring, and sent a telegraph of thanks to Hugo von Hofmannsthal. Delivered on July 15, 1929, the day of the librettist's death, it was never read.

◄ **Karita Mattila** delivers Arabella, a role created by the diva Lisa Della Casa, at a Théâtre du Châtelet production in Paris, 2005.

# Capriccio

Conversation piece for music in one act, 2¼ hours • Composed: 1940–1941 • First performed: October 28, 1942, Nationaltheater, Munich, Germany • Libretto: Clemens Krauss and Richard Strauss

*Capriccio* was inspired by *Prima la musica e poi le parole* (1786), a comical work by Antonio Salieri and librettist Giovanni Battista Casti about tensions among opera artists. Before Nazi annexation drove him from Austria, Jewish librettist Stefan Zweig had proposed the subject to Strauss. While strikingly modern, *Capriccio* revisits Classical forms. It was popular in wartime Munich, until Allied bombs destroyed the opera house in 1943.

A poet, composer, theater director, and performers gather in the château of a Countess and her brother. A string sextet composed by Flamand prompts poet Olivier to ask which the Countess will prefer: words or music; poet or composer. Olivier reminds that words come first, then music. Flamand sees things the other way around. The director, La Roche, says they are both wrong: people go to operas for the scenery. The actress Clairon reads a scene with the enamored Count, and Olivier presents a love sonnet to the Countess. When Flamand puts the poem to music, the Countess praises the marriage of words and music. La Roche is invited to describe his theater project. But quarreling breaks out as Flamand and Olivier suggest the title "Flying Machines and Trapdoors". The director defends his art, and pleads for the stage to be peopled "with beings like us, who speak our language!" ("Holà! Ihr Streiter in Apoll!"). The Countess, moved, commissions an opera on the spot, and her brother finds the perfect story: "Today's events!" He escorts Clairon back to Paris, as other guests depart. Composer and poet leave reconciled, already at work on the new opera. The Countess ponders how it will all end ("Morgen mittag um elf!"). Who is the victor: poet or composer? Called to supper, she hums Flamand's melody, inspired by Olivier's sonnet.

## PRINCIPAL ROLES

**Countess** *soprano*
A young widow

**Count** *baritone* Her brother

**Flamand** *tenor* A composer

**Olivier** *baritone* A poet

**La Roche** *bass* A theater director

**Clairon** *contralto*
A famous Parisian actress

The opera's opening string sextet premiered in the Viennese home of Nazi controller Baldur von Schirach in recognition of the tranquility he assured the part-Jewish Strauss family. They had moved from Bavaria to Vienna in 1941.

◀ **Kiri Te Kanawa**, famous for her Countess in Mozart's *Figaro*, lavishes her creamy voice on Strauss's Countess at the Glyndebourne Festival in 1998.

# 5

# FRENCH OPERA
## (c. 1790–1900)

# French opera c. 1790–1900

Founded as the Royal Academy of Music by Louis XIV in 1669, what is today the Paris Opéra has long played a prominent role in French society. Yet opera music only assumed a distinct French personality in the 19th century with the arrival of *grand opéra*, a five-act spectacle more lavish than anything ever staged before. In reaction, *opéra comique* and operetta also flourished.

## A royal beginning

Until the 1789 Revolution, opera in France was dominated by three great musicians: Jean-Baptiste Lully, the Italian-born court composer to Louis XIV; Jean-Philippe Rameau, court composer to Louis XV; and Christoph Willibald Gluck, the German-born reformer of *opera seria*. The fact that only Rameau was French-born was not accidental. France had always welcomed foreign composers, even after the Revolution demanded patriotic operas. Indeed, the dominant musicians of the Napoleonic era were both Italian: Gaspare Spontini and Luigi Cherubini, who is best remembered for *Médée*.

## The rise of *grand opéra*

With *La Muette de Portici* in 1828, Daniel-François-Esprit Auber persuaded the Paris Opéra that *grand opéra* was its destiny. The composer most identified with this operatic extravaganza, however, was Giacomo Meyerbeer, a German-Jewish immigrant who dominated French opera more than any composer since Rameau. Through works such as *Robert le diable* and *Les Huguenots* he established the model for *grand opéra*: five-act works with ballet and recitatives (that is, no spoken dialogue), accompanied by large casts, mass choruses, rich costumes, elaborate decor, even pyrotechnics.

Italian composers, who considered acclaim in Paris to be the ultimate form of recognition, were quick to take note. In 1829, Rossini, by then settled in Paris, presented *Guillaume Tell*, his final opera and his only *grand opéra*. In 1843, Donizetti, also an expatriate in Paris and eager for attention, tried his hand at *grand opéra* with *Dom Sébastien*. Years later, Verdi, too, made his entry to Paris through *grand opéra* with *Les vêpres siciliennes* in 1855 and with *Don Carlos*

◄ **The new Paris Opéra** at the Palais Garnier, opened in 1875, underlined the important role opera played in the city's social life.

in 1867. After the Franco-Prussian war of 1870 and Paris Commune of 1871, *grand opéra* began to lose popularity. And despite Meyerbeer's earlier prominence, his operas had vanished from the stage by 1900 and are only very occasionally revived today.

The Opéra itself, albeit tradition-bound, was hardly grand: after the Salle du Palais-Royal went up in flames in 1763, it had seven homes before it occupied the Salle Le Peletier in 1821. After Emperor Napoleon III narrowly escaped assassination as he left this theater in 1858, he ordered construction of a large stand-alone opera house in the heart of Paris. By the time the Palais Garnier opened in 1875, Napoleon had been overthrown, but opera's magnificent new home was nonetheless soon where *le tout Paris* gathered.

Other theaters welcomed composers who resisted the Paris Opéra's strict rules. Rossini, Bellini, and Donizetti all preferred the Théâtre-Italien, while the Théâtre-Lyrique first presented Charles-François Gounod's popular mid-century operas, *Faust* and *Roméo et Juliette*, as well as Georges Bizet's first major opera, *Les pêcheurs de perles*. The Opéra-Comique in turn premiered Bizet's *Carmen* and Massenet's *Manon*, although it rejected Massenet's *Werther* as too gloomy; it premiered in Vienna. These three composers turned away from historical tableaux toward more intimate drama. They also embraced melodies with an Italianate lyricism, which was perhaps not surprising since all three spent lengthy periods in Italy as winners of the prestigious French prize, the Prix de Rome.

## A lighter touch

Just as *opera buffa* had parodied *opera seria* in the 18th century, the operetta appeared in reaction to *grand opéra*. In Paris, Jacques Offenbach, a German-Jewish immigrant, became operetta's reigning composer, with a series of farcical and tuneful shows, starting in 1858 with *Orphée aux enfers*. This lively entertainment soon caught on across Europe and spawned the no-less popular Viennese operetta. Then, 23 years later, with *Les contes d'Hoffmann*, a work that is frequently performed today, Offenbach demonstrated that he, too, could write opera. Around the turn of the century, another French composer, Claude Debussy, made a major contribution to opera's development with *Pelléas et Mélisande*, with its through-composed score flowing around a mysteriously poetic libretto. The work is now viewed as Romantic opera's bridge to modernity.

# Luigi Cherubini

Born: September 14, 1760, Florence, Italy • Died: March 15, 1842, Paris, France

Italian-born composer Luigi Cherubini made his name in Paris and set the stage for the rise of 19th-century French opera. A prolific composer of sacred music and operas, renowned for his innovative orchestration and choral writing, he is best known today for his *Requiem in C minor.* Arriving in Paris two years before the French Revolution, Cherubini responded skilfully to the political convulsions of the 1790s in four popular operas: *Lodoïska, Eliza, Médée,* and *Les deux journées.* From 1822 until his death, he was director of the Paris Conservatoire of Music, where the opera composers Daniel Auber and Fromental Halévy were among his students.

▲ **Anna Caterina Antonacci** as Médée
confronts Giuseppe Gipali as her errant
husband Jason in Yannis Kokkos's production
at the Théâtre du Châtelet, Paris, in 2005.

# Médée

MEDEA Opera in three acts, 2¼ hours • Composed: 1796–1797 • First performed: March 13, 1797, Théâtre Feydeau, Paris, France • Libretto: François Benoît Hoffmann, after Corneille's 1635 tragedy, itself after Euripides' *Medea*, 5th century BCE

*Médée* is Cherubini's operatic masterpiece, a work of daunting intensity, which uses the power of music to transform a Greek myth into a very human drama. Inspired by Euripides' 431 BCE tragedy, it tells of the princess from the ancient region of Colchis who commits murder to help her lover Jason steal the Golden Fleece, and then kills their children to punish his betrayal. Musically, *Médée* bridges Gluck's Classicism and 19th-century dramatic opera. It is dominated by the large demands on its lead soprano, who drives the narrative with forceful arias and duets. But it also skilfully explores Médée's vacillation between love and hate, life and death. The only one of Cherubini's operas still to be performed today, often in its Italian version, *Médée*'s importance also lies in its influence on both Beethoven and Weber.

### Act I
Dircé, King Créon's daughter, is preparing to marry Jason, who has abandoned Médée, the mother of his two children. Sailors bring in the Golden Fleece, stolen by Jason from Colchis, as a gift for Dircé. As Jason promises to protect Dircé from Médée's wrath ("Eloigné pour jamais"), Médée herself arrives to reclaim him. Warning that she will kill Dircé if Jason's marriage goes ahead, she begs him to return to her, reminding him of their love and children ("C'est la mère de tes enfants"). Rebuffed, Médée vows revenge. Briefly united, they recognize the terrible suffering unleashed by the Fleece.

### Act II
As a crowd calls for Médée's death, she worries about losing her children. Créon orders her to leave Corinth, but she begs for one day's grace so she can see them again. When Créon reluctantly agrees, Médée decides to use the day to kill Dircé. Jason tells her that the children can stay with her until she leaves. Néris, Médée's maid, anticipating doom, promises her undying loyalty ("Ah, nos peines"). With mounting fury, Médée instructs Néris to take as wedding gifts for Dircé a robe and diadem given to her by Apollo. As she watches Créon and his followers enter the Temple of Hera for Jason's wedding to Dircé, Médée seizes a blazing torch from the altar and awaits her moment of revenge.

### PRINCIPAL ROLES

**Médée** *soprano* A sorceress princess

**Jason** *tenor* Father of Médée's children

**Créon** *bass* King of Corinth

**Dircé** *soprano* Créon's daughter

**Néris** *mezzo-soprano* Dircé's maid

**Captain of the Guard** *baritone*

### Act III
Imagining herself being strangled by serpents, Médée takes a dagger to kill her children, but Néris intercedes. Néris has delivered the gifts to Dircé, who is preparing to wear them to please Jason. But Médée believes the children must die because Jason, their father, is a traitor ("Eh quoi! Je suis Médée"). Suddenly Jason is heard mourning Dircé, who has been poisoned by Médée's gifts. As a crowd calls for her death, Médée grabs her two children and locks herself in the temple. Néris rushes out, screaming that Médée is about to slay the children. The sorceress appears, accompanied by three Furies, waving a bloodied dagger. "Their blood has avenged me," she cries. As the temple bursts into flames, Médée and the Furies disappear into the fire.

Maria Callas, who frequently performed *Médée*, once warned students at a masterclass of the perils of high-powered soprano roles: "In opera, passion without intellect is no good. You will be a wild animal, not an artist."

# Giacomo Meyerbeer

Born: September 5, 1791, Berlin, Germany • Died: May 2, 1864, Paris, France

Giacomo Meyerbeer stands out for the popularity that he enjoyed in his lifetime and the neglect that he suffers today. But he merits a place in the history of opera as the originator of French *grand opéra*, a five-act extravaganza of ballet, elaborate decor, rich costumes, and heroic stories and music. The colossal sound and scale of Meyerbeer's operatic works inspired both Verdi and Wagner.

Born in Berlin to a wealthy German Jewish family, Jakob Liebmann Meyer Beer was a child prodigy as a pianist. He changed his name when he moved to Italy in his twenties to study opera. There, he won plaudits in 1824 for *Il crociato in Eggito*. He moved to Paris where, with *Robert le diable* in 1831, he established *grand opéra* as the dominant operatic form for much of the 19th century. Five years later, working with the librettist Eugène Scribe, he triumphed with *Les Huguenots*. In 1842, he became music director to the Prussian court in Berlin, but he was never fully embraced by Germanic composers. Despite having helped the young Wagner, he was maliciously targeted in Wagner's vitriolic essay "Judaism in Music." In 1849, Meyerbeer returned to Paris to present *Le prophète*. His final opera, *L'africaine*, was in rehearsal when he died unexpectedly in Paris in 1864. It premiered at the Paris Opéra the following year.

◀ **Set design** for the premiere of Meyerbeer's final opera, *L'Africaine*, at the Paris Opéra, France, in 1865.

## FIRST PERFORMANCES

- 1824 *Il crociato in Egitto*
- 1831 *Robert le diable*
- 1836 *Les Huguenots*
- 1849 *Le prophète*
- 1854 *L'étoile du nord*
- 1859 *Dinorah*
- 1865 *L'Africaine*

# Robert le diable

ROBERT THE DEVIL *Grand opéra* in five acts, 4 hours ▪ Composed: 1828–1831 ▪ First performed: November 21, 1831, Paris Opéra, France ▪ Libretto: Eugène Scribe

*Robert le diable*, Meyerbeer's first *grand opéra*, won him overnight recognition as a major composer and, within a decade, the opera had been performed across Europe. The wrenching struggle between good and evil is accompanied by daring orchestration and dramatic solo roles, with the score pitting two "good" sopranos against an "evil" bass who fight for the soul of the tenor. The opera's final trio announces the happy outcome.

## Act I

Robert, the Duke of Normandy, is in Sicily to court Princess Isabelle. He is enraged when a minstrel recounts that he was born of the Devil. Alice, Robert's half-sister, brings their mother's last testament but says he is unworthy to receive it. When Robert's father, Bertram, arrives, Alice recognizes him as the Devil. Encouraged by Bertram to gamble, Robert loses everything, including armor needed to joust for Isabelle.

## Act II

Isabelle gives Robert fresh armor for his duel against the Prince of Grenada. Bertram lures Robert away by sending him on a fruitless mission and, as a result, he misses the tournament and loses Isabelle.

## Act III

Alice overhears Bertram summoning evil spirits and flees, protecting herself with a cross. Bertram tells Robert he can win Isabelle if he collects a magic branch from a tomb. Then Bertram awakens dead nuns ("Nonnes qui reposez") to guide Robert to the branch.

## Act IV

Robert decides to kidnap Isabelle, but when she pledges her love for him ("Robert, toi que j'aime"), he makes the decision to break the magic branch, destroying its power to create sleep.

### PRINCIPAL ROLES

**Robert** *tenor* Duke of Normandy

**Bertram** *bass* His father, the Devil

**Isabelle** *soprano*
A Sicilian princess and Robert's beloved

**Alice** *soprano* Robert's half-sister

**Raimbault** *tenor* A minstrel

▶ **A 19th-century** costume design gives a dapper air to the evil Robert le diable.

## Act V

Outside Palermo Cathedral, Bertram tells Robert that he can recover his power if he signs an irrevocable pact with the Devil before midnight. Robert is willing, but Alice distracts him. When church bells ring out midnight, Bertram vanishes and Isabelle appears before Robert in a bridal gown.

Meyerbeer and his librettist, Eugène Scribe, risked Roman Catholic wrath when, in Act III, they had "fallen" nuns resuscitated from their tombs and recruited to do the Devil's work.

# Les Huguenots

THE HUGUENOTS *Grand opéra* in five acts, 4 hours • Composed: 1832–1836 • First performed: February 29, 1836, Paris Opéra, France
• Libretto: Eugène Scribe and Émile Deschamps

*Les Huguenots*, Meyerbeer's finest work, was also the most successful *grand opéra* of its age, with more than 1,000 performances at the Paris Opéra by 1900. It was bold for a Jewish composer to address the St. Bartholomew's Day Massacre of August 24, 1572, when thousands of Protestants, or Huguenots, were slain by Catholics. But, rather than offending his audiences, Meyerbeer thrilled them with a vast spectacle, involving seven major roles as well as huge choruses representing soldiers, students, and church congregations. The demands of this opera—both the cost of staging it and the complexity of the score—explain why it is rarely performed today.

## PRINCIPAL ROLES

**Marguerite de Valois** *soprano* Sister of Charles IX

**Raoul de Nangis** *tenor* A Protestant noble

**Valentine** *soprano* Raoul's Catholic beloved

**Le Comte de Nevers** *baritone*
Valentine's Catholic betrothed

**Le Comte de Saint-Bris** *bass*
Valentine's Catholic father

**Marcel** *bass* A devout Huguenot henchman

**Urbain** *soprano* Page to Marguerite

**Maurevert** *bass* A Catholic noble

### Act I
With Charles IX trying to end France's religious wars, the Count of Nevers receives a Protestant, Raoul de Nangis, in his castle. Raoul tells of falling for a lady whom he saved from rascals ("Plus blanche que la blanche hermine"). Marcel, Raoul's follower, provokes Catholic guests with a Huguenot ditty. A woman arrives and Raoul recognizes her as the lady he rescued. Nevers reports that she was his fiancée, who came to call off their wedding. A page, Urbain, passes Raoul an invitation to go blindfolded to a mysterious destination ("Une dame noble et sage"). Nevers recognizes Queen Marguerite's Navarre crest on the envelope.

### Act II
Frolicking with her ladies by a river ("O beau pays"), Marguerite is pleased that Valentine can now marry Raoul. But Valentine says her father, the Count of Saint-Bris, objects. Raoul arrives and, while enchanted by Marguerite's beauty, learns he is to marry Saint-Bris's daughter. But on recognizing the woman as Nevers' former fiancée, he refuses, insulting the Catholic nobles.

▼ **Still often evoked**, the St. Bartholomew's Day Massacre remains a dark stain on French history four and a half centuries later.

### La Reine Margot

Although she is only sketchily portrayed in *Les Huguenots*, Marguerite de Valois, or more familiarly La Reine Margot, was a woman equally skilled in love affairs as politics. Her brother, Charles IX, chose her to wed the Protestant Henri de Navarre in the hope of ending France's Wars of Religion. But their marriage, in August 1572, was immediately followed by the massacre of Huguenots in Paris. In 1589, Margot's husband became Henri IV and, by converting to Catholicism, finally brought peace to France.

## Act III

Nevers and Valentine enter a church for their wedding, but only Nevers emerges, saying Valentine wants to pray alone until dusk. Marcel delivers a challenge from Raoul to Saint-Bris, who then orders the nobleman Maurevert to ambush Raoul. Overhearing this, a veiled Valentine warns Marcel ("O terreur!"), who does not recognize her. As Raoul prepares for the duel, Maurevert appears with armed men. Arriving unexpectedly, Marguerite demands an explanation for the commotion. Marcel points to Valentine as his informant and tears off her veil. Even Raoul is shocked, but Marguerite says that Valentine wanted to avoid an unhappy marriage. Saint-Bris announces that Valentine is already married to Nevers.

## Act IV

Valentine is lamenting her unhappy fate and continuing love for Raoul ("Je suis seule chez moi") when Raoul bursts in, determined to see her one last time. When the sound of footsteps forces him into hiding, he hears Saint-Bris tell Catholic nobles of the plan to massacre Protestants, although Nevers refuses to join the plot. Raoul must warn his coreligionists, but Valentine begs him to stay, confessing her love for him. Raoul now imagines escaping with Valentine. But when church bells signal that the massacre has begun, Raoul rushes away.

## Act V

Huguenot nobles are receiving Marguerite, when Raoul brings word of the massacre. Finding him, Valentine promises him royal protection if he will convert, but he refuses. She accepts Raoul's Protestant faith instead ("Ainsi je te verrai périr?"). Marcel then pronounces them married. Catholics open fire on fleeing Protestants. Spotting a woman with two wounded men, Saint-Bris demands their identity. When they say they are Huguenots, he orders them shot. As Valentine falls, Saint-Bris recognizes his daughter. Marguerite appeals for calm, but the killing goes on.

To evoke Huguenot worshippers, Meyerbeer quotes from Bach's famous setting of the hymn *A Mighty Fortress Is Our God*, written by Martin Luther in 1529 after a friend was burned at the stake by Catholics.

# PALAIS
# GARNIER

The Palais Garnier, the legendary home of the Paris Opéra, is unquestionably one of the most extravagant theaters in the world, with its vast marble foyer, sweeping staircase, sculpted balconies, and grand gallery leading to a 1,979-seat Italianate auditorium lit by a 7-ton (6.4-metric ton) chandelier and decorated with a ceiling painting by Marc Chagall. Indeed, such is the weight of the building that a lake in its basement serves to secure its stability, the same lake that inspired Gaston Leroux's novel and Andrew Lloyd Weber's musical, *The Phantom of the Opera.*

As intended, it is a monument fit for a king: the opera company it houses was founded as the Académie Royale de Musique by Louis XIV in 1669 and construction of the building itself was ordered by Emperor Napoleon III after he narrowly escaped assassination outside an earlier opera house, the Salle Le Peletier. The 1870–1871 Franco-Prussian war and Napoleon's ejection delayed the opening of the Palais Garnier—so named after its architect Charles Garnier—until 1875, but the letters N (for Napoleon) and E (for Empress Eugénie) still adorn the facade.

The theater soon stood at the heart of both the musical and social life of late 19th-century Paris, with the dancers of the Paris Opéra Ballet Company memorably portrayed by the artist Edgar Degas. One measure of its importance is that opera and ballet performances continued during both world wars, even as Paris was occupied by German forces between 1940 and 1944. Since the 1970s, the company's traditional prestige has been matched by the quality of its productions.

Since a second opera house—the 2,745-seat Opéra Bastille—opened in the Place de la Bastille in 1989, the Palais Garnier has focused on ballet, although it still presents more intimate operas requiring chamber orchestras. With these two jointly managed opera houses, plus the independent Opéra-Comique, opera lovers in Paris are spoiled for choice.

"From the first downbeat, my experience with the artists of the Paris Opéra was simply magnificent."

GUSTAVO DUDAMEL, MUSIC DIRECTOR, PARIS OPÉRA

◀ **Home to the Paris Opéra** since the 1870s, the Palais Garnier is breathtaking in its opulence, with the Grand Foyer overlooking the Place de l'Opéra the scene of dazzling gala dinners.

# Hector Berlioz

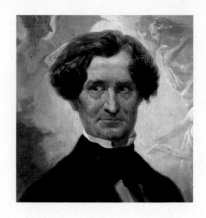

Born: December 11, 1803, La Côte-Saint-André, France ▪ Died: March 8, 1869, Paris, France

Hector Berlioz was an enormously influential composer, considered by many to be the creator of the modern orchestra, yet his work has always been better appreciated in Britain and Germany than in France. Berlioz's career in opera proved particularly frustrating, with the Paris Opéra refusing to receive him after the failure of *Benvenuto Cellini* in 1838.

Although Berlioz played and wrote music in his teens, his parents sent him to Paris to study medicine. He was 21 before he finally devoted himself entirely to composition, writing a *Messe solennelle* that same year. He followed with symphonies, cantatas, and songs, and, in 1830, at his fourth attempt, won the Prix de Rome. Upon his return from Rome, by using literary works as the inspiration for choral symphonies, he established himself as a leader of musical Romanticism.

With the hostile reception given to *Benvenuto Cellini*, however, Berlioz's opera career began badly, and he soon felt excluded from the social heart of Paris musical life. His next theater piece, *La damnation de Faust*, was presented in concert in 1846 and was not staged until 1893. Even his greatest opera, *Les Troyens*, had a troubled birth, with only Acts III to V performed in his lifetime. *Béatrice et Bénédict*, which premiered in Baden-Baden in 1862, was well received, but it reached Paris only

◀ **A blood-splattered Mark Bruce** as the Ghost of Hector in Richard Jones's 2003 production of *Les Troyens* at the English National Opera, in London.

### FIRST PERFORMANCES

- 1823 *Estelle et Némorin (lost)*
- 1838 *Benvenuto Cellini*
- 1846 *La damnation de Faust*
- 1862 *Béatrice et Bénédict*
- 1863 *Les Troyens (Acts III–V)*
- 1890 *Les Troyens (Acts I–II)*

in 1890. Berlioz struggled to win recognition as an opera composer, but he could not be ignored as a music critic. He was often scathing of fellow composers, although he evidently listened carefully to their work. Thus, while disliking much of Meyerbeer's music, he singled out elements for praise. Only the long-forgotten Gaspare Spontini could do no wrong: Berlioz ranked the Italian opera composer alongside Beethoven and Weber as the modern masters who most influenced him.

"I gave myself over entirely to the study and cult of great dramatic music."

HECTOR BERLIOZ

# La damnation de Faust

THE DAMNATION OF FAUST *Légende dramatique* in four parts, 2¼ hours ▪ Composed: 1829 and 1845–1846 ▪ First performed: December 6, 1846, Opéra-Comique, Paris, France ▪ Libretto: Hector Berlioz and Almire Gandonniére, after Goethe's *Faust Part I*

*La damnation de Faust*, while first performed in concert and never intended as an opera, is now frequently staged with success. In his twenties, already intrigued by the Faust legend, Berlioz set eight scenes from Goethe's *Faust Part I*, which he later incorporated into *La damnation de Faust*. This *légende dramatique* is more a succession of tableaux than a flowing narrative, but it is distinguished by powerfully romantic songs and expressive orchestration.

**Part I**

Faust wanders the Hungarian plains and, while happy over the coming of spring, is disturbed by the sound of dancing peasants and army bugles. He cannot share the pleasure of others.

**Part II**

At home in Leipzig, Faust prepares to drink poison, but is cheered to hear Easter hymns. Méphistophélès appears and, promising him pleasure, leads him to a tavern. But Faust is put off by the drunken scene ("Une puce gentille"). Beside the Elbe River, Méphistophélès has him dream of the beautiful Marguerite. When he awakens, he yearns for her.

**Part III**

Through Méphistophélès's magic, Faust enters Marguerite's chamber as she dreams of a lover ("Autrefois un roi de Thule"). As she sleeps, Méphistophélès further enchants her. Awakening to find Faust beside her, she surrenders to his advances.

**Part IV**

Learning that Marguerite is to die for murdering her mother, Faust wants to save her and begs Méphistophélès for help. Méphistophélès demands Faust's soul in exchange and, once Faust agrees, they mount black horses and charge into a flaming abyss. Faust is forever damned, while Marguerite is welcomed to heaven by angels.

A talented writer, Berlioz took the liberty of inventing an opening scene and locating it in Hungary so that he could make use of *Rákóczi's March*, an orchestral piece written years earlier.

▶ **The bass-baritone** José Van Dam as Méphistophélès at the Opéra Bastille, Paris, in 2001.

---

**PRINCIPAL ROLES**

**Faust** *tenor* An elderly philosopher

**Méphistophélès** *bass* A Satanic man

**Marguerite** *mezzo-soprano* An innocent victim of Méphistophélès

**Brander** *bass* A drinker

# Benvenuto Cellini

*Opera semi-seria* in two acts, 2¾ hours • Composed: 1836–1838 (rev. 1851–1853) • First performed: September 10, 1838, Paris Opéra, France • Libretto: Léon de Wailly and Auguste Barbier, after Benvenuto Cellini's late 16th-century autobiography, *Vita*

*Benvenuto Cellini* flopped at its premiere and never recovered. Its story, loosely adapted from Cellini's life as a sculptor and adventurer, is absurd, but the public objected mainly to the score's innovative rhythms and orchestration. Even in rehearsals, Berlioz faced what he later called "the indifference and obvious distaste" of most singers. While the opera is still rarely performed, its daring inventiveness is now recognized and applauded.

## PRINCIPAL ROLES

**Benvenuto Cellini** *tenor*
A sculptor and adventurer

**Giacomo Balducci** *bass*
Pope Clement's treasurer

**Teresa** *soprano* Balducci's daughter

**Ascanio** *mezzo-soprano* Cellini's apprentice

**Fieramosca** *baritone* Cellini's rival

**Pompeo** *baritone* Fieramosca's friend

### Act I: The fall of Troy

The Pope has commissioned a statue from Benvenuto Cellini. But Balducci, the Pope's treasurer, favors a rival sculptor, Fieramosca, because Cellini is courting his daughter, Teresa. With Carnival in full swing, Cellini proposes eloping with Teresa ("O mon bonheur"), but Fieramosca overhears Cellini's plan to dress as a monk. Balducci appears and, as Cellini slips away, Fieramosca hides. When Teresa speaks of seeing a strange man, Balducci discovers Fieramosca in her room. Ascanio, Cellini's apprentice, brings money from the Pope to finish the statue. Fieramosca and his friend Pompeo, in monks' habits, join the festive crowd. A fight erupts, and Cellini kills Pompeo. As cannon shots announce the end of Carnival, Cellini escapes.

### Act II

Cellini is preparing to flee with Teresa ("Ah! Le ciel, cher époux") when Balducci announces that she will marry Fieramosca. The Pope then threatens to withdraw Cellini's commission if the statue is not completed by nightfall. While workers hurry to finish the statue, Fieramosca challenges Cellini to a duel. Teresa is shocked when Fieramosca reappears, but he has come to disrupt work on the statue. Finally, the Pope arrives to witness the casting. A shortage of metal forces Cellini to use every object he can find, and, with an explosion, the statue finally appears. The Pope is satisfied with the result and Balducci cedes Teresa to Cellini.

Berlioz brought a revised version of *Benvenuto Cellini* to Covent Garden, London, in 1853 in the hope of rescuing it from oblivion, but even Queen Victoria's presence at the opening did not shield him from boos.

◀ **Paul Charles Clarke** as Cellini embraces Anne-Sophie Duprels's Teresa in Renaud Doucet's 2005 production at the Opéra National du Rhin in France.

# Les Troyens

THE TROJANS *Grand opéra* in five acts, 3¾ hours ▪ Composed: 1856–1858 (rev. 1859–1860) ▪ First performed: Acts III–V: November 4, 1863, Théâtre-Lyrique, Paris, France; Acts I–II concert performance: December 7, 1879, Théâtre du Châtelet, Paris, France ▪ Libretto: Hector Berlioz, after Virgil's *Aeneid* (c. 30–19 BCE)

Long fascinated by Virgil's *Aeneid*, Berlioz finally adapted the epic for *Les Troyens*, a spectacular five-act opera, with 22 roles, huge choruses, and ballet. Today, the two-part work is often presented on successive evenings: Acts I and II, which were never staged in Berlioz's lifetime, as *The Fall of Troy*; and Acts III to V, which recount the tragic love story of Dido and Aeneas, as *The Trojans in Carthage*.

Fearing new rejection by Paris opera-goers, Berlioz was only convinced to write *Les Troyens* by the insistent encouragement of Liszt's mistress, Princess Carolyne Sayn-Wittgenstein, who, like Liszt, admired Berlioz's work.

### PRINCIPAL ROLES

**Cassandre (Cassandra)** *mezzo-soprano*
A Trojan prophetess

**Chorèbe (Corebus)** *baritone* An Asian prince

**Priam** *bass* King of Troy

**Énée (Aeneas)** *tenor* Trojan hero

**Didon (Dido)** *mezzo-soprano*
Widowed Queen of Carthage

◄ **Plácido Domingo as Énée** (right) leads a chorus of Trojans in a 1983 production of *Les Troyens* at the Metropolitan Opera in New York.

## Act I: The fall of Troy

The Greeks withdraw from Troy after a long siege, but leave behind a large wooden horse. Cassandre, the prophetess, warns that Troy is doomed, but her beloved, Chorèbe, ignores her. Énée reports the death of a priest who called for the destruction of the horse. In a procession ("Du roi des dieux, ô fille aimée"), the horse, carrying Greek soldiers, enters the city.

## Act II

The ghost of Hector, a Trojan leader, urges Énée to flee and found a new Troy in Italy. At the fall of Troy, Chorèbe dies and Cassandre stabs herself. As Énée escapes, his palace is consumed by flames.

## Act III: The Trojans in Carthage

Didon's subjects vow to protect her from Iarbas, the Numidian king. The Trojans arrive. When Iarbas attacks Carthage, Énée comes to the city's defense.

## Act IV

Didon and Énée are in love, but satyrs call out "Italy!" to Énée. As dancers celebrate Carthage's victory over Iarbas, Didon and Énée rejoice in their happiness ("Nuit d'ivresse et d'extase infinie").

## Act V

Didon begs Énée to stay, but the ghosts of Trojan heroes tell him to go. As Énée's fleet sails, Didon ascends a funeral pyre and stabs herself with his sword.

# Charles-François Gounod

Born: June 17, 1818, Paris, France ▪ Died: October 18, 1893, Saint-Cloud, Paris, France

Charles-François Gounod was famous in his lifetime for both his choral music and his operas. Among his sacred works, *La Rédemption* and *Ave Maria*, derived from a Bach prelude, are still popular. But he is best remembered for his two most successful operas, *Faust* and *Roméo et Juliette*, which are regularly performed around the world.

I n his life as in his music, Gounod was divided between religion and more worldly interests. After studying church music in Rome, he spent two years in the seminary of Saint-Sulpice in Paris. But he was later renowned for his circle of female admirers. When he tried his hand at opera, he won critical praise for *Sapho*. His career then took off after he met the librettists Jules Barbier and Michel Carré, with whom he adapted works by Molière (*Le médecin malgré lui*), Goethe (*Faust*), and Shakespeare (*Roméo et Juliette*). All three operas stand out for their melodic arias and innovative orchestration. Gounod's opera about Provence, *Mireille*, also created a fashion for regional themes. When the 1870–1871 Franco-Prussian War interrupted his career, he moved to London, and, for some years, "Gounod's Chorus" became the official choir at the Royal Albert Hall. In the mid-1870s, he returned to Paris and wrote three more operas. But by then, younger composers were making their mark.

## FIRST PERFORMANCES

- 1851 *Sapho*
- 1858 *Le médecin malgré lui*
- 1859 *Faust*
- 1860 *Philémon et Baucis*
- 1862 *La reine de Saba*
- 1864 *Mireille*
- 1867 *Roméo et Juliette*

◀ **The mansion** at Saint-Cloud, outside Paris, where Gounod spent his retirement after his return from London in the mid-1870s, and where he died.

# Faust

Opera in five acts, 3½ hours • Composed: 1856–1859 • First performed: March 19, 1859, Théâtre-Lyrique, Paris, France • Libretto: Jules Barbier and Michel Carré, after Carré's 1850 play *Faust et Marguerite* and Goethe's *Faust Part I*

*Faust* secured Gounod's reputation as a major composer and soon became enormously popular worldwide, even being chosen to inaugurate the Metropolitan Opera in New York in 1883. While the plot is disturbingly cynical, a richly expressive score transforms the opera into a romantic tragedy. Orchestration and choruses highlight the battle that is taking place between good and evil. The composer then reserves his sweetest melodies for love duets between Marguerite and Faust.

### Act I
Contemplating suicide, Faust summons Satan. Méphistophélès answers, promising him wealth, power, and youth in exchange for his soul. After Méphistophélès conjures up a vision of Marguerite, Faust accepts the pact.

### Act II
Valentin asks friends to protect his sister, Marguerite, while he is away at war. When Méphistophélès mocks Marguerite, Valentin draws his sword, but Méphistophélès snaps it. Faust offers Marguerite his arm, but she turns away.

### Act III
While Faust dreams of love ("Oui, c'est toi! Je t'aime"), Méphistophélès leaves Marguerite a jewel box. Her delight encourages Faust to declare his love for her. She begs him to leave, then calls him back. As he returns to her, Méphistophélès laughs with sadistic glee.

### Act IV
Now the abandoned mother of Faust's child, Marguerite prays to God, but Méphistophélès replies. Back from the front, Valentin rushes to Marguerite's cottage. Méphistophélès urges Faust to follow. Valentin tries to avenge his sister, but Faust wounds him. Before dying, Valentin curses Marguerite.

*Faust*'s depiction of the destructive power of love moved Charles Dickens, who wrote: "It has affected me and sounded in my ears like a mournful echo of things that lie in my own heart."

### Act V
Surrounded by dancing witches, Faust has a vision of Marguerite in jail for killing their child. He enters her cell and again they dream of love. But Marguerite refuses to leave with him. As she expires, her soul rises to heaven.

▼ **Australian soprano** Nellie Melba included Marguerite among her favorite roles.

> **PRINCIPAL ROLES**
>
> **Faust** *tenor* An elderly philosopher
>
> **Méphistophélès** *bass* A satanic man
>
> **Marguerite** *soprano*
> An innocent victim of Méphistophélès
>
> **Wagner** *baritone* A student
>
> **Valentin** *baritone*
> A soldier and Marguerite's brother

# Roméo et Juliette

ROMEO AND JULIET Opera in a prologue and five acts, 3¼ hours • Composed: 1865–1867 • First performed: April 27, 1867, Théâtre-Lyrique, Paris, France • Libretto: Jules Barbier and Michel Carré, after Shakespeare's tragedy *Romeo and Juliet* (c. 1595)

*Roméo et Juliette* is a lushly romantic opera, which, while remarkably faithful to Shakespeare's tragedy, dwells even more closely on the ill-fated couple. In Act V, set in the Capulets' vault, Gounod and his librettists also bow to operatic tradition: they keep Roméo alive long enough so that he and Juliette can die in each other's arms. While the libretto borrows freely from Shakespeare's language, it also prolongs the lovers' reunions to allow ample time for four long, touching duets. Roméo and Juliette also have stirring arias, while Stéphano the page, a soprano "trouser role," invariably wins applause for "his" single aria. The generational dimension to this tragedy is underlined by the strong bass roles of Lord Capulet and Frère Laurent, who contribute to the fatal denouement.

## PRINCIPAL ROLES

**Roméo** *tenor* The heir to the Montaigu family

**Juliette** *soprano* Lord Capulet's daughter

**Capulet** *bass* The head of the Capulet family

**Mercutio** *tenor* Roméo's closest friend

**Tybalt** *tenor* Lord Capulet's nephew

**Pâris** *baritone* Juliette's designated husband

**Frère Laurent** *bass* A local monk

**Gertrude** *mezzo-soprano* Juliette's nurse

**Stéphano** *soprano* Roméo's page

### Prologue

The Chorus announces that only the death of two young lovers ended the centuries-old feud between the Montaigus and the Capulets.

### Act I

Hosting a masked ball, Lord Capulet introduces his young daughter, Juliette, to the guests, who include his nephew, Tybalt. Roméo, a hated young Montaigu, enters the party with Mercutio. Roméo is upset by a dream, but Mercutio teases him. Suddenly Roméo sees Juliette and falls madly in love with her. Juliette's nurse, Gertrude, suggests Count Pâris as an ideal husband, but Juliette says she will follow only her heart ("Ah! Je veux vivre"). Taking her aside, Roméo begins wooing her. But they are interrupted by Tybalt, who threatens Roméo. Lord Capulet prevents a fight.

### Act II

Hiding from Capulet guards, Roméo stands below Juliette's bedroom waiting for dawn ("Ah! Lève-toi, soleil"). Appearing on the balcony, Juliette laments that Roméo's Montaigu name could separate them. Roméo then appears and they declare their love for each other. Capulet servants search for a Montaigu, but they find no one. Alone again, Juliette asks Roméo to send word of when and where they will marry.

### Act III

Frère Laurent, seeing a chance for peace between the families, agrees to marry the couple secretly. Still waiting in the Capulet's

◀ **The bedroom balcony** in old Verona where, according to popular myth, Juliet first heard Romeo's words of love.

Thanks to *Roméo et Juliette*, Gounod became known as the "musician of love," a title he happily embraced when, at 70, he said that love was at the heart of his life and his art.

garden, Roméo's page, Stéphano, imagines turtle-doves kissing ("Que fais-tu, blanche tourterelle"). But he is caught by the Capulet servants. Mercutio defends the boy, then Tybalt arrives and fights Mercutio. Roméo tries to separate them, saying the time for hatred is over. But the fighting resumes and Tybalt kills Mercutio. Furious, Roméo slays Tybalt. The Duke of Verona denounces both families for feuding, then sends Roméo into exile.

## Act IV

Together on their wedding night, Juliette forgives Roméo for killing her cousin ("Nuit d'hyménée"). As dawn breaks, Roméo leaves Verona. Lord Capulet informs Juliette that she is to marry Pâris. When she resists, he decides that

Frère Laurent should persuade her of her duty. Instead, the friar offers a potion that simulates death. But, a day later, she will reawaken to find Roméo at her side. Juliette fears waking up beside Tybalt's corpse, but she finally takes the potion ("Amour, ranime mon courage"). Dressed in her bridal gown, Juliette is about to marry Pâris when she collapses and is pronounced dead.

## Act V

Frère Laurent learns that his letter explaining Juliette's "death" never reached Roméo. Believing Juliette to be dead, Roméo breaks into the Capulet vault and finds her inert body. Devastated, he kisses her, then drinks poison. Suddenly, Juliette stirs and, briefly, they imagine fleeing together. But Roméo confesses that, thinking her dead, he took poison ("Console-toi, pauvre âme"). As he grows weaker, Juliette stabs herself with a dagger. Begging God for forgiveness, the lovers die in each other's arms.

▲ **Eidé Norena** (1884–1968), one of the finest sopranos of the interwar years, played Juliette to great acclaim.

# Jacques Offenbach

Born: June 20, 1819, Cologne, Germany ▪ Died: October 5, 1880, Paris, France

Jacques Offenbach, the son of a cantor at Cologne's synagogue, became the master of French operetta. With their farcical plots and witty scores, Offenbach's *opéras-bouffes*, as they were also known, were the toast of mid-19th century Paris. *La belle Hélène* was his biggest success, but *Les contes d'Hoffmann*, which was first performed a year after his death, is considered his operatic masterpiece.

◀ **Jane Rhodes in the title role** of *La belle Hélène*, one of Offenbach's best-loved operettas, in a 1976 production at the Bouffes-Parisiens in France.

Offenbach was just 13 when he moved to Paris, first to study, then to join an orchestra as a cellist, and finally to compose. In this, he looked to Mozart and Schubert for inspiration, yet instinct and a need to survive led him to write vaudeville and salon pieces. To reach a wider audience, he founded the Bouffes-Parisiens, where he presented 30 of his one-act operettas before the triumph of *Orphée aux enfers* in 1858. Over the next decade, thanks to *La belle Hélène*, *La vie parisienne*, and other crowd-pleasers, his fame also spread across Europe, to London and Vienna. Immensely prolific, he wrote more than 600 works of music, 130 of them for the theatre.

The 1870–1871 Franco-Prussian War disrupted Offenbach's life. A Catholic convert and member of France's Légion d'Honneur, a man known for his wit and generosity, he was suddenly vilified as a German Jew. After briefly leaving Paris, he returned to an unwelcoming city. In 1873, he became director of the Gaîté Lyrique, but it soon went bankrupt. His own situation was increasingly desperate. In 1876, he toured the United States to raise some money, but his health was failing him. His last unfinished work, *Les contes d'Hoffmann*, completed by friends, reflects the pessimism of his final years.

### FIRST PERFORMANCES

- 1858 *Orphée aux enfers*
- 1864 *La belle Hélène*
- 1866 *Barbe-bleue*
- 1867 *La Grande-Duchesse de Gérolstein*
- 1868 *La Périchole*
- 1881 *Les contes d'Hoffmann*

*"What else is 'opéra comique,' in fact, but sung vaudeville?"*

JACQUES OFFENBACH

# Orphée aux enfers

ORPHEUS IN THE UNDERWORLD *Opéra-bouffe* in four acts, 1¾ hours (rev. 2¾ hours) ▪ Composed: 1858 (rev. 1874) ▪ First performed: October 21, 1858, Bouffes-Parisiens, Paris, France ▪ Libretto: Hector Crémieux and Ludovic Halévy

*Orphée aux enfers*, Offenbach's first major success, created the Paris fashion for full-evening operettas. A delicious parody of both antiquity and Baroque opera, it also pokes fun at the Orpheus myth so beloved of 17th- and 18th-century opera-goers. With catchy tunes and absurd situations, it also captured the fun-loving spirit of the times, even ending with the famous can-can "Ce bal est original."

### Act I

Eurydice is bored with her husband, Orphée, whose flute-playing no longer amuses her. Annoyed, Orphée threatens her with a violin concerto. Pluton, in the guise of the shepherd Aristée, has won Eurydice's heart and leads her to the underworld. She leaves a note informing Orphée of her death. At the insistence of Public Opinion, Orphée follows her.

### Act II

On Mount Olympus, Jupiter is not pleased that Pluton has abducted Eurydice. Other gods defend Pluton and mock Jupiter for his tyranny and ugliness. Accompanied by Public Opinion, Orphée comes in search of his wife. Jupiter offers to look for Eurydice in the underworld. All the gods follow him.

### Act III

Eurydice is being held in the underworld's prison, when Jupiter arrives to court her. To enter the locked cell, Cupid turns Jupiter into a fly who immediately charms Eurydice ("Il m'a semblé sur mon épaule"). Confident of his conquest, Jupiter identifies himself.

### Act IV

Jupiter turns Eurydice into a reveling Bacchante and, after she entertains with a song, everyone dances the can-can ("Ce bal est original"). While Pluton and Jupiter compete for Eurydice, Orphée arrives and is told he can recover his wife if he leads her away without glancing back. But when Jupiter throws a thunderbolt, Orphée looks around. With that, Eurydice remains a Bacchante and the gods celebrate.

### PRINCIPAL ROLES

**Orphée (Orpheus)** *tenor* A musician

**Eurydice** *soprano* Orphée's wife

**Jupiter** *baritone* King of the gods

**Aristée/Pluton (Pluto)** *tenor*
God of the underworld

**John Styx** *tenor* Prison guard in Hades

**Mercury and Mars** *tenor* Gods

Such was the popularity of *Orphée aux enfers* that a gala performance was organized for Emperor Napoleon III and Empress Eugénie, no small honor for the composer of operettas for popular audiences.

◀ **Madame Méaly** was a striking Eurydice in a 1902 production at the Théâtre des Variétés in Paris.

# La belle Hélène

BEAUTIFUL HELEN *Opéra-bouffe* in three acts, 3 hours ▪ Composed: 1864 ▪ First performed: December 17, 1864, Théâtre des Variétés, Paris, France ▪ Libretto: Henri Meilhac and Ludovic Halévy

*La belle Hélène* echoes *Orphée aux enfers* by parodying the Greek classics. While using all the tricks common to farces, Offenbach also satisfies the 19th century's appetite for sweet melodies, starting with Hélène's opening paean to love, *"Amours divins."* Choruses are important as lyrical cheerleaders to the romantic action. *La belle Hélène* was an immediate success, becoming so popular that it was soon the one operetta regularly performed in mainstream opera houses.

## PRINCIPAL ROLES

**Paris** *tenor* Prince of Troy

**Hélène (Helen)** *mezzo-soprano* Queen of Sparta

**Ménélas (Menelaus)** *tenor* King of Sparta

**Calchas** *bass* Jupiter's high priest

### Act I

Hélène has joined a ceremony at the Temple of Venus, but her mind is on Venus's vow that Paris, Prince of Troy, will win the most beautiful woman in the world. A shepherd learns that he has won the contest. Recognizing the shepherd as Paris, Calchas the high priest asks him to praise Venus ("Au mont Ida"). Hélène is attracted to the shepherd, but their flirtation is interrupted by Ménélas, Hélène's husband. A game of charades follows and the "shepherd" wins Hélène. To further Venus's scheme, Jupiter orders Ménélas to leave for Crete.

### Act II

Paris asks to see Hélène in her chambers, and, after a very brief hesitation, she agrees. While she is sleeping, Paris arrives disguised as a slave, and, thinking she is dreaming, Hélène welcomes him warmly ("Oui, c'est un rêve"). Ménélas arrives unannounced and protests wildly, but Hélène turns the tables on him, complaining that husbands should always give warning before returning.

### Act III

Taking a holiday by the sea, Ménélas and other kings complain of the crowds and worry about Venus's influence over their women. Ménélas, who feels cuckolded by Hélène, summons a priest to restore order. Paris arrives disguised as the priest. He orders Hélène to accompany him to Cythera to honor Venus. After Paris reveals himself, a chorus wishes them bon voyage.

In Hortense Schneider, who created Hélène, Offenbach not only found a mistress but also a talented soprano who contributed to the success of later operettas, including *La Grande-Duchesse de Gérolstein.*

◀ **Felicity Lott** as Hélène is courted by Yann Beuron's Paris in Laurent Pelly's hit production at the Théâtre du Châtelet, Paris, in 2003.

# Les contes d'Hoffmann

THE TALES OF HOFFMANN *Opéra fantastique* in a prologue, three acts, and an epilogue, 2¾ hours • Composed: 1877–1880 • First performed: February 10, 1881, Opéra-Comique, Paris, France • Libretto: Jules Barbier, after a play by Barbier and Michel Carré, based on several tales of E. T. A. Hoffmann

*Les contes d'Hoffmann*, Offenbach's final and finest work, recounts an old poet's four ill-fated love affairs. The opera has a complex theatrical structure, with the same singers ideally used for each of the four soprano and four bass roles to underline the idea that the same love affair keeps repeating itself. The music is at once glittering and melancholic, notably with its most famous song, the lilting barcarole in Act III.

### Prologue

Lindorf, an unscrupulous politician, lusts after Hoffmann's mistress, the singer Stella. At the urging of drinking students, Hoffmann tells the stories of his unhappy love for three other women, who all exist in Stella.

### Act I

In Paris, Hoffmann falls for Olympia, a mechanical doll made by Spalanzani, an inventor. At the touch of her shoulder, she sings ("Les oiseaux dans la charmille")

and dances. Coppélius, who has provided her eyes, feels cheated by Spalanzani and destroys Olympia. Only then does Hoffman realize she is an automaton.

### Act II

In Munich, Crespel forbids his daughter, Antonia, from singing for fear she will die of the same disease as his opera-singer wife. In love, Hoffmann and Antonia decide to marry. Dr. Miracle comes to treat Antonia and has a portrait of

Antonia's mother tell the girl to sing. When she does, she expires. Dr. Miracle vanishes and Crespel blames Hoffmann.

### Act III

In a Venetian bordello, Giulietta sings of love ("Belle nuit, ô nuit d'amour"), but the evil Dapertutto has other plans. In exchange for a diamond ring, she is to capture Hoffmann's reflection. Easily seduced, the poet surrenders his reflection. He then kills Dapertutto, but he loses Giulietta anyway.

### Epilogue

With his stories told, Hoffmann is by now quite drunk. Stella returns and finds him fast asleep. While Lindorf leads her away, she looks back sadly at Hoffmann.

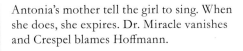

**PRINCIPAL ROLES**

**Hoffmann** *tenor* A poet

**La Muse/Nicklausse** *mezzo-soprano* Hoffman's muse and protector

**Stella/Olympia/Antonia/Giulietta** *soprano* Women loved by Hoffmann

**Lindorf/Coppélius/Miracle/Dapertutto** *bass* Hoffmann's enemies

Unfinished at the time of Offenbach's death, *Les contes d'Hoffmann* was completed by several different hands, with the result that no definitive version of the opera exists, especially of Act III and the Epilogue.

◀ **Natalie Dessay's** Olympia is coached by Sergio Bertocchi's Spalanzani in the Paris Opera's production in 2000.

# Georges Bizet

Born: October 25, 1838, Paris, France ▪ Died: June 3, 1875, Bougival, near Paris, France

Georges Bizet's extraordinary celebrity as an opera composer is the fruit of just one work, *Carmen*. He wrote other operas, with one or two still occasionally performed. But none has come close to enjoying *Carmen*'s enduring popularity around the world. His early death, at 36, cut short a blossoming career.

A child prodigy, Bizet was just nine when he entered the Paris Conservatoire and only 17 when he wrote his fine Symphony in C. After three years in Rome, where he focused on *opera buffa*, his return to Paris brought frustration. He won a competition for a comic opera with *Le docteur Miracle*, and it was presented at Offenbach's Bouffes-Parisiens in 1857. This brought commissions for other operas, which were not produced in his lifetime. Eventually, in 1863, *Les pêcheurs de perles* reached a major stage.

Four years later, *La jolie fille de Perth* earned Bizet some plaudits, but success fell short of his talent. He kept busy writing orchestral music and piano works, with his incidental music to Daudet's Provençal tragedy *L'Arlésienne* still popular today. But many

◀ **Evgueniy Alexiev as Zurga**, leader of the pearl fishers, in an atmospheric scene from Antoine Bourseiller's production of *Les pêcheurs de perles* staged at the Opéra National du Rhin in France.

of his operatic projects were never completed. After the disruption of the Franco-Prussian War of 1870–1871, Bizet wrote an Orientalist comic opera, *Djamileh*, but soon he was absorbed by *Carmen*. With it, he hoped to answer critics who had accused him of being complicated and obscure. "Well, this time I have written a work that is all clarity and vivacity, full of color and melody," he remarked. But the premiere was a flop, and, although *Carmen* was soon hailed as a masterpiece, Bizet did not live to savor his achievement.

## FIRST PERFORMANCES

- **1863** *Les pêcheurs de perles*
- **1867** *La jolie fille de Perth*
- **1872** *Djamileh*
- **1875** *Carmen*

"As a musician, I tell you that if we were to suppress adultery, fanaticism, crime, evil, the supernatural, there would no longer be the means of writing one note."

GEORGES BIZET

# Les pêcheurs de perles

THE PEARL FISHERS Opera in three acts (four tableaux), 2 hours ▪ Composed: 1863 ▪ First performed: September 30, 1863, Théâtre-Lyrique, Paris, France ▪ Libretto: Eugène Cormon and Michel Carré

*Les pêcheurs de perles* launched Bizet's operatic career, although it was not enthusiastically received at its premiere. The composer himself described it as "an honorable, brilliant failure." Today, however, it is "the other" Bizet opera—not *Carmen*—that is still regularly performed. Written when he was only 25, *Les pêcheurs de perles* shows Bizet influenced by Gounod and Verdi and still searching for his own voice. Thus, while this opera's story is set in Ceylon, the music offers no local color. Rather, through wonderfully melodic arias, duets, and choruses, Bizet evokes a dreamlike world of pure romance, one presided over by a virgin priestess and convulsed by human passions. The opera is considered difficult to stage because of its minimal action, but the lush score is a permanent delight.

## Act I

Gathered on a beach, pearl fishers choose Zurga as their leader while they await the virgin priestess who will protect them. Nadir, Zurga's childhood friend, arrives unexpectedly. They recall when they saw a beautiful veiled woman and both fell for her. But to avoid conflict, they renounced their love for her and swore eternal friendship ("Au fond du temple saint"). The priestess is received by Nourabad, the high priest, while Zurga reminds her to remain veiled and to take no lover. Suddenly Nadir recognizes her as his beloved Leïla. That night, he remembers how he betrayed Zurga and followed her ("Je crois entendre encore"). In his sleep, he hears Leïla singing ("O Dieu Brahma"). Following her voice, he finds her on a rock. As her face is briefly revealed, he rejoices.

## Act II

The boats return safely and Nourabad tells Leïla she can sleep peacefully if she has kept her vow to remain pure. Leïla recalls that she once saved the life of a man who gave her a necklace in thanks. Alone, Leïla senses Nadir's presence ("Me voilà seule dans la nuit"). When he appears, they are both overwhelmed by love ("Leïla! Leïla!"). Leïla begs him to leave, as they are both at risk. Shots sound and Nourabad identifies Nadir as the stranger who violated the sacred sanctuary. The pearl fishers are enraged, vowing to kill Leïla and Nadir. Zurga, declaring that only he can decide their fate, tells the couple to flee. But as Nourabad tears off Leïla's veil, Zurga understands the depth of Nadir's betrayal.

## Act III

Zurga regrets ordering Nadir to die at dawn, but when Leïla appears his passion for her is rekindled ("Je frémis, je chancelle"). Leïla begs him to punish only her, saying she met Nadir by chance. But Zurga says he cannot reprieve his friend because she loves him. Admitting that he, too, loves her, he is torn by jealousy. Cursing him, Leïla defies him to take her life. Light in the sky announces the hour of execution. Saying she is ready to die, Leïla asks a fisherman to give her necklace to her mother. Zurga seizes the necklace and runs after her. At the foot of the pyre, Nadir bids emotional farewell to Leïla. Zurga suddenly arrives, saying that the light in the sky is a fire sent down from heaven. As the people scatter in fear, Zurga reveals that he lit the fire to allow the lovers to escape. Showing the necklace that he once gave Leïla, he says he will now save both their lives. As they flee, Zurga feels he has done his duty.

....................

This opera's loveliest melody, the tenor–baritone duet "Au fond du temple saint," becomes a leitmotif that returns, at times echoed only by the orchestra, whenever the friendship between Zurga and Nadir is recalled.

....................

### PRINCIPAL ROLES

**Zurga** *baritone* The leader of the pearl fishers

**Nadir** *tenor*
Pearl fisher and Zurga's childhood friend

**Leïla** *soprano* A mysterious virgin priestess

**Nourabad** *bass* The high priest

### Alfredo Kraus

Less renowned outside the opera world than Luciano Pavarotti and Plácido Domingo, the Spanish lyric tenor Alfredo Kraus was considered the post-war master of *bel canto*. One of his earliest recordings was as Nadir in *Les pêcheurs de perles*, a role that also suited his high tenor voice and refined artistry. Famous for conserving his voice, he was 70 years old when he sang "La donna è mobile" at the reopening of Madrid's Teatro Real in 1997, two years before his death.

◀ **An ornate costume** designed by Umberto Brunelleschi for a production of Bizet's opera at La Scala, Milan.

# Carmen

*Opéra comique* in four acts, 2¾ hours ▪ Composed: 1873–1875 ▪ First performed: March 3, 1875, Opéra-Comique, Paris, France ▪ Libretto: Henri Meilhac and Ludovic Halévy, after Prosper Mérimée's 1845 novella *Carmen*

*Carmen* ranks high among the world's most beloved operas. Yet, as so often with such favorites, it was not instantly recognized as a masterpiece: at its premiere, its indecency shocked the Opéra-Comique's conservative audience. Soon, though, *Carmen* worked its seductive magic through the charm of its melodies, Spanish "exoticism" of the score, and strength of its characters. The work is described as an *opéra comique* because it has spoken dialogue but, beneath its exuberance, it always hints at a tragic denouement. Here, the rich color of the choruses and orchestration plays a central role. But while Don José, Escamillo, and Micaëla have fine arias, Carmen is the fickle Gypsy diva of this opera, nowhere more brilliantly expressed than in her Act I *habanera*.

## PRINCIPAL ROLES

**Carmen** *mezzo-soprano* A rebellious cigarette girl

**Don José** *tenor* A corporal in the dragoons

**Escamillo** *baritone* A matador

**Micaëla** *soprano* A peasant girl

**Zuniga** *bass* A captain

**Moralès** *baritone* An officer

**Lillas Pastia** *spoken role* An innkeeper

## Act I

In a square crowded with soldiers, a peasant girl seeks out a corporal, Don José, but cannot find him. Don José arrives afterward, guessing it is Micaëla. Meanwhile, new to Seville, Captain Zuniga learns that hundreds of women work in the tobacco factory. When a bell rings, the women spill out noisily, while Carmen sings of her untamed love ("L'amour est un oiseau rebelle"). She then tosses a flower at Don José. Micaëla delivers a letter, which Don José reads aloud. His mother says it is time he married and suggests Micaëla as a bride. Suddenly, a fight erupts in the factory and Carmen is blamed. After

Zuniga orders her tied up, she flirts with Don José, proposing a tryst and persuading him to loosen the rope ("Près des remparts de Séville"). As she is led away, she escapes.

## Act II

Two months afterward, Carmen is entertaining officers in a tavern ("Les tringles des sistres tintaient") when she learns that Don José has served his prison term for freeing her. Escamillo the toreador arrives and boasts of his exploits ("Votre toast, je peux vous le rendre"). He tries to win over Carmen, but she brushes him off. As the tavern empties out, smugglers seek help to distract border guards. Carmen refuses, saying she is in love. Don José appears and Carmen dances for him. But when he hears bugles calling him back to the barracks, she mocks him. To prove his love, he shows the flower she threw at him ("La fleur que tu m'avais jetée"). Zuniga arrives to woo Carmen and is disarmed. Don José now realizes he must flee.

## Act III

At the smugglers' hideout, Carmen is losing interest in Don José. The Gypsy girls read their fortunes in cards; when it is Carmen's turn, the cards predict death for herself and Don José. Don José is left on guard. Nearby, Micaëla is building up courage to enter the camp ("Je dis que rien ne m'épouvante"). Escamillo appears, announcing he has come for Carmen. Don José challenges him. In the fight, Escamillo has the upper hand at first, but he then falls. After Carmen saves

◀ **Spanish mezzo-soprano** Teresa Berganza, seen here in a 1981 production at the San Francisco Opera, carried her sensuous interpretation of Carmen around the world.

### Carmen revisited

In 1943, American theatrical producer Oscar Hammerstein II, turned *Carmen* into an African-American story, setting it around a Southern military base and renaming it *Carmen Jones*. It was made into a popular film by Otto Preminger in 1954. A South African *Carmen* was brought to the screen in 2005 as *U-Carmen eKhayelitsha*. Set in a poor township, it won the Golden Bear for best film at the 2005 Berlin International Film Festival.

▶ **Dorothy Dandridge** as Carmen Jones plays up to Harry Belafonte's Joe in Otto Preminger's screen adaptation.

his life, he invites her to his next bullfight. Don José is furious but, learning from Micaëla that his mother is dying, he leaves. He vows to meet Carmen again.

### Act IV

Outside the bullring, children welcome Escamillo, accompanied by Carmen. Her friends warn her that Don José is also there. When Don José finds her, he begs her to return to him, insisting that he loves her. Carmen rebuffs him, declaring that she was born free. Finally, he stabs her. When a triumphant Escamillo appears, Don José tearfully confesses to having killed his "beloved Carmen."

▶ **While a matador may personify** brash virility, his gamble when confronting a fighting bull also symbolizes his fear of being rejected if he falls in love.

Bizet may have modeled Carmen on Céleste Vénard, a nightclub singer and former prostitute known as "La Mogador." After a chance meeting on a train, they became close friends in the mid-1860s, although in her memoirs Céleste Vénard denied that they were ever lovers.

**The American mezzo-soprano** Denyce Graves, one of the most exciting Carmens of her generation, reaches out to the audience at the Arena di Verona in Italy in 1999.

# Jules Massenet

Born: May 12, 1842, Montaud, France ▪ Died: August 13, 1912, Paris, France

Jules Massenet, the dominant French opera composer of the late 19th century, wrote more than 30 operas, in styles ranging from intimate tragedy and *verismo* to *opéra comique* and *grand opéra*. Of these, only *Manon* and *Werther* are regularly performed. Yet both are so popular that they have carried the French flag to theaters around the world.

Like Gounod and Bizet before him, Massenet won the Prix de Rome, which took him to Italy. There, he developed a strong interest in religious music, and he composed several sacred works when he returned to Paris. However, it was opera that consumed his life: he wrote his first in 1867 and his last in 1912. And he wrote for Vienna, Brussels, London, and Monte Carlo as well as Paris, where he was viewed as Meyerbeer's successor.

His two finest works came in the middle of his career—*Manon* in 1884 and *Werther* in 1892—but many others were popular in their day, including *Le roi de Lahore*, *Hérodiade*, *Le Cid*, *Thaïs*, and *Sapho*. Massenet often found inspiration in beautiful sopranos, while he wrote *Don Quichotte* for the great Russian bass Feodor Chaliapin. During his lifetime, he was viewed sceptically by some of his peers, above all after he published his memoirs, considered by many as highly inventive. Nonetheless, a century later, his reputation rests comfortably on his gift for fine tunes and touching stories.

◀ **Jules Massenet** working in the study of his Paris home in the early years of the 20th century.

## FIRST PERFORMANCES

- 1877 *Le roi de Lahore*
- 1881 *Hérodiade*
- 1884 *Manon*
- 1885 *Le Cid*
- 1889 *Esclarmonde*
- 1892 *Werther*
- 1894 *Thaïs*
- 1897 *Sapho*
- 1899 *Cendrillon*
- 1910 *Don Quichotte*

# Manon

*Opéra comique* in five acts (six tableaux), 2½ hours • Composed: 1882–1884 • First performed: January 19, 1884, Opéra-Comique, Paris, France • Libretto: Henri Meilhac and Philippe Gille, after Abbé Provost's 1731 novel *Manon Lescaut*

*Manon*, Massenet's most popular opera, daringly explores a young woman's sexuality. Only nine years earlier, Bizet's *Carmen* was considered scandalous, but this work won public approval. Termed an *opéra comique* for its spoken dialogue, *Manon* is notably tragic, with a fast-paced story accompanied by exceptionally beautiful music. The score, with its famous arias and duets, is above all a gift to singers and audiences.

## Act I

Guillot, a financier, is drinking with an aristocratic friend, Brétigny. Outside the tavern, Lescaut receives his cousin, Manon, who is on her way to a convent ("Je suis encore tout étourdie"). Guillot starts wooing the girl, but Lescaut chases him away. Le Chevalier des Grieux falls for Manon and persuades her to live with him in Paris.

## Act II

Des Grieux wants his father's consent to marry Manon. Their hideaway is discovered by Lescaut and Brétigny, who warn Manon that her lover will be abducted. Brétigny reassures her that if she says nothing, she can then live in luxury with him. Alone, Manon bids farewell to her little table ("Adieu, notre petite table"). On his return, Des Grieux is kidnapped.

## Act III

Now as Brétigny's mistress, Manon learns that Des Grieux is to enter a seminary and hurries to see him. Des Grieux's prayers show he has not forgotten Manon. When she reiterates her love, they flee together.

## Act IV

Manon encourages Des Grieux to gamble. He wins, but Guillot accuses him of cheating and summons the police. Des Grieux is released, but Manon is ordered to be deported to Louisiana.

## Act V

Des Grieux and Lescaut still hope to free Manon. Guards are bribed and the lovers are reunited. But Manon is too exhausted to move. And as they remember their happiness together, she dies in Des Grieux's arms.

One year after Puccini wrote his *Manon Lescaut*, Massenet returned to the story in a one-act opera called *Le portrait de Manon*, in which Des Grieux relives his love for Manon through his nephew.

### PRINCIPAL ROLES

**Manon Lescaut** *soprano* A fickle young woman

**Le Chevalier des Grieux** *tenor* A young noble

**Le Comte des Grieux** *bass* Le Chevalier's father

**Lescaut** *baritone* A soldier and Manon's cousin

**Guillot de Morfontaine** *tenor* A rakish financier

**Brétigny** *baritone* A rich noble and farmer-general

▶ **Anna Netrebko** as Manon Lescaut and Vittorio Grigolo as Le Chevalier des Grieux in Laurent Pelly's 2010 production at the Royal Opera House in London.

# Werther

*Drame lyrique* in four acts, 2 hours • Composed: 1885–1887 • First performed: February 16, 1892, Hofoper, Vienna, Austria • Libretto: Édouard Blau, Paul Milliet, and Georges Hartmann, after Goethe's novella *Die Leiden des jungen Werthers* (1774)

*Werther*, although less frequently performed than *Manon*, is Massenet's finest opera. Adapted from Goethe's novella, itself a pillar of the Romantic movement, it portrays a hopeless love story, which ends in the most tragic of ways: a man's suicide with pistols provided by his beloved. Indeed, *Werther* was initially rejected by the Opéra-Comique in Paris as too depressing. As a result, one of the most celebrated French operas was first presented at the Vienna Court Opera. Massenet himself seemed eager to match Goethe's novella in opera. Thus he offers no relief from the emotional voyage through, say, choruses. Instead, with continuous music evocative of Wagner, Werther's desperate love and Charlotte's emotional disarray are portrayed through the poetry of recitatives and the lyricism of intense arias and duets.

## PRINCIPAL ROLES

**Werther** *tenor* A 23-year-old poet

**Le Bailli** *bass* A bailiff

**Charlotte** *mezzo-soprano*
The bailiff's 20-year-old daughter

**Albert** *baritone* Charlotte's betrothed

**Sophie** *soprano*
The bailiff's 15-year-old daughter

**Schmidt** *tenor* The bailiff's friend

**Johann** *baritone* The bailiff's friend

The role of Charlotte is popular among woman singers, not least because, for once, they do not expire on stage. "Charlotte reverses the roles," Victoria de los Ángeles noted; "it's the man who dies for her."

### Act I

The bailiff, a widower, is rehearsing Christmas songs with his younger children—in July. His friends Johann and Schmidt wander by and learn that his 20-year-old daughter, Charlotte, is dressing for a ball. Talk turns to Werther, a melancholy young man. There is also praise for Albert, Charlotte's fiancé, who is away on business. Werther arrives, cheered by the children's singing. The bailiff introduces him to Charlotte and they go together to the ball, leaving 15-year-old Sophie caring for the smaller children. Hoping to surprise Charlotte, Albert arrives unexpectedly. Hours later, Charlotte and Werther return, arm-in-arm. Werther declares his love, but Charlotte does not respond ("Mais vous ne savez rien de moi"). Hearing that Albert is back, Charlotte says she promised her dying mother to marry him. Devastated, Werther tells her to keep the promise.

### Act II

Now married three months, Charlotte and Albert enter the town church. From afar, Werther watches them in despair ("Un autre est son époux"). As he slumps on a bench, Albert arrives to console him by acknowledging how he once felt for Charlotte. Werther insists that he no longer suffers, but Sophie remarks on his troubled spirit. Werther decides to leave town but then sees Charlotte and again pours out his feelings. She tells him to go away and not to return before Christmas ("Lorsque l'enfant revient"). Seeing him go, Sophie tells Charlotte and Albert, who now knows that Werther still loves Charlotte.

◀ **After *Werther's* opening success** in Vienna, the Opéra-Comique in Paris quickly forgot its objections to the opera and began presenting it regularly.

## Act III

It is Christmas Eve and Charlotte cannot forget Werther, constantly rereading his letters. Seeing her sister's red eyes, Sophie says she knows her sadness began when Werther left. Finally, Charlotte bursts into tears ("Va! Laisse couler mes larmes"). Sophie begs her to join the family. Suddenly Werther arrives. Charlotte says nothing has changed. He recognizes the case of pistols. She points to the love poem he was translating before he left. But when he reads it aloud ("Pourquoi me réveiller"), Charlotte begs him to stop. He tries to kiss her, and she faints. When he embraces her, she flees. A servant brings Albert a letter from Werther, asking to borrow his pistols for a long journey.

Albert orders Charlotte to hand them to the servant. As he storms out, Charlotte grabs her cloak.

## Act IV

Charlotte finds Werther mortally wounded. He opens his eyes and asks for forgiveness. She wants to seek help, but he prefers to die, telling her of his love. Finally, she confesses her love for him and, for the first time, they kiss. Gradually, Werther loses consciousness ("Ah! Ses yeux se ferment"). As he dies, children can be heard singing, "Jesus is born."

▼ **Charlotte Hellekant as Charlotte** resists Paul Charles Clarke as Werther in the Sebastian Baumgarten production staged at the Deutsche Oper Berlin, in 2002.

### In Wagner's shadow

In adapting Goethe's 1774 narrative fiction *The Sorrows of Young Werther*, Massenet assumed no small risk. By the late 19th century, Wagner's *Tristan und Isolde* had redefined tragic love, and even French composers were being measured against the great operas of German Romanticism. Nonetheless, *Werther* was warmly received in Vienna in 1892 as "not too French," and, within a year, it was presented in Paris. Although the music is often unabashedly sentimental, Massenet considered the opera his greatest achievement.

# Claude Debussy

Born: August 22, 1862, Saint-Germain-en-Laye, near Paris, France • Died: March 25, 1918, Paris, France

Claude Debussy marked his era with sensuous and inventive music in all styles. While he is best remembered for his piano compositions and symphonic poems, his *Pelléas et Mélisande* stands as a monument in the history of opera, a work that broke with 19th-century tonal structures and harmonies, and paved the way for 20th-century modernity.

Debussy entered the Paris Conservatoire at the age of 11, and, at 18, he was hired as an accompanist by a widowed Russian millionairess. From then on, his life was a constant adventure. He won the Prix de Rome in 1884 but, pining for his married mistress, he returned to Paris early. Indeed, until he was 40, his personal life was stormy: both a later mistress and his first wife tried to take their own life. Still, he remained productive, creating such memorable works as *Clair de lune* (1890), *Prélude à l'après-midi d'un faune* (1894), and *La Mer* (1905). *Pelléas et Mélisande* was his only opera, although *Le Martyre de Saint-Sébastien*, with his incidental music, is occasionally staged. Debussy's premature death from cancer at 55 cut short a remarkable career.

▼ **Claude Debussy** sitting at the piano beside Jeanne Chausson, wife of his composer friend, Ernest Chausson, at the Chaussons' Paris home.

### A man of many arts

Debussy found musical inspiration in Wagner and Mussorgsky, but he also reached out to other arts, viewing creative expression as a whole. He has been called a "musical Impressionist" because of the influence of Monet and J. M. W. Turner on his music, while he also composed works triggered by Pre-Raphaelite paintings. "I love painting almost as much as music itself," he once noted. Literature, too, intrigued him: he set Symbolist poems to music, while—ever curious—he long hoped to adapt two Edgar Allan Poe stories as operas.

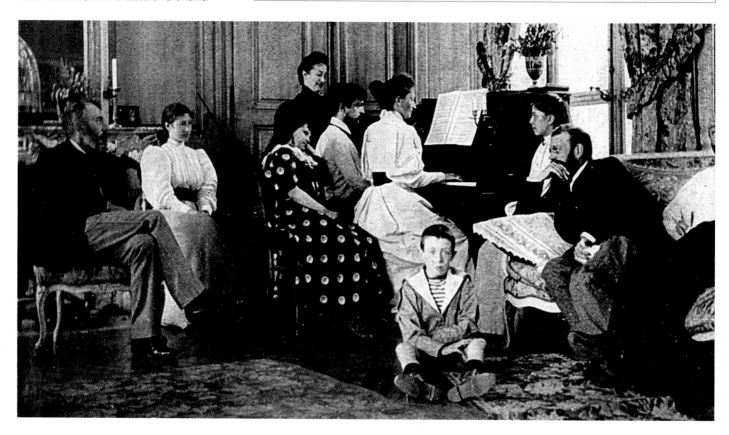

# Le Martyre de Saint Sébastien

THE MARTYRDOM OF SAINT SEBASTIAN *Drame sacré* in five windows, 2 hours • Composed: 1910–1911 • First performed: May 22, 1911, Théâtre du Châtelet, Paris, France • Libretto: Gabriele d'Annunzio

*Le Martyre de Saint-Sébastien* expressed Debussy's ideal of total art: D'Annunzio's mystery play had Ida Rubinstein dancing Michel Fokine's choreography to Debussy's music in decor painted by Léon Bakst. The one-hour score includes solos, choruses, and accompaniment. While the work was poorly received at its premiere, public interest has been maintained by St. Sebastian's homoerotic image as Emperor Diocletian's lover.

### Window One: *La Cour des lys/* The Court of Lilies

The narrator invites the public to view Sébastien's life as if studying five stained-glass windows. The first shows the twins Marc and Marcellien being tortured in a public place while Sébastien calls for a sign from God. As he dances on hot embers, lilies emerge from the ground.

### Window Two: *La Chambre magique/* The Magic Chamber

Sébastien overturns the false idols, enters the Temple of the Virgin Erigone, and defeats pagan forces. Another virgin sings a lament ("Qui pleure mon enfant si doux").

### Window Three: *Le Concile des faux dieux/* The Council of False Gods

In the council of false gods, Emperor Dioclétien hails Sébastien as a "beauteous youth" whom he wants crowned. Sébastien claims he carries a crown, one forged by faith and prayer. The infatuated Dioclétien still wants to make Sébastien a god. When the young man dances the Lord's Passion and refuses the emperor's lyre, Dioclétien orders him put to death ("Il est mort, le bel Adonis").

### Window Four: *Le Laurier blessé/* The Wounded Laurel

In Apollo's laurel grove, Sébastien receives each arrow, crying "Encore!" Alone, he sees stigmata appear on his hands and surrenders to holy ecstasy.

### Window Five: *Le Paradis/* Paradise

Saint-Sébastien's soul is received in heaven by choirs of martyrs, virgins, apostles, and angels singing in unison.

Before the premiere, the Archbishop of Paris warned Christians against a semi-pagan show in which a Jewish woman danced the role of Saint-Sébastien and, when killed by arrows, cried out, "More, more, more!"

**PRINCIPAL ROLES**

**Narrateur** *spoken role* A narrator

**Sébastien** *spoken and danced role* A Roman army officer

**Dioclétien** *spoken role* Emperor of Rome

**Marc** *soprano* A sacrificial victim

**Marcellien** *contralto* A sacrificial victim

**La Vierge Érigone** *soprano*

▶ **Éric Vu-An,** in the spoken and danced role of Saint-Sébastien, faces death by arrows in this 1986 production, which toured Milan, Salzburg, and Brussels.

# Pelléas et Mélisande

PELLEAS AND MELISANDE *Drame lyrique* in five acts (12 tableaux), 3¼ hours ▪ Composed: 1893 (rev. 1900–1902) ▪ First performed: April 30, 1902, Opéra-Comique, Paris, France ▪ Libretto: Hector Berlioz, after the 1891 play by Maurice Maeterlinck

*Pelléas et Mélisande* enjoys a unique place in the history of opera as the gateway to the 20th century. Although Debussy fought to escape Wagner's shadow, there are echoes of *Tristan und Isolde* and *Parsifal* in this work. But, inspired by Maeterlinck's play, a landmark work of Symbolist theater, Debussy went further, creating a timeless world in which the characters communicate in the symbolic language of restrained passion. Indeed, as a lover of poetry, Debussy allows the flow of words to lead the uninterrupted music. Thus, in place of set-piece arias, the lyrics become an exquisite blend of declamatory chant and recitative, with the score playing the role of "musical scenery," as Debussy put it. The effect is a sensual, dreamlike, almost hypnotic atmosphere, one perfectly suited to the slow-motion tragedy that unfolds.

## PRINCIPAL ROLES

**Mélisande** *soprano*
A mysterious and fragile young woman

**Golaud** *baritone* A prince who marries Mélisande

**Pelléas** *tenor* or *baritone* Golaud's half-brother

**Arkel** *bass*
King of Allemonde and grandfather to Pelléas and Golaud

**Geneviève** *mezzo-soprano*
Arkel's daughter, mother to Pelléas and Golaud

**Yniold** *soprano*
Golaud's young son from an earlier marriage

**Un médecin** *bass* A doctor

**Un berger** *baritone* A shepherd

### Act I

Lost in a forest, Prince Golaud comes across a weeping girl. He offers to recover her crown from a pool, but the terrified girl no longer wants it. Finally, giving her name as Mélisande, she nervously follows Golaud out of the forest. Six months later, Geneviève learns that Golaud, her widowed son, has married Mélisande and wants to make peace with Arkel, his grandfather. Golaud asks his half-brother Pelléas to light a lantern on the castle tower signaling if he can return. Later, residing in the castle, Mélisande is walking with Geneviève when Pelléas joins them. He is disturbed to meet her. As they watch a ship set sail, Pelléas announces that he, too, will soon leave.

### Act II

Pelléas leads Mélisande to an old well. When she tries to touch the water, her ring, given to her by Golaud, falls into the well. At the same moment, Golaud is thrown from a horse. As Mélisande

Maurice Maeterlinck tried unsuccessfully to sabotage Debussy's adaptation of his play after the Scottish soprano Mary Gardon was cast as Mélisande at the premiere, instead of Maeterlinck's mistress, Georgette Leblanc.

▶ **Mireille Delunsch** as Mélisande and José van Dam as Golaud in Robert Wilson's production at the Opéra Bastille, Paris, in 2004.

nurses him in bed, he notices her ring is missing. When she says she lost it in the cave by the sea, he tells her to find it and instructs Pelléas to accompany her. Mélisande is afraid, but Pelléas insists they enter the dark cave.

### Act III

Mélisande is combing her hair by her window when Pelléas calls to her ("Mes longs cheveux descendent"). He wants to kiss her hand, but cannot reach it. Suddenly her long hair tumbles down and Pelléas wraps himself in it passionately. Golaud appears and chides them. Outside the castle vaults, Golaud warns Pelléas to stay away from Mélisande, who is pregnant and fragile. Golaud questions his son, Yniold, about Mélisande and Pelléas. He then holds the boy to peer into Mélisande's room. Yniold sees her with Pelléas, but they are looking at a light in silence.

### Act IV

Pelléas must see Mélisande alone and they agree to meet by the well. Arkel is trying to lift Mélisande's spirits. Golaud bursts in and, insulting her to her face, drags her across the floor by her hair. Pelléas finally tells Mélisande of his love. "I love you, too," she responds ("On dirait que ta voix"). They hear a noise and realize that they are doomed. As they kiss, Golaud kills Pelléas.

### Act V

Mélisande lies wounded in bed and asks to see the setting sun through the window ("Ouvrez la fenêtre"). She calls Golaud to her side and he asks for her forgiveness ("Est-ce vous, Golaud?"). He then interrogates her. "Did you love Pelléas?" he asks. "Why yes," she replies. Was it "forbidden" love? Mélisande assures him it was not, but he does not believe her. Her baby is brought to her, but she is too weak to hold it. And without a sound, Mélisande dies. Arkel takes the child, saying, "It must live now, in her place."

▶ **In a pool or a well or at sea**, water serves as this opera's emotional vein, leading from the amorous to the tragic.

# RUSSIAN OPERA
## (c. 1830–1960)

# Russian opera c. 1830–1960

Russian opera emerged in the 1830s as a nationalist reaction to domination by imported European culture. To compete with Italian opera in particular, young composers mined Russian history, religion, and folklore for stories and melodies. The result was opera with a distinctly Russian sound and style, at once patriotic and mournful, dramatic and romantic.

## Imperial roots

In 1712, Peter the Great moved his capital to St. Petersburg from Moscow in order to open up Russia to Europe's modernizing influence. This process was accelerated by the Prussian-born Catherine the Great, who modeled her court—its architecture and its culture—on Versailles. In 1783, with opera all the rage in Western Europe, she had a new Bolshoi Theatre built in St. Petersburg to perform opera—inevitably Italian—and drama.

## Literature leads the way

In the early 19th century, poets, led by Aleksandr Pushkin, discovered a native Russian voice in folklore and pre-Romanov history. Their work inspired a new Russian-language opera, which turned to literature as its primary source. Mikhail Glinka won acclaim as the "father" of Russian opera thanks to *Ivan Susanin*, or *A Life for the Czar*, a patriotic story about a peasant who saves a czar; and *Ruslan i Lyudmila*, a fairy-tale opera based on a Pushkin poem. Both echoed folk melodies and Russian Orthodox's sung liturgies. The new boast was that Russian music owed nothing to Italy or Germany, a conviction that inspired the opening of the Mariinsky Theatre in St. Petersburg in 1860.

## The mighty five

Romantic nationalism became the leitmotif of a group of young, self-taught composers known to the West as "The Five." Mily Balakirev, the group's leader, and César Cui gave political voice to the movement, while the others—Modest Mussorgsky, Aleksandr Borodin, and Nicolai Rimsky-Korsakov—set about transforming Russian opera. Of these, Mussorgsky became the unchallenged

◀ **The sumptuously ornate Mariinsky Theatre** in St. Petersburg, the cradle of Russian opera, has followed the example of the Royal Opera House in London by renovating its backstage areas.

"Verdi" of Russia thanks to *Boris Godunov* and *The Khovansky Affair* (completed by Rimsky-Korsakov after the composer's death). These vast historical tableaux, rich in choruses and spectacle, stand as monuments to the Russian soul.

Rimsky-Korsakov, the most prolific of the group, also turned to Russian history for his first opera, *The Maid of Pskov*, also known as *Ivan the Terrible*. His most popular work, *The Golden Cockerel*, a fairy tale about a foolish czar, can readily be interpreted as political satire.

## Tchaikovsky's lush romanticism

While Pyotr Tchaikovsky could hardly ignore "The Five," he found a more cosmopolitan voice of his own, composing deeply romantic ballet and orchestral music as well as "tragic love" operas of universal appeal. Two won worldwide acclaim: *Eugene Onegin*, first performed in 1879, and *The Queen of Spades*, which premiered in 1890.

In the 20th century, three Russian composers stand out. Igor Stravinsky joined Diaghilev's Ballets Russes in Paris and, after the 1917 Russian Revolution, made his home in France until he left for the US in 1940. His early vocal works were radically modernist: *Solovyei*, or *The Nightingale*, was described as a lyrical story, while *Oedipus Rex* was an opera-oratorio. In contrast, his only full-length opera, *The Rake's Progress*, was undisguisedly Mozartian.

## Stalin's shadow

Sergey Prokofiev also left Russia and, while away, wrote several operas, including *The Gambler*, *The Love for Three Oranges*, and *The Fiery Angel*. Although he never broke with Moscow, his return home in 1936 was traumatic. "Socialist realism" had just been declared the official doctrine, while executions and disappearances were decimating the artistic world. Even Prokofiev's patriotic adaptation of Tolstoy's great novel, *War and Peace*, was considered politically suspect.

Prokofiev should perhaps have noticed how in 1936 Dmitri Shostakovich was denounced for his avant-garde opera, *Lady Macbeth of the Mtsensk District*. Soon, only melodic "Russian" music was acceptable. Then, in 1948, Prokofiev and Shostakovich were among the composers attacked for neglecting beauty in favor of "formalism." With intimidation suffocating creativity, no Russian composer of importance emerged until the Soviet Union collapsed.

# Mikhail Ivanovich Glinka

Born: June 1, 1804, Novospasskoye, Russia • Died: February 15, 1857, Berlin, Germany

Mikhail Ivanovich Glinka is the acknowledged father of Russian opera. After studying music in St. Petersburg, he traveled to Italy, where he came under the sway of Bellini and Donizetti. But when he returned home, he set out to write an opera in Russian, about Russia, with echoes of Slavic folk songs and church music. The result, *Ivan Susanin*, or *A Life for the Czar*, was an immediate success. Glinka's next opera, the fairy tale *Ruslan and Lyudmila*, took five years to write and was initially poorly received. Yet the Russian color of its arias, choruses, and orchestration came to define Russian "nationalist" music for the 19th century.

# Ruslan and Lyudmila

Opera in five acts, 3¼ hours ▪ Composed: 1837–1842 ▪ First performed: December 9, 1842, Bolshoi Theatre, St. Petersburg, Russia ▪ Libretto: Konstantin Bakhturin, Valerian Shirkov, and others, after the poem by Aleksandr Pushkin

*Ruslan and Lyudmila* is considered the cornerstone of Russian opera. In truth, it was neither Russia's nor Glinka's first opera, yet its influence on later Russian composers was fundamental. Until Glinka, Italian opera dominated St. Petersburg's musical taste. Indeed, echoes of Italian *bel canto* can still be heard in this score. Yet, along with its fairy-tale plot and richly attired cast, the opera's melancholic arias, stirring choruses, and riotous dances all conspire to place *Ruslan and Lyudmila* firmly in Russia. The libretto, written by five amateurs, is famously uneven, but this does not detract from a succession of delightful arias. One of the finest is *"I zhar, i znoi smenila nochi ten,"* sung by a contralto in the "trouser role" of Ratmir.

## PRINCIPAL ROLES

**Svetozar** *bass* Grand Prince of Kiev

**Lyudmila** *soprano* His daughter

**Ruslan** *baritone*
A warrior and Lyudmila's beloved

**Ratmir** *contralto*
A suitor to Lyudmila

**Gorislava** *soprano*
An enslaved woman

**Naina** *mezzo-soprano* An evil fairy

◀ **Yevgeny Nikitin as Ruslan** (left) waits for Svetozar (Gennady Bezzubenkov) and Lyudmila (Lyudmila Dudinova), at St. Petersburg's Mariinsky Theatre.

▼ **An elaborate set designed** by Boris Bilinsky for a 1930 Paris production represents the castle of the Grand Prince of Kiev. This is where, in Act I, the suitors of Lyudmila court her.

### Act I
Svetozar, Prince of Kiev, has summoned his court to celebrate the betrothal of his daughter, Lyudmila. She has chosen the warrior Ruslan over Ratmir, an Asian prince, and Farlaf, another warrior, who are also present. After the minstrel Bayan sings of the travails of love, Lyudmila tells of her sadness to leave home, ("Grustno mne, roditel' dorogoi") and her happiness to marry Ruslan. Suddenly the court is plunged into darkness, and, when light returns, Lyudmila has disappeared. Distraught, Svetozar offers her hand—and half his kingdom—to the man who rescues her.

### Act II
The good magician Finn tells Ruslan that Lyudmila has been abducted by Chernomor, an evil dwarf. Finn also warns Ruslan against the sorceress Naina. After Naina orders Farlaf to wait, Ruslan finds himself on a desolate battlefield and is consumed by melancholy ("O pole, pole"). Suddenly a giant head appears, identifying itself as Chernomor's brother. In a brief combat, Ruslan recovers a sword, which will enable him to defeat the dwarf.

### Act III
Arriving in Naina's palace, Ratmir is wooed by Naina's dancing maidens ("I zhar, i znoi smenila nochi ten") and quickly loses interest in Gorislava, an enslaved girl who loves him. Instead, under Naina's spell, Ruslan falls for her. Finally, Finn restores Ratmir to Gorislava and sends Ruslan in search of Lyudmila.

### Act IV
In captivity in Chernomor's castle, Lyudmila yearns for Ruslan and laments her fate ("Vdali ot milogo"). When Ruslan approaches, Chernomor puts her to sleep and rushes out to fight the warrior. Ruslan enters, holding Chernomor's long beard triumphantly in his hand. But Lyudmila cannot be awoken. Ruslan worries that she has betrayed him, then decides to take her home to Kiev.

### Act V
Ratmir, again with Gorislava, is now Ruslan's ally. On the way to Kiev, Farlaf steals Lyudmila, but she sleeps on. Finn then gives Ratmir a ring that will break Chernomor's spell. And when Ruslan finds Lyudmila in Kiev, the ring works its magic. As they finally marry, the court rejoices.

Pushkin's untimely death in a duel prevented him from turning his poem into an opera libretto. Another reason for the confused plot, however, is that Konstantin Bakhturin reportedly sketched the scenario in three hours while drunk.

# Modest Petrovich Mussorgsky

Born: March 21, 1839, Karevo, Russia ▪ Died: March 28, 1881, St. Petersburg, Russia

Modest Petrovich Mussorgsky, the most nationalistic of Russian composers, is best known for his operatic epic *Boris Godunov* and for song cycles depicting ordinary life. Rejecting "art for art's sake," he wrote vocal music that echoed the inflections and intonations of the spoken language. He did this through declamatory arias and choruses shaped by the Orthodox Church and popular tradition.

◄ **Vladimir Matorin exudes** the God-given power that Boris Godunov believes is his gift in a production by Moscow's Bolshoi Ballet at the London Coliseum in 1999.

Mussorgsky was destined for a military career and, at 17, entered the Imperial Guard. From childhood, though, his mother gave him piano lessons, and his wealthy father encouraged his love of music. Later, the composer Mily Balakirev helped him, but he was largely self-taught. At 19, after a nervous breakdown, he left the army.

A first visit to Moscow, the discovery of Mikhail Glinka's music, and his encounter with Balakirev awakened Mussorgsky's patriotic feelings for Russia. This led to his song cycle *Detskaya* and the immense challenge of *Boris Godunov*. After initial rejection and extensive revision, *Boris Godunov* finally premiered to popular—though not critical—acclaim in 1874. By that time, his life was increasingly disrupted by alcoholism. Periods of temperance allowed him to compose his major works before his final years were again dominated by drinking.

In early 1881, Mussorgsky was diagnosed with alcoholic epilepsy. He died just one week after his 42nd birthday. He planned *The Khovansky Affair* as the second in a trilogy of historical operas, but it was unfinished at his death and was completed by Rimsky-Korsakov. Mussorgsky's legacy includes the popular piano suite *Pictures at an Exhibition*, but it was *Boris Godunov* that secured his place in opera history.

## FIRST PERFORMANCES

- **1874** *Boris Godunov*

- **1886** *Khovanshchina* (*The Khovansky Affair*)

- **1908** *Zhenit'ba* (unfinished)

- **1917** *Sorochinskaya Yarmarka* (unfinished)

"Enough of writing for pleasure. You must give your whole self to the people. That is what art needs."

MODEST PETROVICH MUSSORGSKY

# The Khovansky Affair

KHOVANSHCHINA National music drama in five acts, 3 hours • Composed: 1872–1880 (completed by Rimsky-Korsakov 1884–1886)
• First performed: February 21, 1886, Kononov Auditorium, St. Petersburg, Russia • Libretto: Modest Petrovich Mussorgsky

*The Khovansky Affair*, inspired by the success of *Boris Godunov*, plunges into the late 17th-century turmoil that accompanied Peter the Great's rise to power and the birth of modern Russia. Planned as the second in a trilogy, this spectacle interweaves individual passions with political and religious disputes central to the Russian identity. Mussorgsky spent eight years on the opera and died before finishing it. It was completed by Nikolay Rimsky-Korsakov and was reorchestrated by Dmitri Shostakovich in 1960. It nonetheless retains Mussorgsky's distinct musical color, with declamatory arias driving the narrative and powerful choruses evoking Russia. Mussorgsky took most of his characters from history, but he invented the pivotal role of Marfa.

### Act I
After the death of Czar Alexis, his daughter, Sophia, is acting as regent for the young Czars Ivan and Peter. Sophia and her former lover, Prince Golitsyn, are fighting the Old Believers, who oppose religious reforms. Some Old Believers support the Streltsy militia, headed by Prince Ivan Khovansky, which defends feudalism. Shaklovity, a nobleman, warns Sophia anonymously of Khovansky's plot to put his son, Andrey, on the throne. As a scribe reads out graffiti describing Streltsy atrocities, Khovansky arrives and, to cheers, denounces the Western ideas assailing Russia ("Deti, deti moi"). Andrey is pursuing Emma, a German girl. When he tries to kiss her, he is stopped by Marfa, his former mistress and now an Old Believer. Khovansky also desires Emma, but Dosifey, the leader of the Old Believers, protects the girl and calls on Khovansky to save the true faith.

### Act II
Golitsyn reads a letter from Sophia recalling their passion and seeking his help. Marfa then tells his fortune and predicts disgrace and exile for him. Enraged, he orders her drowned. Khovansky and Dosifey arrive and the three men argue over Russia's destiny. Marfa returns, claiming a Golitsyn servant tried to kill her. She is followed by Shaklovity, who announces that Czar Peter is investigating the Khovansky conspiracy.

### Act III
Marfa relives her love for Andrey ("Iskhodila mladyoshen'ka"), but Susanna, another Old Believer, accuses her of heresy. Dosifey tells Marfa to gain comfort by fighting to save her country. As Shaklovity mourns Russia's unhappy lot ("Spit streletskoye gnezdo"), drunken Streltsy arrive, chased by their wives. The scribe brings word that Streltsy families are being attacked. Recognizing Czar Peter's new power, Khovansky orders the militiamen home.

### Act IV
Dancing girls are entertaining Khovansky, when he learns he is in danger. He dismisses the threat. Shaklovity invites him to a Council of State convened by Sophia, then kills him. Dosifey watches Golitsyn head for exile and learns of orders to destroy the Old Believers. When Andrey comes looking for Emma, Marfa tells him that she has left Moscow and that Khovansky is dead. At first furious, Andrey then begs Marfa to save him. As she hides him, a herald announces that the Czars have pardoned the Streltsy.

### Act V
Dosifey summons the Old Believers. Andrey and Marfa recall their love ("Ya ne ostavlyu tebya"). As trumpets announce Czar Peter's troops, the Old Believers build a funeral pyre and Dosifey, Marfa, and Andrey are consumed by flames.

▼ **Ornate costumes designed** by the Russian artist Léon Bakst in 1913 reflect the religious and historical importance of this opera to Czarist Russia.

One of this opera's peculiarities is that its principal hero never appears: at the time, no Romanov could be portrayed on stage, so the young Peter the Great plans his victory out of public view.

# Boris Godunov

National music drama in a prologue and four acts, 3¼ hours • Composed: 1868–1869 (rev. 1871–1872) • First performed: February 8, 1874, Mariinsky Theatre, St. Petersburg, Russia • Libretto: Modest Petrovich Mussorgsky, after Pushkin's historical drama

*Boris Godunov* is in many ways the most Russian of operas, a somber and grandiose spectacle in which the Russian people, both long-suffering and invincible, play the central role. Mussorgsky devoted great energy to this work, not only writing its libretto, which involved condensing Aleksandr Pushkin's drama, but also totally revising the score after it was first rejected by the Mariinsky Theatre. The opera's plot was acceptable to the Romanovs because it described Russia's disorder in the early 17th century, well before their rise to power. It was also patriotic, since it portrays resistance to a Polish invasion. Above all, with Russian folk songs and Orthodox chants echoing through choruses and melancholic arias, *Boris Godunov* evokes a vast *tableau vivant* of Russia's troubled history and anguished soul.

## PRINCIPAL ROLES

**Boris Godunov** *bass* Czar of Russia

**Fyodor** *mezzo-soprano* His son

**Xenia** *soprano* His daughter

**Grigory** *tenor* The Pretender Dimitry

**Marina Mniszek** *mezzo-soprano* Daughter of a Polish governor

**Prince Shuysky** *tenor* Adviser to Boris Godunov

**Pimen** *bass* A monk

**Simpleton** *tenor* A Holy Fool

## Prologue

Guards outside the Novdevichy Monastery order the crowd to beg Boris Godunov to accept the nomination to succeed Czar Fyodor. In Moscow, bells ring as a procession moves into the cathedral. The crowds cheer when the newly crowned Czar appears, but Boris is filled with foreboding.

> Mussorgsky extracted his libretto from Pushkin's play, but he was also influenced by Shakespeare's *Macbeth*, the story of another tyrant who murdered his way to power and provoked a foreign invasion of his land.

## Act I

Six years later in the Chudov Monastery, Father Pimen is writing his chronicle of Russian history ("Yeshcho odno"). Grigory, a fellow monk, wakes, and Pimen reminisces about Ivan the Terrible and his son, Fyodor. Pimen says the murderers of Dimitry, Fyodor's young half-brother, confessed they were sent by Boris. He notes that Dimitry would now be Grigory's age. At an inn near the Lithuanian border, Grigory, who is in fact the Pretender Dimitry, arrives with two mendicant monks. Police appear with a warrant for his arrest, and he escapes.

## Act II

Boris comforts his sad daughter and tells his son to study hard. He then despondently contemplates his destiny, his sleep haunted by images of a bloodied child ("Dostig ya vysshei Vlasti"). Shuysky brings news of a false Pretender to Boris's throne called Dimitry, who is supported by Rome and Lithuania. Boris says a dead child cannot challenge a crowned Czar, but then wonders if the murdered boy really was Dimitry. When Shuysky describes the wounds on his body, Boris sees Dimitry's ghost. In panic, he begs God's mercy for the "guilty Czar Boris."

## Act III

In a castle in Poland, Marina, the governor's daughter, dreams of becoming Czarina ("Skuchno Marine, akh kak skuchno-to!"). The Jesuit Rangoni urges her to convert

◄ **A set design** by Alexandr Jakovlevic Golovin shows the sumptuous staging long associated with Russian productions of this ever-popular opera.

## Feodor Chaliapin

The great Russian bass Feodor Chaliapin made the title role of *Boris Godunov* his own (below). Still in his early twenties when he first sang the part in 1895, he returned to it frequently over the next three decades across Europe and the United States. Acclaimed for his remarkable voice and great stage presence, he was also famous for his interpretation of operas by Rimsky-Korsakov, Verdi, Rossini, and Mozart. Chaliapin left the Soviet Union in 1922 and died in Paris in 1938.

▶ **Evgeny Akimov** as the Simpleton sings his lament for Russia's future in the Mariinsky's production, presented at London's Royal Opera House in 2005.

Orthodox Russia to Catholicism. For that, he says, she must seduce the Pretender Dimitry. Marina objects, but Rangoni rebukes her. Nearby, Dimitry yearns for Marina ("V polnoch', v sadu, u fontana"). Marina announces that only the Russian throne tempts her. Angered, Dimitry responds that, once crowned, he will laugh at her. Suddenly Marina pledges her love.

### Act IV

When urchins steal the Simpleton's last kopeck, he begs Boris to kill the urchins, just as he killed young Dimitry. Boris asks for his prayers, but the Simpleton says he cannot pray for Herod. A deranged Boris appears at the boyar's council, imagining little Dimitry alive. Pimen the monk recounts a miracle at the child's tomb. Suddenly suffocating, Boris names his son the new Czar and dies ("Ostav'te nas! Ujdite vse"). In a forest, the Pretender calls on the people to follow him. As the mob leaves, the Simpleton weeps bitter tears for Russia ("Leytes, leytes, slyozy gor'kiye").

# MARIINSKY THEATRE

In her eagerness to Europeanize Russia, Catherine the Great brought Italian opera to St. Petersburg, leading to the opening in 1783 of the city's first theater for opera and dance, the Imperial Bolshoi Kamenny Theatre. Other theaters were built and destroyed by fire before the inauguration in 1860 of the Italianate Mariinsky Theatre, named after Empress Maria Alexandrovna. In the years that followed, it was Russian rather than imported culture that dominated its stage, with premieres of Mussorgsky's *Boris Godunov*, Tchaikovsky's *Queen of Spades*, and Rimsky-Korsakov's *The Golden Cockerel*.

It was also at the Mariinsky that the choreographer Marius Petipa created innovative works that revolutionized ballet across Europe and continue to be performed today. Little wonder that the Mariinsky ballet school spawned such immense figures as Vaslav Nijinsky and George Balanchine and later, as defectors from the Soviet Union to the West, the star dancers Rudolf Nureyev and Mikhail Baryshnikov.

During the Soviet era, the company was renamed the Kirov Theatre, and most leading artists were restricted from traveling abroad, although the nation continued to maintain a high standard of musical education. As a result, following the collapse of the Soviet Union in 1991, opera in the West has benefited enormously from a massive injection of Russian vocal talent. Since the star soprano Anna Netrebko was discovered at the Mariinsky, opera managers around the world are constantly on the alert for new voices making their name in St. Petersburg.

The guiding light for this renaissance has been the tireless Valery Gergiev, the artistic and general director of the Mariinsky, who has added two buildings to the Mariinsky complex—a Concert Hall inaugurated in 2006 and a second 1,830-seat opera house known informally as Mariinsky II, which opened in 2013. In St. Petersburg's historic cultural competition with Moscow, the Mariinsky's flag is flying high.

> "Valery Gergiev, the longtime artistic director of the Mariinsky Theatre, in St. Petersburg, has attained a level of worldly power perhaps unmatched by any living classical musician."

ALEX ROSS, MUSIC CRITIC, *THE NEW YORKER*

◀ **The Mariinsky Theatre** has played a key role in St. Petersburg's resurgence as a cultural capital since the collapse of the Soviet Union in 1991.

# Pyotr Ilyich Tchaikovsky

Born: May 7, 1840, Votkinsk, Russia ▪ Died: November 6, 1893, St. Petersburg, Russia

Pyotr Ilyich Tchaikovsky is best known for his symphonies, concertos, and ballet music, but he paid enormous attention to operas and, with *Eugene Onegin* and *The Queen of Spades*, he wrote two masterpieces, both inspired by Aleksandr Pushkin. He composed several other operas that were popular in his lifetime, but they are now rarely performed outside Russia.

▲ **Marina Ivanova as Chloe** in Graham Vick's production of *The Queen of Spades* (*Pikovaya Dama*) at the Glyndebourne Festival, England, in 1995.

Tchaikovsky was eight when his family moved to St. Petersburg, the center of court and musical life in Russia. Only six years later, his beloved mother died. He was 22 by the time he entered the St. Petersburg Conservatory and was quick to try his hand at opera. His first, *The Voyevoda*, went largely unnoticed, while his second was never staged. But his third, *The Oprichnik*, won him plaudits in St. Petersburg.

Tchaikovsky's fourth opera, *Vakula the Smith*, was influenced by the "nationalist" school of music, but he turned back to a more European style for *Eugene Onegin*, which would become Russia's most popular opera. While instrumental music was earning him fame abroad, he continued writing operas for Russia, including *Mazeppa* and *The Enchantress*. Meanwhile, his personal life was often complicated and unhappy. In 1877, he was persuaded to get married, with disastrous results. At the same time, his letters suggest he felt guilty about his homosexuality. Still, with *The Queen of Spades*, an unusual work that dwells on the obsessions of a man rather than the loves of a woman, Tchaikovsky again achieved operatic greatness. Completed three years before his death, it soon joined *Eugene Onegin* in the standard opera repertoire.

---

### FIRST PERFORMANCES

- 1869 *Voyevoda* (The Voyevoda)
- 1874 *Oprichnik* (The Oprichnik)
- 1876 *Kuznets Vakula* (Vakula the Smith)
- 1879 *Onegin Yevgeny* (Eugene Onegin)
- 1881 *Orleanskaya Deva* (The Maid of Orleans)
- 1884 *Mazepa* (Mazeppa)
- 1887 *Charodeika* (The Enchantress)
- 1890 *Pikovaya Dama* (The Queen of Spades)
- 1892 *Iolanta* (Iolanthe)

---

"Truly there would be reason to go mad were it not for music."

PYOTR ILYICH TCHAIKOVSKY

# The Queen of Spades

PIKOVAYA DAMA Opera in three acts, 2¾ hours ▪ Composed: 1890 ▪ First performed: December 19, 1890, Mariinsky Theatre, St. Petersburg, Russia ▪ Libretto: Modest Tchaikovsky, after Pushkin's short story *Pikovaya dama* (1834)

*The Queen of Spades* reached the stage almost by accident. Borrowing from an eponymous story by Pushkin, Tchaikovsky's brother, Modest, wrote the libretto in 1886 for a different composer, who then lost interest. Finally, four years later, Tchaikovsky was persuaded to take it on. Written in 44 days during a sojourn in Italy, it became his own favorite opera. The libretto presents a less cynical hero than in Pushkin's short story: Herman shows genuine affection for Liza, rather than simply using her. Tchaikovsky also sets the action some 40 years earlier than Pushkin so that he can introduce Mozartian dance music. Finally, while Pushkin's Herman ends up in an asylum, here Herman chooses to take his own life. The opera's music is unabashedly romantic even as its story grows ever darker.

## Act I

In St. Petersburg's Summer Garden, army officers discuss their colleague, Herman, and his obsessive gambling. Nearby, Tomsky remarks on Herman's gloominess. Herman explains he is in love with a woman but does not know her name ("Ya imeni yeyo ne znayu"). Prince Yeletsky is congratulated on his engagement to Liza, who arrives with her grandmother, the Countess. Herman recognizes Liza as his beloved, while she is intrigued by Herman as a mysterious stranger. As the women leave, Tomsky tells how, years earlier, having gambled away all her money, the Countess gave herself to Count St. Germain in exchange for the secret of three winning cards. Then, after sharing the secret with her husband and a young man, an apparition warned her that the next person she told would kill her. Girlfriends entertain Liza, who insists she is not sad. But, alone, she bursts into tears ("Otkuda eti slyozy"), realizing she has fallen for the stranger. Suddenly, Herman arrives. When she begs him to leave, he proclaims his love for her ("Prosti, nebesnoe sozdanye"). He takes her in his arms and they declare their love.

### A likable villain

Although Herman, the opera's anti-hero, is a manic obsessive, Tchaikovsky described him as "a real, alive, and even likable person" and wept when he scored the character's death. One reason may be that, to the end, Herman remains true to his belief that gambling is more important than love. Thus, he becomes fixated with extracting the secret of the winning cards from the old Countess. But while he succeeds, their dramatic confrontation leads to the denouement that Tchaikovsky so lamented.

## Act II

At a masked ball, Yeletsky and Liza enter and, noticing her sadness, the prince reiterates his love for her ("Ya vas lyublyu"). After a pastoral intermezzo, a masked Liza slips Herman the key to her grandmother's bedroom, which leads to her own. In her bedroom, after the ball, the Countess dozes off. She awakens to find Herman demanding the secret of the winning cards ("Yesli kogda nibud' znali vy chuvstvo lyubvi"). When she remains silent, he draws a revolver and she dies of shock. Hearing Herman complain that the Countess did not reveal the secret, Liza feels betrayed and expels him.

## Act III

At his army barracks, Herman receives a letter from Liza absolving him of her grandmother's death. Distraught, Herman recalls that the dead Countess winked at him from her coffin. Her ghost then appears and, telling him to marry Liza, finally shares the gambling secret. Awaiting Herman, Liza is plunged in sorrow ("Akh! Istomilas ya gorem"). When he arrives, they fall into each other's arms. But before eloping, he says, he must test the Countess's secret. When Liza accuses him of killing the Countess, he mocks her. As he leaves, Liza drowns herself in a canal. At the gambling table, Herman raises the stakes. He calls out three—and wins. He calls out seven—and again wins. But when he calls out ace, the Queen of Spades instead appears in his hand. Seeing the Countess's ghost, a terrified Herman stabs himself. With his dying breath, he begs for forgiveness.

▶ **A set design** by the Russian artist Sergei Alimov from 1999 adds a Surrealist tone to this strange story.

### PRINCIPAL ROLES

**Herman** *tenor* An army officer

**The Countess** *mezzo-soprano*

**Liza** *soprano* Her granddaughter

**Polina** *contralto* Liza's companion

**Prince Yeletsky** *baritone* Liza's betrothed

**Count Tomsky** *baritone* An army officer

**Chekalinsky** *tenor* An army officer

**Surin** *bass* An army officer

Tchaikovsky wrote this opera with a particular singer in mind. But he then worried whether the tenor Nicolai Figner could handle the demanding role of Herman, who appears in every scene.

# Eugene Onegin

YEVGENY ONEGIN Lyrical scenes in three acts and seven scenes, 2½ hours • Composed: 1877–1878 • First performed: March 29, 1879, Little Theatre, Imperial College of Music, Moscow, Russia • Libretto: Pyotr Tchaikovsky and Konstantin Shilovsky

*Eugene Onegin* is considered Russia's most popular opera, inspired by one of Aleksandr Pushkin's most beloved poems. Yet while it evokes bourgeois country life under the Czars, its music is decidedly Western, with little of the spectacle and none of the religious and folk color preferred by other Russian composers of Tchaikovsky's era. Indeed, with its numerous introspective arias, this is essentially an intimate opera. It is also a love story that is stained by tragedy and ends unhappily. Tatyana's famous and lengthy "letter scene" captures the dreams of a young woman whose imagination is shaped as much by literature as by the yearning for love. Onegin's callous response to her love then establishes the dark tone of the opera.

## PRINCIPAL ROLES

**Mrs. Larina** *mezzo-soprano* The estate owner

**Tatyana** *soprano* Her eldest daughter

**Olga** *contralto* Her youngest daughter

**Eugene Onegin** *baritone* Tatyana's beloved

**Lensky** *tenor* Olga's fiancé

**Prince Gremin** *bass*
A retired general and Tatyana's husband

**Filipyevna** *mezzo-soprano* Tatyana's nurse

Tchaikovsky's fear of failure led him to premiere *Eugene Onegin* with students from the Moscow Conservatory, although in practice their young voices were not equipped to meet the emotional challenges posed by its central roles. The opera's success soon attracted more mature singers.

### Act I

As her daughters Tatyana and Olga sing about love and sorrow, Mrs. Larina reminisces with her maid, Filipyevna. Peasants arrive to dance and sing for Mrs. Larina. Tatyana says the songs make her dream, but Olga says she prefers to dance to them. Tatyana attributes her own pallor to the sad love story she is reading. Olga's fiancé, Lensky, arrives with a friend, Yevgeny (Eugene) Onegin, who tells Lensky he chose the wrong sister. Tatyana is excited ("Skazhi, kotoraya Tatyana?"). Onegin wonders if life is not boring in the country, but she says she reads and dreams. That evening, Tatyana tells Filipyevna that she is in love. She then takes pen and paper and, with hesitation and fear, writes a long love letter to Onegin ("Puskai pogibnu ya"). Sealing it, she notes, "It's too frightening to read over." The following morning, it is delivered. A few days later, Tatyana awaits Onegin in her garden. Promising frankness equal to hers, he says that he is not made for marriage and predicts that she will soon turn her ardor elsewhere ("Kogda bi zhizn domashnim krugom"). Tatyana is shattered.

### Act II

Guests at a party for Tatyana include Lensky and Onegin, who decides to break the tedium by flirting with Olga. Lensky is irritated, but Olga scoffs at his jealousy. A Frenchman toasts Tatyana's beauty and health but, as the dancing resumes, Lensky broods. When Onegin suggests he is mad, they start arguing. Finally, to everyone's horror, Lensky challenges Onegin ("V vashem dome!"). He then bids Olga farewell forever. The following morning, as he awaits Onegin, Lensky again dreams of Olga ("Kuda, kuda, kuda vi udalilis"). Finally, Onegin arrives, and the two men ask themselves why they are fighting not laughing. In the duel, Onegin fires and Lensky falls dead.

### Act III

Years later, Onegin is bored at a ball in St. Petersburg. Prince Gremin enters with his wife, and Onegin recognizes Tatyana. The elderly Gremin sings of his great love for Tatyana and introduces Onegin to her. She recalls having previously met Onegin, then asks to leave. Onegin realizes he loves her.

◀ **Apple blossoms** announce spring, but when the heat of summer arrives and their petals fall, the promise of love may prove false.

▲ **Oleksiy Palchykov as Lensky** and Roderick Williams as Eugene Onegin prepare for their ill-fated duel in Garsington Opera's 2016 production, directed by Michael Boyd.

In Gremin's house, Tatyana feels her passion for Onegin returning. When Onegin appears, she wonders if he is now attracted by her new status ("Onegin! Ya togda molozhe"). Onegin declares his love for her, but she asks him to leave. She admits she still loves him, but will never betray her husband. Onegin is left alone with his remorse.

### Love, in life and art

Tchaikovsky had already begun work on Tatyana's "letter scene" in May 1877, when he received a passionate love letter from Antonina Milyukova, a former student at the Moscow Conservatory. Shaken by the coincidence, Tchaikovsky accepted Antonina's marriage proposal, saying he would not play Onegin to her Tatyana. The marriage, perhaps intended to conceal the composer's homosexuality, lasted barely three months and drove Tchaikovsky to attempt suicide. Somehow, through all of this, *Eugene Onegin* was completed.

# Nikolay Rimsky-Korsakov

Born: March 18, 1844, Tikhvin, Novgorod region, Russia • Died: June 21, 1908, Lyubensk, near St. Petersburg, Russia

A prolific composer of lushly melodic music, Nikolay Rimsky-Korsakov was also an influential teacher who shaped a generation of Russian composers, including Prokofiev and Stravinsky. Outside Russia, he remains best known for his orchestral pieces *Capriccio Espagnol* and *Sheherazade*, but he was also active in opera. He edited *Boris Godunov* and completed *Khovanshchina*, both by his friend Mussorgsky, and he wrote 15 stage works of his own, starting with *Pskovityanka*, or *The Maid of Pskov*, a tragic love story set in the time of Ivan the Terrible. But *Zolotoy petushok*, or *The Golden Cockerel*, a satire on war, is Rimsky-Korsakov's only opera regularly performed outside Russia.

# The Golden Cockerel

ZOLOTOY PETUSHOK Opera in three acts, with prologue and epilogue, 1¾ hours ▪ Composed: 1906–1907 ▪ First performed: October 7, 1909, Solodovnikov Theatre, Moscow, Russia ▪ Libretto: V. I. Belsky, after the 1834 fairy tale, *The Tale of the Golden Cockerel*, by Pushkin

*Zolotoy petushok*, or *The Golden Cockerel*, is a fairy tale with a political message critical enough for Russian censors to demand cuts. Since Rimsky-Korsakov refused to comply, the opera was performed only after his death—with cuts required by officials. The libretto, adapted from a Pushkin fairy tale in verse, fits into a Russian folk tradition, but the score is nonetheless sophisticated, notably in its orchestration. The vocal parts are particularly testing because of the high register of the Astrologer and Golden Cockerel roles and the requirement that king and queen dance while they sing in Act II. This work's best-known aria is the queen's "Hymn to the Sun" in Act II, while the bridal procession in Act III is a musical *tour de force*.

## PRINCIPAL ROLES

**Czar Dodon** *bass* The ruler of Russia

**Prince Gvidon** *tenor* The Czar's son

**Prince Afron** *bass* The Czar's second son

**General Polkan** *bass* The Czar's chief of staff

**Astrologer** *very high tenor*

**Queen of Shemakha** *soprano*

**Golden Cockerel** *very high soprano*

This opera mocks a monarch who attacks a neighboring country and is defeated. Understandably, Russian authorities were upset: two years earlier, the Russo–Japanese War proved to be equally disastrous for Czar Nicholas II.

◀ **In a 2002 production** at the Théâtre du Châtelet in Paris, Olga Trifonova as the Queen of Shemakha sings till dawn.

### Prologue
The Astrologer announces that his fairy tale has a moral.

### Act I
Czar Dodon summons his chief of staff, General Polkan, and his sons, Gvidon and Afron, for advice on fighting the country's enemies so that he can retire to bed. Gvidon and Afron make suggestions, which Polkan dismisses. The Astrologer presents Golden Cockerel, who will perch on a steeple and warn if an invasion is imminent ("Slaven bud', velikiy tsar'!"). Delighted, the czar offers payment, but the Astrologer says he will name his price later. After the czar's maid sings him to sleep ("Veshnim dnyom sosnut' zdorovo"), he dreams of an Asian princess. Shaken from his slumber by the Cockerel, he dispatches his sons to the war front and goes back to sleep. But the Cockerel again sounds the alarm. This time, Dodon reluctantly dons his rusty armor and sets off with his army to save the country, cheered on by his people.

### Act II
On a foggy night, Dodon discovers that his army has been defeated and that his sons have killed each other. As dawn breaks, a richly decorated tent comes into view. Emerging from it, the Queen of Shemakha celebrates the rising sun ("Otvet' mnye, zharkoye svetilo"). She then proclaims her desire to conquer Dodon's kingdom and orders the czar to sing and dance, until he collapses in exhaustion. Now in the queen's sway, the czar proposes to her. While the queen's servants mock him, she prepares to take over his land.

### Act III
Dodon returns home, accompanied by the queen and a procession of enslaved people, dwarfs, giants, and bizarre animals. The Astrologer arrives and, reminding the czar of his promise to pay any price for the Cockerel, he says he wants to marry the queen ("Tsar' velikiy, eto ya!"). Dodon tries to dissuade him, then kills him with his scepter. As the queen laughs, the Cockerel flies down and, with one peck, kills the czar. A fierce storm erupts, and, when it passes, the queen, the Astrologer and the Cockerel have vanished. The people lament.

### Epilogue
The Astrologer announces that only he and the queen were real and that everyone else was an illusion.

◀ **The stage design** for an early production of Rimsky-Korsakov's opera uses architecture to suggest a fantasy world that is not too distant from Russia itself.

# Igor Fyodorovich Stravinsky

Born: June 17, 1882, Lomonosov, Russia ▪ Died: April 6, 1971, New York, US

Igor Fyodorovich Stravinsky had a major influence on modern music. He came out of a Russian musical tradition, but spent most of his life in France and the United States. The son of an opera singer, he studied under Rimsky-Korsakov before composing numerous scores for Diaghilev's Ballets Russes. Of these, *The Firebird* and *The Rite of Spring* caused a shock with their fierce rhythms and lively orchestral coloring. Although Stravinsky remained close to the stage throughout his life, three of his four operas—*The Nightingale*, *Mavra*, and *Oedipus Rex*—were short. *The Rake's Progress*, written after he fled France for the United States in 1940, is his only full-length opera.

# The Rake's Progress

Opera in three acts and an epilogue, 2¼ hours • Composed: 1947–1951 • First performed: September 11, 1951, Teatro La Fenice, Venice, Italy • Libretto: W. H. Auden and Chester Kallman, after William Hogarth's etching and engraving series *A Rake's Progress* (1735)

*The Rake's Progress* took Stravinsky on an unlikely journey. Having discovered Hogarth's prints in Chicago in 1947, he met the poet W. H. Auden and his partner, Chester Kallman, a playwright. From the eight engravings in *A Rake's Progress*, the couple created a brilliant verse libretto. Around this 18th-century plot, Stravinsky decided to write a pastiche of a late 18th-century opera in his own Neo-Classical style. For this, he unabashedly took inspiration from Mozart, notably *Così fan tutte*. Mozartian touches include accompanying the recitative with a harpsichord, inserting a coloratura soprano aria, and ending the opera with a *Don Giovanni*–like epilogue. The result is Stravinsky's most lyrical score, a far cry from the pulsating rhythms of *The Rite of Spring* nearly 40 years earlier.

## Act I

Anne Trulove is to marry Tom Rakewell. Her father has found work for him, but Tom prefers to live off his wits. When he wishes for money, Nick Shadow appears, announcing that Tom has been left a fortune by a mysterious uncle. As he hurries to London, Tom promises Anne that she will soon follow ("Laughter and light"). At Mother Goose's brothel in London, Tom and Shadow are discussing beauty, pleasure, and love. Tom wants to leave, but Shadow persuades him to join the drinking and dancing. Mother Goose then takes him to bed. Meanwhile, with no word from Tom, Anne leaves for London ("I go, I go to him").

## Act II

Tom has tired of wine and women ("Vary the song"). When he yearns for happiness, Shadow shows him a picture of Baba the Turk. Tom scoffs at the idea of marrying her, but quickly changes his mind. Anne sees Tom arriving in a sedan chair. He tells her to return home, but she refuses. A veiled Baba emerges from the sedan chair and is introduced as Tom's wife. As Anne leaves, the crowd asks Baba to remove her veil and show her long beard. Tom's room is crowded with strange gifts collected by Baba. When he tires of her, she starts breaking them in rage. Tom silences her by putting her wig on her back-to-front. Shadow arrives with a machine to resolve the world's problems.

## Act III

The contents of Tom's house are being auctioned. When the auctioneer tears off Baba's wig, she expels everyone except Anne. She tells Anne to rescue Tom and announces her return to her life as an entertainer. Shadow says he now expects payment for his services. And since Tom is broke, the payment is Tom's soul—unless he can correctly identify three hidden cards. When he succeeds, a furious Shadow makes him insane. Now in a psychiatric hospital, Tom believes he is Adonis. When Anne arrives, he sees Venus and asks her to sing a lullaby ("Gently, little boat"). As he sleeps, Anne bids him farewell. Awakening, Tom begs the other madmen to weep for Adonis.

## Epilogue

The players warn: "For idle hands/ And hearts and minds/ The Devil finds/ A work to do."

### PRINCIPAL ROLES

**Trulove** *bass* A country gentleman

**Anne Trulove** *soprano* His daughter

**Tom Rakewell** *tenor* A rake loved by Anne

**Nick Shadow** *baritone* Tom's servant

**Mother Goose** *mezzo-soprano* A brothel-keeper

**Baba the Turk** *mezzo-soprano* Tom's wife

Show business glamour drew Stravinsky to Hollywood after he fled Europe in 1940, yet *The Rake's Progress* might never have been written if he had succeeded in his ambition to compose movie scores.

▼ **The final plate** of Hogarth's morality tale, *Scene in Bedlam*, is reflected in Act III of this opera when Tom Rakewell goes mad.

◀ **In a production designed** by David Hockney, Victoria Vergara reveals herself as Baba the Turk at the San Francisco Opera in 1988.

# Sergey Prokofiev

Born: April 23, 1891, Sontsovka, Ukraine • Died: March 5, 1953, Nikolina Gora, near Moscow, Russia

Sergey Prokofiev wrote memorable music in many genres: sonatas, symphonies, film scores, and ballet music, including *Romeo and Juliet* and *Cinderella*. He also wrote a dozen operas. Of these, *War and Peace* is now judged the most significant, but only his fairy tale, *The Love for Three Oranges*, was a success in his lifetime.

Prokofiev studied under Rimsky-Korsakov at the St. Petersburg Conservatory, where his talent as a pianist led to his first compositions. While there, he also wrote five operas, although none were immediately staged. After the 1917 Revolution, he left for a lengthy tour of the United States. Later, living in Europe, Prokofiev wrote magical symphonies and ballet music, although a new opera, *The Fiery Angel*, was not staged until 1955. He returned to Moscow in 1936, but difficult times lay ahead. During World War II, his "patriotic" opera *Semyon Kotko* was poorly received. He spent years composing *War and Peace*. In 1948, he was attacked by the regime. Even his death went largely unnoticed because Stalin had died a few hours earlier.

## In America

To escape the disarray of post-revolutionary Russia, Prokofiev traveled to the United States in mid-1918. His American sojourn would prove tumultuous. While he was well received in Chicago, where the Lyric Opera commissioned *The Love for Three Oranges*, New York critics labeled him the "Bolshevik pianist" and criticized his "orgy of discordant sounds." In fact, even after he settled in Europe, his American tours followed this pattern: a hit in Chicago and a flop in New York. Had he felt more appreciated in the United States, Prokofiev might have made his home there and averted the pain of his return to Moscow. It served him little to feature on the cover of TIME magazine in 1945.

◀ *The Fiery Angel* is a provocative opera about religious hysteria in 16th-century Germany. Nuns try to calm a sister possessed by spirits in this 1965 production at Sadler's Wells Opera, London.

# The Love for Three Oranges

LYUBOV' K TREM APEL'SINAM Opera in a prologue and four acts, 1¾ hours ▪ Composed: 1919 ▪ First performed: December 30, 1921, Chicago Auditorium, US ▪ Libretto: Sergey Prokofiev, after Carlo Gozzi's 1761 play *L'amore delle tre melarance*

*The Love for Three Oranges* is a delightful fairy tale inspired by *commedia dell'arte*. While the story could not be sillier, it is a response to the bombast of 19th-century opera. First performed in French in Chicago, its huge cast and fast pace leave little room for arias or set pieces, although the score is full of life and humor. The opera's most famous melody is provided by the "March" in Act II.

### Prologue
Tragedy, Comedy, Lyric Drama, and Farce are boasting, when the audience (The Ridiculous People) chases them off.

### Act I
The king learns that his son's hypochondria can be cured only by laughter, but Leandro wants the prince to die so Princess Clarissa can be queen.

### Act II
The Prince finally laughs when Fata Morgana slips and tumbles ("Kha-kha Kha-kha-kha"). Furious, she makes him fall in love with three oranges.

### Act III
Tchelio, a magician, helps the Prince steal the oranges. When he falls asleep, Truffaldino the clown cuts open two of the oranges and finds two princesses. When they die of thirst, he flees. The Prince awakens, opens the third orange, and falls in love with Princess Ninetta ("Truffaldino, Truffaldino"). Fata Morgana turns Ninetta into a rat.

### Act IV
As Tchelio turns the rat back into Ninetta, the king orders Clarissa and Leandro put to death. But Fata Morgana helps them escape. The Ridiculous People then toast the happy Prince and Princess.

---

**PRINCIPAL ROLES**

**King of Clubs** *bass*

**The Prince** *tenor* His melancholic son

**Princess Clarissa** *contralto*
The king's ambitious niece

**Leandro** *baritone* Clarissa's henchman

**Truffaldino** *tenor* The court clown

**Fata Morgana** *soprano* An evil sorceress

---

The idea that love can cast a magic spell takes on a whole new meaning in this opera: the Prince falls madly in love with three large oranges, unaware that each contains a princess.

▼ **Martial Defontaine as the Prince**
sleeps while François Le Roux's Truffaldino opens two oranges in a 2005 production at the Netherlands Opera.

# War and Peace

VOINA Y MIR Lyric dramatic scenes in two parts, 4¼ hours ▪ Composed: 1941–1943 (rev. 1946–1952) ▪ First performed: June 12, 1946, Maly Theatre, Leningrad, Russia (heavily cut concert version) ▪ Libretto: Sergey Prokofiev and Mira Mendelson, after Leo Tolstoy's novel (1865–1869)

Adapted from Leo Tolstoy's monumental novel of the same name, *War and Peace* is Prokofiev's operatic masterpiece. Planned as a small-scale work focused on the vagaries of love, it assumed a patriotic dimension after Nazi Germany invaded the Soviet Union in June 1941. As a result, a romantic "peace," which dwells on Natasha's fickle love, is followed by a "war," which exalts the suffering and heroism of the Russian people in the tradition of Mussorgsky's *Boris Godunov*. This is reflected in the score: Part I offers a Tchaikovsky-like lyricism, while Part II evokes "eternal" Russia through rousing choruses that were designed to please the Kremlin. To add authenticity, Prokofiev researched military music of the era. However, although he imagined it being performed over two evenings, the opera is rarely produced because of its prohibitive length and the need for 70 soloists.

## PRINCIPAL ROLES

**Natasha Rostova** *soprano*
The daughter of an impoverished landowner

**Prince Andrey Bolkonsky** *baritone*
Natasha's betrothed

**Prince Nikolai Bolkonsky** *bass-baritone*
His father

**Count Pyotr Bezukhov (Pierre)** *tenor*
Prince Andrey's friend

**Hélène Bezukhova** *mezzo-soprano* His wife

**Prince Anatole Kuragin** *tenor* Lover of Natasha

**Lieutenant Dolokhov** *baritone*
Prince Anatol's friend

**Field Marshal Prince Mikhail Kutuzov** *bass*
Russian army commander

**Napoleon Bonaparte** *baritone* French emperor

### Part I
**Peace** The widowed prince, Andrey Bolkonsky, is moved by hearing Natasha Rostova sing of the joys of spring ("Ja ne budu, ja ne magu spat"). Months later, at a New Year's Eve ball, they fall in love and become engaged. But Andrey's father, objecting to their marriage, sends his son away for a year in the hope that Andrey will forget her. Natasha worries that their love may not survive the separation. In May, during a party at Count Pierre's house, Natasha meets Prince Anatole Kuragin, who declares his love for her and kisses her ("Chudo, kak khorosha ona, krasavitsa takaia"). Natasha's cousin warns her of Anatole's disrepute, but she has been won over. The next night, before eloping with Natasha, Anatole visits his friend, Dolokhov.

▶ **At the start of Part II**, peasants and volunteers prepare to defend Mother Russia against Napoleon's invading forces at the Paris Opéra in 2000.

When Dolokhov reminds him that Natasha is engaged and that he is married, Anatole laughs and says that he cannot resist young women. Natasha's plan to elope has been discovered by Madame Akhrosimova, in whose house she is residing. The grande dame chastises Natasha for her foolishness and recruits Pierre to tell her that Anatole is married ("Natalya Ilyinichna"). Suddenly remorseful, Natasha begs Pierre to ask Andrey to forgive her. Pierre, in turn, wishes that he could marry someone like Natasha. He then orders Anatole to give up Natasha and leave Moscow. As word arrives that Napoleon has advanced on Russia, volunteers prepare to join the army.

## Part II

**War** It is August 1812 and Russia's army of peasants and volunteers is confident of defeating Napoleon in the Battle of Borodino. Aware of Natasha's betrayal, Andrey is ready to die, even refusing a safe post at Field Marshal Kutuzov's headquarters. As the battle begins, Napoleon is impressed by Russian resistance, but he wins the day. Kutuzov debates whether to defend Moscow or to withdraw and regroup. Reluctantly, he decides to abandon Moscow ("Kogda zhe, kogda zhe reshilos' eto strashnoye delo?"). After Napoleon's forces take Moscow, Muscovites set fire to the city ("Pred vragom Maskva"). Pierre learns that Natasha's family has fled with some wounded Russian soldiers, including Andrey. Pierre sets out to assassinate Napoleon but is arrested. Meanwhile, a delirious Andrey recalls his love for Natasha. She recognizes him and begs him for his forgiveness ("Neuzheli tol'ko lish zatem sud'ba segodnya"), but his life cannot be saved. Forced to retreat by the fierce Russian winter, the French army escorts Russian prisoners along the Smolensk road. Armed partisans free some prisoners, including Pierre. Hearing of the death of Andrey and his own wife, Pierre believes he can now love Natasha. As Kutuzov announces Russia has been saved, the people sing the glory of the motherland.

...................................................

*Tolstoy might not have welcomed Prokofiev's opera: in his final years, the increasingly irascible novelist proclaimed Russian folk songs to be superior to classical music and dismissed opera as absurd.*

...................................................

### A painful birth

Once Communist Party officials grasped the parallels between Napoleon/Hitler and Kutuzov/Stalin, meddling in Prokofiev's operatic project was inevitable. A concert version of Part I ("Peace") was performed in 1946. But after the dress rehearsal of Part II ("War") in 1947, officials canceled the production, saying it lacked heroism. It was only in 1959, six years after Prokofiev's death, that the opera was finally staged as written (below).

**Olga Guryakova as Natasha** meets Irina Bogacheva's Madame Peronskaya (left) in Francesca Zambello's 2000 production of *War and Peace* at the Opéra Bastille, Paris.

# Dmitri Dmitryevich Shostakovich

Born: September 25, 1906, St. Petersburg, Russia • Died: August 9, 1975, Moscow, Russia

Dmitri Dmitryevich Shostakovich was the most important composer to emerge from the Soviet era. While he was forced to adapt to the regime's changing artistic diktats, his music engaged Russian tradition even as it forged Russian Modernism. His best-known work was orchestral, notably his Symphony No. 5, but he also wrote ballet and film music as well as one major opera.

Born into a cultivated St. Petersburg family, Shostakovich's teenage years were accompanied by both political turmoil and artistic ferment. At 19, he was acclaimed for his Symphony No. 1. And, just four years later, in 1929, he presented his first opera, *Nos*, or *The Nose*. His next opera, *Ledi Makbet Mtsenskogo Uyezda*, or *Lady Macbeth of the Mtsensk District*, was initially well received. But after it was attacked by the official press in 1936, Shostakovich largely abandoned opera.

He was hailed as a patriot for his Symphony No. 7, written during Nazi Germany's siege of Leningrad. But in 1948 he was attacked for "formalism." Then, after Stalin's death, he was again treated as a Soviet hero.

### Brave or cowed?

Decades after his death, Shostakovich's political views remain a topic of heated debate: admirers note that he was denounced by the Soviet regime in 1936 and 1948, while critics recall that he joined the Communist Party in 1960 and accepted state honors, such as the Lenin Prize. The fairest assessment may be that, unwilling to defect, he became a survivor: his desire to enjoy any artistic freedom led him to find ways of coexisting with the dictatorship.

◀ **Shostakovich (right) joins** firemen on the roof of the Leningrad Conservatory in 1941 during the prolonged siege of Leningrad in World War II.

# The Nose

NOS Opera in three acts, 1¾ hours ▪ Composed: 1927–1928 ▪ First performed: January 18, 1930, Maliy Opera Theatre, Leningrad, Russia ▪ Libretto: Dmitri Shostakovich, after the short story "The Nose" by Gogol (1836)

*The Nose* is a decidedly eccentric work, above all for a young composer writing his first opera. Combining the avant-garde influence of Berg, Schoenberg, and Hindemith with a bizarre libretto inspired by Gogol, this work at times verges on the anarchic. With a huge cast swarming the stage and more than 70 named roles squeezed into a fast-paced score, ensembles take precedence over arias, expressionism over lyricism.

## Act I

Kovalyov, a civil servant, is being shaved. The next morning, Yakovlevich the barber finds a nose in his bread roll and is ordered by his wife to dispose of it. He drops it in the river but is spotted by the Police Inspector, who arrests him. Kovalyov discovers that his nose is missing and, after a fruitless search, decides to report the loss to the police. At the St. Isaak Cathedral, he sees that his nose has become a state councilor, but it escapes.

## Act II

Unable to find the inspector, Kovalyov tries to place an advertisement in the local newspaper, but the clerk suspects it contains a coded message and refuses him ("Ya ne mogu vam skazat', kakim obrazom"). He returns home in despair.

## Act III

The inspector believes that the nose may flee town. As a coach prepares to leave, the nose tries to stop it. The crowd beats the nose. Finally, it reverts to its nasal shape and is taken to Kovalyov. But the nose refuses to return to its proper place, persuading Kovalyov that Madame Podtochina has cursed him for rejecting her daughter ("Vinoyu etogo dolzhen byt' nikto drugoy"). Meanwhile, amid scenes of confusion, the entire town is still looking for the nose. Kovalyov wakes up with his nose back on his face. When a young woman responds to his advances, he is sure that he is again whole.

### PRINCIPAL ROLES

**Platon Kuzmich Kovalyov** *baritone* A civil servant

**Ivan Yakovlevich** *bass-baritone* A barber

**Police Inspector** *very high tenor*

**Nose** *tenor*

**Madame Podtochina** *mezzo-soprano*

**Her daughter** *soprano*

While this opera is clearly allegorical, Shostakovich shielded himself from criticism by suggesting it recounted a genuine human misfortune. "Why laugh at a poor wretch who has just been so disfigured?" he asked.

▶ **Jeremy Huw Williams** as Kovalyov tries to reattach his nose in the Opera Group's 2001 production.

# Lady Macbeth of the Mtsensk District

LEDI MAKBET MTSENSKOGO UYEZDA Opera in four acts and nine scenes, 2½ hours • Composed: 1930–1932 (rev. 1935; and as *Katerina Ismailova* 1956–1963) • First performed: January 22, 1934, Maly Opera Theatre, Leningrad, Russia • Libretto: Dmitri Shostakovich and Alexander Preys

*Lady Macbeth of the Mtsensk District* was a daring venture for a composer in his mid-twenties. It may even have verged on reckless for Shostakovich to present the Lady Macbeth–like murderess of Nikolay Leskov's original story as "an affectionate woman, a deeply sensitive woman, by no means lacking in feeling." Certainly, by giving Katerina moments of both passion and reflection, he tries to explain her crime. The Shabby Peasant; an Old Convict; and Boris, Katerina's father-in-law, all sing lively arias, but they are generally parodied in Shostakovich's orchestration. Although some critics found the opera coarse, it had more than 100 performances in the two years before it was banned. Shostakovich later revised it as *Katerina Ismailova*. Today, opera houses prefer the original *Lady Macbeth*.

## PRINCIPAL ROLES

**Boris Ismailov** *high bass*
A prosperous merchant

**Zinovy Ismailov** *tenor* His son

**Katerina Ismailova** *soprano* Zinovy's wife

**Sergey** *tenor* One of Ismailov's laborers

**Aksinya** *soprano* A maid

**The Shabby Peasant** *tenor*

**Sonyetka** *contralto* A convict

**Old Convict** *bass*

**Police sergeant** *bass*

### Act I

Katerina is weary of life ("Akh, nye spitsa bol'she"). Boris, her father-in-law, complains she has produced no heir, but she blames her husband, Zinovy. Boris orders her to find rat poison. As he leaves on business, Zinovy introduces a new laborer, Sergey. Boris tells Katerina to swear to be faithful to her husband. Aksinya, the maid, warns Katerina that Sergey is a womanizer. Laborers, Sergey, and the Shabby Peasant molest Aksinya. Katerina mocks them for pretending to be brave. Sergey suggests wrestling with her. Boris discovers them on the floor and threatens to inform Zinovy. Naked in her bedroom, Katerina wishes someone would come to her. Sergey arrives and makes a pass at her. At first, she resists, then surrenders to wild lovemaking.

### Act II

Boris reminisces about his philandering youth and imagines satisfying Katerina ("Pod oknamiu chuzhikh"). When he spots Sergey leaving her room, his servants beat Sergey and lock him in a storeroom. Katerina serves Boris mushrooms with rat poison. Feeling ill, he summons a priest. Boris tells the priest that Katerina has poisoned him—then dies.

Unconcerned, the priest sings a quick requiem. In bed with Sergey, Katerina demands more passion, but he says their affair must end when Zinovy returns because he cannot share her ("Katerina Lvovna"). She promises to marry him. Katerina is awakened by Boris's ghost, who curses her. She then hears noises in the house. As Sergey hides, Zinovy appears, accuses her of infidelity, and beats her. She cries out for Sergey, who kills Zinovy with a candlestick and hides him in the cellar.

### Act III

The Shabby Peasant sings the praises of vodka and sets out looking for more drink ("U menya byla kuma"). Breaking into the cellar, he finds Zinovy's rotting corpse. The police sergeant is annoyed that he was not invited to Katerina's wedding party. When the Shabby Peasant brings word of the body, the police rush off to fill up on food and drink at the wedding. Everyone is drunk except Katerina. Noticing that the cellar's door is open, she prepares to flee with Sergey when the police arrive. She promptly invites them to handcuff her.

### Act IV

In a labor camp, an Old Convict laments his unhappy lot. Katerina finds Sergey, still yearning for his love, but he rejects her ("Nye lekhko posle pochota da poklonov".) Instead, he desires Sonyetka, but she at first rejects him, saying she wants stockings as proof of his love. Claiming he is ill, Sergey borrows Katerina's stockings and disappears with Sonyetka. Then, seeing Sonyetka standing on a bridge, Katerina pushes her into the river and jumps in herself. An officer announces they have drowned, and the prisoners move off, singing.

## Stalin as music critic

*Lady Macbeth of the Mtsensk District* was popular until Stalin attended a performance in December 1935. The following month, the Communist Party daily paper called it "Muddle instead of music," and complained that "singing is replaced with screaming." As for the work's popularity abroad, "is it not explained by the fact that it tickles the perverted tastes of the bourgeoisie with its fidgety, screaming, and neurotic music?"

**▲ Larisa Gogolevskaya**
interprets Katerina opposite Viktor
Lutsyuk as her lover Sergey in a
2002 production at the Mariinsky
Theatre in St. Petersburg.

The famous lovemaking scene between Katerina and Sergey need not be staged explicitly since
the orchestration in the final scene of Act I, which makes heavy use of the brass section and
includes suggestive trombone slides, portrays sexual passion with unusual vividness.

# 7

## CZECH OPERA
### (c. 1860–1940)

# Czech opera c. 1860–1940

As nationalism spread through 19th-century Europe, opera played a key role in preparing Czech independence. Centuries of rule by the German-speaking Hapsburgs had smothered the Czech identity. But, as part of a cultural renaissance known as the Czech National Revival, opera gave pride of place to the Czech language, history, and folklore.

## A folk legacy

After the ancient kingdoms of Bohemia, Moravia, and Slovakia were absorbed into the Hapsburg Empire in 1526, Prague and Brno were dominated by Viennese culture and the German language. Music, though, was an exception. While Czech folk music survived in rural communities, Italian opera was performed in Prague as early as 1627, with two of Mozart's "Italian" operas—*Don Giovanni* and *La clemenza di Tito*—premiering there.

## The rise of Czech consciousness

The French Revolution and the Napoleonic wars shook European monarchies by spreading liberal ideas and encouraging rebellion. Although the Hapsburgs survived, the convulsion inspired Czech aristocrats, artists, and intellectuals to start forging a sense of nationhood.

In 1826, František Škroup presented *The Tinker*, the first Czech-language opera. Then, in 1848, accompanying fresh political unrest across Europe, a failed Czech uprising spawned the Czech National Revival. With the abolition of serfdom, migration from rural areas began to swell Prague's Czech-speaking population. Soon the Czechs were bent on building a National Theatre, paid for by citizens.

In the interim, the Czech-language Provisional Theatre opened in 1862, challenging the official Estates Theatre, with its German-language programming. And it was at the Provisional Theatre that Czech opera as such was born. The first work to make an impact, in 1866, was Bedřich Smetana's *The Brandenburgers in Bohemia*, which portrayed the horrors of foreign occupation, albeit pre-Hapsburg. A few months later, Smetana staged *The Bartered Bride*, a rural romance filled with folk melodies and dances.

◀ **Prague's National Theatre** on the banks of the Vltava River has long been a monument to Czech nationalism.

## Smetana as a father figure

Through these two Czech-language operas, Smetana came to personify cultural nationalism, which, in musical terms, meant rejecting Wagner and other German influences. Strangely, Smetana was himself more fluent in German than in Czech, yet he found a way of using the Czech language to create a distinctively Czech musical sound. In 1868, his new historical opera, *Dalibor*, included a song to freedom that became an informal Czech anthem.

The long-awaited National Theatre finally opened in June 1881 with yet another Smetana opera, *Libuše*. But just two months later, it was destroyed by fire. This was considered such a national catastrophe that money was quickly collected for its reconstruction, aided by the popularity of Smetana's patriotic symphonic poem, *Má Vlast*, or *My Country*.

By the time Smetana died, in 1884, Prague was enjoying a lively and increasingly autonomous cultural life, with several younger composers fueling the Czech National Revival. Antonín Dvořák, in contrast, was winning acclaim across Europe and in the United States, where he wrote his ever-popular Symphony No. 9 (*From the New World*). His reputation as an opera composer was also contested at home by Smetana loyalists. His sin was to echo "old" French and Italian influence, while Smetana was modern and authentically Czech. That said, even among Czechs, Dvořák's wonderfully melodic fairy tale *Rusalka* is as popular as *The Bartered Bride*.

## Janáček the Moravian maestro

Dvořák died in 1904, the same year that a little-known Moravian composer, Leoš Janáček, staged the first of his operatic masterpieces, *Jenůfa*. Janáček's problem was that he did not belong to the cultural and political elite of Prague. Further, *Jenůfa* was adapted from a play that had provoked moral outrage in 1890. As a result, Janáček was not recognized as a major Czech composer until the opera reached the National Theatre in Prague in 1916.

After Czechoslovakia became independent in 1918, the country enjoyed two decades of cultural ebullience before it entered a dark half-century of foreign domination. Unfortunately, Janáček's reputation did not recover until the 1950s. Today, even after the separation of the Czech Republic and Slovakia in 1993, the people of the region still look to Smetana, Dvořák, and Janáček as guardians of their nationalist sentiments.

# Bedřich Smetana

Born: March 2, 1824, Litomyšl, Bohemia, Czech Republic • Died: May 12, 1884, Prague, Czech Republic

Bedřich Smetana was the first great Czech opera composer, although he struggled to win recognition in his lifetime. In his twenties, out of frustration, he moved to Sweden. Then, in 1862, he returned home to write opera for Prague's new Provisional Theatre, starting with *The Brandenburgers in Bohemia*. This was followed by *The Bartered Bride*, the village opera that made him famous. His next work, *Dalibor*, was criticized as too Wagnerian, but is now considered a patriotic epic. In 1882, Smetana wrote his great symphonic tone poem, *Má Vlast*, or *My Country*. Soon afterward, chronic syphilis brought on lunacy and he died in a psychiatric hospital in 1884.

# The Bartered Bride

PRODANÁ NEVĚSTA Comic opera in three acts, 2¼ hours ▪ Composed: 1863–1866 (rev. 1869–1870) ▪ First performed: May 30, 1866, Provisional Theatre, Prague, Czech Republic ▪ Libretto: Karel Sabina

*The Bartered Bride* is a delightful pastoral opera, but it took time for its distinctly Bohemian character to be accepted in a Prague still under Italian, French, and German musical influence. Indeed, the opera's initial lukewarm reception prompted Smetana to carry out a drastic revision, which he presented four years later, with three acts instead of two and sung voices replacing spoken dialogue. This version won over the Czech people. Its polka dances, rousing choruses, and traditional clothing evoke an idyllic and bucolic past, while its charming love story deftly captures the intrigues of village life. Musically, a succession of fine duets and Mařenka's "broken heart" aria in Act III provide lyrical stepping stones through twists and turns in the plot.

## Act I

Mařenka reassures Jeník of her love, but reveals that her father wants her to marry Mícha's son, Vašek. She asks Jeník about his past and he recounts that, after his mother's death, his father remarried and he was driven from his home by his stepmother. He then wandered the world. Mařenka and Jeník vow undying love ("věrné milováni"). Kecal, the local marriage broker, tells Mařenka's parents that, while Mícha's son from an earlier marriage has disappeared, Mícha's other son, Vašek, would make a fine son-in-law. But Mařenka declares she only loves Jeník. As the villagers dance the polka, Kecal plots his next move.

## Act II

Vašek, a stammering simpleton, builds up courage to woo Mařenka by reminding himself of his mother's warning: the entire village will mock him if he does not marry Mařenka ("Má-ma-ma-matička"). But he does not recognize Mařenka when she sweetly warns him against marrying the dreadful Mařenka, who will be the death of him. She makes Vašek swear not to marry this Mařenka ("Známt' já jednu dívčinu").

Meanwhile, Kecal offers Jeník a bribe if he renounces Mařenka. Jeník takes the money on condition that Mařenka marry only "Mícha's son" and that her father's debts to Mícha be cleared. The villagers condemn Jeník for "selling" Mařenka, while Jeník is amazed that Kecal has been so easily duped.

## Act III

The circus comes to town, but the "dancing bear" is hopelessly drunk, and Esmeralda, an acrobat, persuades Vašek to play the role. Vašek worries that marrying Mařenka will kill him, but when he recognizes her, he wants to wed her. Mařenka is stunned by Jeník's betrayal ("Ten lásky sen"). But Jeník presents himself as Mícha's missing son and claims his right to marry Mařenka. She understands the ruse and forgives him: Jeník keeps the bribe and wins the bride. Panic erupts because the bear has escaped. But when Mícha recognizes the foolish Vašek, he approves Jeník's marriage to Mařenka.

### PRINCIPAL ROLES

**Mařenka** *soprano* Village girl

**Jeník** *tenor* Mařenka's beloved

**Mícha** *bass* His father, the wealthiest villager

**Vašek** *tenor* Mícha's son

**Kecal** *bass* A scheming marriage broker

**Esmeralda** *soprano* An acrobat

◀ **Tomáš Černý as Jeník** makes peace with Maria Haan as Mařenka in a production of this beloved Czech opera at the National Theatre in Prague in 2005.

▶ **This frontispiece** of a piano score of the ever-popular "People's March" from *Prodaná Nevěsta* shows traditional clothing and dancing.

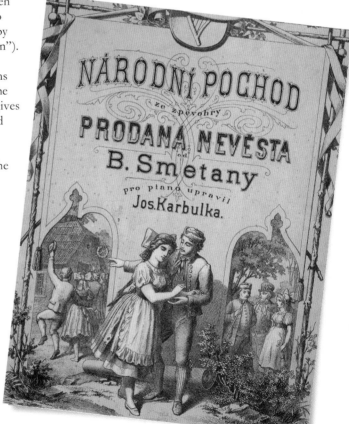

Operas traditionally traveled from Vienna to Prague, but *The Bartered Bride* reversed this practice when it reached Vienna in 1892. From there, its popularity quickly spread, with productions in Chicago in 1893 and London in 1895.

# Antonín Dvořák

Born: September 8, 1841, Nelahozeves, Czech Republic • Died: May 1, 1904, Prague, Czech Republic

Antonín Dvořák is the Czech composer with the widest international following, thanks mainly to his symphonic work, notably his Symphony No. 9 (*From the New World*). But he met with less success as an opera composer. While he wrote 11 operas, both comic and serious, his only lasting triumph was the romantic fairy tale, *Rusalka*, presented three years before his death. More ambitious was *Dimitrij*, written 20 years earlier, in which the composer continues the story of Mussorgsky's *Boris Godunov*. But, except for *Rusalka*, Dvořák's operas were viewed by many Czechs as dramatically weak. In that sense, he failed in his lifelong ambition to be recognized as Smetana's heir.

# Rusalka

Lyric fairy tale in three acts, 3 hours ▪ composed: 1900 ▪ First performed: March 31, 1901, National Theatre, Prague, Czech Republic ▪ Libretto: Jaroslav Kvapil, after *Undine*, by F. H. C. de la Motte Fouqué and folk tales compiled by K. J. Erben

*Rusalka*, a dreamily melodic opera about a water nymph who falls in love with a real prince, has its roots in northern European forest lore. The tale had already been used by La Motte Fouqué in *Undine*; by Hans Christian Andersen in *The Little Mermaid*; and by Pushkin in *Rusalka*. Kvapil then included some Slavonic features of the myth in his libretto. Dvořák's beautiful score occasionally evokes both Wagner and Debussy, but it, too, has earthier passages, which underline its Czech identity. As a love story, it remains unusual: since Rusalka cannot speak to her prince, there is no conventional love duet. Nonetheless, the opera's finest arias—including the famous "Song to the Moon"—belong to Rusalka.

## Act I

Rusalka rests in a willow tree while three wood nymphs tease a water goblin. She confides in the goblin that she has fallen for a man who swims in the lake and whom she embraces as a wave. If she were human, she says, he could kiss her, too. Alarmed, the water goblin suggests she consult the witch Ježibaba. Alone, Rusalka asks the Moon to shine on her beloved ("Měsíčku na nebi hlubokém"). She then tells Ježibaba why she wants to become human. The witch warns that she will have no voice and, if betrayed, will be forever damned. Rusalka drinks a magic potion. At the lake, the Prince finds Rusalka standing before him and is overwhelmed by her beauty ("Ustaňte v lovu, na hrad vrat'te se"). When he questions her, she falls into his arms. Incredulous, he leads her to his palace.

## Act II

Servants gossip about the Prince's infatuation with the mysterious mute woman and hope a visiting Foreign Princess can distract him. The Prince enters with Rusalka, complaining of her cold embraces. When the new Princess presents herself, the Prince tells Rusalka to dress for the ball. Upset to see the Prince courting the Princess, Rusalka finds the water goblin and pours out her sorrows. She returns to embrace the Prince, but he pushes her aside. The water goblin tells him that he can never escape Rusalka. As Rusalka vanishes into a pond, the Prince collapses at the feet of the Foreign Princess.

### PRINCIPAL ROLES

**Rusalka** *soprano* A water nymph

**Water goblin** *bass*
The "father" of the water nymphs

**Ježibaba** *mezzo-soprano* A witch

**The Prince** *tenor*

**The Foreign Princess** *soprano*

▶ **The Czech soprano** Gabriela Beňačková as the lovestruck water nymph Rusalka in Otto Schenk's 1993 production at the Metropolitan Opera in New York.

## Act III

Rusalka lies by the lake, dejected ("Necitelná vodní moci"). Offering her a dagger, Ježibaba says she can save herself if she slays the man who seduced her, but Rusalka throws the weapon into the lake. Furious, Ježibaba leaves her to her fate. Rusalka plunges into the water, but her nymph sisters ignore her. Meanwhile, the Prince's servants inform Ježibaba that their master is under Rusalka's spell. The Prince arrives, asking for Rusalka's forgiveness and begging for a kiss ("Milačku, znáš mne, znáš?"). She warns that it will doom him, but he insists. She kisses him and he dies happily. As the water goblin laments that her sacrifice was in vain, Rusalka again kisses the Prince and disappears into the lake.

◀ **This set design** for *Rusalka* perfectly captures the opera's distinctive underwater fairy tale ambience.

Dvořák came to write *Rusalka* by chance: after three of Jaroslav Kvapil's composer friends turned down his libretto, it was recommended to Dvořák, who agreed to set it without even reading the text.

# Leoš Janáček

Born: July 3, 1854, Hukvaldy (Czech Republic) ▪ Died: August 12, 1928, Ostrava, Czech Republic

Leoš Janáček, the most widely performed Czech opera composer, is now ranked among the giants of 20th-century opera. While his music often embraced folk traditions, his operatic scores were strikingly modern. He was 62 before he won national recognition, but his final years were enormously productive and included his masterpiece, *Katya Kabanova*.

◄ **The Dutch soprano** Eva-Maria Westbroek in the tragic title role of *Katya Kabanova* in a 2014 production at Berlin Staatsoper directed by Andrea Breth and conducted by Sir Simon Rattle.

"To deny the development of opera is to deny the development of the human spirit."

LEOŠ JANÁČEK

Janáček attended musical conservatories in Prague, Leipzig, and Vienna before settling in the Moravian city of Brno. There he taught at a teachers' training college and the Brno Organ School, of which he became director. In 1884, the opening of the Brno Provisional Theatre awakened his interest in writing for the stage, but his first operas were either failures or not produced.

Finally, in 1904, after the success of *Jenůfa* in Brno, he devoted himself entirely to writing opera scores, using his own librettos. Even so, because of political intrigues and jealousies, *Jenůfa* only reached Prague in 1916. In the decade that followed, with a young married woman as his muse, he reached his prime, moving Czech opera far beyond the patriotic model established by Smetana. His music was notable for echoing the "speech melody" of the Czech language, while his often-somber librettos touched on universal emotions.

Janáček's reputation quickly spread to Austria and Germany, but he was largely ignored in the rest of Europe and the United States until the 1960s. Since then, however, his operas have entered the repertory of lyric theaters around the world. In fact, rare is the opera house today that does not include one Janáček work in every season.

## FIRST PERFORMANCES

- 1894 *Počátek románu* (The Beginning of a Romance)

- 1904 *Jenůfa*

- 1920 *Výlety páně Broučkovy* (The Excursions of Mr. Broucek)

- 1921 *Káťa Kabanová* (Katya Kabanova)

- 1924 *Příhody lišky bystroušky* (The Cunning Little Vixen)

- 1926 *Věc Makropulos* (The Makropulos Affair)

- 1930 *Z mrtvého domu* (From the House of the Dead)

- 1958 *Osud* (Fate)

# Jenůfa

Opera in three acts, 2 hours ▪ Composed: 1894–1903 (rev. 1907–1908) ▪ First performed: January 21, 1904, National Theatre, Brno, Czech Republic) ▪ Libretto: Leoš Janáček, after Gabriela Preissová's 1890 play, *Její pastorkyňa* (*Her Stepdaughter*)

*Jenůfa*, the opera that made Janáček's name, took him 10 years to complete. Adapted from a bleak play by Gabriela Preissová, it borrows from Italian *verismo*, or realism, to portray a calamitous family conflict in a remote Czech village. To evoke rural life, the opera includes folk dances and choruses, but a dark mood gradually engulfs the work. Its most tragic figure is the Kostelnička, who commits murder to "save" Jenůfa. The opera's violent subject partly explains the refusal by Prague's National Theatre to present it until 1916.

### Act I
Jenůfa loves the mill owner, Števa, and worries that, if he is drafted into the army, they cannot marry before her pregnancy is discovered. Laca, Števa's half-brother, who loves Jenůfa, is unhappy when Števa is not conscripted. Jenůfa's stepmother, known as the Kostelnička, "the female sacristan," decrees Števa and Jenůfa cannot marry for one year. Crazed with jealousy, Laca slashes Jenůfa's face.

### Act II
Jenůfa has borne a son. While she sleeps, the Kostelnička shows Števa the baby and begs him to marry Jenůfa, but he refuses. Laca, who believes Jenůfa is in Vienna, still wants to marry the girl. But he is put off when the Kostelnička reveals Jenůfa gave birth to a baby who died. Alone, the Kostelnička grimly decides she must drown the infant ("Co chvíla, co chvíla"). Jenůfa awakens and prays to the Virgin ("Zdrávas královno"). The Kostelnička announces that the baby has died of fever, leaving Jenůfa saddened but willing to marry Laca.

### Act III
As the Kostelnička prepares to bless the couple, a boy brings news that a baby's frozen body was found in the millstream. The crowd blames Jenůfa, but the Kostelnička confesses her crime. At first stunned, Jenůfa forgives her stepmother. As the woman is led away, Laca says he still wants to marry Jenůfa.

### PRINCIPAL ROLES

**Jenůfa** *soprano* A village girl

**Kostelnička Buryjovka** *soprano*
The female sacristan and Jenůfa's stepmother

**Grandmother Buryjovka** *contralto*
Jenůfa's grandmother

**Števa Buryja** *tenor* Jenůfa's cousin and lover

**Laca Klemeň** *tenor* Jenůfa's cousin and suitor

**Karolka** *mezzo-soprano* The mayor's daughter

Jenůfa's sad story had echoes in Janáček's life. Having already lost an infant son, his 21-year-old daughter died while he was composing this opera. Devastated, he vowed to tie the score with black ribbons.

# Katya Kabanova

KÁŤA KABANOVÁ Opera in three acts, 1¾ hours ▪ Composed: 1919–1921 ▪ First performed: November 23, 1921, National Theatre, Brno, Czech Republic ▪ Libretto: Leoš Janáček, after Alexandr Ostrovsky's 1859 play *Groza* (*The Storm*), translated by V. Cervinka

*Katya Kabanova* is considered Janáček's greatest opera. Its story is Russian in both setting and mood, with Katya's impossible love and uncontainable guilt leading her irrevocably toward suicide. Janáček, himself a devoted Russophile, fell in love with his tragic heroine, imagining her to be as pure and gentle as his own muse, Kamila Stösslová. The opera is often viewed as a natural successor to *Jenůfa*, but in fact Katya is a far more developed character, one whose solitude and unhappiness are expressed with almost painful realism. Although the score is through-composed, Janáček underlines his emotional attachment to Katya through the flowing lyricism of her role, as if she alone had true feelings.

## PRINCIPAL ROLES

**Káťa (Katya) Kabanová** *soprano*
An unhappily married woman

**Tichon Ivanyč Kabanov** *tenor* Her husband

**Marfa Ignatěvna Kabanová (Kabanicha)** *contralto* Tichon's evil mother

**Boris Grigorjevič** *tenor* Katya's lover

**Savël Prokofjevič Dikoj** *bass* A rich merchant and Boris's uncle

**Varvara** *mezzo-soprano* Kabanicha's foster daughter

**Váňa Kudrjáš** *tenor* Varvara's lover

**Kuligin** *baritone* A friend of Váňa

▼ **Patricia Racette as Katya Kabanova** (left) shares her worries with Anna Grevelius's Varvara in an English National Opera's production at the London Coliseum in 2010.

### Act I

Kudrjáš asks his friend Boris why he tolerates the insults of his uncle, Dikoj. Boris explains glumly that Dikoj controls his inheritance. Now, adding to his troubles, Boris says, he loves Katya Kabanova. Katya arrives with her husband, Tichon, and her mother-in-law, Kabanicha, who is complaining, as always. This time, Kabanicha warns Tichon that Katya will never respect him if he keeps proclaiming his love. Alone with her friend Varvara, Katya reminisces on her sweet life before marriage ("Viš, co mi napadlo"). But now she is anxious. At night, someone whispers lovingly to her, but it is a sin to love another man. Alarmed, she begs Tichon not to go on a trip. Kabanicha demands Katya's obedience while he is away.

### Act II

Preparing for a tryst with Kudrjáš, Varvara gives Katya the key to the garden gate. At first terrified, Katya persuades herself that it is not a sin to talk to Boris. As she leaves for the garden, a drunken Dikoj arrives, hoping to seduce Kabanicha. Kudrjáš sings a love song while waiting for Varvara ("Nikohu te není!"). Boris arrives and Varvara brings word that Katya will soon be there. When she appears, Boris immediately declares his love for her ("Jste to vy, Katěrino Petrovno?"). She asks if he is leading her to sin, but he promises to obey her wishes. Throwing herself into his arms, she says she is now ready to die. Soon, Katya and Boris can be heard singing of their love in the darkness ("To jste si vymysleli pěknou věc").

### Act III

Sheltering from a storm, Kudrjáš notes that there are no lightning conductors to absorb the electric charges, but Dikoj insists that lightning is punishment from on high. Varvara warns Boris that Tichon has returned and that Katya is distraught. Katya herself arrives and asks Boris if he is satisfied with her suffering. When Kabanicha and Tichon appear, Katya throws herself at her husband's feet, crying that she sinned from the first night he left. When Kabanicha demands the identity of her lover, Katya blurts out Boris's name and flees into the storm. Hours later, Katya now regrets her confession ("Vidět se s ním rozloučit"). Hearing her voice, Boris runs into her arms ("Svedl nás Bůh!"). But he has been ordered to leave town by his uncle. Devastated, Katya leaps into the Volga. Dikoj brings in her body and Tichon angrily blames his mother. Kabanicha is unmoved.

## Janáček's young muse

During a long marriage Janáček had many passions, but none was more important than his love for Kamila Stösslová, a married woman 38 years his junior whom he met when he was 63. Overnight, she became his muse and, while it is thought that their relationship was never consummated, Janáček remained obsessed with her until his death. Kamila excited his romantic imagination and inspired the principal female roles in his late operas. After completing *Katya Kabanova*, he wrote: "You know it's your opera."

Long an admirer of Puccini, Janáček was struck by the parallel between Katya's fate and that of *Madama Butterfly*'s heartbroken Cio-Cio-San, who also prefers suicide to living in shame.

# The Makropulos Case

VĚC MAKROPULOS Opera in three acts, 1½ hours ▪ Composed: 1923–1925 ▪ First performed: December 18, 1926, National Theatre, Brno, Czech Republic
▪ Libretto: Leoš Janáček, after the 1922 comedy by Karel Čapek

*The Makropulos Case* is a strange and powerful opera. Its central character is a woman who was born in Crete in 1575 as Elina Makropulos and who, at the age of 337, appears in Prague in 1912 as an arrogant opera diva called Emilia Marty. In between, to conceal that an elixir extended her life by 300 years, she adopted different names, always using the initials "E. M." Karel Čapek called his play of the same name a philosophical comedy, but Janáček's opera is a far darker meditation on life.

## Act I

Gregor has a century-old claim to an estate owned by Jaroslav Prus. Emilia Marty, an aloof opera singer, arrives with the lawyer Kolenatý, who has just lost the case. Emilia says a document in Jaroslav's house could reverse the verdict. Emilia explains that in 1827 Baron Prus left the estate to his illegitimate son with Ellian MacGregor. Gregor is descended from that son. Kolenatý finds the document.

## Act II

At the opera house, a crowd is congratulating Emilia, who treats everyone rudely except for an old man who recognizes her as Eugenia Montez. Jaroslav says Gregor cannot claim the estate ("Dovolte mi dřive otázku") because the mother of Baron Prus' illegitimate son was recorded as Elina Makropulos. Emilia asks Janek, Jaroslav's son, to steal another document. But Jaroslav offers it in exchange for a night with Emilia.

## Act III

At dawn, Jaroslav hands over the envelope, before learning that Janek has killed himself for love of Emilia. In Emilia's bags, Kolenatý and others find her many names, all with the initials "E. M." Emilia declares she is Elina Makropulos. She has lived 337 years thanks to an elixir of life, which her father tested on her ("Pro lékaře!"), but she now believes a long life is pointless. As she dies, the elixir's formula is burned.

### PRINCIPAL ROLES

**Emilia Marty (Elina Makropulos)**
*dramatic soprano*

**Dr. Kolenatý** *bass-baritone* A lawyer

**Albert Gregor** *tenor* A Makropulos descendant

**Jaroslav Prus** *baritone* A nobleman

**Janek** *tenor* His son

**Kristina** *soprano* Janek's girlfriend

The opera has long provoked speculation that Janáček created the cold and distant character of Emilia Marty out of frustration that his own muse, Kamila Stösslová, refused to reciprocate his love.

▶ **German soprano Anja Silja**, won acclaim as Emilia Marty at Glyndebourne, England, in 1997.

# The Cunning Little Vixen

PŘÍHODY LIŠKY BYSTROUŠKY Opera in three acts, 1½ hours • Composed: 1922–1923 • First performed: November 6, 1924, National Theatre, Brno, Czech Republic • Libretto: Leoš Janáček, after the 1920 novel *Liška Bystrouška* by Rudolf Těsnohlidek

*The Cunning Little Vixen* is a delight, for both its poetic music and its fairy-tale world where human and animal lives are entwined. Inspiration for the opera came from a serialized novel, itself built around 200 sketches about an adventurous little vixen. Using his own libretto, Janáček then created singing and dancing roles for countless animals, who are in turn given human attributes—in the case of the vixen, the need to love. Thus, through them and a half-dozen countryfolk, Janáček evokes the cycles of rural life. Long instrumental passages set different moods—comic, erotic, nostalgic, and tragic—while the melodies echo the rhythms of the human voice and animal sounds. In this way, Janáček gives the forest its own musical language.

## PRINCIPAL ROLES

**Animals**

**Bystrouška** *soprano* A vixen cub

**Zlatohřbítek** *soprano* A fox

**Lapák** *mezzo-soprano* A dog

**Humans**

**The Forester** *bass-baritone*

**The Schoolmaster** *tenor*

**Harašta** *bass* A poacher

## Act I

On a warm afternoon, as animals bustle around him, the Forester takes a nap. He wakes when Bystrouška the vixen cub chases a frog onto his nose. He grabs the cub to raise as a pet. Locked up with other animals, Bystrouška learns to defend herself. She also calls on the hens to mutiny. When they ignore her, she kills them and escapes.

◀ **Dawn Upshaw** as Bystrouška, the cunning little vixen, at the Royal Opera House, London, in 2003.

## Act II

Back in the woods, Bystrouška evicts the Badger from his home. At the inn, the Forester passes the time ("Ano, ve Stráni bude daleko lépe") teasing the Schoolmaster for not conquering his beloved Terynka. Later, the tipsy Schoolmaster takes Bystrouška for Terynka. The Forester fires at the vixen, but misses. Bystrouška then falls in love with Zlatohřbítek the fox. All the animals celebrate their marriage.

## Act III

Harašta the poacher is to marry Terynka. The Forester sets a trap for Bystrouška, but she and her cubs dance around it. She attracts Harašta's attention. When he trips, the foxes eat his chickens. He fires a shot and Bystrouška is killed. The Forester leaves the Schoolmaster weeping over Terynka and walks home through the wood. He sits down to rest and reminisces on the cycles of life ("Hoj! Ale není to Bystroušky!"). Falling asleep, he imagines chasing a little vixen, but instead he catches a frog.

Janáček was so fond of this opera that the final scene was performed at his funeral in August 1928, sung by his friend Arnold Flögl.

# From the House of the Dead

Z MRTVÉHO DOMU Opera in three acts, 1½ hours ▪ Composed: 1927–1928 ▪ First performed: April 12, 1930, National Theatre, Brno, Czech Republic ▪ Libretto: Leoš Janáček, after Dostoevsky's *Memoirs from the House of the Dead* (1862)

*From the House of the Dead*, Janáček's final opera, is a work of heavy atmosphere and little plot. Adapted from Dostoevsky's own account of his time in a labor camp, it evokes the tedium and violence of prison life as well as the elusive dream of freedom. A wounded eagle becomes a symbol of hope: it lives with the prisoners until it can fly away. Perhaps unfinished when Janáček died, the opera was given a more cheerful ending by friends. But his original libretto and score are used today.

## Act I
Gorjančikov, a deported politician, arrives at the camp. When he protests, the prison governor orders him whipped. An inmate teases an injured eagle, but others proclaim the eagle to be czar of the jungle. As prisoners leave for work, singing mournfully ("Neuvidi oko již těch krajů"), Skuratov recalls his life as a cobbler. Luka Kuzmič then recounts how he murdered a prison officer. Gorjančikov returns, barely able to stand.

## Act II
One year later, Gorjančikov offers to teach young Aljeja to read and write. Skuratov explains that he is in Siberia because he loved a German girl ("Přešel den, druhý, třetí"). When she married a rich relative, he was heartbroken and killed the man. The inmates improvise two plays, which provide brief respite from the boredom. As a prostitute arrives for a young prisoner, Gorjančikov and Aljeja drink tea. A prisoner attacks Aljeja and wounds him.

### PRINCIPAL ROLES

**Prison Governor** *bass*

**Alexandr Petrovič Gorjančikov** *baritone*
A nobleman

**Skuratov** *tenor* A jailed cobbler

**Luka Kuzmič (alias of Filka Morozov)** *tenor*
A jailed murderer

**Šiškov** *bass* A jailed murderer

**Aljeja** *mezzo-soprano* A Tartar boy

## Act III
Gorjančikov cares for Aljeja. Luka is also ill. Šapkin, another inmate, recalls how a police officer tortured him by pulling his ears. Šiškov says he killed his fiancée because she still loved Filka Morozov. When Luka dies, Šiškov recognizes him as Filka. Gorjančikov is summoned, and the governor apologizes to him. As Gorjančikov leaves, the eagle is released. The prisoners are ordered back to work.

Even for an opera set among prisoners jailed for life in a Siberian labor camp, Janáček looked for the humanity in the story, noting that there are "bright places in the house of the dead."

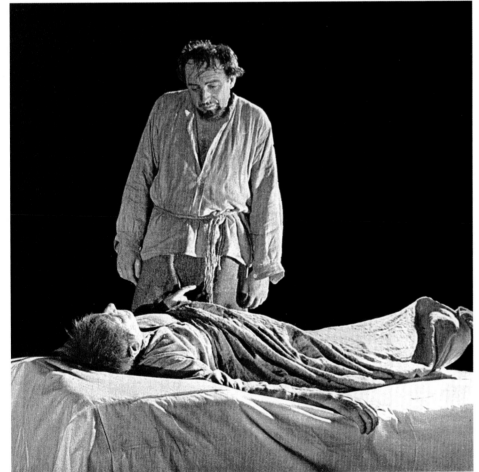

◀ **Šiškov recognizes** the dead Luka as Filka Morozov in a scene from Act III of a Brno production in 1958.

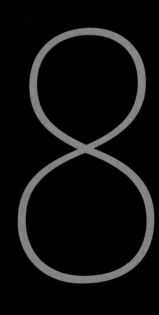

# MODERN OPERA

## (c. 1900– )

# Modern opera c. 1900–

The modern era sent opera in two fresh directions. Innovations in technology carried the melodies of earlier opera to mass audiences, and turned charismatic singers into recording stars. At the same time, opera began to address the complexities of modern life, its fragmented nature, its rush toward change, and the new sounds of its urban landscapes.

## Modern times for opera

For 300 years, great singing was enjoyed in live performances. But, in the 20th century, the gramophone brought opera stars into drawing rooms. The thrill of being in an opera house was sacrificed for the pleasure of immediate access to the most popular arias and singers. At the same time, composers, performers, and audiences of opera were required to adjust to a fast-changing world and the disturbing isolation of modern life.

## Schoenberg and European serialism

Until Arnold Schoenberg rewrote the rules of tonality in 1909, "beautiful" music remained loyal to a basic key anchoring the notes. But, with his "12-tone method," Schoenberg established what became known as the Second Viennese School. Alban Berg, the movement's most important opera composer, explored the human condition in *Wozzeck* and *Lulu*. Experimentation rippled through Europe's opera capitals until Fascism forced Schoenberg, Kurt Weill, Bertolt Brecht, and a generation of opera creators to flee. After World War II, composers in Europe extended Schoenberg's method of atonality to embrace other variables, including electronic music.

## Britten's Britain

In England, Benjamin Britten inaugurated a one-man renaissance of opera with *Peter Grimes* in 1945. The country's first operatic master since Henry Purcell 250 years earlier, Britten was a deeply human composer, melding influences as diverse as Romantic opera, atonal compositions, sacred music, and Asian music theater. His 15 operas ranged from the tragic *Billy Budd* to the comic *Albert Herring*.

◀ **In 1948, designer Tanya Moiseiwitsch** works with a miniature model for an opera set while the British composer Benjamin Britten looks on.

Performed around the world, they place him alongside Richard Strauss as the 20th century's most significant opera composer. Leading British opera composers of recent decades—John Tavener, Judith Weir, Mark-Anthony Turnage, Thomas Adès, and George Benjamin, among them—owe much to Britten.

## Operas made in America

The United States imported opera until the early 20th century, when American composers began to find their own voices. The first to do so was Scott Joplin, a Black American composer, who set his ragtime opera *Treemonisha* in a Black rural community two decades after the abolition of slavery. Virgil Thomson tuned his music to the rhythms of American speech in *Four Saints in Three Acts*. And in *Porgy and Bess*, George Gershwin echoed the music and language of Black American communities. After World War II, Leonard Bernstein maintained this popular touch with his operetta, *Candide*, and his most cherished musical, *West Side Story*.

Reacting against Broadway, from the 1970s composers such as Philip Glass and John Adams chose the repetitive rhythms of minimalism. As the flag-carrier of American opera, though, New York's Metropolitan Opera remained surprisingly conservative. One exception was Terence Blanchard's *Fire Shut Up In My Bones*, the first opera composed by a Black American in the opera house's history, which opened the Met's 2021–2022 season.

## Global opera

After the fall of the Berlin Wall in 1989, talents of the former Soviet Bloc and the West intermixed freely in opera houses. Newly unified, Berlin suddenly boasted three opera houses, and St. Petersburg again came alive with opera. And making opera accessible to distant audiences at a fair price, major opera houses now routinely stream live productions into movie theaters or onto home screens. To stay alive as an art form, though, opera still counts on the talent of international composers such as the Hungarian Péter Eötvös, the Belgian Philippe Boesmans, the Frenchman Pascal Dusapin, the Finn Kaija Saariaho, the South Korean Unsuk Chin, and the Chinese-American Tan Dun. Tan's first major opera, *Marco Polo*, happened to honor a founding figure of global culture: like opera itself, Marco Polo set out from Venice to travel farther than anyone could have thought possible.

# Ethel Mary Smyth

Born: April 22, 1858, Sidcup, England ▪ Died: May 8, 1944, Woking, England

Ethel Mary Smyth was an English composer who earned her place on the English music scene at a time when being a "woman composer" was a great disadvantage. Although her father opposed her musical ambitions, Smyth studied at the Leipzig Conservatory and moved in circles that included Dvořák, Grieg, and Tchaikovsky. Her compositions ranged from concertos and chamber music to a Mass in D and six operas, three of them comic operas. *Der Wald*, a one-act opera staged in New York in 1903, was for more than a century the only opera by a woman presented at the Metropolitan Opera. She abandoned music for two years to devote herself to the suffragette cause, going to jail for her actions. In later years, while still composing, she became deaf. Smyth is best known for her opera *The Wreckers*.

# The Wreckers

Opera in three acts, 2 hours ▪ Composed: 1902-1904 ▪ First performed: November 11, 1906, Neues Theater, Leipzig, Germany ▪ Libretto: Henry Brewster

Henry Brewster's high-voltage libretto for *The Wreckers* was inspired by Smyth's own experience of hearing stories of villagers provoking shipwrecks so that their cargoes could be plundered. Much like Benjamin Britten's later *Peter Grimes*, the opera is set among deeply poor fishermen who are trapped in a world of betrayal, violence, and religious fanaticism.

## Act I

Pascoe, the local preacher, tells villagers that they have had no wrecked ships to loot because the Lord is punishing them for their heavy drinking. Lawrence, the lighthouse keeper, says he has seen bonfires lit to warn off ships. Mark, a young fisherman once devoted to Lawrence's daughter Avis, switches his attention to Pascoe's wife, Thirza. While Pascoe's sermon justifies the plundering of shipwrecks, Avis spreads word that Pascoe is the traitor who has been lighting beacons.

## Act II

Mark, the true traitor, is gathering driftwood on a beach, preparing to light a fire. Warning him that the villagers might catch him, Thirza declares her love for him. They agree to run away together. As they escape, Thirza is recognized by Pascoe, who collapses on the beach. The villagers see the unlit fire and decide that the preacher is the traitor.

## Act III

Defending Pascoe at his trial, Avis says he is under the spell of Thirza's witchcraft. As the villagers prepare to condemn him, Mark arrives and confesses to have lit the bonfires. Thirza says she, too, is guilty. Avis invents an alibi for Mark, but he rejects her. Pascoe also tries to save Thirza, but to no avail. Accepting death, Mark and Thirza are chained together inside a cave, doomed to drown at high tide.

Although Smyth's earlier opera, *Der Wald*, was produced at the Metropolitan Opera in 1903, the first performance of *The Wreckers* in the United States took place only in 2015 at Bard SummerScape festival in New York State.

### PRINCIPAL ROLES

**Pascoe** *baritone* The local preacher

**Thirza** *mezzo-soprano* The preacher's wife

**Lawrence** *baritone* The lighthouse keeper

**Mark** *tenor* A young fisherman

**Avis** *soprano* Lawrence's daughter

**Chorus** Villagers and fishermen

▶ **Sky Ingram's Avis tries to save** the life of Mark, sung by Neal Cooper, in the Bard SummerScape production at Bard College in New York, in 2015.

◀ **Neal Cooper as Mark declares** his love for Katharine Goeldner's Thirza in the Bard SummerScape production at Bard College.

# Scott Joplin

Born: November 24, 1868, Texas, United States • Died: April 1, 1917, New York, United States

An American pianist and composer, Scott Joplin was celebrated in his lifetime for creating "classical" ragtime music and acclaimed long after his death for his opera, *Treemonisha*. Born to a formerly enslaved father and a freeborn mother, Joplin's family had a love for music. Initially a self-taught pianist, by the turn of the 20th century he had earned himself the nickname of "King of Ragtime." Joplin completed *Treemonisha* around 1911, but could not find a publisher. After his death, his work was largely forgotten until a revival of interest in ragtime led to the first full production of *Treemonisha* in 1972. Then, after "The Entertainer" and other ragtime melodies were used in the soundtrack of the 1973 movie *The Sting*, Joplin once again became a household name.

# Treemonisha

Opera in three acts, 1 hour 25 minutes • Composed: 1911 • First performed: January 27, 1972, Atlanta Memorial Arts Center, Georgia, United States • Libretto: Scott Joplin

*Treemonisha* is a feel-good opera, where even the villains are entertaining. It gives a rose-tinted view of life on a Southern plantation two decades after the abolition of slavery. Treemonisha—so named because she was found by Monisha under a tree—personifies hope, since she can read and write and preaches forgiveness. Joplin also pokes fun at religious fanaticism and satirizes those taken in by conjurers.

### Act I
Zodzetrick, a conjurer, tries to trick Monisha, but her husband Ned stops him. Their daughter Treemonisha is teaching Remus to read when Zodzetrick approaches her, but Ned chases him away. Plantation workers arrive to husk corn, and Treemonisha leads a celebration dance. When Treemonisha reaches for flowers from a nearby tree, Monisha stops her, saying the tree is sacred. It was there, 18 years earlier, that she found Treemonisha as an abandoned baby ("One Autumn night I was in bed lying"). The young woman is sad that Monisha and Ned are not her real parents, but Monisha says that proof of their love is that they arranged for her education by a "white lady." Pastor Alltalk arrives to exchange corn for blessings. Meanwhile the conjurers kidnap Treemonisha, and Remus rushes off to rescue her.

### Act II
A few days later, another conjurer, Simon, warns the villagers that every superstition should be heeded because bad luck is always near. Meanwhile, Zodzetrick and his sidekicks are discussing how to punish

Treemonisha for fighting superstition. As they prepare to throw her into a wasp's nest, Remus arrives wearing a devil's mask, and the kidnappers flee. He and Treemonisha stop at another plantation to ask directions. The cotton pickers end their day's work and dance ("Aunt Dinah has blowed de horn").

### Act III
As Ned consoles Monisha, Remus arrives with Treemonisha, and the plantation celebrates. Two of the kidnappers are caught, and the villagers start beating them until Treemonisha stops them. When the criminals are again beaten, Treemonisha begs for mercy for them. Remus says, "wrong is never right" ("Never treat your neighbors wrong"). The community chooses Treemonisha as its new leader and celebrates with a rousing final dance.

▶ **Soprano Adina Aaron as Treemonisha** rests her head on the lap of mezzo-soprano Grace Bumbry in the role of her mother, watched over by bass-baritone Willard White as her father in a 2010 production at the Théâtre du Châtelet, Paris.

> ## "When I'm dead twenty-five years, people are going to begin to recognize me."
>
> SCOTT JOPLIN

### PRINCIPAL ROLES

**Treemonisha** *soprano* An educated young woman

**Monisha** *contralto* Her mother

**Ned** *bass* Her father

**Zodzetrick** *baritone* A conjurer

**Remus** *tenor* Treemonisha's rescuer

**Parson Alltalk** *baritone* Local preacher

**Simon** *bass* A conjurer

◀ **A celebration of the triumph** of good over evil led by soprano Adina Aaron as Treemonisha at the Théâtre du Châtelet, Paris, in 2010.

# Arnold Schoenberg

Born: September 13, 1874, Vienna, Austria • Died: July 13, 1951, Los Angeles, California, US

Arnold Schoenberg was the first composer to give voice to a modern idiom within the language of classical music. As the 20th century dawned, he paved the way for opera to express contemporary experience. He fashioned new musical building blocks with his 12-tone method, and established the Second Viennese School, whose chief opera composer would be Alban Berg.

At 19, Schoenberg played cello in an ensemble led by Austrian composer Alexander Zemlinsky, who became his teacher. Over the following decade, Schoenberg discovered that, when notes were given equal weight—rather than made to serve a musical key or chord, as in traditional harmony—the door to a new realm of "atonal" expression was opened. Among his short works for the stage were *Erwartung*, or *Expectation*; *Die glückliche Hand*, or *The Fateful Hand*; and *Von Heute auf Morgen*, or *From One Day to the Next*. His sole attempt at a full opera came with *Moses und Aron*, but it was never completed. Persecuted as a Jew while teaching in Berlin, Schoenberg fled to the United States in 1933.

### Der Blaue Reiter

In Munich in 1911, Wassily Kandinsky heard Schoenberg's *Three Piano Pieces*, which inspired him to explore musical ideas through abstract painting. With other painters, Kandinsky formed a group known as *Der Blaue Reiter* (The Blue Rider). Schoenberg exhibited his own paintings with the group in Vienna, and corresponded copiously with Kandinsky about relationships between musical and visual art forms.

▼ **Arnold Schoenberg** (seated, second from left) gathers with his wife Gertrud, the architect Adolf Loos (left), and the artist Oskar Kokoschka at a bar in Berlin.

# Moses and Aaron

MOSES UND ARON Opera in three acts (incomplete), 1¾ hours ▪ Composed: 1930–1932 ▪ First performed: June 6, 1957, Stadttheater, Zurich, Switzerland ▪ Libretto: Arnold Schoenberg

*Moses and Aaron*, an incomplete opera which is challenging to stage, is rarely given. To convey the frustrations of a prophet who deems himself inarticulate, Schoenberg set the role of Moses in *Sprechgesang* or "speak-singing." The tenor voice of the eloquent Aaron is by contrast all the more penetrating. Choral passages and Act I's "Dance around the Golden Calf" are highlights of this intense opera based on the biblical Exodus. In the United States in 1945, Schoenberg's application for funding to complete the opera was rejected.

## Act I
God instructs Moses to lead the Israelites to the Promised Land. Moses claims himself incapable, but God promises that signs will aid him. In the wilderness, Moses meets Aaron. Israelites favor Moses's God, but a priest warns of Moses as a murderer. Moses and Aaron arrive. Aaron interprets the new god as infinite, but the Israelites reject God's invisibility. Aaron produces signs persuading the Israelites to challenge Pharaoh ("Ein Wunder erfüllt uns mit Schrecken"). The people wonder what they will eat in the desert. Aaron reassures them. The Chosen People celebrate their seeking the Promised Land.

## Interlude
The Israelites ask after Moses, who has been absent for 40 days.

## Act II
The Israelites refuse to wait for Moses to return from the Mount of Revelation with the new law. The people are agitated ("Wo ist Moses?") and claim they will slaughter their priests. Aaron promises them an image of God. At Aaron's invitation, people worship the Golden Calf. Sacrifices are followed by orgiastic excesses, with virgins slaughtered by priests. Moses descends from the mountain, and the people flee. Aaron tries to justify the idol to Moses, claiming that the tablets are also "visible" forms of God. Moses smashes the tablets. Alone, Moses is anguished.

▼ **Frode Olsen** plays the reluctant prophet Moses, a spoken role, at the Hamburg Staatsoper in 2004.

### PRINCIPAL ROLES

**Moses** *spoken* A prophet of God

**Aaron** *tenor*
Interprets Moses's God for the Israelites

**Young Girl** *soprano* She embraces the new god

**Young Man** *baritone* He embraces the new god

**Priest** *bass* He warns the Israelites against Moses

**Naked virgins** *two sopranos/two contraltos*
They are slaughtered by priests

The name "Aaron" would normally have been spelled the same way in German. Schoenberg changed the spelling to Aron because he believed that the title *Moses und Aaron* would be inauspicious: it contains 13 letters.

# Alban Berg

Born: February 9, 1885, Vienna, Austria • Died: December 24, 1935, Vienna, Austria

Since World War II, Alban Berg has been hailed as a key figure of 20th-century avant-garde music. He wrote only two operas: *Wozzeck* and *Lulu*. The latter remained unfinished at the time of his death. These works—atonal, passionate, and shocking—sent opera music on a startling new path.

B
erg was born in Vienna and lived there until his death from blood poisoning at the age of 50. He showed early strength as a composer of songs, writing dozens of them in his teenage years. But Berg's formal music education was scant until 1904, when in the burgeoning arts scene of Vienna he met Arnold Schoenberg, originator of the 12-tone method of composition. He then studied with Schoenberg, whose rejection of Romantic definitions of music and beauty, along with the radical lyricism of fellow Viennese composer Gustav Mahler, strongly influenced Berg's distinct style. He moved freely among forms and effects, from folk music to tightly wound dissonance.

Berg's life and work were hit hard by historical circumstances. Progress on the opera *Wozzeck* was delayed by World War I, when he worked for the War Ministry. And from 1933, as Berg was composing *Lulu*, Nazi authorities took steps to ban performance of his music in Germany and Austria.

Berg is often remembered as the leading opera composer of the Second Viennese School led by Schoenberg; its other chief composer was Anton Webern. Both the music and themes of Berg's operas influenced composers throughout the 20th century. His inarticulate antihero Wozzeck, in particular, captured new problems of listening and being heard, and spawned tragic opera heroes of a distinctly modern kind.

> ## "Berg's music is saying farewell to life."
>
> THE PHILOSOPHER THEODOR ADORNO

## FIRST PERFORMANCES

- 1925 *Wozzeck*

- 1937 *Lulu*

- 1979 *Lulu* (completed)

▼ **Sets designed by** Stefanos Lazaridis add a chilling realism to a 2002 *Wozzeck* for London's Royal Opera House, with German baritone Matthias Goerne as Wozzeck, and Swedish soprano Katarina Dalayman as Marie.

# Lulu

Opera in a prologue and three acts, 2¾ hours ▪ Composed: 1928–1935; Act III completed by Friedrich Cerha, 1974 ▪ First performance of two-act version: June 2, 1937, Zurich Opera, Switzerland; first performance of complete three-act version: February 24, 1979, Palais Garnier, Paris ▪ Libretto: Berg, from Frank Wedekind's plays *Erdgeist* (1895) and *Die Büchse der Pandora* (1904)

*Lulu* has been hailed a landmark atonal opera, although Berg had only scored the first two acts by the time of his death in 1935. The third and final act was supplied by the Austrian composer Friedrich Cerha some 40 years later. Formally precise and complex, but also seething with psychological luxuriance, *Lulu* has since Berg's day remained a shocking opera built around the sexually mesmerizing "black angel" Lulu. The subjects of obsession, lust, disfiguring disease, and violence have struck some as gratuitously outrageous. But Berg worked on the piece in Sigmund Freud's Vienna, where tight-laced hypocrisy fed on unspoken desires. The intrepid *Lulu* still takes to stages like a savage creature just released from its cage. Since 1979, the complete version has been given in major opera houses worldwide.

### Prologue
An Animal Tamer welcomes the audience to his tent, where he promises a show of wild rather than domesticated beasts.

### Act I
Lulu poses for the Painter in his studio while her lover, Dr. Schön, observes. Sexual tension coils when Schön departs ("Sie bekommen mich noch lange nicht"). The Painter confesses love for Lulu just as her husband arrives; the husband dies on the spot. Married to her worshipful Painter, Lulu meets Schön at home in secrecy. He aims to end their long affair and marry Countess Geschwitz. When the Painter discovers Schön with Lulu, he takes his own life. Three years later, in the dressing-room of a theater where Lulu dances, she argues with Schön, still unmarried ("Das hättest du dir besser erspart!"). Taking dictation from Lulu, Schön, still as bewitched by her as ever, pens a letter renouncing his engagement. The task complete, he finally breaks down.

### Act II
Married now to Schön, Lulu entertains her lesbian admirer, the Countess Geschwitz. When Schön enters the drawing room with a revolver, Lulu takes him to bed. She returns to flirt with visiting lovers, who hide when Alwa, Schön's son, woos her with passion. Discovering them, Schön urges Lulu to kill herself, but she refuses ("Wenn sich die Menschen"). Instead, she fires on Schön and promises Alwa love. But, his father dead, Alwa has contacted the police.

A silent film portrays Lulu spending a year in prison and contracting cholera. As the staged action resumes, the Countess leaves for the cholera ward to change places with Lulu. When Lulu returns in the Countess's stead, the Acrobat who was to marry her is revolted by her diseased features. Alone with Alwa, Lulu rejoices in her freedom as he praises her body ("Durch dieses Kleid").

### Act III
In a Paris casino, all are gambling when the Marquis, a sex-trafficker, warns Lulu he will betray her unless she agrees to be sold. Others return from gambling, and Lulu quarrels with the Countess ("Brilliant! Es geht brilliant!"). She escapes with Alwa before the police arrive. In a London attic room, Lulu, now a prostitute, returns with a client, a professor. When he leaves, the Countess arrives with Lulu's portrait by her dead husband. Terrified, Lulu returns to the street, and reappears with a second client, who is violent and soon departs. The Countess, lovesick for Lulu, toys with suicide. Lulu returns with a third client, Jack. They wrangle about money and prepare for moonlit sex ("Wer ist das"). From her room, Lulu shrieks wildly. Jack emerges with a bloodied knife and stabs the Countess, who dies calling for Lulu ("Lulu! Mein Engel").

▶ **Evelyn Lear plays Lulu** to Dietrich Fischer-Dieskau's Schön in 1968 at the Deutsche Oper, West Berlin.

The Royal Riding School in the Christiansborg Palace of Denmark was the venue for Travis Preston's 1996 production. In the theater dressing-room scene of Act I, American soprano Constance Hauman sang Lulu naked.

### PRINCIPAL ROLES

**Lulu** *soprano* A bewitching dancer

**Dr. Schön/Jack the Ripper** *baritone*
An editor-in-chief/Murderer

**Countess Geschwitz** *mezzo-soprano*
Schön's lesbian fiancée

**Alwa** *tenor* A composer and Dr. Schön's son

**Schigolch** *bass*
An old man who passes as Lulu's father

**The Painter/Second client** *tenor*
Lulu's second husband/Sex client

**The Prince/Marquis** *tenor*
Wooer of Lulu/Sex-trafficker who betrays Lulu

**Animal Tamer/Acrobat** *bass*
Presenter of the opera/Man in love with Lulu

# Wozzeck

Opera in three acts, 1½ hours ▪ Composed: 1914–1922 ▪ First performed: December 14, 1925, Staatsoper, Berlin, Germany ▪ Libretto: Alban Berg, from the play *Woyzeck* (1837) by Georg Büchner

*Wozzeck* is a masterwork of the modern era, and its influence on subsequent composers is difficult to exaggerate. Based on Georg Büchner's 1837 play, itself based on a true story, the opera presents a disturbed murderer as a sympathetic man struggling to preserve his dignity. Musically, the opera is a *tour de force*. Each of its 15 scenes is built on forms such as the lullaby, the military march, the rhapsody, and the fugue. Berg's signature music creates maximum theatrical effect, as does his pacing. Indeed, a central subject in the opera is haste, and it exerts stress on the troubled Wozzeck from the first scene. The 1925 premiere of *Wozzeck* was a triumph, and, until it was banned in 1933, the opera was a success in Germany.

## PRINCIPAL ROLES

**Wozzeck** *baritone* A poor soldier

**Andres** *lyric tenor* Wozzeck's friend

**Tambourmajor** *tenor (Heldentenor)* Drum Major

**Hauptmann** *tenor (buffo tenor)* Captain

**Doktor** *bass (buffo bass)* Doctor

**Der Narr** *tenor* The Idiot

**Marie** *soprano* Mother to Wozzeck's child

**Mariens Knabe** *treble* Their son

**Margret** *contralto* Marie's neighbor

The opera famously took Berg nearly eight years to write. Preparation for the premiere was also time-consuming. Conductor Erich Kleiber called 137 rehearsals, including 34 for the orchestra alone.

▼ **To those who are lost**, a forest evokes the unknown, where even streams of light can seem ominous.

### Act I

As Wozzeck shaves his Captain, the officer berates him for immorality for having a child out of wedlock with Marie. Cutting brush with Andres, his fellow soldier, Wozzeck believes the place is haunted. When night falls, the men depart fearfully. Margret, a neighbor, taunts Marie for admiring the Drum Major who leads a military band in the street. Slamming her window on Margret, Marie sings her child a lullaby ("Mädel, was fangst du jetzt an?"). When Wozzeck appears, she holds their son out to him. But, disturbed by visions, he leaves. Wozzeck complains of hallucinations to the Doctor, who grows ecstatic imagining his fame for treating Wozzeck's strange illness ("Oh! meine Theorie!"). Marie eyes the Drum Major as he marches before her. At first she resists his advances, then falls into his arms.

### Act II

Admiring her new earrings, a gift from the Drum Major, Marie prevents her son from seeing them ("Was die Steine glänzen!"). When Wozzeck asks her how she obtained the jewelery, Marie lies to him. He gives her his earnings and leaves. In a street, the Doctor discusses his medical cases with the Captain. Wozzeck passes by, but rushes away when they needle him about the Drum Major. Wozzeck reaches Marie's home. Crazed, he lunges at her, but she takes refuge in her room. Wozzeck watches the Drum Major dance gropingly with Marie in a garden. Andres joins others in song ("Ein Jäger aus der Pfalz"), and a drunkard delivers a sour sermon ("Jedoch, wenn ein Wanderer"). Wozzeck is warned of a smell of blood by an Idiot. In the barracks, he is sleepless. The Drum Major arrives drunk, bragging about his conquest. After they fight, Wozzeck is left bleeding on the floor as the Drum Major exits.

### Act III

Studying the Bible, Marie pushes her child away in self-disgust, then calls him back. At dusk, Marie and Wozzeck walk in the woods. With a red moon rising, he plunges a knife into her throat. Marie dead, Wozzeck hurries off. In a tavern, Wozzeck sings, then watches others dance. Margret notices blood on his hand. Wozzeck rushes out. In the woods, Wozzeck stumbles on Marie's corpse while looking for his knife ("Das Messer?"). He throws the knife into a pond, then wades in to throw it further. The Doctor and Captain hear a man drown as they pass, but they do nothing. Marie's son plays with other children. They tell him his mother is dead, but he does not understand. Hopping along on a toy horse, he follows the children as they go to inspect Marie's body.

▶ **At the Santa Fe Opera** in 2001, in the opera's second act, Håken Hagegård plays Wozzeck (left), Michael Smallwood is Andres (center), and Anthony Laciura portrays the Idiot (right).

# Kurt Weill

Born: March 2, 1900, Dessau, Saxony, Germany • Died: April 3, 1950, New York, US

Kurt Weill rejected distinctions between high and low art to write dozens of inspired works of music theater. His masterpieces in German, *Die Dreigroschenoper* and *Aufstieg und Fall der Stadt Mahagonny*, created an earthier species of opera in Weimar Germany, while his later American pieces elevated the Broadway musical to new heights.

Weill was born to a cantor in the synagogue of Dessau and began composing music as a boy. He later studied under various teachers, including Wagner's protégé, Engelbert Humperdinck. By the late 1920s, he was writing operas marked by new European music as well as American dance music. Collaboration with writer Bertolt Brecht then generated *Die Dreigroschenoper* (*The Threepenny Opera*) and *Aufstieg und Fall der Stadt Mahagonny* (*Rise and Fall of the City of Mahagonny*). Both works found wide popularity in Weimar Germany, but

Weill's operas of the early 1930s provoked riots. The Nazis' rise to power in January 1933 prompted him to flee, first to Paris, and then, in 1935, to the United States. There, Weill gained renown for his musicals, from *Johnny Johnson* and *Lady in the Dark* to *One Touch of Venus* and *Street Scene*.

◀ **At the Music Box Theatre** in New York, Weill plays tunes from his musical *Lost in the Stars*.

## FIRST PERFORMANCES

- 1926 *Der Protagonist*

- 1927 *Royal Palace*

- 1928 *Der Zar lässt sich photographieren* • *Die Dreigroschenoper*

- 1930 *Aufstieg und Fall der Stadt Mahagonny* • *Der Jasager*

- 1932 *Die Bürgschaft*

- 1933 *Der Silbersee* • *Die sieben Todsünden*

- 1936 *Johnny Johnson*

- 1937 *The Eternal Road*

- 1938 *Knickerbocker Holiday*

- 1941 *Lady in the Dark*

- 1943 *One Touch of Venus*

- 1945 *The Firebrand of Florence*

- 1947 *Street Scene*

- 1948 *Down in the Valley* • *Love Life*

- 1949 *Lost in the Stars*

# The Threepenny Opera

DIE DREIGROSCHENOPER Play with music in a prologue and three acts, 1¼ hours (music only) ▪ Composed: 1928 ▪ First performed: August 31, 1928, Theater am Schiffbauerdamm, Berlin, Germany ▪ Libretto: Bertolt Brecht, from John Gay's *The Beggar's Opera* (1728)

*The Threepenny Opera* became one of the most popular operas ever to hit the German stage. Irresistible numbers, such as the "Cannon Song" in Act I and the "Song of Sexual Dependency" in Act II, pepper the opera, and each act ends in a show-stopping finale. Weill and librettist Bertolt Brecht mined the flexibility of the English ballad-opera, whose 1728 archetype, John Gay's *The Beggar's Opera*, was their chief source.

## Prologue
A Street Singer introduces the opera with the "Ballad of Mac the Knife" ("Die Moritat von Mackie Messer").

## Act I
Mr. and Mrs. Peachum, who head a gang of beggars and petty criminals, disapprove of their daughter Polly's eloping with Macheath (Mac). Polly and Mac celebrate their marriage in Soho, but Polly's parents want the Sheriff of London to arrest Mac.

## Act II
Polly puts on a show of lamenting Mac's flight from the law. Mac takes up with Jenny, a prostitute bribed by Mrs. Peachum to betray him to the police. In the law courts, Mac escapes with help from Lucy, the Sheriff's daughter. In a finale, the company sings of survival in a world where "Mankind is kept alive by bestial acts" ("Denn wovon lebt der Mensch?").

## Act III
Mr. Peachum threatens the Sheriff: Mac must be arrested, or beggars will upset the imminent coronation. Mac, visits brothels again, is returned to court, where he is condemned to death by hanging. But Mr. Peachum informs the audience that, since this is an opera, humanity will prevail over justice. The Sheriff pronounces Mac free, bestows a peerage on him, and all propose that injustice be spared from persecution.

### PRINCIPAL ROLES

**Polly Peachum** *soprano*
Daughter to Mr. and Mrs. Peachum

**Mrs. Peachum** *mezzo-soprano* Polly's mother

**Jonathan Jeremiah Peachum** *baritone*
Polly's father

**Macheath** *tenor* Also known as Mac the Knife

**Jenny** *soprano*
A prostitute, and Mac's former lover

*The Threepenny Opera* was single-handedly responsible for introducing Weill to a wide American public when, in the monumental New York revival of 1954, its run lasted 2,611 performances.

▶ **Bertolt Brecht's granddaughters** Johanna and Jenny Schall directed and costumed this production at the Maxim Gorki Theater, Berlin, in 2004.

# Béla Bartók

Born: March 25, 1881, Nagyszentmiklós, Hungary (now Sânnicolau Mare, Romania)
▪ Died: September 26, 1945, New York, US

Béla Bartók is now recognized as a major 20th-century composer, although in his lifetime he was better known outside Hungary as a concert pianist. Today, his most popular work is instrumental, although his only opera, *A kékszakállú herceg vára*, or *Duke Bluebeard's Castle*, has also earned a place in the repertory. As a young man, Bartók explored folk music, and this is echoed in his work. But he was also influenced by Debussy, Liszt, and Richard Strauss. Then, in the 1920s, he recognized Stravinsky and Schoenberg by including dissonance in some quartets. In 1940, he took refuge in the United States, where he wrote his monumental *Concerto for Orchestra*. He died there in 1945.

# Duke Bluebeard's Castle

A KÉKSZAKÁLLÚ HERCEG VÁRA Opera in one act, 1 hour • Composed: 1911 (rev. 1912, 1918, 1921) • First performed: May 24, 1918, Royal Hungarian Opera, Budapest, Hungary • Libretto: Béla Balázs, after Charles Perrault's story *La Barbe Bleue* (1697)

*Duke Bluebeard's Castle*, Bartók's only opera, is a Gothic tale set to a masterful score. For the libretto, Béla Balázs adapted Charles Perrault's *La Barbe Bleue*, itself a retelling of a popular folk tale. But he added a dark ending—Bluebeard's latest wife joins the others in death—and used the stark, emotional language of Symbolist poets to create a mood of permanent tension. The powerful score combines the harmony, melody, and *parlando-rubato* rhythm of Hungary's folk music, with nods to Wagner, Richard Strauss, Debussy, and Ravel. The result, notably the "tone poem" orchestration, is highly original. Bluebeard and Judith are engaged in dialogue throughout, leaving no room for traditional arias, yet their vocal parts vividly capture the ever-changing colors of the opera.

### PRINCIPAL ROLES

**The Storyteller** *spoken*

**Duke Bluebeard** *baritone* A baron

**Judith** *mezzo-soprano* His newest wife

**Three murdered wives** *silent*

◀ **Willard White's Duke Bluebeard** terrorizes Judith, sung by the Russian mezzo-soprano Elena Zhidkova, in a 2010 production at the Mariinsky Theatre, St. Petersburg, Russia.

▼ **Béla Bartók is photographed** with his composer friend Zoltán Kodály and a quartet of folk musicians (far right). Both men were inspired by Hungary's music traditions.

The Storyteller announces that "old is the castle, and old the tale that tells of it." Duke Bluebeard leads his new wife, Judith, into his castle. She wonders why it is "always icy, dark, and gloomy" and vows to let in warmth and light. For this, she points to seven bolted doors, which she must open. Bluebeard discourages her, recalling rumors about his sinister past, but she insists, saying she loves him. The first door reveals daggers, racks, and branding irons, all covered with blood: it is Bluebeard's torture chamber. As a crimson sunrise brings the first rays of light into the castle, Judith asks for another key. The next door leads to the armory, where spears are also splashed with blood. Judith presses on, ignoring Bluebeard's warnings. The third door opens to gold, diamonds, and pearls, again blood-stained ("Oh, be sok kincs!"); it is Bluebeard's

treasury. A fragrant garden stands behind the fourth door, and still more light pours in. Judith asks about white roses spotted with blood, but Bluebeard will answer no questions. The fifth door leads to Bluebeard's sunny kingdom ("Ah! Kékszakállú Lásd ez az én birodalmam"), but even here clouds are streaked in blood red. Bluebeard says the castle glitters with light now that Judith has achieved her aim. But if she continues, he cautions that darkness will return. "Though I perish, I fear nothing," she replies. Opening the sixth door, she sees a white sheet of water ("Csendes fehér tavat látok"). "Tears, my Judith, tears, tears," says Bluebeard. He tries to distract her with a kiss, but she asks about his former lovers. When he again refuses to answer, she says she can explain all the blood: as long rumored, he killed all his former wives. He gives her the key to the seventh door and announces his former lovers ("Lásd a régi aszszonyokat"). As three finely attired women emerge, Judith is stunned by their beauty. The first wife, Bluebeard explains, he found at daybreak; the second at noon; the third in the evening. And, turning to Judith, he adds, the fourth at midnight—and darkness will be hers forever. Suddenly terrified, Judith is dressed in diamonds as the "queen of all my women." And, still pleading for her life, she passes through the seventh door. Henceforth," he says, "all shall be night, night, night."

After the socialist Béla Balázs was driven into exile by a rightist regime in 1919, Bartók refused to take Balázs's name off this opera. He was not again credited with the libretto in Budapest until 1955.

# George Gershwin

Born: September 26, 1898, Brooklyn, New York, US ▪ Died: July 11, 1937, Los Angeles, California, US

The leading Broadway composer of the 1920s and '30s, George Gershwin teamed up with his lyricist brother, Ira, to create unforgettable songs that America would adopt as its own. *Porgy and Bess*, his only opera, changed the sound of stage music in the United States, where composers are still under its jazzy spell.

George Gershwin became a professional pianist at age 15, and as a young man began composing songs absorbed into musicals signed by other talents. His career soon skyrocketed. He composed a string of Broadway hits, from musical comedies like *Strike Up the Band* to his sole operatic work, *Porgy and Bess*. From 1924 onward, George and Ira Gershwin created countless numbers whose very titles, such as "'S Wonderful"

from *Funny Face* and "I Got Rhythm" from *Girl Crazy*, still trigger popular recollection of entire songs. The dance team Fred and Adele Astaire were among America's top stage talents who appeared repeatedly in Gershwin's musical comedies. Many of these works were influenced by the operetta form, but Gershwin's masterpiece, the opera *Porgy and Bess*, was most indebted to traditional African-American music. Gershwin was

inspired by DuBose Heyward's novel *Porgy*, and his resulting "folk opera" was meant to premiere at the Metropolitan Opera in New York. But when those plans fell through, it opened in Boston before enjoying a run of 124 performances at New York's Alvin Theatre. Less than two years after the 1935 premiere of *Porgy and Bess*, Gershwin's blossoming career was cut tragically short. He died of a brain tumor at age 38.

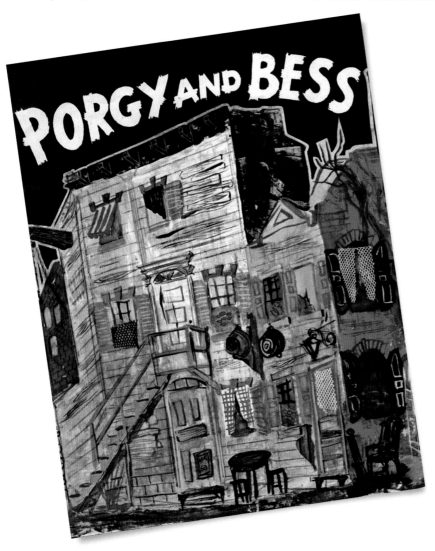

### Leontyne Price

Born in Mississippi in 1927, soprano Leontyne Price studied at the Juilliard School in New York and made her debut in 1952 in Virgil Thomson's *Four Saints in Three Acts*. Price rose to fame as Bess in a revival of *Porgy and Bess*, touring America, Europe, and Russia, and married her onstage Porgy, William Warfield. Her 1961 Metropolitan Opera debut was no less glamorous—her Leonora in Verdi's *Il trovatore* earned a 42-minute ovation.

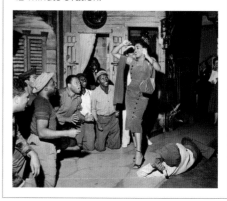

◀ **The front cover of the program** for Gershwin's well-loved masterpiece *Porgy and Bess* from the Everyman Opera production that toured the world from 1952 to 1956.

# Porgy and Bess

Opera in three acts, 3 hours ▪ Composed: 1934–1935 ▪ First performed: September 30, 1935, Colonial Theater, Boston, US ▪ Libretto: DuBose Heyward, from the play *Porgy* (1927) by DuBose and Dorothy Heyward based on DuBose Heyward's 1925 novel; additional lyrics by Ira Gershwin

Many hit songs from *Porgy and Bess*—"A Woman Is a Sometime Thing," "It Ain't Necessarily So," "Bess, You Is My Woman Now"—have been recorded by great jazz and blues singers. Gershwin traveled to South Carolina to take in the atmosphere and music of the opera's setting. His score integrated African-American gospel music, blues, and jazz to create worlds of sound that Broadway had never heard the likes of before 1935.

### Act I
The mood in the tenement on Catfish Row is trance-like ("Summertime"). Porgy, a disabled beggar, is in love with Bess, whose boyfriend, Crown, joins other men to gamble. When Robbins gets lucky with the dice, Crown stabs him in a burst of anger. As police close in, Crown flees, and Bess finds refuge with Porgy. Serena and others mourn Robbins' death in her room. A detective questions them, then detains a guiltless suspect.

### Act II
Porgy and Bess fall in love. But during a picnic on an island, where Crown is in hiding, Bess is again seduced by her old lover. Back on Catfish Row, a distraught Bess assures Porgy of her love for him. As a hurricane threatens, all sing for the Lord's protection. Suddenly, Crown returns for Bess, but then risks his own life to save a fisherman in the storm.

### Act III
All console the dead fisherman's wife. When Crown reclaims Bess, Porgy stabs him. The detective leads Porgy away to identify Crown's body. Returning from jail time, Porgy learns that Bess has run off to New York with the drug dealer Sportin' Life. Porgy has no idea where New York is, but begins his journey to find Bess ("Oh Lawd, I'm on my way").

## PRINCIPAL ROLES

**Porgy** *bass-baritone*
A disabled man in love with Bess

**Bess** *soprano* Crown's girlfriend

**Crown** *baritone* Her boyfriend

**Robbins** *tenor* A gambling patron

**Serena** *soprano* His wife

**Sportin' Life** *tenor* A drug dealer

◀ **In 1985, American bass-baritone** Simon Estes was the first Porgy ever to appear at the Metropolitan Opera in New York.

The original Porgy, Todd Duncan, recalled George and Ira Gershwin singing through the opera to interest him in the role. In spite of their "awful, rotten voices," Todd was seized by the melodies.

# Francis Poulenc

Born: January 7, 1899, Paris, France • Died: January 30, 1963, Paris, France

Francis Poulenc, the reigning *enfant terrible* of French music in the 1920s and '30s, following World War I was drawn into the Surrealist movement. He set poems by Paul Éluard, Jean Cocteau, and Guillaume Apollinaire, whose play *Les mamelles de Tirésias*, or *The Breasts of Tiresias*, also served as the source for his first opera, in 1947. A decade later, Poulenc's operatic masterpiece, *Dialogues des Carmélites*, showed that his youthful piquancy had given way to genuine sentimental depth. It and his final opera, *La voix humaine*, or *The Human Voice*, struck some contemporaries as too Romantic, but both have entered the repertoire as major 20th-century works.

# Dialogues of the Carmelites

DIALOGUES DES CARMÉLITES Opera in three acts and twelve scenes, 2½ hours • Composed: 1953–1955 • First performed: January 26, 1957, La Scala, Milan, Italy • Libretto: Francis Poulenc, after the play by Georges Bernanos

The tragic events recounted in this opera prompt Poulenc to avoid a lush sound in favor of a lean score that cuts to the heart of the drama. The music's searing clarity owes more to Stravinsky than Massenet, though Poulenc retains Massenet's elegant way with a melody. For the finale, one of the opera's few ensembles, nuns sing a lyrical hymn, "Salve Regina," with voices dropping out one by one to the sound of a falling guillotine.

**Act I**
**Scene 1:** Blanche tells her father she wants to become a nun and escape the fearful excitement of the world. **Scene 2:** Blanche tells the prioress, Madame de Croissy, she wishes to take the name "Sister Blanche of the Agony of Christ." **Scene 3:** Blanche chastises Constance for her irreverence on the subject of death. **Scene 4:** De Croissy blasphemes as she suffers a horrible, tedious death. She asks Mère Marie to watch over Blanche. She bids Blanche goodbye ("Relevez-vous, ma fille") and dies.

**Act II**
**Scene 1:** De Croissy lies in state, as Blanche minds her. Blanche fearfully tries to leave the room, but Marie arrives and chides her. Later, Constance muses that someone else will receive the graceful, unafraid death God intended for de Croissy. **Scene 2:** The new prioress, Madame Lidoine, greets the order. **Scene 3:** The Chevalier bids his sister Blanche goodbye before going to war and asks her to care for their father. She refuses, citing her duty to God. **Scene 4:** A commissioner arrives and orders the Convent to disband.

**Act III**
**Scene 1:** The Carmelites vote anonymously whether to take a vow of martyrdom. After Constance retracts her initial objection, they take the vow. Blanche then flees. **Scene 2:** Marie urges Blanche to return. She declines. **Scene 3:** Jailed, the Carmelites await execution. **Scene 4:** The nuns chant as they advance to the guillotine. As Constance awaits her turn, a serene, accepting Blanche joins them ("Salve Regina").

◀ **A scene from Poulenc's opera** in a spare and moving production staged by Francesca Zambello for the Opéra Bastille, Paris, in 2004.

▶ **Francis Poulenc** (left) reads through the libretto of *Dialogues of the Carmelites* with two members of the cast at a rehearsal for a 1958 production at the Royal Opera House, London.

**PRINCIPAL ROLES**

**Blanche de la Force** *soprano*
A timorous woman

**Chevalier** *tenor* Her brother

**Madame de Croissy** *contralto*
Prioress of the Carmelite Convent

**Mère Marie (Mother Mary)** *mezzo-soprano*
Assistant Prioress

**Madame Lidoine** *soprano* The new Prioress

**Sœur Constance (Sister Constance)** *soprano*
A very young nun

Blanche and de Croissy share the ambitious name "Sister of the Agony of Christ," referring to the moment when Jesus expressed fear of death in Gethsemane. De Croissy capitulates to her fear, but Blanche transcends it.

# Benjamin Britten

Born: November 22, 1913, Lowestoft, Suffolk, England • Died: December 4, 1976, Aldeburgh, Suffolk, England

Benjamin Britten was the first major English opera composer since Henry Purcell almost three centuries earlier. He was also the first ever to demonstrate the full operatic potential of the English language. In 1945, post-war England discovered new cultural life in his landmark opera *Peter Grimes*. But it was only the beginning of a career that would dominate late 20th-century opera.

B ritten was born in 1913 in Suffolk, where his father was a dentist. He began composing at 6, and at 15 studied with composer Frank Bridge before attending the Royal College of Music in London. His career blossomed amid the political upheavals that scarred Europe in the 1930s. Still a teenager, he was recognized as an exceptional talent and by age 22 was employed by the Government Printing Office, where he worked as a composer with the Film Unit. During the late 1930s, he met the poet W. H. Auden and the tenor Peter Pears, who remained Britten's muse, collaborator, and partner throughout the remainder of his life. A committed pacifist, Britten traveled with Pears just before the outbreak of World War II to live in exile in the United States. There, with Auden his librettist and Pears his lead tenor, he created *Paul Bunyan*, an opera about the American folk hero. The work was largely ignored after its New York premiere in 1941, yet Britten himself was noticed. That same year, he was awarded a Library of Congress Medal for his services to chamber music in the United States, and received a commission from the library's Koussevitzky Music Foundation to write an opera. The result, *Peter Grimes*, proved to be Britten's first masterpiece, and cause for celebration in England.

### Early operas 1945–1955
When Britten returned with Peter Pears to England in 1942, they were already at work sketching *Peter Grimes*. The country was at war, but both young men were recognized as conscientious objectors and were exempted from military service. *Peter Grimes* premiered in London in 1945 mere weeks after V-E Day in Europe, with Pears singing the title role Britten had written for him. The opera was instantly embraced as a work heralding a new era for the war-tattered

## FIRST PERFORMANCES

- 1941 *Paul Bunyan*
- 1945 *Peter Grimes*
- 1946 *The Rape of Lucretia*
- 1949 *The Little Sweep*
- 1951 *Billy Budd*
- 1953 *Gloriana*
- 1954 *The Turn of the Screw*
- 1958 *Noye's Fludde*
- 1960 *A Midsummer Night's Dream*
- 1964 *Curlew River*
- 1966 *The Burning Fiery Furnace*
- 1968 *The Prodigal Son*
- 1971 *Owen Wingrave*
- 1973 *Death in Venice*

country. The following years brought *The Rape of Lucretia*, based on the poem by Shakespeare; *Albert Herring*; and *The Little Sweep*, a children's opera. But of all operas from this period, many today consider *Billy Budd*, which premiered in 1951, to be the composer's finest. Subsequent operas were the controversial *Gloriana*, about Queen Elizabeth I, and *The Turn of the Screw*.

### Later operas 1956–1976
In 1956, Britten and Pears traveled to Bali and Japan, where new horizons in sound and drama marked the composer for subsequent operas. *Noye's Fludde*, a miracle

▲ **At the historical premiere** of Benjamin Britten's *Peter Grimes* in 1945, the tenor Peter Pears (left) held London audiences spellbound in the unsettling title role.

"It is cruel that music should be so beautiful. It has the beauty of loneliness and of pain, of strength and freedom."

BENJAMIN BRITTEN

▲ **Benjamin Britten** (second from right) on a boating expedition in 1949 with friends, including the novelist E. M. Forster, who was one of his librettists.

play, and *A Midsummer Night's Dream*, based on Shakespeare's play, sparkle with Eastern effects, as do the three "church parables" of the 1960s: *Curlew River*, *The Burning Fiery Furnace*, and *The Prodigal Son*. In this era, too, Britten's legendary pacifism grew more explicit in his music. The much-loved *War Requiem* of 1962 was followed by *Owen Wingrave*, an anti-war opera of 1971 based

on a story by Henry James. Britten's final opera, *Death in Venice*, was written as he struggled with a heart ailment. He was too sick to attend the premiere at the Aldeburgh Festival, which he and Pears had founded in 1948. But he did hear his beloved Pears give a *tour de force* interpretation of the extraordinary role of Aschenbach at Covent Garden in London. By the time of his death in 1976, the composer was Baron Britten of Aldeburgh, a life peer named by Queen Elizabeth II. By then, too, his operatic oeuvre was formidable and sure to be enduring.

▶ **Benjamin Britten** appeared on the cover of *Time* magazine in 1948. Fishing nets in the background suggest his opera *Peter Grimes*.

# Peter Grimes

Opera in a prologue and three acts, 2¼ hours ▪ Composed: 1944–1945 ▪ First performed: June 7, 1945, Sadler's Wells, London, England ▪ Libretto: Montagu Slater, after the poem collection *The Borough* (1810) by George Crabbe

*Peter Grimes* is the first operatic masterpiece by Benjamin Britten. He was living in the United States during World War II when he read George Crabbe's *The Borough*, a set of poems from 1810 about the people of Britten's beloved Aldeburgh, including a fisherman called Peter Grimes. Work on adapting the Grimes story began before his return to Britain, where the opera premiered after the war. It would become the first major opera written in English since Purcell's 17th-century *Dido and Aeneas*. With Peter Pears singing the title role, *Peter Grimes* proved a tremendous success. The threads of its dark and stirring story—of injustice, hatred, dashed hopes, and a man's struggle with his poisoned fate—are woven into a musical web of heartrending orchestral beauty and vocal transcendence.

## PRINCIPAL ROLES

**Peter Grimes** *tenor* A fisherman

**Ellen Orford** *soprano* A widowed schoolmistress

**Captain Balstrode** *baritone*
Retired merchant sea captain

**Auntie** *contralto*
Owns The Boar, a tavern and brothel

**Bob Boles** *tenor* A righteous Methodist fisherman

**Mr. Swallow** *bass* Mayor, coroner, and lawyer

**Mrs. Sedley** *mezzo-soprano* An unpopular widow

**Reverend Horace Adams** *tenor* The parson

**Ned Keene** *baritone* The apothecary

▼ **Benjamin Britten** (left) and the opera's producer Eric Crozier examine a model for the stage set of the 1945 premiere of *Peter Grimes*.

### Prologue
At a coroner's inquest, Peter Grimes gives evidence about the death of his most recent apprentice. He is warned not to take another, and gossip instantly shapes his reputation.

### Act I
Several days later, fishermen work on their boats. Ned Keene, the apothecary, has found Grimes a new apprentice from an orphanage. The village, called the Borough, responds with fear, but Ellen Orford, the schoolmistress, vouches for Grimes. Balstrode, a retired captain, spies a gale force storm approaching, and the Borough prepares ("Now the flood tide"). Grimes tells Balstrode that he hopes to become rich fishing, to gain respect and marry Ellen. Grimes enters The Boar tavern, thinking aloud about fate ("Now the Great Bear and the Pleiades"). The Methodist Boles, drunk, tries to strike him, but Balstrode blocks the effort. When John, the new apprentice, is delivered, Grimes takes him home directly.

### Act II
Villagers sing hymns in church while Ellen sits outside with John. Seeing his wounded neck, she realizes that Grimes has hurt him ("Let this be a holiday"). Grimes arrives in a state of excitement, eager to profit from waters teeming with fish. When Ellen objects, Grimes strikes her. They part ways, and villagers soon form a mob to head to Grimes's hut. In the hut, Grimes reflects on his life's plans ("In dreams I've built myself some kindlier home"). Hearing the mob, he leads John to the back door, where a landslide caused by the storm has created a precipice over the sea. The boy falls out of sight, and Peter rushes after him. The villagers burst in, but realize that their search is pointless. All leave as they came, save Balstrode, who follows the route Grimes took.

### A marginal hero

Peter Grimes is an antihero, but Britten made him a sympathetic and deeply human one. When Grimes adds his voice to those of villagers singing together in Act I, they break off to leave his voice alone. Emotional impact is heightened by Grimes's exclusion, and by his urgent desire to be accepted. The rapport between Grimes and his community is a central concern in the opera's score.

▶ **Peter Pears** played Peter Grimes numerous times after he created the role in 1945.

### Act III
A few evenings later, villagers dance in the town hall. But Mrs. Sedley leaves to sit on the shore. She listens unnoticed as Balstrode discovers Grimes's boat, and Ellen recognizes the missing boy's jersey ("Embroidery in childhood was"). Mrs. Sedley gives the news to Swallow, who gathers a posse. The Borough erupts with hatred and disperses in search of Grimes ("Who holds himself apart"). Hours later, Grimes returns to an empty town. He rehearses the accidental losses of his apprentices and accepts his fate. Ellen and Balstrode arrive to offer solemn help. Balstrode instructs Grimes to take his boat out to sea and sink it. As the town comes to life the next day, Swallow notes that a boat is sinking at sea, but is too far off to be rescued.

▲ **Eerie staging by David Pountney**
marks a 2005 production of *Peter Grimes*
at the Opernhaus in Zurich, Switzerland,
with Christopher Ventris as Peter Grimes.

The opera company of the Sadler's Wells Theatre was initially hostile to the
idea of premiering *Peter Grimes*. Company members, who found the work grim
and unmusical, were astounded by its success.

# Billy Budd

Opera in four acts (revised version: two acts with prologue and epilogue), 2¾ hours ▪ Composed: 1950–1951; rev. 1960 ▪ First performed: December 1, 1951, Royal Opera House, London, England ▪ Libretto: E. M. Forster and Eric Crozier, from the short novel *Billy Budd, Foretopman* (1891) by Herman Melville

*Billy Budd* is considered among the finest operas of the 20th century, a flawless work about human flaws. Tension builds from the outset as an English warship enters enemy waters to fight the French. But the real war occurs among the English: both outwardly and inwardly the seamen are in perpetual conflict. Further, alluring ideas about "the rights of man" lead officers to fear that their own crew plots mutiny, inspired by the revolutionary French enemy. Tension was no less present in the opera's creation. Britten wrestled with his librettists, E. M. Forster and Eric Crozier, until he was satisfied with the work.

## PRINCIPAL ROLES

**Billy Budd** *baritone* Able seaman

**Captain Vere** *tenor* Captain of HMS *Indomitable*

**Claggart** *bass* Master-at-arms

**Mr. Redburn** *baritone* First Lieutenant

**Mr. Ratcliffe** *bass* Second Lieutenant

**Mr. Flint** *bass-baritone* Sailing Master

**Dansker** *bass* An old seaman

**Squeak** *tenor* Ship's corporal

◀ **The American** Theodor Uppman created Billy Budd at the Royal Opera House in London in 1951.

### Prologue

Captain Vere looks back on his life and recalls the French wars of 1797, when he commanded the warship *Indomitable*. He searches for meaning in the balance of good and evil, and notes that even good is always marred by imperfection.

### Act I

Mr. Flint, the Sailing Master, treats his crew harshly. When three recruits arrive, Claggart, Master-at-arms, interrogates them. Only the third appears promising. He declares himself to be Billy Budd, able seaman. But he stammers helplessly when asked about his home. Officers find this a flaw, but Claggart sees Billy as goodness incarnate. Assigned to the foretop, Billy rejoices, and bids a spirited farewell to his previous ship, the *Rights o' Man* ("Billy Budd, king of the birds!").

Officers fear that Billy's evocation of the "rights of man" could incite mutiny. Meanwhile, fellow crew members warn Billy against Claggart and praise Captain Vere ("Starry, Starry Vere"). A week later, Redburn and Flint are invited to Vere's cabin, where they note that a Novice on board cheered the "rights of man." But Vere has no fears about Billy Budd. Ratcliffe reports that the *Indomitable* has entered enemy waters. On the berth-deck, Squeak provokes Billy to fight. Claggart puts Squeak in irons but, alone, aims to destroy Billy ("O beauty, o

handsomeness, goodness"). Under Claggart's orders, the Novice offers Billy money to wage mutiny. When Billy's anger produces stammering, the Novice flees.

### Act II

Captain Vere worries about enveloping mists as his men grow impatient for battle. Suddenly, a French frigate is sighted, and the crew excitedly prepares for action ("This is our moment! The moment we've been waiting for!"). But exhilaration wanes when Vere gives orders to abandon the chase. Claggart informs Vere that mutiny is being fomented by Billy Budd. Dismayed, Vere summons Billy. In Vere's cabin, Claggart accuses Budd of mutiny. Billy stammers and, in frustration, strikes the officer. When Claggart proves to be dead, Vere realizes he has no choice but

to put Billy on trial ("The mists have cleared"). After speaking in his own defense, Billy is taken away, crying for Captain Vere to save him. But the law requires Billy's execution, and Vere reluctantly accepts his officers' verdict. Billy explains to Dansker that fate has determined his death. But, alone, he discovers an inner strength—stronger than fate—that allows him to embrace death ("And farewell to ye, old Rights o' Man!"). At first light, Billy blesses Captain Vere, then is hanged. The crew reacts with groaning sounds, and tension builds until the officers cause the men to disperse.

## Epilogue

Years later, the elderly Captain Vere reflects that he could have saved Billy from death, but instead it was Billy who saved and blessed him.

### Good vs. evil

Britten's score for Billy Budd explores a mysterious realm beyond good and evil, where acceptance offers tranquility and salvation. Costume designers usually convey the good Billy and the evil Claggart by dressing them in white and black respectively (right). Many designers also relish the challenge of working with additional elements to capture a director's broader vision of the interaction of good and evil.

▲ **Christopher Oram's** set design for a Glyndebourne production in 2010 made audience members feel they were on board the ship with Billy Budd.

The opera calls for three principals, a full male chorus, and a children's chorus, also male, who form part of the crew aboard the *Indomitable*. There are no female roles in *Billy Budd* because no women were admitted on Royal Navy warships in the late 18th century.

**Francesca Zambello's staging**—at the Dorothy Chandler Pavilion in Los Angeles, in 2014—of Benjamin Britten's *Billy Budd* was visually striking and charged with symbolism.

# ROYAL OPERA
# HOUSE

England's attachment to opera has been at best sporadic, perhaps because the country produced no important opera composer in the three centuries between Henry Purcell and Benjamin Britten. But Handel, the German who composed Italian operas for the English, did make his mark, presenting seven operas at the Theatre Royal in Covent Garden in the mid-18th century. That theater was destroyed by fire in 1808 as was its successor in 1856. The building housing today's Royal Opera House opened on the same site two years later.

Known initially simply as the Covent Garden, the theater became the Royal Opera House in 1892, presenting German and Italian operas performed in English. Without a reliable audience of opera lovers, the 2,200-seat theater was also used for plays, pantomimes, and even ice shows. During World War II, the auditorium became a dance hall. The theater was then rescued for opera, although as important was the arrival of the Sadler's Wells Ballet company, soon to become the Royal Ballet.

A major turning-point for the Royal Opera House came in the late 20th century when, thanks to grants from the Arts Lottery, it gained extensive additional space for opera and ballet rehearsal, a large foyer, and a 400-seat theater below ground.

By then, under successive acclaimed choreographers, the Royal Ballet had won a place among the world's top companies. Similarly, with Antonio Pappano as music director for more than two decades from 2002, the opera company's post-1960s reputation for excellence was consolidated.

For its financing, the opera house falls between the European and American models, receiving a government subsidy for administration but needing private sponsors for its productions. Even so, thanks to the English National Opera; numerous opera festivals; and opera companies in Scotland, Wales, and northern England, more musical theater is being performed in Britain than ever before.

> " I think in the opera world the conductor has to love the words as much as the music. The music certainly has the drive, but the words and situations, based on the ideas of struggle, loss, love, death, or hatred, are to be taken for real."

ANTONIO PAPPANO, MUSIC DIRECTOR, ROYAL OPERA HOUSE

◀ **Standing beside the classical facade** of the Royal Opera House, the glass-fronted Paul Hamlyn Hall offers the theater space for receptions, exhibitions, and concerts.

# The Turn of the Screw

An opera in a prologue and two acts, 1¾ hours ▪ Composed: 1954 ▪ First performed: September 14, 1954, Teatro La Fenice, Venice, Italy ▪ Libretto: Myfanwy Piper, after Henry James's story *The Turn of the Screw*

In this chamber opera, a governess attempts to save two children haunted by a dead man. Music associated with the governess is stark, percussive, and neurotic. But the ghost's hypnotic vocal lines and dreamy music thread through the opera, and even dominate at the end of Act I. The prologue establishes a musical theme, and orchestral interludes return in increasingly demented variations to create ever-deepening suspense.

## PRINCIPAL ROLES

**The governess** *soprano* Cares for the children

**Miles** *treble* Boy in her charge

**Flora** *soprano* His sister, also in her charge

**Mrs. Grose** *soprano* The housekeeper

**Quint** *tenor* A former valet

**Miss Jessel** *soprano* A former governess

The libretto borrows a line from poet W. B. Yeats, "The ceremony of innocence is drowned," which not only refers to the abused children, but also illuminates the governess's shattered idealism.

### Prologue
A governess has agreed to care for two children who live at Bly, a country mansion. Their guardian insists that she not contact him.

### Act I
Riding in a coach, the governess anxiously anticipates her arrival at Bly. Mrs. Grose and the children, Miles and Flora, welcome her. Later, the governess receives notice of Miles's dismissal from school, but she and Mrs. Grose do not believe that Miles could be bad. The governess sees the figure of a man upon a tower. Hearing the description, Mrs. Grose verifies it is Peter Quint, who had abused the children and former governess, Miss Jessel. Both Quint and Miss Jessel are dead now. Miles rehearses Latin ("Malo, Malo, Malo"). The governess and Flora sit beside the lake, where the governess sees Miss Jessel and rushes Flora away. At night, Miss Jessel and Quint beckon to Miles and Flora. The governess hurries them inside.

### Act II
Quint and Miss Jessel describe what they seek in the children ("I seek a friend"). Mrs. Grose goes to church with the children, and the governess decides to write to their guardian. Miles steals the letter. Later, Miles plays the piano, and Flora sneaks off. The governess confronts Flora, who calls her cruel and hateful. She then questions Miles who, increasingly distraught and frightened, blurts out "Peter Quint, you devil," then falls lifeless into the governess's embrace.

▼ **Mireille Delunsch portrays** the overwhelmed governess in Luc Bondy's production at Théâtre des Champs-Élysées, 2005, with haunting sets by Richard Peduzzi.

# A Midsummer Night's Dream

Opera in three acts, 2½ hours ▪ Composed: 1959–1960 ▪ First performed: June 11, 1960, Jubilee Hall, Aldeburgh, Suffolk, England ▪ Libretto: Benjamin Britten and Peter Pears, adapted from Shakespeare's play (1595–1596)

The opera is divided into three distinct spheres. For the fairy realm, Britten makes extravagant use of celesta, glockenspiel, harps, and even harpsichord to achieve an orchestral texture of enchantment. The lovers constitute a balanced vocal quartet despite the improbable story unfolding onstage. But the show often goes to the rustics, who win over audiences with their comic timing, playful harmonies, and tight ensemble work.

### Act I
Oberon and Tytania quarrel over a changeling left in Tytania's care. Oberon instructs the trickster Puck to obtain a love potion. Hermia and Lysander pledge their love for each other, while Helena futilely pursues Demetrius. A simple group of men, the rustics, plan a play for the Duke of Athens' wedding celebration. Puck administers his potion to Lysander, making him fall in love with Helena. She interprets his attention as mockery.

### Act II
As the rustics rehearse, Puck bewitches Bottom, the lead of their troupe, by fitting him with the head of an ass. Tytania, charmed with the same potion as Lysander, falls in love upon seeing the ass-headed Bottom. She instructs the fairies to dote on him ("Be kind and courteous to this gentleman"). Puck lastly gives the potion to Demetrius, who also falls in love with Helena. Helena and Hermia quarrel, as the men ally themselves with Helena.

### Act III
Oberon releases Tytania from the spell and arranges the lovers into two suitable pairs. Upon waking, they celebrate their love ("Helena!" "Hermia!" "Demetrius!" "Lysander!"). The rustics perform their ridiculous play for the Duke's wedding festivities.

> **PRINCIPAL ROLES**
>
> **Oberon** *countertenor* King of the Fairies
>
> **Tytania** *coloratura soprano* Queen of the Fairies
>
> **Lysander** *tenor* In love with Hermia
>
> **Demetrius** *baritone* In love with Hermia
>
> **Hermia** *mezzo-soprano* In love with Lysander
>
> **Helena** *soprano* In love with Demetrius

The rustics put on a play that parodies 19th-century *bel canto* style. At the premiere, Pears, as Flute, imitated the diva Joan Sutherland to perfection, leaving the assistant conductor, George Malcolm, in stitches.

▶ **Director Simon Phillips** gave the opera's Shakespearean action a fresh and modern feel for a 2006 production at the Staatsoper in Hamburg.

# Leonard Bernstein

Born: August 25, 1918, Lawrence, Massachusetts, US • Died: October 14, 1990, New York, US

Leonard Bernstein redefined American music theater in much-loved works over a span of four decades from the 1940s. His unmistakable signature, at once declarative, life-loving, and sophisticated, galvanizes his comic operetta, *Candide*. Bernstein's two other operatic works, *Trouble in Tahiti* (1952) and its sequel, *A Quiet Place* (1983), portray life in suburban America.

Bernstein burst onto the American music scene as a conductor with the same flair that came to characterize his compositions. On November 14, 1943, the New York Philharmonic required a conductor to fill in at the last moment. Only 25, Bernstein picked up the baton and stepped into American music history. His charisma enthralled New York, and he went on to dazzle audiences worldwide. From 1956 to 1966, he would serve as the first American-born conductor of the New York Philharmonic. By then, he had long established himself as a composer. His first musical comedy came in 1944 with *On the Town*, to a libretto by the legendary Broadway duo Betty Comden and Adolph Green. They teamed up again for the 1953 musical *Wonderful Town*. But it was the sensational *West Side Story*, in 1957, that would become the quintessential American musical. With all of his works for the stage, including the remarkable operetta *Candide*, Bernstein injected into American theaters and opera houses a fresh mix of classical and popular sound.

◀ **A program cover** for Bernstein's *West Side Story* shows the hit musical's lovers, Maria and Tony, in happier times before tragedy strikes.

**West Side Story**

*A New Musical*

## The communicator

Leonard Bernstein reached audiences with his infectious enthusiasm for music. The first concert he conducted was broadcast nationally from Carnegie Hall. It mesmerized America, and captured worldwide interest. Within a decade, he would lead orchestras in London, Prague, Tel Aviv, and Milan, where he was the first American to conduct an opera at La Scala. From 1958, and for 14 years, his TV program *Young People's Concerts* opened countless American ears to classical music.

▲ **Bernstein flamboyantly** conducts Mahler in 1970 during the Tanglewood Festival in Lenox, Massachusetts, US.

# Candide

Comic operetta in two acts, 2½ hours ▪ Composed: 1954–1956 (rev. 1973, 1988–1989) ▪ First performed: December 1, 1956, Martin Beck Theater, New York, US ▪ Libretto: Lillian Hellman, based on the 1759 novel *Candide* by Voltaire; lyrics by Richard Wilbur

*Candide* has suffered a rocky production history, but since the 1970s it has been regarded as one of Bernstein's greatest works. The French 18th-century novel by Voltaire is treated in high comedic style of a distinctly American stripe that joyfully mocks Old World ideas and musical traditions. Beloved numbers are "Glitter and Be Gay" and "The Best of All Possible Worlds," but the most famous passage is the winsome overture.

### Act I

Candide is an adopted boy living with his cousins, Cunegonde and Max, in Westphalia. He loves Cunegonde and she him. Their tutor, Pangloss, instructs them to find "the best of all possible worlds" in all situations. When the Bulgar Army brings war, all but Candide are slain. Candide sets out to wander the world. He discovers Pangloss, not dead after all and now a beggar. They witness atrocities, but Candide remains optimistic even when Pangloss is hanged. Candide wanders to Paris ("It must be me"), where Cunegonde has become a prostitute. When she inadvertently stabs a man, she and Candide flee with her brothel-keeper, the Old Lady, and eventually set sail for South America.

### Act II

Candide and the others discover Max and the former family servant Paquette miraculously alive and residing in Buenos Aires. Later, in a jungle, Candide stabs Max by mistake and, following extraordinary events, rediscovers Pangloss. Accompanied by the tutor, Candide, Cunegonde, and the Old Lady reach Venice. There, the group rediscovers Max and Paquette, and all throw themselves into Carnival gambling. Finally, in a farmhouse near Venice, Candide celebrates his love for Cunegonde and realizes that life is neither good nor bad ("Make our garden grow").

The opera was so often revised that, after the final changes of the 1988–1989 version, the noted *Candide* conductor John Mauceri joked: "The last time I saw Lenny, I said, 'Now you've really screwed everything up!'"

## PRINCIPAL ROLES

**Candide** *tenor* Naive young man

**Cunegonde** *soprano* His wealthy foster sister

**Max** *baritone* Brother to Cunegonde

**Pangloss** *baritone* Tutor to the three children

**Paquette** *soprano* A dissolute servant

**Old Lady** *mezzo-soprano* A Parisian brothel-keeper

▶ **The Neue Oper** in Vienna put on a cabaret-influenced production of the opera in 2000.

# György Ligeti

Born: May 28, 1923, Diciosânmartin (now Târnăveni), Romania • Died: June 12, 2006, Vienna, Austria

György Ligeti injected a new world of sound into avant-garde music of the late 20th century. Fleeing Communist Hungary in 1956, he settled in Vienna, where in the 1960s his experiments with polyphony distinguished him from even the most innovative composers of the day. While Europeans like Luciano Berio, Karlheinz Stockhausen, and Pierre Boulez explored serialism derived from Arnold Schoenberg's 12-tone method, Ligeti was drawn to surrealism. His 1962 *Poème symphonique* was scored for 100 wound metronomes, its duration dependent on the time needed for all of the contraptions to unwind. *Le Grand Macabre*, his only full-length opera, is equally playful and provocative.

# Le Grand Macabre

Opera in two acts (original version); opera in four scenes (revised version), 2 hours ▪ Composed: 1972–1976; revised 1996 ▪ First performed: April 12, 1978, Royal Opera, Stockholm, Sweden; July 28, 1997, Festspielhaus, Salzburg (revised) ▪ Libretto: György Ligeti and Michael Meschke

*Le Grand Macabre* is an intrepid, exuberant opera based on the 1934 farce *La balade du grand macabre* by Michel de Ghelderode. Brimming with impish humor and coursing with shock, it pleads that life must not be lived in fear of death—or lived in fear of anything. The opera's "Terminator" is in theory Nekrotzar, or Lord Macabre, whose divine purpose is to annihilate the world. But even he is a clown, one of cosmic proportions. Whichever time-honored operatic morsel the work devours, from the love duet to the death scene, it is spat back out as rebellious entertainment. After the 1978 premiere, the opera was revised for 1997. Marks of its double life remain, not least in a mix of postmodern and Cold War era elements. But the music—by turns raucous, heart-grabbing, wizardly, and flippant—makes the opera irresistible in any period.

## Scene I

In a graveyard, the drunken Piet praises the paradise that is Breughelland. Amanda and Amando, lovers, want to die together. Nekrotzar warns that all will perish at midnight ("Heute noch, um Mitternacht"). Piet recognizes Nekrotzar as Lord Macabre and begs for his mercy. Spirits warn of destruction ("Es naht schon das Verderben"). The lovers vow love unto death.

## Scene II

Mescalina tortures her husband, Astradamors. She petitions Venus for a night of sex, then falls asleep. Nekrotzar arrives, riding on Piet's back. In a dream, Mescalina asks Venus for a "well-hung" man. Nekrotzar has violent sex with the unconscious Mescalina; she comes to, then falls dead. Nekrotzar prepares for his mission ("Feuer und Feuersnot"). He rides off atop Piet. Astradamors notes: "At last I am master in my own house."

## Scene III

Two ministers exchange insults in alphabetical order. They place their sovereign prince, Go-Go, atop a rocking

horse. He falls. Gepopo, Chief of the Secret Police, reports turmoil. The ministers court the people of Breughelland, but they hail Go-Go instead ("Uns'ren Fürsten!"). Informed of a comet, the ministers abandon Go-Go, who notes that he is finally master of his own house. Gepopo and others flee, fearing Lord Macabre. A siren sounds. Nekrotzar enters atop Piet. People panic. Piet, Astradamors, and Go-Go feast, drink, and mock Nekrotzar, who asks to sip human blood from a chalice ("Ex! Trink! Ex!"). He drinks to excess, relishing his career of destruction. Lightning strikes, and Nekrotzar renews his motivation. But, when placed on the rocking horse, he falls off, drunk.

## Scene IV

In the graveyard, Piet and Astradamors, now ghosts, float away. Ruffians massacre everyone, but Go-Go bounces back up. At sunrise, Nekrotzar melts into the earth. Amanda and Amando are heard making love in a tomb. The lovers explain that the world came to an end for them as well, only that they were in ecstasy. All praise life lived without fear of death.

### PRINCIPAL ROLES

**Piet the Pot** *buffo tenor* A life-loving drunk

**Nekrotzar** *baritone* Lord Macabre

**Astradamors** *bass* A transvestite court astrologer

**Mescalina** *mezzo-soprano* His sadistic wife

**Go-Go** *countertenor* Sovereign prince of Breughelland

**Gepopo** *soprano* His Chief of the Secret Police

▼ **The cover image taken from** the CD of Ligeti's *Le Grand Macabre* shows a rocking horse, a key image in stagings of the opera.

GYÖRGY LIGETI
Le GRAND MACABRE
PHILHARMONIA ORCHESTRA
ESA-PEKKA SALONEN

In the opera's otherworldly Breughelland, all is subject to musical mockery, including life after death. When Piet the Pot and Astradamors return as ghosts of their former selves in Scene 4, ironic harp music accents the action.

# Philip Glass

Born: January 31, 1937, Baltimore, Maryland, US

Philip Glass became the most popular opera composer to emerge from among the American minimalist composers of the late 20th century. His *Einstein on the Beach*, a collaboration with director Robert Wilson, took opera to new conceptual heights in 1976.

lass earned a master's degree from the Juilliard School of Music in New York and then studied with Nadia Boulanger in Paris. But the sitar player Ravi Shankar and travels to India also influenced Glass. In New York in the 1960s, he used electronic instruments to experiment with combinations of Western and Indian musical ideas. Among the distinctive features of his minimalist style is the deliberate, trancelike repetition of notes or chords. Glass has scored more than 20 major works for the stage, including *Satyagraha* and *Akhnaten* (operas completing the "Portrait Trilogy" begun with *Einstein on the Beach*); the *CIVIL warS*; *The Juniper Tree*; *The Fall of the House of Usher*; and *The Voyage*.

### Robert Wilson

Born in 1941, Robert Wilson attended the Pratt Institute in Brooklyn, New York, and studied painting with George McNeil in Paris, France. Influenced by the choreography of Merce Cunningham and Martha Graham, Wilson applied visual ideas to onstage movement. While his work with Glass has been legendary, Wilson has inspired numerous illustrious collaborators, including Susan Sontag, William S. Burroughs, Lou Reed, David Byrne, Laurie Anderson, and Jessye Norman.

◀ **Robert Wilson** (left) and Philip Glass formed a new approach to opera with *Einstein on the Beach*. Wilson has since staged operas worldwide.

◀ **Shown rehearsing** in New York in 1993 with the Philip Glass Ensemble, Glass has also composed for films such as Errol Morris's *The Thin Blue Line* (1988).

# Einstein on the Beach

Opera in four acts and five "knee plays", 4½ hours ▪ Composed: 1974–1975 ▪ First performed: July 25, 1976, Théâtre Municipal, Avignon, France ▪ Libretto: Philip Glass, Robert Wilson, Christopher Knowles, Samuel M. Johnson, and Lucinda Childs

*Einstein on the Beach* is an avant-garde opera of wide influence. Electronically repeated at high speed, some musical passages can have a hypnotizing or disorienting effect. The opera's nonlinear action keeps attention on its atmospheres, and on reverberating visual and musical motifs. Einstein, incarnated by a costumed onstage violinist, presides loosely over the work's logic. His theory of relativity serves as a source of conceptual surprises, at once visual, musical, and ultimately theatrical.

*Einstein on the Beach* is unusual for being a nonnarrative opera. Its building blocks are visual, musical, and verbal repetitions rather than plot elements. The opera explores myriad ideas: Einstein's theory of general relativity, a train's motion as a metaphor for the theory, and law court exchanges as portals into concepts of prejudice and judgment. These are presented in lyrical juxtapositions rather than in narrative fashion.

The work's atypical structure is reinforced in performance: with no intermission, the long piece invites audience members to come and go freely, and without missing key moments in any "story." The opera is partly shaped by what Glass and Wilson called "knee-plays," or "knees" for short. These appear between scenes requiring major set changes. The opera opens with Knee play 1: the ensemble builds a hypnotic web of effects by vocalizing digits ("One, two, three, four, five..."). Act I includes a train scene and a trial scene with lyrics about Mr. Bojangles, and concludes with Knee play 2. Act II offers a dance, and revisits the train thread in a variation called "Night Train." After Knee play 3, Act III revisits the trial thread in relation to the theme of "Prison." A Witness recites text by Lucinda Childs into a dense sound cloud of mechanical choral chanting ("I was in this prematurely air-conditioned supermarket"). A second dance is followed by Knee play 4. Act IV visits themes of "Building," "Bed," and "Spaceship." And the opera concludes with Knee play 5, in which a Bus Driver sings of "Two Lovers on a Bench."

Most opera composers initially respond to a libretto. Glass took a different starting point in his collaboration with Wilson, who engaged the composer's imagination with drawings and visual elements.

▶ **Robert Wilson** designed the opera for a third time at the progressive MC93 Bobigny theater outside Paris in 1992.

> ### PRINCIPAL ROLES
>
> **Einstein** *violinist* Author of the theory of relativity
>
> **Ensemble** *soprano, alto, tenor*, actors, dancers

# Satyagraha

Opera in three acts, 2 hours 10 minutes ▪ Composed: 1979 ▪ First performed: September 5, 1980, Stadsschouwberg, Rotterdam, Netherlands ▪ Libretto: Philip Glass and Constance DeJong

*Satyagraha* is the second of Philip Glass's "Portrait Trilogy," focusing on Mahatma Gandhi's struggle for Indian minority rights in South Africa between 1893 and 1914. Meaning "holding firmly to truth," satyagraha was the name given to Gandhi's nonviolent policy. The libretto comprises short phrases sung in Sanskrit from the sacred Hindu poem, *Bhagavad-Gita*, itself part of the *Mahabharata*. Each director must decide how to stage the narrative. The score, limited to woodwinds and strings, is again minimalist, characterized by repetition of musical phrases, building up to moments of high drama.

### Act I—TOLSTOY

In Scene 1, *Kuru, the field of justice,* two royal families, symbolizing the Indians and Europeans, engage in battle in the presence of Krishna. In Scene 2, *Tolstoy's Farm (1910)*, Gandhi's followers—known as satyagrahis— enjoy the harmonious life of an ashram. In Scene 3, *Swearing of the Oath (1906)*, Indians vow to resist to the death a British order for them to carry residence permits at all times.

### Act II—TAGORE

In Scene 1, *Confrontation and rescue (1896)*, Gandhi risks being lynched when he returns to Durban after denouncing discrimination against Indians in South Africa. In Scene 2, *Indian Opinion (1906)*, the movement's newspaper promotes satyagraha principles. In Scene 3, *Protests (1908)*, after the British government refuses to withdraw a repressive law, Gandhi organizes a passport-burning ceremony.

### Act III—KING

In *The Newcastle March (1913)*, the British government again breaks its promise to withdraw a racist law, and Gandhi calls for support from the coal miners in Newcastle in South Africa's KwaZulu-Natal province. The miners' families are to join a satyagrahi march. If stopped, they will flood the prisons and embarrass the government; if not, it will be a victory for satyagraha.

 **Tenor Sean Panikkar as Mahatma Gandhi** against a background of the *Indian Opinion newspaper*, established by Gandhi, in a 2021 production at the English National Opera, London.

> The continuing relevance of nonviolent resistance has insured that *Satyagraha* is frequently revived, notably in the United States, as a commentary on social and political injustice.

### PRINCIPAL ROLES

**Gandhi** *tenor*

**Miss Schlesen** *soprano*

**Mrs. Naidoo** *soprano*

**Kasturbai** *mezzo-soprano*

**Mrs. Alexander** *mezzo-soprano*

**Mr. Kallenbach** *baritone*

**Prince Arjuna** *baritone*

**Parsi Rustomji** *bass-baritone*

**Lord Krishna** *bass-baritone*

# Akhnaten

Opera in three acts, 2 hours ▪ Composed: 1980–1984 ▪ First performed: March 24, 1984, Staatstheater, Stuttgart, Germany ▪ Libretto: Philip Glass with Shalom Goldman, Robert Israel, Richard Riddell, and Jerome Robbins

*Akhnaten*, the third of Glass's "Portrait Trilogy" operas, tells the story of an Egyptian pharaoh who is credited with introducing monotheism. Scrubbed from history by his successors, Akhnaten was resuscitated when his city, Amarna, was unearthed and the famous bust of his wife Nefertiti was discovered. *Akhnaten*'s libretto is taken from ancient Egyptian, Akkadian, and Hebrew sources, with a Scribe speaking passages in today's languages.

## PRINCIPAL ROLES

**Akhnaten** *countertenor*

**Nefertiti** *mezzo-soprano* His wife

**Queen Tye** *soprano* His mother

**Aye** *bass* Nefertiti's father

**High Priest** *tenor*

**General Horemhab** *baritone*

**Akhnaten's six daughters**
*sopranos and contraltos*

### Act I—Year 1 of Akhnaten's reign: Thebes

Lengthy funeral rites prepare Amenhotep III's journey to the afterlife. Once his body is embalmed, his son Akhnaten steps forward to be crowned. He soon proclaims monotheism and exclusive devotion to the sun god Aten. He also changes his name from Amenhotep IV, meaning "spirit of Amon," to one meaning "spirit of Aten." His wife, Nefertiti, and his mother, Queen Tye, join him in worshiping Aten.

### Act II—Years 5 to 15: Thebes and Akhetaten

Akhnaten and his mother banish old religions, while Akhnaten and Nefertiti celebrate their love in song. A new city—Akhetaten (Amarna)—is built as the capital of their new religion.

### Act III—Year 17 and the present: Akhetaten

Queen Tye is alarmed that Akhnaten and Nefertiti and their six daughters live in isolation from Egypt. Crowds gather at the city gates before the priests of Amon break into the palace and kill Akhnaten. His son is crowned, but even now the voices of Akhnaten, Nefertiti, and Queen Tye still echo from the ancient world.

For all the superficial simplicity of the score, this opera invites an elaborate production, an occasion to display costumes, crowns, and decor reminiscent of Verdi's grandiose Egyptian opera, *Aïda*.

◀ **Anthony Roth Costanzo** as Akhnaten exudes the majesty of one of Egypt's most powerful rulers in an English National Opera production at the London Coliseum in 2019.

# John Adams

Born: February 15, 1947, Worcester, Massachusetts, US

John Adams and his fellow American collaborator, the director Peter Sellars, have taken contemporary opera down a new path. Before Adams, minimalist composers such as Philip Glass built their opera music around interrelated concepts and images rather than on story threads. Working with Sellars, Adams pressed beyond the minimalist idiom of repetition and symmetry to embrace a narrative opera form replete with characters who feel and evolve. In 1985, Adams and Sellars captured attention with *Nixon in China*, arguably the first opera to address audiences raised on television culture. Subsequent operas include *The Death of Klinghoffer*; *El Niño*; and *Doctor Atomic*, to a Sellars libretto.

# Nixon in China

Opera in three acts, 2½ hours ▪ Composed: 1985–1987 ▪ First performed: October 22, 1987, Brown Theater, Wortham Theater Center, Houston Grand Opera, Texas, US ▪ Libretto: Alice Goodman

*Nixon in China* is about President Richard M. Nixon's 1972 visit to Beijing (Peking) for meetings with the Chinese leader Mao Zedong. The opera benefits from a remarkable libretto by Alice Goodman. Spectacular ceremonial action is balanced by private exchanges. But attention is also paid to the subtler inner workings of political figures. Music moves fluidly and relentlessly forward, yet can be suddenly transformed by the drama of the moment, switching from the reflective to the explosive. *Nixon in China* awakened excitement in opera circles when it premiered in Houston in 1987. Like early operas, this one offered a story that audiences were likely to know and, since it was based on recent history, even find relevant to their own lives. The opera was an overnight success.

### Act I

On an airfield in Beijing, Chinese military personnel greet President Richard Nixon ("The people are the heroes now"). As Premier Zhou Enlai introduces key officials, Nixon privately thrills to the idea that "the world is listening" before descending into delusional fantasies ("It's prime time in the USA"). In Mao's study, Nixon struggles to bond with the philosophical Chairman. Dr. Kissinger, National Security Adviser, adds awkward remarks. In the Great Hall, the Nixons are feeling light-hearted. Zhou toasts the Americans ("Ladies and gentlemen, Comrades and friends"), and Nixon the Chinese. A tide of goodwill washes over all ("Cheers!"). When the First Lady, Pat, reminds everyone that it is George Washington's birthday, they are galvanized, Zhou and Nixon reinforce their toasts.

### Act II

Touring Beijing, Pat pauses to foresee a time of simple virtues. That night, the Nixons and Jiang Qing, Mao's wife, attend the premiere of a revolutionary ballet. Its heroine is whipped by a counterrevolutionary, Lao Szu, surprisingly performed by Kissinger. Upset by the action, Pat rushes onstage to alter its course. The president follows, consoling her in his way. But the heroine is beaten senseless. Following a storm scene, the now-armed heroine, prompted by Jiang Qing from the audience, stuns the ballet ensemble by opening fire on Lao Szu and his lot ahead of her cue. Jiang Qing joins the stage to deliver her revolutionary vision ("I am the wife of Mao Zedong").

### Act III

On the President's last night in Beijing, all save Chairman Mao are weary. When Jiang Qing calls for music, a solo piano sparks Pat's nostalgia for California. The Maos dance. Zhou directs Kissinger to the toilet. Nixon reminisces about World War II. In a searching final solo, Zhou notes that "Everything seems to move beyond/ Our remedy."

◀ **Air Force One deposits** Nixon and his entourage in China as the opera begins during its premiere in Houston, Texas, in October 1987.

---

**PRINCIPAL ROLES**

**Richard Nixon** *baritone*
President of the United States

**Pat Nixon** *soprano* The First Lady

**Henry Kissinger** *bass*
American National Security Adviser

**Zhou Enlai** *bass* Chinese Premier

**Mao Zedong** *tenor* Chairman of the Party

**Jiang Qing** *soprano* Wife of Mao Zedong

---

The opera's creative team—Adams, Sellars, Alice Goodman, and choreographer Mark Morris—remained intact for *The Death of Klinghoffer* in 1991.

# Tan Dun

Born: August 18, 1957, Si Mao, Hunan Province, China

The Chinese-American Tan Dun has become the most successful and outspoken composer to represent global opera culture in the 21st century. From his first two operas, *Nine Songs* and *Marco Polo*, his works for the stage have combined classical and Asian resources and themes to explore a kind of opera beyond music tradition.

Tan grew up in rural China, where he was a rice planter during the Cultural Revolution. As a violin player and arranger, he worked for a provincial opera ensemble before entering the Central Conservatory of Beijing. In 1986, he traveled to New York to study at Columbia University with Chou Wen-chung and Mario Davidovsky. Tan's operas integrate his diverse backgrounds into a singular realm of expression that explores Eastern and Western traditions. He scores for standard orchestral ensembles, enhanced by Chinese instrumentalists and vocalists. Tan also intermixes Chinese forms, such as those of *kunqu* opera with, say, European medieval chant. While Western composers like Britten and Glass have for decades injected Asian elements into native resources, Tan has made the intermarriage of East and West a musical priority. His second and third operas, *Marco Polo* and *The Peony Pavilion*, premiered in the West. His fourth, *Tea*, was first given in Tokyo's Suntory Hall. But wherever staged, Tan's operas have reopened definitions of music theater for a global era.

▼ **Costumes and staging** invite audiences into the ceremonial world of Tan Dun's fourth opera, *Tea*, at the Netherlands Opera, Amsterdam, in 2005.

## East meets West

Like Bright Sheng, a fellow American opera composer born in China, Tan was influenced by the late Toru Takemitsu, the Japanese composer who freed Asian and Western instruments and musical idioms from the strictures of their independent traditions. Tan's operas call for such instruments as the Chinese pipa (left), the Indian sitar, and the Tibetan horn to augment Western orchestras. Sheng's most eclectic opera, *The Silver River*, employs Asian dancers as well as vocalists and instruments alongside Western resources.

▲ **For the opera's premiere** in Munich in 1996, director Martha Clarke responded to Tan's music by combining traditional and modernist elements in her staging.

# Marco Polo

An opera within an opera, 1¾ hours ▪ Composed: 1995 ▪ First performed: May 7, 1996, Muffathalle, Munich, Germany ▪ Libretto: Paul Griffiths, after his novel *Myself and Marco Polo* (1989)

Tan describes *Marco Polo*'s central theme of travel in his notes: "Paul Griffiths and I conceived of three journeys: Physical, Spiritual, and Musical." The central character, Marco Polo, is here split into two figures: Marco is the hero's active self, while Polo is his memory, a contemplative voice. Griffiths' libretto, with its literary allusions and sources, is in English, but Chinese and other languages are also used.

## PRINCIPAL ROLES

**Marco** *mezzo-soprano* Marco Polo's active self

**Polo** *tenor* Marco Polo's memory

**Rustichello** *Chinese opera singer* A questioner

**Water** *soprano* Lover of Marco Polo

**Dante** *baritone* A guide

**Kublai Khan** *bass* Mongol Emperor

### The Book of Timespace: Winter

Marco reads his past in his Book and, with Polo, his other self, finds the story incomplete. **PIAZZA** Dante and Shadows compel Polo to emerge again into light and life. Meanwhile, Kublai Khan prepares his own journey. Marco invites Polo, his memory, to take him on travels.

### The Book of Timespace: Spring

When Marco and Polo hesitate to depart, Shadows remind them of "gold" and "silk." **SEA** Marco sets out on Water ("Such a moment"), as Polo recalls past travels. A storm threatens, then recedes. **BAZAAR** Marco sees a market, and Dante fears it is dangerous. But, as Marco and Polo fuse, all proceed.

### The Book of Timespace: Summer

Marco and Polo are speechless. Rustichello urges them on. **DESERT** Marco and Polo are separated as Sheherazada, the desert seductress, tries to win Polo. **HIMALAYA** In a ritual ambience, Polo is silent while others sing. Marco and Polo are bound with silk scarves. **THE WALL** Marco and Polo advance toward the Wall.

### The Book of Timespace: Autumn

Rustichello asks whether the Wall was in the Book. All attempt to recall the journey, and suggest that life is a dream. **THE WALL** Before the Wall, Polo sings to the Khan's Queen ("song gou feng"). The Khan and Queen invite Marco and Polo to remain in their realm. But at Polo's prompting, Marco breaks through the Wall.

Tan Dun structured the opera so that its multilayered journey would lead the music through distinct soundscapes: Medieval, Middle Eastern, Indian, Tibetan, Mongolian, and, finally, Chinese.

# Thomas Adès

Born: March 1, 1971, London, England

Thomas Adès burst onto the music scene in his native England as a teenager with his Chamber Symphony of 1990. A pianist and conductor as well as composer, Adès studied at London's Guildhall School of Music and with Hungarian composer György Kurtág. His first opera, *Powder Her Face*, premiered in 1995. To a libretto by Philip Hensher, it told the story of the scandal of Margaret Sweeny's divorce from the Duke of Argyll in 1963. But with *The Tempest*, Adès gained a calling card to an international audience, and with *The Exterminating Angel* reinforced his reputation as one of the most admired opera composers of his generation.

# The Tempest

Opera in three acts, 2 hours ▪ Composed: 2002–2004 ▪ First performed: February 10, 2004, Royal Opera House, London, England ▪ Libretto: Meredith Oakes, after the 1611 play by William Shakespeare

Shakespeare's *The Tempest*, an inherently musical play, has inspired instrumental music by great composers far and wide: Beethoven, Debussy, and Tchaikovsky are among them. Operas based on the play include Fromental Halévy's *La Tempesta* in 1850 and Luciano Berio's *Un re in ascolto* in 1984. Adès breathed new life into the beloved play with music that captured the story's scintillating magic while preserving its darker ambience. His librettist, Meredith Oakes, aroused controversy by departing freely from the Bard's sacrosanct language and even introducing some plot twists. But Shakespeare is never far away, even when characters such as Prospero and Caliban express themselves in sing-song rhymes. A highlight is the spirit Ariel, whose high soprano vocal acrobatics shimmer at every turn in the opera.

## Act I
Following a tempest depicted in the opera's overture, shipwreck victims cry out on a remote island. Moved by their voices, Miranda questions her father, Prospero. He explains that fate has delivered his enemies: his brother, Antonio, who usurped him as Duke of Milan, and the King of Naples. While Miranda sleeps, Prospero commands his captive spirit Ariel to retrieve the victims. Caliban, a monster native to the island, claims to be its king, but Prospero accuses him of lunacy ("Abhorrent slave"). Ariel reports saving the victims, and reminds Prospero that he promised freedom ("Five fathoms deep"). Miranda awakens to fall in love with a shipwreck survivor, Ferdinand, the king's son. Prospero uses magic to immobilize Ferdinand.

## Act II
The shipwrecked rejoice to be alive ("Alive, awake"). Prospero observes his enemies as Ariel sows confusion. Caliban meets the new arrivals and promises to show them the island's secrets ("Friends don't fear"). The king's entourage searches for Ferdinand while Caliban and his new friends, Stephano and Trinculo, imagine themselves siring "a nation" when the king dies. Elsewhere on the island, Prospero observes the power of love as Miranda frees Ferdinand.

◀ **Ian Bostridge created Caliban** (left) and Simon Keenlyside created Prospero for the opera's premiere at the Royal Opera House in London in 2004.

## Act III
Caliban and Trinculo drunkenly cheer Stephano's reign as King. Elsewhere, Antonio and Sebastian, the real King's brother, nearly slay the sleeping King. Ariel awakens the court and magically presents a feast, but, in harpy form, admonishes Prospero's enemies ("You are men of sin"). Prospero savors the sight of the King and Antonio realizing they have wronged him. Miranda and Ferdinand announce their marriage. Prospero's hunger for revenge is sated. "King Caliban" returns, intent on Miranda as his Queen. Prospero grants Ariel freedom. Under Prospero's spell, the King marvels to behold his son and Miranda. The visitors anticipate sailing home in their magically restored ship; Prospero breaks his magic stave. Alone, Caliban wonders if he dreamed of humans.

▼ **Deserted beaches and gentle waves** can seem welcoming, but visitors exploring farther onto tropical islands may be confronted by unpleasant surprises.

### PRINCIPAL ROLES

**Prospero** *high baritone*
The ousted Duke of Milan, versed in magic arts

**Miranda** *mezzo-soprano* His daughter

**Ariel** *high soprano* A spirit in Prospero's captivity

**Caliban** *tenor* A monster in Prospero's captivity

**King** *tenor* King of Naples

**Ferdinand** *tenor* His son

Such was the success of *The Tempest* when it premiered at the Royal Opera House in London that Thomas Adès, still only 32 at the time, was immediately proclaimed by critics as Benjamin Britten's long-awaited successor as a British opera composer with global appeal.

# The Exterminating Angel

Opera in three acts, 2 hours 30 minutes ▪ Composed: 2007–2015 ▪ First performed: July 28, 2016, Haus für Mozart, Salzburg, Austria ▪ Libretto: Tom Cairns with Thomas Adès, based on Luis Buñuel's film *The Exterminating Angel*

The opera is based on Luis Buñuel's Spanish-language film *El ángel exterminador*, released in 1962. Like Buñuel's early movies, *L'Age d'or* and *Un perro andaluz*, it is surreal to the point of defying all logic. A group of bourgeois opera-goers who attend a post-performance dinner find themselves unable to leave, even though no visible obstacle blocks them. In the days that follow, their "civilized" behavior disintegrates. While surrealist effects are easier to create on the screen, Adès's moody score underlines the story's disturbingly unnatural dimension.

## PRINCIPAL ROLES

**Edmundo de Nobile** *tenor* Host

**Lucía de Nobile** *soprano* Hostess

**Leticia Meynar** *soprano* Opera singer

**Leonora Palma** *mezzo-soprano* Pianist

**Colonel Álvaro Gómez** *tenor* Lucia's lover

**Señor Russell** *baritone* Dying guest

**Dr. Carlos Conde** *bass-baritone* Family doctor

**Julio** *baritone* The butler

**Blanca Delgado** *mezzo-soprano* Dinner guest

**Silvia de Ávila** *soprano* Dinner guest

**Beatriz** *soprano* Dinner guest

**Eduardo** *tenor* Dinner guest

### Act I

Sheep and a bear arrive at the house just as the kitchen staff walk off the job, leaving only Julio, the butler, to manage the guests. The opera-goers arrive in elegant attire— only the host, Edmundo de Nobile, notices that they arrive twice—and sit down for dinner. A waiter bringing the first course trips and scatters food everywhere. The host's wife, Lucía, sends the sheep into the garden. After dinner, Blanca plays the piano, the soon-to-be-married Beatriz and Eduardo dance, and Dr. Conde's patient, Leonora, kisses him. Leticia, the opera star, is encouraged to sing, but Señor Russell says she has sung enough. Lucía kisses her lover, Colonel Gómez. Guests yawn at the late hour and prepare to leave, but find reasons to stay. Edmundo de Nobile offers beds for the night, but instead the men take off their jackets and settle down. Beatriz and Eduardo find a discreet corner and spend the night in each other's arms.

Buñuel had a simple explanation for including sheep in the film: while they appear designed to add surrealism, they were in fact merely a device to ensure that those trapped in the mansion did not go mad or die of starvation.

◀ **Mezzo-soprano Alice Coote** as Leonora Palma shows signs of falling apart as party guests increasingly despair in a 2017 production at the Royal Opera House, London.

## Act II

The following morning, Silvia says she slept badly, while Dr. Conde concludes Russell is dying. When Lucía and some friends try to leave, they are blocked by an invisible force. Blanca is worried about her children, but Silvia says Father Sansón will care for her boy. With no fresh food delivered, Julio brings coffee and leftovers, then finds he ,too, is trapped. As the day advances, Russell's condition worsens and the mood in the salon turns sour. Russell opens his eyes and says he will be pleased to die before the "extermination." During the night, he dies, and Beatriz and Eduardo watch his body being dragged out of the room.

## Act III

A crowd has gathered outside the mansion, but no one can enter. Julio punctures a water pipe so everyone can drink, but many guests are crazed with hunger. Leonora cries out for Dr. Conde and the Virgin Mary. Hallucinating, she sees a hand floating around the room; she grabs a knife, but it is Blanca's hand that she stabs. In despair, Beatriz and Eduardo take their own lives. A fight erupts and Edmundo is injured. The sheep wander in from the garden. They are slaughtered and everyone is fed, but new quarrels follow. Someone suggests a sacrifice is needed.

Edmundo offers himself, but Leticia notices they are in the same places as they were on their first night together. Repeating their motions, they are able to cross the threshold. Once freed, they give thanks in a church, where they again become trapped.

▼ **Mezzo-soprano Christine Rice** as Blanca Delgado (left), soprano Audrey Lunaz as Leticia Maynar (center), and soprano Sally Matthews as Silvia da Ávila share alarm over their predicament in a 2017 production at the Royal Opera House, London.

# Unsuk Chin

Born: July 14, 1961, Seoul, South Korea

Unsuk Chin is an acclaimed South Korean–born composer whose works have been performed across the world under the batons of leading conductors, from Sir Simon Rattle and Gustavo Dudamel to Kent Nagano and fellow Korean Myung-whun Chung. A self-taught pianist, Chin studied composition from an early age, first at Seoul National University and later in Hamburg with the Hungarian composer György Ligeti. A resident of Berlin, Chin's compositions range from electronic music to full orchestra symphonic works. So far, she has written only one opera, *Alice in Wonderland*.

# Alice in Wonderland

Opera in seven scenes, two interludes, and a finale, 2 hours ▪ Composed: 2004–2007 ▪ First performed: June 30, 2007, Bayerische Staatsoper, Munich, Germany ▪ Libretto: David Henry Hwang and Unsuk Chin, after Lewis Carroll's *Alice's Adventures in Wonderland* and *Through the Looking-Glass*

Unsuk Chin's *Alice in Wonderland* follows the broad lines of Lewis Carroll's two novels. Although the nature of opera demands a small number of scenes and pared-down language, most of the familiar characters from the Alice stories are present. On stage, surrealism becomes the obvious instrument for interpreting the nonsensical narrative.

### Scene I—Dream I
Alice opens a book in the library, which becomes a treasure chamber. She asks two old men to flee before the door to the treasure chamber closes. They don't.

### Scene II—The Pool of Tears
Alice follows the White Rabbit down a hole and is confronted by locked doors. Opening one, she sees a garden full of flowers, but she is too big to enter. After sipping from a bottle with the words "Drink Me," she becomes too small to handle the big key. She eats a cake labeled "Eat Me" and grows too big to pass through any door. Her size shocks the White Rabbit. Alice fills a pool with her tears, upsetting a mouse by talking about cats. The mouse tells the driest story ever to dry everyone off.

### Scene III—In the House of the White Rabbit
The White Rabbit sings Alice a song as she again grows.

### Interlude I—Advice from a Caterpillar
The caterpillar encourages Alice to change.

### Scene IV—Pig and Pepper
Alice meets the Fish and the Frog, footmen in livery, the Duchess with the Baby, the Cook, and the Cheshire Cat. Upset at how the Baby is being treated, Alice sings a lullaby and the Baby becomes a pig. The Cheshire Cat points Alice toward the March Hare.

### Scene V—A Mad Tea Party
Alice meets the March Hare, the Dormouse, and the Mad Hatter, but soon she has to leave the tea party.

### Scene VI—The Croquet Ground
Gardeners are trying to turn white roses into red ones to give to the Queen of Hearts. The Queen invites Alice to play croquet with no rules, and it ends in confusion. The Queen orders the cat be beheaded, but the head has no body.

### Interlude II
The Queen rescues Alice from the Duchess and they eat Mock Turtle soup until people arrive for a trial.

### Scene VII—The Trial or Who Stole the Tarts?
Alice is not scared of testifying about what happened to the tarts because she understands the Queen of Hearts and her Court are just playing cards.

### Finale—Dream II
Alice cannot find seeds in the infertile soil of the garden, until the invisible man gives her some. She sows them, and the flowers become bright shining lights.

---

**PRINCIPAL ROLES**

**Alice** *soprano*

**Cheshire Cat** *soprano*

**Mad Hatter/Duck** *baritone*

**White Rabbit/Badger/March Hare** *countertenor*

**Mouse/Pat/Cook/Dormouse/Invisible Man** *tenor*

**Ugly Duchess/Owl/Two** *mezzo-soprano*

**Queen of Hearts** *dramatic soprano*

**King of Hearts/Old Man #2/Crab** *bass*

**Frog-Footman/Seven/Dodo** *bass*

**Caterpillar** *solo bass clarinet*

**Eaglet/Old Man #1/Executioner/Fish-Footman/Five** *tenor*

◀ **Sally Matthews** in the role of Alice sings to her own mask in a 2007 production at the Bayerische Staatsoper, Munich, Germany.

▶ A masked **Sally Matthews** in the role of Alice prepares to follow the White Rabbit down a hole at the Bayerische Staatsoper.

> "Music for [Chin] is amazement and play, and communication that can be tender or fizzing: wild worlds without words (or with them)."

PAUL GRIFFITHS, MUSIC CRITIC

# Mark-Anthony Turnage

Born: June 10, 1960, Corringham, England

Mark-Anthony Turnage is a prolific English composer whose works stretch from orchestral, choral, and chamber music to ballet and opera. His affection for jazz, notably music by Miles Davis, can often be heard in his classical compositions. Turnage was just 28 when his first opera, *Greek*, a modern retelling of Sophocles's *Oedipus Rex*, marked him as a major new talent. His next opera, *The Silver Tassie*, was adapted from a Sean O'Casey play set during World War I. Turnage followed this with a piece of musical theater, *Coraline*, is a dark fantasy children's story based on a novella by Neil Gaiman. *Anna Nicole*, commissioned by the Royal Opera House in London, tells the story of Anna Nicole Smith, a B-movie actress and former *Playboy* magazine Playmate, who at the age of 26 married an American billionaire 63 years her senior. He died a year after their wedding, and Smith spent the rest of her life fighting for a share of the inheritance.

# Anna Nicole

Opera in two acts, 2 hours ▪ Composed: 2009–2011 ▪ First performed: February 17, 2011, Royal Opera House, London, England ▪ Libretto: Richard Thomas

*Anna Nicole* is a tragedy set in the garish world of celebrity culture and tabloid newspapers, where everything from breast implants to drug overdoses can be exploited. With its strong undertones of jazz, Turnage's score is the perfect match for the fast-paced libretto, written by Richard Thomas, also composer and librettist for *Jerry Springer: The Opera*. The vulgarity of the story makes this an opera for our times, although the BBC received an avalanche of complaints when it rebroadcast *Anna Nicole* from the Royal Opera House, London, in March 2011.

## Act I

Anna Nicole introduces herself to a mob of reporters. She was born in a rundown Texas town to a family comprising a foul-mouthed mother and brutish father. Her life is a mess: a high-school dropout, married at 17, she has a son, Daniel, and is divorced at 23. She heads for Houston to "rape the American dream." To succeed in a Gentleman's Club, she undergoes breast enhancement surgery. This brings her chronic back pain and the infatuation of an octogenarian oil magnate, J. Howard Marshall. Now her every wish is granted. She marries Marshall, enjoys a life of wealth, and becomes addicted to pain pills.

## Act II

Rich and famous, Anna enjoys the limelight. Her lawyer, Stern, is now in love with her. She throws a lavish party, where Marshall collapses and dies, leaving no will. Marshall's sons ensure Anna gets nothing. Stern urges her to sue the family. Ten years later, and now overweight, Anna orders Stern to bring her painkillers. He warns that she is harming herself. Daniel, now grown, rubs her back. Larry King interviews Anna and Stern about the inheritance dispute; she claims she has stopped taking drugs. Stern tells reporters that Anna is pregnant and he sells live images of the baby's birth to a TV station. While visiting Anna, Daniel collapses and dies. Anna is heartbroken and loses the will to live. She lies back, throws a final kiss to the audience, and zips herself into a body bag.

### PRINCIPAL ROLES

**Anna Nicole** *soprano*

**Virgie** *mezzo-soprano* Her mother

**Daddy Hogan** *bass* Her father

**J. Howard Marshall** *tenor* Billionaire and her second husband

**Kay** *mezzo-soprano* Her aunt

**Sheller** *mezzo-soprano* A cousin

**Stern** *bass-baritone* Her lawyer

**Teenage Daniel** *baritone* Her son

**Larry King** *tenor* Television show host

◀ **Eva-Maria Westbroek** as Anna Nicole (center) enjoys a party for her aged husband, J. Howard Marshall, sung by Alan Oke (sitting behind Anna).

▲ **The Dutch soprano** Eva-Maria Westbroek as Anna Nicole receives the media as part of her climb to fame and fortune in a 2014 production at the Royal Opera House, London.

"Mr. Turnage, whose modernist music is brashly accessible and run through with jazz, has written a pulsing, wild, and, when called for, yearning score."

ANTHONY TOMMASINI, MUSIC CRITIC

# George Benjamin

Born: January 31, 1960, London, England

George Benjamin is an English composer and conductor whose operas have won him worldwide acclaim. Drawn to composing before reaching his teens, Benjamin studied in Paris with Olivier Messiaen. An orchestral piece written when he was still at King's College, Cambridge was performed at a Promenade Concert at the Albert Hall, London, in 1980. Benjamin's first three operas were collaborations with the playwright Martin Crimp, beginning with *Into the Little Hill*, a 40-minute piece for soprano and contralto based on the legend of the Pied Piper of Hamelin. After *Written on Skin*, they wrote *Lessons In Love and Violence*, which explores, King Edward II's intimate relationship with his favorite, Piers Gaveston.

# Written on Skin

An opera in 15 scenes, 95 minutes ▪ Composed: 2009–2012 ▪ First performed: July 7, 2012, Grand Théâtre de Provence, Festival d'Aix-en-Provence, France ▪ Libretto: Martin Crimp, based on a legend about the 13th-century Occitan poet Guillem de Cabestaing

The theme of *Written on Skin* is borrowed from the popular legend of a French troubadour, Guillem de Cabestaing, whose lover is forced to eat his heart after he is murdered by her cuckolded husband. In this opera, which combines modern-day angels with events taking place in the 13th century, the troubadour is identified only as the Boy, who is seduced by the Protector's wife, Agnès.

## Part I
### Scene 1: Chorus of Angels
The chorus recalls when books were written on "skin," or parchment. The Protector, a violent landowner, treats his wife, Agnès, as his property. The Boy illustrates manuscripts.

### Scene 2: The Protector, Agnès, and the Boy
The Protector asks the Boy to paint his enemies in Hell and his family in Paradise.

### Scene 3: Chorus of Angels
The Angels recall how women were mistreated at the Creation.

### Scene 4: Agnès and the Boy
Agnès secretly visits the Boy and is shown a picture of Eve. She challenges him to portray a woman he covets.

### Scene 5: The Protector, John, and Marie
The Protector notices Agnès has changed. Her sister, Marie, annoys the Protector by asking about the Boy.

### Scene 6: Agnès and the Boy
The Boy shows Agnès an illustration of herself on a bed. She and the Boy make love.

## Part II
### Scene 7: The Protector's bad dream
The Protector hears of a secret page showing Agnès in bed with the Boy.

### Scene 8: The Protector and Agnès
Agnès asks her husband for a kiss, but he refuses, saying she is childish. She tells him to ask the Boy if she is a woman.

### Scene 9: The Protector and the Boy
In the woods, the Protector challenges the Boy. He says he has slept with Marie, not Agnès.

### Scene 10: Agnès and the Boy
The Boy says he was protecting Agnès. To punish her husband, she demands a painting showing her as a woman.

## Part III
### Scene 11: The Protector, Agnès, and the Boy
The Boy shows the Protector images of atrocities portraying Paradise. Agnès asks to see Hell and is shown a written page, but she is illiterate.

### Scene 12: The Protector and Agnès
The page describes the Boy's affair with Agnès. The Protector is furious. Agnès asks to see the word for love.

### Scene 13: Chorus of Angels and the Protector
Angels describe the cruelty of a God who makes man "ashamed to be human." The Protector murders the Boy.

### Scene 14: The Protector and Agnès
The Protector forces Agnès to eat, then tells her she has swallowed her lover's heart.

### Scene 15: The Boy/Angel
The Boy reappears as the First Angel. As the Protector rushes to kill Agnès, she leaps to her death.

PRINCIPAL ROLES

**Agnès** *soprano*

**Protector** *bass-baritone*

**First Angel/Boy** *countertenor*

**Second Angel/Marie** *mezzo-soprano*

**Third Angel/John** *tenor*

**Angels, Archivists**

▼ **Soprano Barbara Hannigan** as Agnès implores the Boy, sung by countertenor Bejun Mehta, to prove she is a grown woman, in the 2012 world premiere at the Festival d'Aix-en-Provence, France.

◀ **Christopher Purves** as the Protector abuses Victoria Simmonds' Marie in the belief she has slept with the Boy, in a 2013 production at the Royal Opera House, London.

"*Written on Skin* is an old story, but we live it very much in the here and now."

MARTIN CRIMP, LIBRETTIST

# Charles Wuorinen

Born: June 9, 1938, New York, United States • Died: March 11, 2020, New York, United States

Charles Wuorinen, an American composer strongly identified with 12-tone serial music, had a strong following from an early age: in 1970, he became the youngest composer to win the Pulitzer Music Prize. Soon afterward, he was given Stravinsky's final sketches for use in *A Reliquary for Igor Stravinsky*, a widely applauded work. Before writing his opera based on the movie *Brokeback Mountain*, his work in musical theater was limited to *The W of Babylon*, which he described as a baroque burlesque, and *Haroun and the Sea of Stories*, based on the novel of the same name by Salman Rushdie. Wuorinen's book *Simple Composition* is a sharp indictment of popular culture.

# Brokeback Mountain

Opera in two acts, 2 hours • Composed: 2008–2012 • First performed: January 28, 2014, Teatro Real, Madrid, Spain • Libretto: Annie Proulx

Charles Wuorinen immediately spotted the operatic possibilities of the movie *Brokeback Mountain*, but he later chose to follow Annie Proulx's short story more closely. Together, Wuorinen and Proulx added new elements to the story, including a ghost and what Wuorinen called his "Greek chorus."

## PRINCIPAL ROLES

**Ennis del Mar** *bass-baritone* Cowboy

**Jack Twist** *tenor* Cowboy

**Aguirre** *bass* Rancher

**Alma Beers** *soprano* Ennis's wife

**Lureen** *mezzo-soprano* Jack's wife

**Mrs. Twist** *alto* Jack's mother

**Bartender** *alto*

**Bill Jones** *spoken*

## Act I

Jack and Ennis meet in a Wyoming bar. It is 1963. The two cowboys have been hired to herd sheep beside Brokeback Mountain. In the camp, they discuss families, religion, and food, and one night they drink too much. At bedtime, Jack pulls Ennis into his tent. The following morning, remembering he is to marry Alma, Ennis says he is not queer.

Nor is he, says Jack. But their lives have changed. Aguirre, the trail leader, tells them to bring the flock down in the morning. After a last night together, Jack insists that Ennis enjoyed their lovemaking, but Ennis loses patience and strikes Jack. He is immediately sorry, and, as Aguirre approaches, they say goodbye: Jack returns to rodeo and Ennis marries Alma. Four years later, a letter from Jack announces he will be visiting.

## Act II

Jack and Ennis hug and kiss. Jack hears Ennis's children at play and says he also has a baby with a Texan girl called Lureen. They head off for a drink, but instead make love in a motel. They wish they were still on Brokeback Mountain. Ennis calls Alma to say he will be away for a few days. The men plan to meet several times a year.

Some months later, Alma insists that Ennis get a proper job and they argue about money. When Alma walks out on him, Jack proposes he and Ennis make a life together on a ranch.

▶ **The bass-baritone Daniel Okulitch** as Ennis del Mar embraces tenor Tom Randle as Jack Twist in the 2014 world premiere of *Brokeback Mountain* at the Teatro Real, Madrid, Spain.

Ennis remembers hearing of an old gay farmer who was murdered. At a Thanksgiving dinner, Alma tells Ennis she always knew he and Jack did something that made her sick. Ennis throws her to the ground and leaves. Twenty years after their first meeting, he and Jack are again together in the mountains. Ennis says he cannot meet again soon and they argue bitterly. Some months later, Ennis sends Jack a card; it is returned, stamped "deceased." Lureen says Jack died in a freak accident and his ashes were scattered on Brokeback Mountain. Ennis visits Jack's parents and is allowed into Jack's room, where he finds his own shirt with Jack's blood on it. Grieving deeply, he vows that no one can ever replace Jack.

"The story, a mostly plotless meditation on the angst of thwarted love, is essentially a working-class same-sex variation on the greatest of all operas, *Tristan und Isolde*."

JAMES JORDAN, MUSIC CRITIC

# Kaija Saariaho

Born: October 14, 1952, Helsinki, Finland

Kaija Saariaho is a Finnish composer whose work has been performed to acclaim around the world. After attending the Sibelius Academy in Helsinki, she studied in Germany and later worked at IRCAM, a musical research unit in Paris, where she added electronic sounds to her compositions. She was also drawn by traditional Japanese instruments, present in her six-part percussion work *Six Japanese Gardens* of 1994. In 2000, Saariaho excited the music world with her first opera, *L'Amour de loin*. With a libretto by the novelist Amin Maalouf, it borrows from a story of "love from afar" by a 12th-century troubadour. She followed in 2006 with two new collaborations with Maalouf: the opera *Adriana Mater*, a tragedy set in a civil war, and the orchestra and choral ensemble *La Passion de Simone*, inspired by the French mystic Simone Weil. *Innocence*, Saariaho's first opera without Maalouf, had its premiere a year later than planned—in 2021—because of the Covid-19 pandemic.

# Innocence

Opera in five acts, 1¾ hours ▪ Composed: 2017–2020 ▪ First performed: July 3, 2021, Festival d'Aix-en-Provence, France ▪ Libretto: original in Finnish, Sofi Oksanen; multilingual version, Aleksi Barrière

A musical thriller set against the background of a school massacre a decade earlier, *Innocence* is considered an operatic masterpiece of the early 21st century. The opera's 13 singers are intended as a nod to Leonardo da Vinci's *Last Supper*, while there are echoes of Richard Strauss's *Elektra* and Berg's *Wozzeck* in its modernist score. The original libretto is by the Finnish novelist Sofi Oksanen, but the staged version by Aleksi Barrière is performed in nine languages—English, Finnish, Czech, Romanian, French, Swedish, German, Spanish, and Greek—accompanied by supertitles in the language of the audience.

**Act I**

At a wedding reception, the groom's mother rejoices that her son Tuomas is marrying Stela. This might help the family overcome a trauma experienced a decade earlier.

The groom's father believes Stela should know about the tragedy, but his wife objects. Several guests recall their own traumas.

**Act II**

A Czech woman, Tereza, is employed as a waitress for the reception. Upon arrival, she discovers that Tuomas's older brother carried out the school massacre that convulsed her life. Some survivors recall the atrocity.

**Act III**

Tuomas's mother and a priest feel guilty that they did not do more to avert the catastrophe. Tereza holds back from telling the bride that her daughter Markéta was among the victims, but reminds the groom's father that the killer used his weapon. Survivors relive how each friend died.

**Act IV**

Tuomas learns why Tereza is behaving oddly. She tells Tuomas's mother that she wants justice. The mother blames Markéta and other boys for harassing her older son.

◀ **Chloe Lamford's striking stage design** captures the multilayered quality of the opera, which had its premiere at the Festival d'Aix-en-Provence, France, in 2021.

### PRINCIPAL ROLES

**Tereza** *mezzo-soprano* Waitress

**Mother-in-law** *soprano*

**Father-in-law** *bass-baritone*

**Stela** *soprano* Bride

**Tuomas** *tenor* Groom

**Priest** *bass-baritone*

**Teacher** *soprano*

**Student 1 (Markéta)** *soprano*

**Student 2 (Lilly)** *soprano*

A teacher regrets not anticipating the tragedy, while a French student says she watched movies of massacres with the killer.

**Act V**

Tuomas hides the truth from Stela, but he worries that Tereza's presence has doomed his marriage. The French student says another person knew about the planned massacre. Tuomas admits he was too cowardly to join his brother, but he still admires him. In an epilogue, Markéta tells her mother it is time to end her grieving.

"This is undoubtedly the work of a mature master, in such full command of her resources that she can focus simply on telling a story and illuminating characters."

ZACHARY WOOLFE, *THE NEW YORK TIMES*

# BEIJING
## OPERA

By giving the National Center for the Performing Arts a dramatic appearance and immense visibility to anyone visiting downtown Beijing, China demonstrated its readiness to embrace Western culture alongside Chinese traditions. Furthermore, it turned to a French architect, Paul Andreu, to design the magnificent complex, soon nicknamed the Egg, that now houses a 2,207-seat opera house as well as a concert hall and theater.

Since the 1990s, Chinese singers educated in Western music have left their mark in China and abroad, with the soprano Ying Huang among the first voices to be noticed, when, in 1995 she sang the lead role in a popular film version of *Madama Butterfly*. This was followed in 1998 by a production of *Turandot* inside the Forbidden City, directed by Zhang Yimou. Since then, several Chinese bass-baritones have stood out, including Shenyang, who won the 2007 BBC Cardiff Singer of the Year competition, and Ao Li, who won the top prize in Plácido Domingo's annual Operalia competition in 2013.

With many of these singers graduates of the Shanghai Conservatory of Music, their success abroad has energized the China Central Opera, the company headquartered in Beijing's performing arts center, which also counts on an in-house orchestra to accompany opera and ballet productions. The Opera Hall now regularly presents the most popular works by Mozart, Verdi, Wagner, Offenbach, and Puccini.

Not to be overlooked is China's own age-old operatic tradition, with Peking Opera perhaps the most popular. Using voice, drums, mime, dance, and acrobatics to recount romantic, epic, or patriotic tales, such as "The Long March," these operas are often raucous and exciting. Interestingly, some of these same stories are now being retold in what is known as Western-style Chinese opera, also performed on the stage of the Beijing performing arts center.

"The Center lies in the heart of Beijing, beside the National Art Museum of China, the Great Hall of the People, and the Forbidden City, all buildings representing power throughout Chinese history. I wanted mine to be of its time and just as strong."

PAUL ANDREU, ARCHITECT

◄ **The National Center for the Performing Arts**, which hosts both Western and Chinese opera, gives a dazzlingly modern face to China's ancient culture.

# Terence Blanchard

Born: March 13, 1962, New Orleans, Louisiana, United States

In 2021, Terence Blanchard's opera, *Fire Shut Up in My Bones*, became the first by a Black composer to be performed in the Metropolitan Opera of New York since its creation in 1883. Blanchard began playing the trumpet at the age of 8, and by the time he was 20, he was a member of the Lionel Hampton Orchestra. Later, he was artistic director of the Thelonious Monk Institute of Jazz (now the Herbie Hancock Institute of Jazz). An acclaimed composer of jazz, Blanchard was twice nominated for an Academy Award for scoring Spike Lee films and has won five Grammys. His father, an amateur opera singer, awakened his interest in classical music. His first opera, *Champion*, told the story of the world champion boxer Emile Griffith.

# Fire Shut Up in My Bones

Opera in three acts, 2 hours 40 minutes ▪ Composed: 2016–2019 ▪ First performed: June 15, 2019, Opera Theatre of Saint Louis, Missouri, United States ▪ Libretto: Kasi Lemmons, based on the memoir *Fire Shut Up in My Bones* by Charles Blow

Set in a segregated southern town, *Fire Shut Up in My Bones* tells the coming-of-age story of Charles Blow, a Black American columnist at *The New York Times*, whose early life was scarred by sexual abuse. Blow's narrative is expanded to include important dance and dream sequences and moments when the older Blow meets and sings a duet with the child Blow. The librettist also introduced two imagined characters, Destiny and Loneliness, performed by a soprano. The score has strong echoes of jazz, but many moments also evoke 19th-century Italian opera. Blanchard considers the work to be "opera in jazz" rather than a jazz opera.

### Act I

Driving through Louisiana with a gun by his side, Charles Blow remembers his impoverished youth, while Destiny sings to him. In a flashback, the seven-year-old Charles, nicknamed Char'es-Baby, struggles to catch the attention of his overworked, strong-minded mother, Billie. Tired of her husband Spinner's womanizing, Billie drives him out of the house at gunpoint. She takes her five sons to live with Uncle Paul, where Char'es-Baby dreams of a better life as Loneliness sings to him. Chester, Charles's cousin, joins him in bed and sexually abuses him. Charles tells no one.

### Act II

Charles becomes an angry and confused adolescent. Learning that God promises forgiveness of sins, he is baptized, but finds no peace. Loneliness reappears to sing to him. He is drawn to Evelyn, a beautiful young woman. This gives him strength to study on his own at a Black college. Billie is both proud and sorry when he leaves, recalling all she has sacrificed and wondering what lies ahead.

### Act III

At college, Charles is subjected to ritual hazing by fellow students, but he is used to pain. He falls in love with Greta, an attractive student, and eventually feels confident enough to tell her about being sexually abused. Her secret—that she is still sleeping with someone else—shatters Charles. He calls his mother for sympathy, but instead learns that Chester has returned home. As in the opening scene, Charles is driving with a gun by his side. Destiny again sings, promising to stand by him if he carries out his dark plan. Reaching home, his younger self, Char'es-Baby, urges him to bury his past anger. Charles must decide between murdering Chester or starting his life afresh.

### PRINCIPAL ROLES

**Charles (adult)** *bass-baritone*

**Char'es-Baby (Charles as a boy)** *treble/soprano*

**Chester** *baritone* Charles's cousin

**Destiny/Loneliness** *soprano* Apparition

**Billie** *soprano* Charles's mother

**Spinner** *tenor* Billie's husband

**Greta** *soprano*

▶ **Soprano Angel Blue as Destiny** reassures Will Liverman's Charles in the 2021 production at the Metropolitan Opera, New York.

◀ **Bass-baritone Will Liverman** as Charles (center) hangs out with pals on a basketball court in the 2021 production at the Metropolitan Opera, New York.

# Other important operas

This directory lists some of the other important works created during the celebrated history of opera. These works were acclaimed by critics and audiences alike—for their gripping themes, curious stories, and evocative music.

▲ MEZZO-SOPRANO LOUISE WINTER INTERPRETS THE LOVE-STRUCK GODDESS DIANA IN *LA CALISTO* AT THE STAATSOPER UNTER DEN LINDEN, BERLIN, IN 2002.

## △ **La Calisto** 1651

Francesco Cavalli

*La Calisto* was the ninth of ten operas written by Cavalli to librettos by Giovanni Faustini. They offered Venice well-mixed cocktails of romantic love, silliness, and a dash of outrage. Here, Faustini combined two Greek myths about sexual love between gods and mortals: one of Jove seducing Calisto, and another of Diana falling for Endymion. The subject is doubly racy when Giove (Jove), disguised as the goddess Diana, enjoys erotic meetings with Calisto. As a musician of the Basilica of St. Mark, Cavalli may seem an improbable composer for such a work, but, like the unfettered Calisto of this opera, the Republic of Venice enjoyed unusual freedom from religious and moral strictures. Cavalli responded to the story with his uniquely sensuous and sweetly varied music.

## **Alceste** 1674

Jean-Baptiste Lully

Lully and his librettist Philippe Quinault marshaled all resources to make *Alceste* a spectacle to please Louis XIV, their Sun King. The opera is framed by the personage of the king, whose absence is lamented in the prologue, and whose symbolic double, the sun god Apollo, glorifies celebrations in the final act. Sets and dazzling special effects by Carlo Vigarani, to be Lully's decades-long collaborator, added further majesty.

## **Atys** 1676

Jean-Baptiste Lully

*Atys* is an exquisitely sensuous and, by French Baroque standards, even erotic opera. Philippe Quinault's libretto builds tension scene by scene with themes of denial, secrecy, betrayal, and the dangers of succumbing to love. The opera abounds in highlights, from solo and choral vocal passages to gorgeous orchestral music, notably in Atys's famous dream sequence of Act III. Atypical of Lullian opera, *Atys* concludes with the tragic deaths of its lovers.

## ▷ **Médée** 1693

Marc-Antoine Charpentier

The ancient Greek story of Medea, the sorceress whose passion drove her to infanticide, is inherently operatic. Indeed, a century after Charpentier's opera, it was the subject of a second masterpiece in French, Luigi Cherubini's *Médée*. Charpentier's *Médée* was a failure in Paris in 1693, possibly because rabid supporters of the late Lully assured a negative response to any opera that was not by him. *Médée* bears heavy marks of the reign of Louis XIV, who is overtly flattered in its prologue. But the opera possesses a timeless brilliance. *Lullistes* would have been outraged to discover that *Médée*, with its breathtaking harmonic palette, is now widely considered to be the greatest opera of 17th-century France.

## ▷ **Tamerlano** 1724

George Frideric Handel

*Tamerlano* joins *Giulio Cesare* and *Rodelinda* as one of the great operas Handel composed in the early 1720s. It pits love against duty in a troubled political context. The historical Asian conqueror Tamerlane, a popular stage subject at the time, is treated dramatically, not factually. Noted for its brilliant structure, the opera opens with captive emperor Bajazet attempting to take his own life, and ends only when his renewed attempt succeeds.

## **Rodelinda** 1725

George Frideric Handel

*Rodelinda* is among Handel's masterpieces for the Royal Academy of Music. Dominated by a series of more than 30 da capo arias—solo pieces meant to show off one singer at a time—it

▲ STEPHANIE NOVACEK'S MÉDÉE IN THE ARMS OF DANCER PATRICK LAVOIE AT A 2002 PRODUCTION OF *MÉDÉE* AT THE ELGIN THEATRE, TORONTO, CANADA.

▲ A SPARE SET DIRECTS ATTENTION TO THE LAVISHLY COSTUMED CHARACTERS IN JONATHAN MILLER'S 2001 STAGING OF *TAMERLANO*.

contains only two duets and one ensemble number. But Handel paced the opera with artistry, using contrasting tempos, keys, and orchestration to build maximum tension. The music for Rodelinda herself is perfectly in tune with her martial devotion to marriage.

## Orlando 1733

George Frideric Handel

With *Orlando*, Handel returned to the enchantment and special effects of his earlier operas, such as the popular *Rinaldo*. Influenced by the English masque, in which spectacle was more important than drama, these operas show little concern for credibility of plots or motivations. But nonetheless, *Orlando* contains some of Handel's finest writing, notable especially in the famous "mad

scene" at the end of Act II, in which the music effortlessly captures the wild delusions of the jealous lover Orlando.

## La serva padrona 1733

Giovanni Battista Pergolesi

*La serva padrona* has been an audience pleaser ever since its premiere in 1733. It then served as a literal intermezzo: it provided diversion "between the acts" of a more solemn main attraction. *La serva padrona*, or *The Maid Turned Mistress*, was sandwiched into *Il prigionier superbo*, an *opera seria* also by Pergolesi, and was the first intermezzo to be performed independently. Within 20 years, its revolutionary portrayal of a man in love with his servant enthralled audiences across Italy and Germany and in Paris and London. In 1752, it ignited Paris's *Querelle des Bouffons*: a politically charged "war" over the

relative merits of reverent French and irreverent Italian music theater. *La serva padrona* sparked reforms that led to Gluck's operas, and opened the way for those of Mozart. Given in Baltimore, Maryland, in 1790, it is also among the earliest operas performed in the United States.

## Iphigénie en Aulide 1774

Christoph Willibald Gluck

*Iphigénie en Aulide* was Gluck's first opera for a Paris audience. It marked a crossroads for French opera, which since Lully had teemed with dances and divertissements. Gluck's sparer approach prompted mixed reactions but created a taste for operas of engrossing drama. This work of love and law colliding in antiquity won acclaim across Europe. Highlights include its magnificent overture, subtle orchestration, and forceful characterizations.

## Mitridate 1770

Wolfgang Amadeus Mozart

*Mitridate*, written when Mozart was only 14, was commissioned by the Austrian governor general of Lombardy. As was common, the composer was given a libretto, one set only three years earlier by Quirino Gasparini. The opera was well received, with Mozart's brilliant coloratura arias bringing cries of "Viva il Maestro, viva il Maestrino" and new commissions. But *Mitridate* was then largely forgotten for two centuries.

## Lucio Silla 1772

Wolfgang Amadeus Mozart

*Lucio Silla* was commissioned for Milan's Teatro Regio Ducale after the success of *Mitridate*. Mozart was given a month to write the opera's

18 arias, but his growing experience shows, notably in how the music reinforces the personalities of the key roles. The score matches the high drama of the story. But *Lucio Silla* was only a moderate success, and Mozart soon left Italy forever.

### *Il re pastore* 1775

Wolfgang Amadeus Mozart

*Il re pastore* was commissioned by the Prince-Archbishop Colloredo of Salzburg to celebrate a visit by the young archduke Maximilian Franz. For this event, Mozart was handed Pietro Metastasio's 1751 *opera seria* libretto, which had already been set by a dozen composers. The score contains some beautiful arias and ensembles, but it did not earn Mozart a fresh commission. Five years would pass before he wrote another opera, which would be his first great stage work, *Idomeneo*.

### *La clemenza di Tito* 1791

Wolfgang Amadeus Mozart

*La clemenza di Tito* is Mozart's penultimate opera, but it resembles his earlier works, especially as it is an *opera seria* based on a stock libretto.

Commissioned at short notice to write an opera for Leopold II's coronation as King of Bohemia, Mozart completed the score in under three weeks. Rich in lively arias and duets, the work places unusual prominence on female voices, including two written as "trouser roles"—women playing men.

### ▽ *Tancredi* 1813

Gioachino Rossini

Written when he was still only 21, *Tancredi* was Rossini's first great opera. While this *opera seria* offers inventive orchestration and remarkable lyricism, its principal innovation is the so-called double aria—an aria that progresses from slow to fast and is repeated. For a new production in Ferrara in March 1813, Rossini replaced his happy ending with a tragic finale closer to Voltaire's original. Today, the Ferrara version is usually preferred.

### *Le Comte Ory* 1828

Gioachino Rossini

*Le Comte Ory*, Rossini's last comic opera, is distantly inspired by a medieval ballad in which knights end up seducing nuns. In the one-act play offered to Rossini

by Eugène Scribe and Charles-Gaspard Delestre-Poirson, however, a knight dresses as a nun to seduce a countess. Rossini then asked for a first act to be added. And thanks to its delightful arias, ensembles, and choruses, the opera was soon immensely popular.

### ▷ *Guillaume Tell* 1829

Gioachino Rossini

*Guillaume Tell*, Rossini's final opera, was also his only attempt at French *grand opéra*, a style that would soon demand monumental spectacles. Rossini did not abandon lyricism, but he took up the new challenge, introducing declamatory recitatives, stripping arias of excessive "Italian" ornamentation, emphasizing "patriotic" choruses, and adding new harmony to the orchestration. Designed to establish his French credentials, *Guillaume Tell* ended Rossini's career on a dramatic note.

### *Il pirata* 1827

Vincenzo Bellini

*Il pirata*, Bellini's first collaboration with Felice Romani, was also his first international success,

▲ THE ITALIAN TENOR GIACOMO LAURI-VOLPI AS ARNOLD IN ROSSINI'S *GUILLAUME TELL*.

performed across Europe within five years of its premiere. Audiences were surprised by the simplicity of its melodic line, immediately distinguishable from Rossini's coloratura-packed scores. While *Il pirata* has dramatic tenor and baritone roles, its tragic tone is set by Imogene's soaring soprano arias and chilling "mad scene" at the end.

### *Maria Stuarda* 1835

Gaetano Donizetti

*Maria Stuarda*, which presents a fictional account of the downfall of Mary Queen of Scots, has a brilliantly lyrical score, one dominated by two great soprano roles, Maria and Elisabetta, but also well supported by the tenor voice of Leicester. Because its plot is rife with conflict, the opera also boasts several stirring duets. No less memorable is the splendid ensemble accompanying Elisabetta's explosive meeting with Maria in Act II.

### *Zar und Zimmermann* 1837

Albert Lortzing

*Zar und Zimmermann*, packed with infectious songs and a beloved "clog dance," premiered in Leipzig to no fanfare but soon became a

▲ AGNIESZKA WOLSKA AS AMENAIDE IN A 2000 PRODUCTION OF *TANCREDI* AT THE POLISH NATIONAL OPERA CONDUCTED BY THE RENOWNED ROSSINI EXPERT ALBERTO ZEDDA.

▲ RENÉE FLEMING AS LOUISE (LEFT) TRIES TO PERSUADE HER FELLOW SEAMSTRESSES SHE IS NOT IN LOVE, IN LOTFI MANSOURI'S 1990 PRODUCTION OF *LOUISE* AT THE SAN FRANCISCO OPERA.

favorite opera in German-speaking Europe. It was then presented to audiences in their own languages from London to Lisbon, and as far as St. Petersburg, reaching the American stage in 1852. This Singspiel playfully transfers a historical Peter the Great—the Russian czar did work incognito in Dutch shipyards—into a tightly woven fictional world of mistaken identities, military secrets, and sweet romantic love.

## La vie parisienne 1866

Jacques Offenbach

Unsurprisingly, Offenbach's first operetta to address the contemporary life of his adopted city is full of mischief. Here, two Parisian dandies fall out over one woman then join forces to chase another. Can Bobinet help his pal Gardefeu seduce a visiting Swedish baroness? With its lively score and a mishap-filled plot, *La vie parisienne* offers an entertaining portrait of how many foreigners imagined Paris in the 19th century.

## La Grande-Duchesse de Gérolstein 1867

Jacques Offenbach

A mischievous parody of war and politics, *La Grande-Duchesse de Gérolstein* was timed to coincide with the 1867 Exposition Universelle in Paris. Censors demanded a few cuts to avoid offending visiting royalty, but the operetta proved a great success. In fact, it finally won over Britons and Americans to Offenbach and *opéra-bouffe*. Banned after the 1870–1871 Franco-Prussian war for its jocular treatment of war, the opera was revived to acclaim in 1878.

## Hänsel und Gretel 1893

Engelbert Humperdinck

Premiering under the baton of Richard Strauss, *Hänsel und Gretel* was an instant success in Germany and has since become one of the world's best-loved operas. The libretto splices regional realism into the more abstract fairy tale.

Humperdinck's score responds brilliantly. Throughout, the orchestra weaves symphonic threads, thick or delicate, yet also delivers isolated tunes derived from traditional songs or sacred hymns. Wagner's influence can be heard in the prelude to Act II, "The Witches' Ride," and Italian *verismo* peppers the score, as shown when Gertrud screeches in frustration, or the Witch cackles unnervingly. The Witch only appears in the final act, but music that is tied to her role menaces from the outset, and even swoops into the opera's final bars, well after the children have destroyed her.

## △ Louise 1900

Gustave Charpentier

Set in 1900, the very year of its creation, *Louise* not only depicted "real" Parisians but, more daringly, it also addressed class differences and a young woman's yearning for the freedom to love. While the score is romantic, melodic, and naturalistic, even including cries

from the streets of Montmartre, the opera represents no musical watershed, with echoes of Berlioz, Wagner, Gounod, and Massenet to be heard throughout. However, having spent more than a decade working on the libretto and score, Charpentier created a powerful theatrical event, with no fewer than 19 female soloists, 20 male soloists, and a large chorus. The accessibility of the music and the story ensure *Louise*'s popularity: it reached its 1,000th performance in 1956, the year of Charpentier's death.

## Il trittico 1918

Giacomo Puccini

*Il Trittico*, or *The Triptych*, is the name given to three hour-long operas—*Il tabarro*, *Suor Angelica*, and *Gianni Schicchi*—now rarely performed together. More often, theaters present just two, or pair one with another short opera. *Gianni Schicchi*, Puccini's only comic opera, is especially popular, with its mischievous depiction of cunning greed.

## Die tote Stadt 1920

Erich Wolfgang Korngold

*Die tote Stadt*, or *The Dead City*, was based on a Symbolist novel of hallucinatory connections between sexual desire and mourning. Bold for its time, the opera was first given at the Staatsoper, Hamburg, in 1920 and, soon after, in New York. With much-loved numbers, including "*Pierrotlied*," it remains popular worldwide today.

## Aufstieg und Fall der Stadt Mahagonny 1930

Kurt Weill

*Aufstieg und Fall der Stadt Mahagonny*, Weill's landmark opera, redefined the sound of modernity. Weill and his librettist, Bertolt Brecht, had written *Kleine Mahagonny* (*Little Mahagonny*) in

1927, about an American city, and it formed the basis of the full opera, also known as *Rise and Fall of the City of Mahagonny*. Weill integrated music-hall tunes and existing music into a visionary score of classical structure that— like the modern experience— magically coheres even as it threatens to disintegrate. With its story of existential misery and political subversion, the opera's career was choppy in the 1930s, particularly as the Nazi regime forced Weill into exile. But it has since found its place as a major opera of the 20th century.

## Four Saints in Three Acts 1934

Virgil Thomson

*Four Saints in Three Acts* enjoyed a run of 60 performances when, in 1934, it opened on Broadway with an all-Black cast. Called a "choreographic spectacle," this

through-composed opera with dialogue celebrated its freedom to engage audiences with emotion-packed staging, vocal virtuosity, and Gertrude Stein's lyrics. A highlight is the powerful choral music informed by hymns that Thomson heard as a child in Missouri.

## Œdipe 1936

Georges Enescu

Arguably Romania's most important 20th-century composer, George Enescu struggled for 25 years to complete his only opera, *Œdipe*. One challenge involved putting to music Edmond Fleg's cumbersome four-act French-language libretto, which covers Oedipus's entire life, from birth to death. Although composition of this opera coincided with the rise of the atonal revolution of the Second Viennese School, Enescu's score owes more to Debussy and other Modernist musicians. After *Œdipe*'s premiere

in Paris in 1936, further productions were disrupted by World War II, but interest in the opera has grown in recent decades, with new productions at the Salzburg Festival as well as in Vienna, Paris, and London.

## ▽ Julietta aneb Snář 1938

Bohuslav Martinů

*Julietta aneb Snář* is Martinů's excellent adaptation of Georges Neveux's Surrealist play, *Juliette*, or *The Key to Dreams*, which was given a stormy reception when it opened in Paris in 1930. At first, the plot seems straightforward: a man returns to a seaside town where three years earlier he fell for a young woman. But when he discovers that neither she nor anyone else has any memory of the past, a complex game of fantasy and reality unfolds. Written in Czech, Martinů's fast-paced libretto names 25 roles and comprises 28 scenes, with the Central Office of Dreams in

▲ PAUL NILON AS MICHEL IS RECEIVED BY JESSICA WALZER'S LITTLE ARAB IN DAVID POUNTNEY'S *JULIETTA ANEB SNÁŘ* AT ITALY'S RAVENNA FESTIVAL IN 2005.

▲ AN INNOCENTLY COSTUMED MARIE IS ENGULFED BY MENACING SOLDIERS IN A PRODUCTION OF *DIE SOLDATEN* AT THE NETHERLANDS OPERA IN 2003.

sacrifice. Britten weaves these into music of deceptive simplicity and refined restraint, bringing all the maturity of his musical experience to bear on the score. The opera belongs to Aschenbach, perhaps the most demanding role in the English repertoire.

### ◁ *Die Soldaten* 1965

Bernd Alois Zimmermann

*Die Soldaten* premiered to great success in 1965 as a profoundly German opera of the post-war era. Although set in no particular time, its very title—*The Soldier*, in English—stirred recent and disturbing memories of World War II: soldiers abuse a young woman in militarized Flanders. Through its formal and thematic links to Alban Berg's 1925 *Wozzeck*, Zimmermann's work also added a new dimension to avant-garde opera in German. *Die Soldaten*'s cinematic pacing, combined with simultaneously projected films in Act IV, redefined the roles of time and place on opera stages. Zimmermann's own musical idiom further upsets expectations of any linear action; Bach chorales, jazz music, a waltz passage, and recorded segments remind audiences that no one world sound is independent of another.

Act III providing the key to the story. Rather than reinforcing the notion of a dream, however, Martinů's score treats events at face value, with lyricism, drama, and even satire.

### Die Kluge 1943

Carl Orff

For *Die Kluge*, or *The Clever Girl*, Orff turned an old folktale into a modern parable, pitting wisdom and love against mindless power. This one-act opera hypnotizes with its mixture of sweet and sour sounds, characters, and story threads. Mischievous vagabonds lighten the mood, while the clever girl's untiring commitment to truth provides solemn entrancement.

### Albert Herring 1947

Benjamin Britten

*Albert Herring* has been called a comical version of the tragic *Peter Grimes*, Britten's earlier opera about

a man stripped of his dignity. Here, the man prevails. Filled with strong characters, *Albert Herring* is often moving, as when Albert struggles against his overbearing mother, or when townspeople mourn his presumed death. The work suffered a poor premiere in 1947, but has since been hailed a comic opera of painfully real dimensions.

### Curlew River 1964

Benjamin Britten

*Curlew River*, one of Britten's three church parables, marries Eastern and Western cultures in both its music and its story. Basing his work on a Japanese Noh play about a mother searching for her child, Britten also harks back to medieval liturgical dramas. Latin plainsong hymns and Balinese gamelan music are among the distinct elements given new life in this short work about a miracle on a river that divides, connects, and heals. Aptly, it premiered in a church.

### ▽ Death in Venice 1973

Benjamin Britten

*Death in Venice* was Britten's final opera. Based on the novella by Thomas Mann, the subjects of this operatic masterpiece are inspiration, beauty, longing, wisdom, and

▲ FOR THE PREMIERE OF *DEATH IN VENICE* AT SNAPE MALTINGS, ALDEBURGH, UK, IN 1973, PETER PEARS (IN WHITE SUIT) PLAYED ASCHENBACH, AND ROBERT HUGUENIN (KNEELING CENTER) WAS TADZIO.

▲ GEORG NIGL IN *UN RE IN ASCOLTO* AT THE GRAND THÉÂTRE DE GENÉVE, SWITZERLAND, 2002.

150 strong—and a vocalist of superhuman stamina in the title role. Saint François's journey into the pain and love experienced by Christ during the Passion takes four hours. The intricate architecture of this ritualistic piece is carefully constructed: solo voices dominate until Saint François comes within reach of God's greatest mystery. Then, massive choruses express the Lord's responses to François' prayers. These reverberating voices lift François into a sphere of stunned divinity, and transfix audiences in an age all too bereft of spiritual intensity.

## ◁ *Un re in ascolto* 1984

Luciano Berio

*Un re in ascolto* takes up a subject that preoccupied Berio throughout his career: listening—noted here in the opera's title in English, *A King Listens*. The opera dwells on the mysterious quest of the character Prospero for a singular voice. In a work dwelling on sound, memory, and the meaning that may be gleaned from a sea of voices, the riveting solos and intense ensemble passages stand out like musical islands.

## *Die Bassariden* 1966

Hans Werner Henze

*Die Bassariden* is a thoroughly modern opera fueled by an ancient Greek storyline. Also known as *The Bassarids*, the tragedy pits Pentheus, the new king of Thebes, against the god Dionysus, who lures the Thebans into sensual pleasures on Mount Cytheron. With a libretto by W. H. Auden and Chester Kallman, Henze's music is dramatic and other worldly.

## *Donnerstag aus Licht* 1981

Karlheinz Stockhausen

*Donnerstag aus Licht* was the first of seven operas Stockhausen composed between 1977 and 2003 for his cycle *Licht*, or *Light*. Three melodies structure the

cycle, and each is linked to a character: Michael, and his parents Eva and Luzifer. This opera, *Thursday from Light* in English, focuses on Michael. The invisible chorus creates atmospheres of layered time and space as Michael journeys from his childhood.

## *Les Boréades* 1982

Jean-Philippe Rameau

Mystery surrounds *Les Boréades*, Rameau's last great opera: the librettist's identity is uncertain, and, while it was rehearsed in 1763, it was not staged until 1982. Some experts have gleaned Masonic themes, and believe that the work was barred as subversive. The music responds to the quick pace of its fairy-tale story of *The Sons of Boreas*, with harmonic innovation and forceful rhythms. It also contains gorgeous vocal parts and spirited dances.

## ▽ *Saint François d'Assise* 1983

Olivier Messiaen

*Saint François d'Assise*, a masterpiece of the late 20th century, is a work of unparalleled musical and theatrical force. However, few are the opera-goers lucky enough to attend the work, since Messiaen called for rare resources—one being a chorus

## *Tri Sestri* 1998

Péter Eötvös

*Tri Sestri*, inspired by Anton Chekhov's *Three Sisters*, is the work of the prolific Hungarian

▲ JOSÉ VAN DAM, SEEN HERE IN PARIS IN 1983, WAS LONG THE REIGNING BARITONE IN THE ROLE OF SAINT FRANCIS IN *SAINT FRANÇOIS D'ASSISE*.2.

composer and conductor, Péter Eötvös, who has written close to a dozen operas since the mid-1990s. In the libretto, which he and Clause H. Henneberg cowrote, the story of each of three siblings—Irina, Andrei, and Masha—is addressed separately, while the third sister, Olga, and Andrei's wife, Natasha, also have central roles. Eötvös wrote these four female roles to be sung by countertenors. And in a further gender reversal, the role of the maid Anfisa is given to a bass. The score reflects the avant-garde influence of Pierre Boulez and Karlheinz Stockhausen, but it also incorporates some of Hungary's folkloric traditions.

## ▽ Faustus, The Last Night 2006

Pascal Dusapin

Most operas devoted to the myth of Faust use Goethe as the source for their libretto, but Pascal Dusapin turned instead to Christopher Marlowe's *Tragicall History of Dr. Faustus*. A French composer of great versatility, whose works include nine operas, Dusapin skips Faust's customary journey from pleasure to pain, focusing on the "last night" of his fateful bargain with Mephistopheles instead. Furthermore, much like a contemporary billionaire or a modern dictator, this Faust thirsts for absolute power rather than knowledge or pleasure. Dusapin describes *Faustus* as "a very pessimistic opera," with the score conveying this mood through extensive use of a *parlando* or speaking style and tuba and brass adding a sense of doom.

## The Trial 2014

Philip Glass

Philip Glass considers *The Trial*, written for a 12-piece orchestra, a chamber opera. But it is also ambitious, as the libretto by the playwright Christopher Hampton seeks to convey the complexity and surrealism of Franz Kafka's novel of the same name. In its simplest form, the plot recounts Josef K's arrest and trial for reasons he never discovers and from which he has no escape. The opera's large number of roles—20, requiring 8 singers—in turn reinforces K's sense of being lost in a crowd of unsympathetic and uncomprehending spectators. Notably, Glass's trademark style of repetitive musical phrases and rhythms seems almost designed for a story about a man whose life has lost all sense of direction.

## Lessons in Love and Violence 2018

George Benjamin

In a powerful follow-up to *Written on Skin*, George Benjamin and his habitual librettist, Martin Crimp, revisit a tragic love story first recounted on stage by Christopher Marlowe in the late 16th century— that of England's King Edward II and his favorite, Piers Gaveston, sung here by baritones. The triangle is completed by the powerful soprano role of Edward's queen, Isabel, who, working with her ally Mortimer, arranges for Gaveston's capture and murder. Edward's own arrest and death—infamously portrayed by Marlowe—soon follow. Benjamin's modernist score is daring yet accessible, a perfect vehicle for conveying the thirst for power as well as the "love and violence" of the opera's title.

## Eurydice 2020

Matthew Aucoin

Matthew Aucoin, an American composer who has quickly made his mark in music circles, retells the myth of Orpheus and Eurydice as a modern story recounted from the woman's point of view. Taking their cue from Sarah Ruhl's play, also *Eurydice*, the composer and the playwright cowrote the libretto with an added twist. To underline Orpheus's immense musical power, his character is sung by two men, one a bass, the other a countertenor, each representing a different side of his personality. *Eurydice*'s mood ranges from the soberly meditative to the surrealistically droll, with the score stretching from the enchanting to the harsh, with echoes of composers as different as Ravel and Thomas Adès.

▼ CAROLINE STEIN (LEFT) AS ANGEL, GEORG NIGL AS FAUSTUS, AND HANNO MÜLLER-BRACHMANN AS MEPHISTOPHELES AT A PRODUCTION OF *FAUSTUS, THE LAST NIGHT* AT THE STAATSOPER UNTER DEN LINDEN, BERLIN, IN 2006.

# Index

Page numbers in **bold** refer to main entries and box features; *italic* numbers denote illustrations.

# Acknowledgments

**Dorling Kindersley would like to thank the following people for their assistance with this book:**

The authors wish to thank Michael Berger-Sandhofer, James Conlon, Sergei Dreznin, Robert Minder, David Stern, and Augusta Read Thomas for their thoughtful readings and comments.

They are grateful to EMI and Mariko Tada for research materials; Opera News for archival access in New York; Liza Vick and the staff of the Loeb Music Library of Harvard University; and John Varney and the Handel House Museum in London.

For loving support and patience, Marlise, Alexander, Jordan, and Naira will never be forgotten.

DK would like to thank John Andrews for proofreading, Robert Weinberg for reading the manuscript, Liz Moore for additional picture research, Nobina Chakravorty and Arshti Narang for design assistance, Anita Kakkar and Suefa Lee for editorial assistance, and Mrinmoy Mazumdar for technical assistance.

Studio Cactus would like to thank Lindsey Brown for proofreading, and Robbie Jack for access to his archives and expertise.

**The publisher would like to thank the following for their kind permission to reproduce their photographs:**

(Key: a-above; b-below / bottom; c-center; f-far; l-left; r-right; t-top)

**2 Rex Features:** Olycom Spa; **4 Lebrecht Music and Arts Photo Library:** Richard Haughton; **6 Rex Features:** Nils Jorgensen; **7 Getty Images:** Keystone / Stringer; **8-9 Státní Opera Praha:** Ondřej Kocourek; **10-11 Alamy Stock Photo:** Mats Silvan / Axiom / Design Pics Inc.; **12 Corbis:** Bettmann (t). **Corbis:** Christie's Images (bl); **13 Bridgeman Art Library:** Yale Center for British Art, Paul Mellon Collection, USA (br). **Lebrecht Music and Arts Photo Library** (tr); **14 Lebrecht Music and Arts Photo Library; 15 Corbis:** Robbie Jack Photography (br). **Lebrecht Music and Arts Photo Library** (bl). **Agence Enguerand:** Marc Enguerand (tr); **16-17 Alamy Stock Photo:** Garry Gay; **18 The Art Archive:** Museo Civico Modena / Dagli Orti (A) (bl). **Bridgeman Art Library:** Private Collection, The Stapleton Collection (tl). **The Art Archive:** Hospital Institute Verona / Dagli Orti (A) (br); **19 Corbis:** Bettmann (tl). **Bridgeman Art Library:** Private Collection, Archives Charmet (cr). **Corbis:** Wally McNamee (br); **20-21 Corbis:** Robbie Jack Photography; **22 Corbis:** Annebicque Bernard / Co Sygma (tr). **Corbis:** Philippe Caron / Sygma (b); **23 Bridgeman Art Library:** Private Collection (bl). **Corbis:** Annebicque Bernard / Co Sygma (br). **Bregenzer Festspiele:** Karl Forster (t); **24-25 Alamy Stock Photo:** Jean-Dider Risler / Onlyfrance.fr.; **26 Bridgeman Art Library:** Civica Raccolta Stampe Bertarelli, Milan, Italy (b). **Corbis:** Origlia / Pizzoli / Co Sygma (tr); **27 Staatsoper Unter den Linden:** bildTeam Berlin (bl). **Archiv der Salzburger Festspiele:** Fritz Haseke (tr); **28-29 Corbis:** Tim Graham / Hulton-Deutsch Collection; **30 Shutterstock.com:** Alastair Muir (t). **Lebrecht Music and Arts Photo Library** (bl). **Getty Images:** Johan Elbers / Time Life Pictures (br); **31 Corbis:** Reuters (tl). **Mary Evans Picture Library:** (br); **32-33 Getty Images:**

Francesco Ruggeri; **34 The Art Archive:** National Portrait Gallery Scotland / Dagli Orti (A); **36 Lebrecht Music and Arts Photo Library** (tr). **Bridgeman Images:** Laurie Lewis (cl); **37 ArenaPAL:** Clive Barda; **38 ArenaPAL:** Stephen Cummiskey / Royal Opera House; **39 Alamy Stock Photo:** Everett Collection Inc / © ADAGP / DACS / Comité Cocteau, Paris 2022 (br). **Festival d'Aix-en-Provence:** Elisabeth Carecchio (t); **40 Staatsoper unter den Linden:** Monika Rittershaus (b); **41 Lebrecht Music and Arts Photo Library:** Colette Masson (t); **42 Lebrecht Music and Arts Photo Library** (tr, bl); **43 Opera Atelier, Canada – The Elgin Theatre:** Bruce Zinger; **44 Lebrecht Music and Arts Photo Library:** Royal Academy of Music Coll (tr), (br); **45 Getty Images:** Robbie Jack / Corbis; **46 Lebrecht Music and Arts Photo Library** (bl); **47 Alamy Stock Photo:** Malcolm MacGregor (tr). **Shutterstock.com:** Alastair Muir (b); **48 Lebrecht Music and Arts Photo Library** (tr, b); **49 State Opera Prague:** Frantisek Ortmann; **50 Lebrecht Music and Arts Photo Library** (tr); **51 TopFoto.co.uk:** Clive Barda / PAL; **52 Getty Images:** George F Mobley; **53 Zurich Opera House:** Peter Schnetz (t). **Agence Enguerand:** Tristan Jeanne-Vales (br); **54 Getty Images:** Robbie Jack / Corbis (bl). **Lebrecht Music and Arts Photo Library** (tr); **55 Bridgeman Art Library:** Guildhall Library, City of London (c). Birmingham Museums and Art Gallery (br); **56 Getty Images:** Johan Elbers / Time Life Pictures; **57 Bridgeman Art Library:** Louvre, Paris, France, Lauros / Giraudon (t). **Lebrecht Music and Arts Photo Library** (br); **58 Topfoto:** Clive Barda / PAL; **59 Lebrecht Music and Arts Photo Library:** Laurie Lewis; **60 Bridgeman Images:** Tristram Kenton (bl). **Lebrecht Music and Arts Photo Library** (tr); **61 Lebrecht Music and Arts Photo Library; 62-63 ArenaPAL:** Glyndebourne Productions Ltd. (b); **63 Bridgeman Art Library:** State Central A.A. Bakhrushin Theatre Museum, Moscow (tr); **64 akg-images:** Marion Kalter (l). **Bridgeman Images:** (br); Lebrecht Music & Arts (cra). **Getty Images:** Imagno / Hulton Fine Art Collection (tr); **65 Alamy Stock Photo:** Lebrecht Music & Arts (br). **Bridgeman Images:** Lebrecht Music & Arts (t); **66 Staatstheater Stuttgart, Opernhaus:** A. T. Schaefer; **67 Alamy Stock Photo:** Arno Burgi / dpa-Zentralbild / dpa picture alliance; **68 Alamy Stock Photo:** Donald Cooper; **69 Getty Images:** Robbie Jack / Corbis (br). **TopFoto:** Roger-Viollet (t); **70-71 Getty Images:** Jean-Marc Zaorski / Gamma-Rapho; **72 akg-images:** (bl); **72-73 Bridgeman Images:** Laurie Lewis (t); **73 Bridgeman Images:** Richard Bebb Collection (b); **74 Lebrecht Music and Arts Photo Library:** (bl); **74-75 TopFoto. co.uk:** Keith Saunders / ArenaPAL (b); **76-77 Getty Images:** Gonzalo Azumendi; **78 Getty Images:** Angelo Cavalli; **79 akg-images:** Erich Lessing (tc). **Lebrecht Music and Arts Photo Library:** Colette Masson (cb); **80-81 PunchStock:** Image Source; **82 Bridgeman Art Library:** Musee Conde, Chantilly, France, Lauros / Giraudon; **84 Lebrecht Music and Arts Photo Library:** Tristram Kenton (cl). **Lebrecht Music and Arts Photo Library:** H.Weidner-Weiden Interfoto (tr). **Lebrecht Music and Arts Photo Library** (bl); **85 Lebrecht Music and Arts Photo Library; 86 Riccardo Musacchio & Flavio Ianniello; 87 Hamburgische Staatsoper:** Karl Forster; **88 De Nederlandse Opera:** Hans Hijmering; **89 Riccardo Musacchio:** (br); **Lebrecht Music and Arts Photo Library:** Private Collection (tl); **90 Royal Danish Opera:** Martin Mydtskov Rønne; **91 Corbis:** Massimo Listri (tc). **TopFoto.co.uk:** Clive Barda / ArenaPAL (br); **92 Ken Howard:** San Diego Opera (cl). **Corbis:** Krause, Johansen / Archivo Iconografico, SA (tr); **93 Corbis:** Mimmo Jodice; **94 Festival Della Valle D'itria; 95 Shutterstock.com:** Alastair Muir; **96 Corbis:** Raymond Gehman; **97 Teatro alla Scala:** Erio Piccagliani (tc). **Lebrecht Music and Arts Photo Library:** HIS Interfoto (br); **98-99 Getty**

Images / iStock: ai_yoshi; **100 Getty Images:** John Snelling (l). **Lebrecht Music and Arts Photo Library** (tr); **101 The Art Archive:** Donizetti Museum Bergamo / Dagli Orti (A); **102 Lebrecht Music and Arts Photo Library** (bl); **102-103 Getty Images:** Robbie Jack / Corbis (t); **104 Bridgeman Images:** Pascal Victor / ArtComPress; **105 Lebrecht Music and Arts Photo Library** (br); **106 Ken Howard / Metropolitan Opera; 107 Lebrecht Music and Arts Photo Library:** Private Collection; **108 TopFoto.co.uk:** Clive Barda; **109 Riccardo Musacchio; 110** TopFoto / Roger-Viollet (cl); **The Art Archive:** Society Of The Friends Of Music Vienna / Dagli Orti (A) (tr); **Lebrecht Music and Arts Photo Library:** TAL RA (br); **111 Lebrecht Music and Arts Photo Library:** ColouriserAL (br); **Mary Evans Picture Library:** (tr); **112 Corbis:** Ira Nowinski; **113 Corbis:** Bill Cooper / epa; **114-115 Dreamstime.com:** Perseomedusa; **116 Lebrecht Music and Arts Photo Library; 117 Lebrecht Music and Arts Photo Library** (br); O. Rotem (t); **118-119 Teatro alla Scala:** Andrea Tamoni (b); **119 Corbis:** Robbie Jack Photography (tr); **120 Alamy Stock Photo:** Photo 12 (crb). **Teatro alla Scala:** Andrea Tamoni (bl); **121 Bridgeman Art Library:** Bibliotheque de la Comedie Francaise, Paris, France, Archives Charmet (tr). **Corbis:** Leonhard Foeger / Reuters (b); **122 Deutsche Oper Berlin:** Bernd Uhlig; **123 Corbis:** Bettmann; **124 Colette Masson; 125 Corbis:** Robbie Jack Photography; **126 Corbis:** Ira Nowinski (bl); **Getty Images:** National Geographic / Kenneth Garrett (cra); **127 Teatro Regio Torino:** Ramella & Giannese; **128-129 Getty Images:** Amr Nabil / AFP; **130 The Lordprice Collection:** Tony Price; **131 Getty Images:** Robbie Jack / Corbis (br). **Shutterstock.com:** Donald Cooper (t); **132 Bridgeman Art Library:** Private Collection (bl); **132-133 Getty Images:** Patrick Riviere (b); **133 Lebrecht Music and Arts Photo Library:** Laszlo Vámos (tr); **134 Lebrecht Music and Arts Photo Library** (tr). **Topfoto:** Ron Scherl / Arena Images (b); **135 Lebrecht Music and Arts Photo Library** (tr). **Topfoto:** ArenPAL (b); **136 Corbis:** Hulton-Deutsch Collection (tr); **137 Bridgeman Art Library:** Bibliotheque de L'Opera, Paris, France; **138 Corbis:** Alinari Archives / Gaetano Puccini (cl). **Lebrecht Music and Arts Photo Library** (tr). **The Lordprice Collection:** Tony Price (br); **139 The Lordprice Collection:** akg-images; **140 Alamy Stock Photo:** Mary Evans Picture Library (bl); **141 Corbis:** Vittoriano Rastelli (t). **Lebrecht Music and Arts Photo Library:** Private Collection (bc); **142 Corbis:** Eduardo Abad / epa; **143 Lebrecht Music and Arts Photo Library:** Tristram Kenton; **144-145 Shutterstock.com:** Apostolis Giontzis; **146 Lebrecht Music and Arts Photo Library:** Private Collection; **147 Corbis:** Gianni Giansanti / Sygma (r); Hulton-Deutsch Collection (bl); **148 Ken Howard / Metropolitan Opera; 149 The Lordprice Collection:** Tony Price (br); **Corbis:** Bettmann (bl); **150 Topfoto:** Clive Barda / ArenaPAL (b); **151 Getty Images:** Hiroyuki Ito / Hulton Archive; **152-153 Corbis:** Robert Matheson; **154 Lebrecht Music and Arts Photo Library; 156 The Art Archive:** Beethoven House Bonn / Dagli Orti (A) (tr). **Corbis:** Sandro Vannini (b); **157 Staatsoper Unter den Linden:** Monika Rittershaus; **158 akg-images:** (b). **The Art Archive:** Musée Bonnat Bayonne France / Dagli Orti (A) (tr); **159 TopFoto.co.uk:** Roger-Viollet; **160 Science Photo Library:** Mike Agliolo; **161 akg-images:** (bc). **Staatsoper Unter den Linden:** (t); **162 Colette Masson** (cl); **Lebrecht Music and Arts Photo Library** (tr); **Alamy Stock Photo:** nagelestock.com (cr); **163 Lebrecht Music and Arts Photo Library** (br); **akg-images:** Richard-Wagner-Museum (tr); **164 Staatsoper Unter den Linden:** Monika Rittershaus; **165 Lebrecht Music and Arts Photo Library:** S.Lauterwasser; **166 Getty Images:** Bryan Peterson (bl); **166-167** Wilfried Hösl (b); **167 Corbis:** Bettmann (tr); **168 Lebrecht Music and Arts Photo Library; 169 Lebrecht Music**

and Arts Photo Library (cl). **Los Angeles Philharmonic:** Kira Perov / Bill Viola (Artist, r); **170 TopFoto.co.uk:** Clive Barda (bl); **170-171 Staatsoper Unter den Linden:** Monika Rittershaus (b); **171 akg-images:** (tr); **172 The Art Archive:** Neuschwanstein Castle Germany / Dagli Orti (A); **173 Corbis:** Christie's Images; **174 Lebrecht Music and Arts Photo Library** (b); **175 Bayreuther Festspiele:** Jorg Schulze (br). **Lebrecht Music and Arts Photo Library:** S Lauterwasser (t); **176 Getty Images:** Robert R. McElroy / Archive Photos; **177 Ken Howard / Metropolitan Opera** (b); **Lebrecht Music and Arts Photo Library** (tr); **178-179 Bayreuther Festspiele:** (b); **179 Lebrecht Music and Arts Photo Library:** Private Collection (tr). **Lebrecht Music and Arts Photo Library** (br); **180** Bayreuther Festspiele (b); **181 Agence Enguerand:** Marc Enguerand; **182 Getty Images:** Ron Scherl / Redferns; **183 Getty Images:** Beatriz Schiller / Time Life Pictures (crb). **Bridgeman Art Library:** Bibliotheque des Arts Decoratifs, Paris, France, Archives Charmet (bl); **184 Lebrecht Music and Arts Photo Library** (tr). **Pat Bromilow:** Cape Town Opera (b); **186 Corbis:** Hulton-Deutsch Collection (tr). **Lebrecht Music and Arts Photo Library** (b); **187 TopFoto.co.uk:** Ron Scherl / Arena Images; **188 Lebrecht Music and Arts Photo Library:** Laurie Lewis (cl). **Lebrecht Music and Arts Photo Library:** (tr), Private Collection (br); **189 Getty Images:** Hulton Archive; **190 akg-images:** Coll. Archiv f.Kunst & Geschichte (bl). **TopFoto.co.uk:** (cr); **191 Lebrecht Music and Arts Photo Library:** Colette Masson; **192 TopFoto.co.uk:** Clive Barda / PAL; **193 Corbis:** Herwig Prammer / Reuters; **194 TopFoto:** Roger-Viollet; **195 Lebrecht Music and Arts Photo Library; 196 Agence Enguerand:** Marc Enguerand; **197 Lebrecht Music and Arts Photo Library:** Laurie Lewis; **198-199 Corbis:** Nathalie Darbellay / Sygma; **200 Corbis:** Gianni Dagli Orti; **202 Corbis:** Bettmann (tr); **202-203 Agence Enguerand:** Ramon Senera / Agence Bernand (b); **204 akg-images:** (bl). **Corbis:** Bettmann (tr); **205 Corbis:** Austrian Archives; **206 Lebrecht Music and Arts Photo Library** (bc); **206-207 Alamy Stock Photo:** Sami Sarkis (b); **208-209 Shutterstock.com:** Songquan Deng; **210 ArenaPAL:** Mark Elliedge (l). **The Art Archive:** San Pietro Maiella Conservatoire Naples / Dagli Orti (A) (tr); **211 Bridgeman Images:** Pascal Victor / ArtComPress; **212 Opéra national du Rhin:** Alain Kaiser; **213 Getty Images:** Beatriz Schiller / Time Life Pictures; **214 Lebrecht Music and Arts Photo Library** (tr). **Réunion des Musées Nationaux Agence Photographique:** Droits réservés / Musée d'Orsay, Paris (b); **215 Lebrecht Music and Arts Photo Library; 216 Corbis:** Ted Spiegel (bl); **216-217 Corbis:** Herwig Prammer / Reuters (b); **217 Lebrecht Music and Arts Photo Library:** Private Collection (tr); **218 Topfoto:** Roger-Viollet (bl). **Corbis:** Hulton-Deutsch Collection (tr); **219 Lebrecht Music and Arts Photo Library; 220 Lebrecht Music and Arts Photo Library:** Colette Masson; **221 Getty Images:** Robbie Jack / Corbis; **222 Agence Enguerand:** Agence Bernand (bl). **The Art Archive:** San Pietro Maiella Conservatoire Naples / Dagli Orti (A) (tr); **223 Lebrecht Music and Arts Photo Library; 224 TopFoto.co.uk:** Ron Scherl / Arena Images; **225 Corbis:** Bettmann (tl). **Photolibrary:** P Berchery (r); **226-227 TopFoto.co.uk:** Gianfranco Fainello / PAL; **228 Corbis:** Gianni Dagli Orti (bl). **Lebrecht Music and Arts Photo Library** (tr); **229 Corbis:** Robbie Jack Photography (cr); **230 Lebrecht Music and Arts Photo Library:** Brian Morris (bl); **230-231 Deutsche Oper Berlin:** Bernd Uhlig (b); **232 Lebrecht Music and Arts Photo Library** (tr, b); **233 Teatro alla Scala:** Lelli & Masotti; **234-235 Agence Enguerand:** Tristan Jeanne-Vales (b); **235 Getty Images:** Bruce Forster (tr); **236-237 Alamy Stock Photo:** Diomedia; **238 Corbis:** Catherine Panchout; **240 Corbis:** Bettmann (tr). **Mariinsky Theatre:** Natasha Razina (b); **241 Mary**

Evans Picture Library; **242 ArenaPAL:** Nigel Norrington (l). **Lebrecht Music and Arts Photo Library** (tr); **243 The Art Archive:** Bibliothèque des Arts Décoratifs Paris / Dagli Orti; **244 akg-images; 245 ArenaPAL:** Marilyn Kingwill (r). **Lebrecht Music and Arts Photo Library** (tl); **246-247 Alamy Stock Photo:** Panoramic Images; **248 ArenaPAL:** Mike Hoban / Glyndebourne Productions Ltd. (l). **Lebrecht Music and Arts Photo Library** (tr); **249 akg-images; 250 Getty Images:** Gary Holscher; **251 Getty Images:** Robbie Jack / Corbis (t). **akg-images** (br); **252 Lebrecht Music and Arts Photo Library** (tr). **Colette Masson:** (b); **253 Bridgeman Art Library:** Pushkin Museum, Moscow, Russia / The **Bridgeman Art Library; 254 Lebrecht Music and Arts Photo Library** (tr). **San Francisco Opera:** Ken Friedman (b); **255 Corbis:** Burstein Collection; **256 Lebrecht Music and Arts Photo Library** (tr). **Topfoto:** Zoe Dominic / Boosey & Hawkes Collection / ArenaPAL (bl). **Getty Images:** Time Life Pictures (br); **257 De Nederlandse Opera:** Hans van den Bogaard; **258-259 ArenaPAL:** Colette Masson / Roger-Viollet / TopFoto (b); **259 Lebrecht Music and Arts Photo Library** (cr). **260-261 Agence Enguerand:** Marc Enguerand; **262 Corbis:** Bettmann (crb); Underwood & Underwood (tr). **Lebrecht Music and Arts Photo Library** (bl); **263 The Opera Group; 264 TopFoto.co.uk; 265 Mariinsky Theatre:** Natasha Razin; **266-267 Corbis:** Ladislav Janicek / Zefa; **268 Corbis:** Liba Taylor; **270 Lebrecht Music and Arts Photo Library** (tr). **Prague National Theatre:** František Ortmann (b); **271 The Art Archive:** Conservatoire Prague / Dagli Orti; **272 Lebrecht Music and Arts Photo Library** (tr). **Bridgeman Art Library:** Private Collection, RIA Novosti (b); **273 Getty Images:** Beatrz / SchillerTime Life Pictures; **274 Getty Images:** Lieberenz / ullstein bild (l). **Lebrecht Music and Arts Photo Library** (tr); **275 Shutterstock.com:** Mary Altaffer / AP Photo; **276 Getty Images:** Robbie Jack / Corbis (bl). **Lebrecht Music and Arts Photo Library:** Moravské Zemské (cr); **277 Getty Images:** Robbie Jack / Corbis; **278 ArenaPAL:** Mark Ellidge Archive; **279 Lebrecht Music and Arts Photo Library; 280-281 Alamy Stock Photo:** OJPhotos; **282 Getty Images:** Denis De Marney / Stringer; **284 Getty Images:** Hulton Archive (tr); **284-285 Cory Weaver:** (b); **285 Cory Weaver:** (br); **286 Getty Images:** Michael Ochs Archives (tr); Bertrand Rindoff Petroff (b); **287 Getty Images:** Joel Saget / AFP; **288 Corbis:** Sylvia Salmi / Bettmann (tr). **Lebrecht Music and Arts Photo Library** (b); **289 Hamburgische Staatsoper:** Hermannund Clächen Baus; **290 ArenaPAL:** Nigel Norrington (b). **Corbis:** Bettmann (tr); **291 akg-images:** Gert Schütz; **292 Getty Images:** Marc Moritsch; **293 TopFoto.co.uk:** Ken Howard / PAL; **294 Corbis:** John Springer Collection (b). **Lebrecht Music and Arts Photo Library:** Kurt Weill Foundation (tr); **295 DRAMA. Agentur fuer Theaterfotografie:** Iko Freese; **296 Bridgeman Images:** Sputnik (b). **Corbis:** Hulton-Deutsch Collection (tr); **297 The Art Archive; 298 Corbis:** Bettmann (tr, br). **Lebrecht Music and Arts Photo Library** (bl); **299 Corbis:** Jacques M. Chenet; **300 Lebrecht Music and Arts Photo Library:** (tr); **300-301 Agence Enguerand:** Pascal Gely / Agence Bernand (b); **301 Corbis:** Hulton-Deutsch Collection (br); **302 Corbis:** Hulton-Deutsch Collection (cl). **Corbis:** Hulton-Deutsch Collection (tr); **303 Corbis:** Hulton-Deutsch Collection (c). **Lebrecht Music and Arts Photo Library:** Time Life Pictures (br); **304 Getty Images:** Kurt Hutton / Picture Post / Hulton Archive (bl). **TopFoto.co.uk:** Zimmermann / Boosey & Hawkes Collection / ArenaPAL (cr); **305 Zurich Opera House:** Suzanne Schwiertz; **306 Lebrecht Music and Arts Photo Library:** Private Collection (bl); **306-307 Corbis:** Robbie Jack Photography (t); **307 Lebrecht Music and Arts Photo Library:** ArenaPAL (bc); **308-309 Getty Images:** Lawrence K. Ho / Los Angeles Times; **310-311 Getty Images:** View Pictures / Hufton+Crow / Universal Images; **312 Agence Enguerand:** Pascal Gely / Agence Bernand; **313 Hamburgische Staatsoper:** Brinkhoff / Mögenburg; **314 Corbis:** Bettmann (br). **Lebrecht Music and Arts Photo Library** (bl); Mike Evans (tr); **316 Bridgeman Images:** Pascal Victor / ArtComPress (b). **Lebrecht Music and Arts Photo Library:** Horst Tappe (tr); **317 Lebrecht Music and Arts Photo Library:** Sony Classical; **318 Corbis:** Nubar Alexanian (bl). **Lebrecht Music and Arts Photo Library:** Betty Freeman (tr). **TopFoto. co.uk:** Richard Mildenhall / Arena Images (crb); **319 Tilde de Tullio; 320 Getty Images:** John Snelling; **321 Getty Images:** Robbie Jack / Corbis; **322 Lebrecht Music and Arts Photo Library:** Betty Freeman (tr); **322-323 TopFoto.co.uk:** Jim Caldwell / Arena Images (b); **324 De Nederlandse Opera:** Hans van den Bogaard (br). **Lebrecht Music and Arts Photo Library:** Laurie Lewis (tr); **325 Regine Koerner; 326 Lebrecht Music and Arts Photo Library:** T. Martinot (tr); **Lebrecht Music and Arts Photo Library:** Alastair Muir (b); **327 Alamy Stock Photo:** Patrick Medd; **328 Getty Images:** Jack Vartoogian (bl); **328-329 Getty Images:** Jack Vartoogian (b); **330 Getty Images:** Johannes Simon (b, tr); **331 Getty Images:** Johannes Simon; **332 Getty Images:** Dave J Hogan (tr); **332-333 Getty Images:** Robbie Jack / Corbis (b); **333 Getty Images:** Robbie Jack / Corbis (br); **334 Getty Images:** Boris Horvat / AFP (tr); Robbie Jack / Corbis (b); **335 Getty Images:** Boris Horvat / AFP; **336 Getty Images:** Carlos R. Alvarez / WireImage; **337 Getty Images:** Gerard Julien / AFP; **338 Getty Images:** Raphael Gaillarde / Gamma-Rapho (tr); **338-339 Jean-Louis Fernandez:** (b); **340-341 Dreamstime.com:** Mirko Kuzmanovic; **342 Getty Images:** Timothy A. Clary / AFP (b); Marvin Joseph / The Washington Post (tr); **343 Getty Images:** Timothy A. Clary / AFP; **344 Staatsoper unter den Linden:** Marion Schöne (cl). **Opera Atelier, Canada:** Bruce Zinger (br); **345 Agence Enguerand:** Ramon SENERA Agence Bernand; **346 Lebrecht Music and Arts Photo Library:** Private Collection (tr); **Teatr Weikl Poland:** Juliusz Multarzyński (bl); **347 San Francisco Opera:** Ken Friedman; **348 Ravenna Festival Foundation; 349 Lebrecht Music and Arts Photo Library:** Nigel Luckhurst (cr). **Hans van den Bogaard:** (tl); **350 Agence Enguerand:** Agence Bernand (br). **Neue Oper Wien:** Peter Grubinger (br). **Grand Théâtre de Genève:** (tl); **351 Alamy Stock Photo:** dpa picture alliance archive.

All other images © Dorling Kindersley
For further information see: www.dkimages.com